Defending Idaho's Natural Heritage

Defending Idaho's Natural Heritage

By Ken Robison

ISBN 978-0-578-14093-3

For additional copies of this book go to:

www.defendingidahosnaturalheritage.com

Dedication

This book is dedicated to all those
who spoke up for fish and wildlife habitat,
for flowing rivers
and for exceptional natural areas.

Personal dedication

For my family.

Acknowledgments

No book is the work of a single person, and this one is no exception to that rule. Many people have provided assistance. Here is the short list:

Without the help of Royce Williams, there would be no book. He has provided counsel, ran down photos and worked with our printer, Caxton Printers, to prepare the book for publication. And Teresa Sales of Caxton Printers helped immensely with guidance and suggestions during the printing process.

Gerald (Jerry) Jayne shared documents and provided information on other conservation leaders. An extensive collection of documents on the formation and early years of the Hells Canyon Preservation Council, along with photos, came to this book from Russell Mager.

H. Tom Davis provided encouragement and allowed us to use some his excellent photos, one on the back cover. Ron Walker provided the artwork for the cover, based on his iconic River of No Return Wilderness poster.

The staff of the Idaho Historical Society made available the Bruce Bowler and Harry Shellworth papers and tracked down many helpful documents, as did the staff at BSU Albertson's Library Special Collections and Archives, who gave us full access to the papers of Sen. Frank Church, Sen. Len B. Jordan, Cecil Andrus and Ted Trueblood. Both provided photos from their files. Julie Monroe of the University of Idaho Library helped with access to the Jerry Jayne, H. Tom Davis and Ralph Maughan papers.

The Idaho Department of Fish and Game helped us with access to issues of the Idaho Wildlife Review and Idaho Wildlife magazines, plus minutes of the Fish and Game Commission meetings.Linda Phillips of the U.S. Forest Service regional office in Missoula also tracked down an important document.

Dan and Donna Day provided some of his father's outstanding Sawtooth photos, those with the Ernie Day credit line. Jane Harvey provided a photo of her father, Floyd Harvey.

Thanks also to all the people who consented to interviews: Cecil Andrus, Bert Bowler, Russell Brown, Stanley Burns, H. Tom Davis, Jerry Jayne, Russell Mager, Floyd Harvey, James Keating, Martel Morache, Bill Platts, Bob Johnson and Monte Richards. Platts, Jayne, Davis, Morache and Bowler also reviewed chapters.

Finally, thanks to members of my family for the assistance and support that made the book possible – Maxene, Jill, Nicholas and Paige.

Ron Walker, a Boise artist, did this line drawing of scenes from the River of No Return Wilderness. It is based on photographs by Ernie Day, Ted Trueblood and H. Tom Davis and was turned into a poster presented to members of the United States Congress before the votes creating the 2,373,331-acre wilderness area in central Idaho. Later, when Sen. Frank Church (D-Idaho) was suffering from terminal cancer in 1984, fellow Sen. James McClure (R-Idaho) pushed a bill through Congress to add Church's name to the wilderness area. The Frank Church River of No Return Wilderness is the largest wilderness in the lower 48 states.

Table of Contents

Introduction

One of the purposes of this narrative is to recognize the efforts of Idahoans and others who worked for wildlife conservation, for the protection of habitat for fish and wildlife, and for the preservation of some of the most spectacular geography on the planet. Because of their efforts, we still have a flowing river in Hells Canyon, a large central Idaho wilderness and a White Cloud Mountain range without open pit mines.

Some of the best of Idaho was saved for present and future generations with Congressional legislation establishing the Sawtooth National Recreation Area (1972), Hells Canyon National Recreation Area (1975) and the River of No Return Wilderness (1980), later renamed the Frank Church River of No Return Wilderness.

All of those conservation victories were achieved because of robust citizen campaigns.

The leaders were motivated by their reverence for the land and the wildlife. Some were also motivated by knowledge of what had been lost, including mountain meadows devastated by dredge mining and salmon spawning waters lost to dams and sediment from forest roads.

The key political figure was Sen. Frank Church, a champion of the Wilderness Act, and a sponsor of the Wild and Scenic Rivers Act. His stature and legislative skills made possible the passage of the Sawtooth, Hells Canyon and Central Idaho wilderness legislation.

Earlier gains for conservation were achieved with designation by the Forest Service of the Idaho, Selway-Bitterroot and Sawtooth primitive areas (1931, 1936 and 1937). In 1938, the 2-year-old Idaho Wildlife Federation sponsored a successful initiative creating a commission system for fish and game management, a significant gain for wildlife conservation.

In 1954, the federation sponsored a successful initiative to curb the damage to fish and wildlife habitat by dredge mining and went on record opposing proposed dams on the Clearwater River. In 1960, it intervened with the Federal Power Commission to prevent construction of a Snake River dam that would have locked salmon and steelhead out of the Salmon River drainage.

Work on this narrative began in 2008 after a friend suggested that I do some writing on Idaho conservation history. It is, at best, only a partial history of Idaho conservation. And the story ends in this book in1980.

Chapter 1

Happy hunting ground
Sportsmen organize for wildlife conservation

"From one end of the state to the other mountain range after mountain range send their towering peaks skyward, piercing the clouds and presenting a skyline of artistic beauty. There are literally hundreds and hundreds of cascading streams and rivers, great forests of all the pine and fir species, myriads of crystal clear lakes nestled in the bosom of mountain fastnesses, and sweeping plains to awe those who traverse these highways and byways of Idaho. Here, indeed, is the happy hunting ground of sportsmen." – From the 13th biennial report of the Fish and Game Warden of Idaho, Richard E. Thomas, 1930.

Idaho's 54 million acres provided habitat for a great variety of wildlife including elk, deer, mountain goats, mountain sheep, antelope, black and grizzly bears, cougars, wolves, coyotes, ducks, geese and grouse. Fish were abundant in thousands of streams and lakes, including huge runs of salmon and seagoing trout that returned annually to the Snake River and its tributaries. Wild game and fish allowed 19th century explorers and fur trappers to sustain themselves and also fed the miners and settlers who arrived after the gold discoveries of the 1860s. Market hunters supplied the mining camps and the railroad construction crews of the 1870s and 1880s. Commercial fishermen using nets took tons of salmon and trout from streams and lakes.

The country that Lewis and Clark explored in 1805-1806 had been inhabited for thousands of years by people skilled in hunting and fishing. The Shoshoni Indians they met near the Salmon River after crossing the Continental Divide and the Nez Perce who succored and assisted them on the Clearwater speared and trapped salmon and seagoing trout, hunted buffalo, deer, bighorn sheep and elk. The lives of the natives were adapted to the seasons, the geography of the country and the migrations and movement of fish and animals.

The journals of fur trappers suggest that the larger animals were abundant in the early 1800s including elk, deer, mountain sheep and bears. The Alexander Ross party found many buffalo in Lemhi Valley in April 1824. In June they killed 17 deer and six elk on the lower Boise River. The Peter Skene Ogden trapping party in 1826 found buffalo by the hundreds near the present town of Salmon. "The plains appear covered by them." Another trapping party found "an open plain of luxurious grass dotted with buffalo in all directions" near present day Idaho Falls. "An Indian came in this day and reported that he and three others had killed 60 buffalo that day."[1]

The first territorial legislature, meeting in Lewiston in 1864, recognized that year-around killing would reduce game populations. Idaho's first wildlife conservation law made it unlawful to kill, pursue or have in possession from February 1 to July 1 any buffalo, deer, elk, antelope, mountain sheep or mountain goat. Any number could be legally taken in the other seven months of the year. Fish could be taken by any method at any time with no limit. Enforcement was left to the county sheriff and there was little enforcement. Sheriffs had better things to do than to trouble their constituents about killing elk or deer out of season. And, if they observed an illegal kill by a neighbor, people were not inclined to complain or testify. More wildlife conservation laws passed before Idaho was admitted as a state in 1890 reflected increasing concern about declining populations of the larger game animals but provided no real remedy. No limits were set on the number of animals or fish that could be taken. Elk and deer were killed for their hides and horns with carcasses left to rot.

In 1873, the legislature established the first bird seasons, limiting the legal killing of quail and partridge to six months and establishing seasons for ducks and geese in Ada and Boise counties.[2] In 1875 came the first fish conservation laws making it illegal to fish with explosives or poisonous chemicals or to obstruct a stream with a weir, net or dam, except for mine, milling or agriculture purposes. Fishing by any method other than hook and line was prohibited for five years in Oneida and Bear Lake counties.[3]

In 1883, killing buffalo, elk, deer, antelope and mountain sheep was limited to four months of the year and it was now illegal to kill them solely for their hides or horns, chase them with dogs or ship them out of the territory for "speculative purposes." Killing of quail or partridge was banned until September 1887 and grouse hunting was closed from February 1 to July 15. Fishing was limited to the use of pole, line and hook on any stream, but salmon, salmon trout (steelhead) and sturgeon could be taken with a seine or spear.[4]

Added fish protection was approved for Bingham and Bear Lake counties in 1885. Idaho's first water pollution law said sawmill operators in those counties would be subject to a $100 fine if they permitted sawdust to be discharged in any body of water containing fish. And any dam in those counties not used for mining or agriculture was to have fish ladders or chutes allowing passage of fish from March 1 through July 31. Also screens were to be provided to prevent fish larger than three inches from entering irrigation ditches. This was the legislature's first attempt to reduce fish losses to dams, canals and ditches, subjects that would be revisited many times.[5]

In 1887, the season on buffalo, elk, deer and mountain sheep was limited to three months, September 1 to December 1.[6] In 1893, three years after Idaho became a state, the legislature approved more restrictions and tougher penalties. Elk, moose and caribou were to be protected with hunting closed for four years, until September 1, 1897. (Idaho had a small caribou herd near the Canadian border.) It was now illegal to hunt elk, deer, buffalo and mountain goats with dogs or to kill them solely for their hides or horns. The meat was not to be sold, bought or shipped except during the designated seasons. The law attempted to curb commercial fishing other than for local markets, prohibiting the shipping of fish by stage line, express or railroad at any time of the year. Fishing was closed from November 1 to April 15 except fish could still be taken year-round for home consumption. Fish must now be taken only with pole, line and hook except salmon, salmon trout (steelhead) and sturgeon could be taken with seines, nets, fences, baskets, traps and spears. It was now illegal statewide to deposit sawdust into any waters known to contain trout. Construction of a fishway could be required for any dam if the county commissioners deemed it necessary. Fish losses were mounting as more dams went in for mining and irrigation. Hunting of quail, prairie chickens, pheasants, partridges and grouse was banned between January 1 and August 1, of ducks, geese and swans between April 15 and August 15.[7]

Penalties were increased, with possible fines of $50 to $100 and up to 60 days in jail. Rather than leaving enforcement to the county sheriff, the revised game law directed county commissioners to appoint a game warden in each county. The warden could appoint additional wardens. There was no pay but wardens were to receive one half of any fines collected with the other half going to the county school fund. Wardens were required to pursue any violation for which they had personal knowledge or "reliable information."

The editor of the Kendrick Gazette was not impressed, pointing out that the new law did nothing if it wasn't enforced. "Right here on the Potlatch this week several men were throwing dynamite into the stream to kill the trout." County commissioners had appointed no warden and the law "is not worth the paper it is written on." The Gazette called for a state game warden with

Ernie Day Photo

Packing in for a Chamberlain Basin elk hunt.

authority to appoint deputies in all parts of the state. In June 1893, an anonymous Boise County writer advised The Idaho Statesmen that "a party of men are engaged in shooting deer for their hides on the South Fork of the Payette," tanning the hides to avoid detection.[8]

Perhaps because few county game wardens had been appointed, the law was changed in 1895, returning responsibility for enforcement to county sheriffs and constables with no mention of wardens. In an effort to promote enforcement the law now said any person could make a complaint, under oath, and the person complained against must be arrested. With a conviction the person making the complaint would be entitled to half of the fine.[9] The 4-year ban on the legal killing of elk, moose and caribou ended in 1897 but hunting for those animals, mountain goat and mountain sheep was limited to the month of September. Deer and antelope could be hunted for four months, from

September 1 to December 31. Killing or trapping beaver was outlawed for five years. The killing of buffalo was banned, too late for the buffalo.[10]

As Idaho approached the end of the century, concern for the state's wildlife was increasing. Enforcement by the counties was not working. "To fish and hunt without limit was considered the right of anyone." Neighbors were not inclined to testify against neighbors. Market hunters were still killing large numbers of elk and deer. Elk were still being slaughtered for their hides, horns and teeth. Commercial fishermen were shipping tons of fish out of the state. In 1899, the legislature gave up on enforcement by the counties and created a new office, state game warden with authority to enforce the game laws statewide. The warden was authorized to appoint a resident of each county as a deputy. For the first time there were limits on the numbers of big game animals legally taken, two elk and four deer, antelope, mountain goat or mountain sheep per person. Hunting for moose and caribou was closed statewide for five years.[11]

Gov. Frank Steunenberg chose a 37-year-old state representative from De Lamar, Charles Arbuckle, as state game warden. Arbuckle faced a huge challenge in attempting to end 40 years of "wanton slaughter" in a state spread over 54 million acres with a population accustomed to unlimited hunting and fishing. In his report to the governor and legislature in December 1900, Arbuckle wrote: "Prior to the creation of this department various laws for the protection of fish and game have been on our statute books. They were framed with the best intent but all have been practically inoperative because no person felt fully authorized to enforce them." Also, "Public sentiment seemed largely against the punishment of offenders and convictions were almost impossible even for the most flagrant violations." Arbuckle reported progress despite "many difficulties and discouragements." While public sentiment was "largely against the punishment of offenders," he had found that there were sportsmen who favored change: "The work of this office, since its creation, has been assisted materially by the sportsmen of this state individually and by their club organizations. To them is due much credit in the education of public sentiment for the protection of our game and fish."[12]

Arbuckle managed to appoint local wardens in all but three counties, Ada, Custer and Shoshone. Their work had been efficient and energetic, he believed, considering that their "remuneration has been contingent only upon securing a conviction." Not all the wardens had reported but he estimated that there had been 60 convictions despite a lack of public support, difficulty in obtaining evidence and reluctant county prosecutors. Even when there was adequate evidence some prosecutors refused to act, he wrote, especially when "the law breakers have been prominent citizens."

Arbuckle believed that the commercial shipping of game and trout to other states had been effectively stopped and sales in the open market in Idaho suppressed. As an example, he said, 50,000 to 90,000 pounds of Henry's Lake trout, mislabeled as whitefish, had been shipped every winter to Butte, Salt Lake City and other points. Arbuckle credited the Idaho attorney general and the cooperation of express and transportation companies with shutting down these shipments. Commercial exploitation of Henry's Lake trout didn't end with Arbuckle's tenure, however, and it would be a challenge for later wardens.

Even more significant than what he accomplished were Arbuckle's recommendations. "We can never effectively enforce the law under the present system," he wrote. The legislature had given him only $300 a year for expenses which included office rent, postage and travel. The office needed a continuing source of revenue. Arbuckle proposed that Idaho require purchase of an annual license to hunt and fish with a $2 fee for residents and $25 for non-residents. He estimated this would provide $8,500 a year, allowing the warden to appoint five regional deputies with sufficient pay "to enable them to devote their entire time and attention to their duties." It would also allow a warden to reimburse counties for the work of prosecutors.

Arbuckle cited his difficulty with the meager expense allowance in his response to a report by Tennyson Wright of Pollock in November 1900 that Indians were slaughtering deer migrating to their winter feeding areas on the Salmon River. Arbuckle went to Weiser to see what could be done but decided to go no further. "With the $300 a year appropriated for the expense of my office, I could not make a complete investigation of the subject. Neither could I go alone and surround the band of Indians, and that is what I would have had to do had I undertaken the job." Arbuckle pointed out that the law allowed every Idahoan to take four deer a year. So if there were 50 Indians, they could legally kill 200.[13] In his report he proposed limits of two for deer and one for elk, mountain sheep and mountain goats along with shorter seasons. The alternative was "practical extinction" for the larger game animals. Arbuckle also called for daily bag limits for game birds and protection for songbirds. As for Indians, he proposed to bar any hunting outside of reservations. (In 1922, the state of Idaho recognized the treaty rights of the Nez Perce allowing them to fish and hunt at "all usual and accustomed places" without a license. The Nez Perce agreed to follow state season and bag limits).[14]

Arbuckle also proposed a pounds per day limit for trout, a ban on all fishing with nets and spears and tightening of the 1899 law allowing the use of private ponds and streams for commercial fish operations. "Springs and streams are dammed up and stocked with fish taken from public waters or permitted to enter these so-called lakes and ponds." The fish were being sold in large quantities as private property, skirting the law barring commercial sale of trout. Arbuckle also called for a law requiring screens to curb the loss of game fish passing into irrigation canals and proposed construction of a state fish hatchery. He asked authority for wardens to hire local counsel when county prosecutors refused to enforce the law and recommended requiring all non-resident hunters to employ local guides who would be deputized to enforce the law.

Arbuckle's plea for a license system and warning about the gloomy prospects with the existing system did not impress the incoming governor or the 1901 legislature. None of his proposals was adopted. And, with a new administration, he was out of a job. His appointment was to expire in May 1901 but he chose to leave in February. Democrat Frank Hunt had been elected governor with the help of Populist support and the Populists demanded a share of state jobs. Arbuckle's successor was a Populist, T.W. Bartley of Moscow.[15] Within a few months The Idaho Statesman was accusing him of neglecting his duties in favor of out of state travel. "In all sections of the state people complain that the fish and game law is not enforced. In some localities there seems to be no attempt to enforce it." When people had attempted to contact Bartley, they could not learn where he was. "He got the office as a political reward" and had done nothing beyond "making a pretense of the discharge of duty." The Statesman backed the Republican nominee, Caldwell attorney John Morrison for governor in 1902, citing lax enforcement of game laws by Bartley as one of the shortcomings of Hunt's administration.[16]

Morrison's narrow election victory meant Bartley was out. He left office in 1903 after submitting a report that repeated many of Arbuckle's recommendations including a license system. Bartley said it had been impossible to employ county wardens to work without pay or expenses in many counties including those where enforcement was most needed. A man does not wish to make enemies "when his services are so meagerly paid for." Also he might spend a week or two working up a case only to have "hostile courts and unfriendly juries set the man free." Although the law required sheriffs and other peace officers to enforce the game law, Bartley reported that not a single arrest had been made by a sheriff in the past two years. In a few instances sheriffs had notified him of violations rather than making arrests themselves. Bartley proposed a $1 hunting license fee for residents and $25 for non-residents, estimating that the proceeds would allow the warden to employ and pay the expenses of five deputies. He proposed reducing from four to two the number of elk, deer, mountain sheep and mountain goats that could be taken in a year, a daily limit of 10 for quail, grouse and pheasants, a daily limit for waterfowl and a pounds-per-day limit for trout.[17]

Frank Fenn, supervisor of the Bitterroot National Forest, gave his support to a license system in a letter to The Idaho Statesman. Idaho's neighboring states required out-of-state hunters to pay a heavy fee for a license, he wrote, but Idaho said "we like visitors. Come in and kill all the game you please and it shall not cost you a cent." Idaho's policy attracted unscrupulous eastern hunters who "kill indiscriminately, slaughter ruthlessly and wantonly. Our present system invites the destruction of our game by these vandals." The Forest Reserve law required forest rangers to help state authorities enforce fish and game laws, Fenn noted, and with a license law the rangers could check hunters for licenses. Fenn also advocated requiring non-resident hunters to employ guides who would be deputized as wardens.[18]

Governor Morrison didn't support the license fee proposal and asked the legislature to abolish the office of state game warden as an economy move. But legislators had heard the complaints about weak enforcement and Rep. C.A. Dilatush of Lincoln County, chairman of the House Fish and Game Committee, was prepared to act. After considering suggestions from "almost every county in the state" he drafted a bill to establish a license system. It became law in March 1903.[19] Male residents over age 12 were to pay $1 for a license to hunt and fish. Non-residents were to pay $5 to hunt birds or $25 to hunt big game. The warden was to be paid $1,200 a year with $600 for expenses. No salaries were authorized for full-time deputies but county wardens were to receive $3 a day for time spent enforcing the law. They would get nothing for expenses. The state warden was now required to appoint a deputy in any county upon petition of 10 or more citizens. And the warden was to be "an active executive officer," taking to the field to perform his duties at all times possible.[20]

Big game limits were reduced; only one elk, mountain sheep, mountain goat or antelope and two deer per year just as Arbuckle had recommended. The number of game birds legally taken in a day was limited; 24 ducks, 18 grouse, quail and partridge. Pheasant hunting was banned for four years and for the first time there was a limit on fish, 20 pounds a day of trout, bass, catfish, grayling or sunfish. (Pheasants were not native to the state but had been introduced by private citizens.)

The task of administering the license law fell to W. Van Iorns of Hagerman, appointed by Governor Morrison to succeed Bartley. Van Iorns was more active than his predecessor, promising to meet with every sheriff in the state to ask their cooperation in enforcing the law. He invited anyone finding evidence of violations to contact him. In Bear Lake County, Van Iorns reported, a deputy had overcome objections to the fish ladder law. When his request to install a ladder was ignored he blew out the dam with a charge of powder. When Spokane, Wash. residents with summer homes in northern

Idaho questioned whether they should be required to purchase a non-resident license, Van Iorns defended the law with the help of an attorney general's opinion. Van Iorns said Utah residents he had spoken to supported the law "believing it would have a marked effect on preserving the game."[21] The entire game law was printed on the back of the license. With the licensing system and a continuing source of revenue Van Iorns and his successors were better able to enforce the game laws. But they were still hampered by popular resistance and indifferent prosecutors.

In 1905, Frank Gooding succeeded Morrison as governor. Gooding's choice for warden was William Stephens, a Republican state representative from Rexburg.[22] Stephens would be the first Idaho game warden to serve for more than two years, continuing during Gooding's second term and during the 2-year term of Gov. James Brady. Stephens named 30 county deputies. He went after the illegal shipping of native trout from Henry's Lake and from fish ponds in the Island Park area near Yellowstone. Deputy Martin Garn managed to seize some of the Henry's Lake trout that were being shipped to Butte and Great Falls, Mont. and to Salt Lake City. Stephens and deputies Garn and A. L. Ellsworth also found thousands of trout from area streams and Henry's Lake shut up in "25 pretended fish ponds." About 75 tons of trout from these ponds had been shipped in each of the past two years to Utah, Colorado and Montana, Stephens reported. Backed by a Fremont County Judge and prosecutor, Stephens persuaded some of the operators to release native fish in the ponds, returning 50,000 trout to Henry's Lake. The wardens tore out a weir extending across Shot Gun River that was being used to divert fish into a private pond. The owner sued but the court sided with the game department, ruling that the owner had not met the requirements for a legal private pond.[23]

Enforcing the law was difficult in remote mountain areas. Stephens received complaints in May 1906 that a party of trappers from Montana had wintered in the upper Clearwater country on the Idaho side of the Bitterroot Mountains and had slaughtered many elk and deer and a few moose for their teeth, hides and horns. Deputy B.T. Livingston traveled by train to Darby, Mont. to attempt to intercept the poachers on their way out over Lost Trail Pass. After receiving a report that they were proceeding down the Clearwater, Livingston traveled to Lewiston only to learn that his quarry had returned to Montana over two lower passes. "This is a very large, wild country," wrote Stephens "and it is almost impossible to capture such poachers unless two or three deputies go in there and stay the winter." Deputies and a forest ranger would spend a month on a fruitless attempt in the same area seven years later.

Even though elk were being protected by the U.S. Army in Yellowstone Park, poachers were still killing elk in the park as well as in adjacent areas in Wyoming and Idaho for their teeth, heads and horns. In October 1906, Deputy

Ellsworth intercepted a shipment of 48 elk scalps being sent from Sugar City to Los Angeles. Two Jackson Hole, Wyo. men were arrested on federal charges and were eventually convicted.[24] In his first two years Stephens also reported that his deputies had gained convictions for killing deer out of season in Bannock, Nez Perce and Idaho counties and in the Hagerman area, killing geese out of season in Kootenai County, fishing without a license in Fremont and Shoshone counties and selling trout in Nez Perce County.

In 1907, the legislature authorized the construction of a fish hatchery and Stephens chose a site on state owned land on Silver Creek, a meandering spring fed stream south of Hailey. Within a few years hatcheries would be added at Sandpoint, Coeur d'Alene and Ashton and by 1921, the Fish and Game Department was producing 13 million tiny hatchery fry a year for planting in streams and lakes, including trout, perch, crappie, catfish and kokanee.[25]

Thousands of trout were passing into canals and ditches and were being lost in irrigated farm fields. In 1907, the legislature attempted to reduce the losses by requiring screens on irrigation canals as Arbuckle had suggested in 1900. But the law said that a screen could not impede the flow of water. Stephens reported in 1909 that he had been unable to find a workable design and his successors would have the same problem.

Idaho now had many local sportsmen's and shooting clubs taking an interest in fish and game. Arbuckle had credited them with supporting his efforts to enforce the law. In 1906, some of the clubs organized the Idaho State Sportsmen's Association. The association, meeting in Boise, adopted resolutions criticizing Stephens for changes in the 1907 game law enacted with his support including an increase in the fee for processing license applications. Dr. E.H. Maberly of the Intermountain Gun Club of Boise said Stephens had failed to consult local clubs in choosing deputies and criticized him for his treatment of the owners of private fish ponds. Stephens replied, citing examples of club endorsements of his deputies including Dr. Maberly's approval of Deputy Livingston.[26]

Complaints about Stephens spilled over into the 1909 session of the legislature. Rep. Robert McCracken of Ada County said the warden had exceeded his authority. McCracken proposed several amendments to the fish and game bill that had been drafted based on Stephens' recommendations. But Fish and Game Committee Chairman Robert McKinlay of Twin Falls disputed McCracken's assertion that sportsmen were unhappy with the bill's provisions. The amendments were rejected. The revised law established standards for private fish ponds and required a license issued by the warden. Despite the criticism of Stephens by the Sportsmen's Association and Rep.

McCracken the newly elected governor, James Brady, appointed him to another 2-year term.[27]

Supervisor Emile Grandjean of the Boise National Forest was troubled by the state's weak enforcement of the game laws and by a decline of elk, deer and game birds. In 1909, he asked the legislature to designate a 220,000-acre game preserve in the Payette River drainage on the west side of the Sawtooth Mountains, making it off limits to hunting and trapping. "A small band of elk inhabiting the proposed game retreat have, in the past, been reduced to 40 head owing to the custom of hunters in killing game late in the fall when the snow is deep and the deer and elk are confined to the valleys," said Grandjean. "The greatest slaughter occurs in the spring when the big game visit the numerous springs for the purpose of licking the salt and the alkali beds. Small game, consisting of blue grouse, Franklin's grouse and ruffled grouse are all common although the fool hen is disappearing. These game birds are killed throughout the year. This wanton destruction is due to the fact that the game department of the state of Idaho has not stationed a deputy in this region. If the retreat is placed under restriction, the ranger force of the Boise National Forest in this district may be detailed as game wardens and protect the game." The Statesman said the preserve would embrace the most beautiful mountain scenery in Idaho. "Great rocky jagged peaks raise their snow-capped summits to an elevation of 12,000 feet and all is covered by coniferous forest from the base to a height of 9,000 feet… At intervals along the streams in the mountains are found boiling springs with a temperature in the neighborhood of 165 degrees."[28]

Grandjean first proposed a game preserve designated by Congress but decided to pursue state legislation instead. He won the support of Gov. Brady after agreeing that the Forest Service would help enforce the game laws. The preserve legislation said forest rangers could act as deputy game wardens, not only in the preserve but in all national forests. To overcome opposition by woolgrowers, Grandjean promised that sheep would not be excluded. Because the preserve "contained approximately 220,000 acres and only about 10,000 head of sheep were allotted to this territory, I felt safe in making the promise."[29] The legislative sponsor was Rep. Robert McKinlay, chairman of the House Fish and Game Committee.

The law took effect March 13, 1909. It banned hunting of game animals and killing or trapping of fur bearing animals in the preserve. Cougars, wildcats, wolves and coyotes could be killed by the wardens.[30] "Sportsmen here feel that the setting aside of the preserve was one of the best pieces of legislation that was ever enacted for the good of game in this state," declared the Statesman. Another forester, Frank Fenn, had suggested the designation of a Bitterroot game preserve in his 1903 letter supporting a game license system.

Grandjean went further, taking a specific proposal to the legislature and negotiating with legislators and the governor to get it passed. The provision allowing the rangers to act as game wardens, augmenting the state's wardens, meant more enforcement in the national forests. Previously the rangers could only advise state wardens of possible violations. Now they could be deputized, gather evidence and make arrests. Grandjean assigned three men to patrol the Boise Forest and one of them reported making an arrest for killing deer out of season only six days after the law took effect.[31]

While he was pleased with the creation of the preserve, Grandjean was dissatisfied with what he considered a lack of cooperation by Warden Stephens. In June 1909, he told a reporter that Stephens had failed to post boundary signs for the preserve and hadn't responded to his reports of game law violations on the forest, including the mass killing of deer outside the preserve near Alexander Flat on the Boise River. Further, Grandjean said the Highland Valley dam fish ladder was clogged with trash and inoperable, no fish ladder had been installed at a dam on the South Fork of the Payette as the law required and fish were dying by the thousands in the absence of screens on irrigation canals. All of this found its way into a Statesman story under the headline "Much Criticism of Warden Stephens--Forest Supervisor Says Fish and Game Department Has Been Negligent."[32]

Governor Brady was incensed. He immediately called Stephens into his office to hear his defense. Then he composed and released to the press a letter to Chief Forester Gifford Pinchot defending his administration and suggesting that Grandjean should be reprimanded. The governor was particularly upset because, as he advised Pinchot, he had cooperated with Grandjean to establish the Payette preserve. "This interview is a very serious reflection, indeed, on the game department and on my administration and, having full confidence in your fairness in such matters, I ask whether or not you approve of his (Grandjean's) action in this matter." The forester had never "called my attention to any of these facts, or abuses, with which he rushes into print, and I feel it is only fair, if such a condition did exist, that he should either inform you of the fact and have you advise and consent with me relative to the same or should at least pay the chief executive of this state the courtesy of calling his attention to it before making public charges of this character." Stephens told Brady that Grandjean had contacted him only once to call his attention to a violation. Snow was too deep at the time to attempt to make an arrest and Stephens said he understood that, when weather permitted, rangers would go in to gather evidence and "the department would assist in every way possible to obtain a conviction." Stephens said there had been no further word from Grandjean. As to trout and ditches, wrote Brady, "I did not know Supervisor Grandjean had been making an investigation of the irrigation headgates of the state." Since the law said no screen could interfere with the flow of water, stopping the fish losses was almost impossible, Brady advised Pinchot, but the state was trying to gain the cooperation of irrigators. He labeled Grandjean's charges "unfair and malicious. It is the desire of this administration and the game department to in every way possible co-operate and work in harmony with the forest service in the preservation of our game, and I think you will agree with me that this end cannot be accomplished if the parties are to take the matter up first with the press instead of with the proper authority."[33]

Asked for reaction, a chastened Grandjean had nothing further to say except that his information on fish losses to irrigation ditches came from sportsmen, not from forest officers as the original story indicated. He met with Brady to make peace. Later the forester would write in his history of the Boise Forest that Brady had acknowledged that the warden was "no good." When he was removed from office by President William Howard Taft in 1910, Pinchot wrote Grandjean and other forest supervisors praising them for their efforts and asking them to "stand by the service." In 1912, at Pinchot's request, Grandjean sent him his recollections of his work with the Forest Service.[34]

After the Grandjean-Brady fracas, Warden Stephens told the press he had printed 1,000 signs to mark the boundaries of the preserve and gave them to Grandjean for posting by his rangers. Stephens also announced a crackdown on game violations: "The department is encouraging the various deputies over the state to make arrests in every possible case of violation of the law that is brought to their attention." Convictions were reported for fishing without a license, selling game fish, fishing with a net and exceeding the 20-pound trout limit.[35]

The Idaho Sportsmen's Association made Grandjean an honorary member in 1910. In his letter of thanks the forester responded to complaints that sheep continued to graze in the preserve, competing with elk and deer for forage. The state surveyor general had said the preserve was almost worthless because sheep would drive out the game. Grandjean said game numbers in the preserve were increasing. While he didn't believe sheep were interfering with game propagation, he had reduced the number from 10,000 to 8,000. Grandjean also called for more Idaho game preserves to protect elk, deer, mountain goats and mountain sheep, suggesting possible locations: Fremont County, Chamberlain Basin between the south and middle forks of the Salmon River, and the upper reaches of the Lost River drainage.[36] No further preserves were established in 1911 but, in the wake of the devastating forest fires of 1910, the legislature imposed a 5-year moratorium on elk hunting in nearly all of the counties north of the Salmon River. And in 1913, the southern Idaho counties of Cassia, Twin Falls, Oneida and Bear Lake were declared a game preserve to restore the deer population.[37]

A change in the governor's office brought an end to Stephens' tenure in 1911. Democratic Gov. James Hawley appointed Ben R. Gray of Hailey as warden and Frank Kendall of Twin Falls as his chief deputy. Hawley said he wanted geographic balance in his appointments and Gray was chosen because he was from central Idaho. Gray resigned to take another job in 1912 and was succeeded by Kendall who served for only a few months because Republican John M. Haines won the governorship. Orrin H. Barber, publisher of a weekly newspaper at American Falls, campaigned statewide for Republican state and national candidates in 1912 and was rewarded with the warden appointment. Haines credited Barber with working hard for Republicans but said he based his choice on his belief that Barber would be a good administrator. Barber named former warden Stephens as his chief deputy.[38]

From 1899 to 1913 Idaho had six governors and eight game wardens, all appointed on the basis of political patronage. No knowledge of wildlife or game management was required. The same applied to operators of fish hatcheries and deputies who were routinely replaced by incoming wardens. Outgoing Warden Frank Kendall called for reform in his biennial report. People who hunted and fished supported the department with their license fees, he wrote, but they had no choice as to who would fill the office or whether he was qualified. The office had been used "primarily for political purposes." Kendall proposed making the warden an elective office with a 4-year term and called for a civil service system for employees. He also proposed the appointment of a trained fish culturist, saying money had been wasted planting fish in non-productive streams. Kendall also responded to complaints that the game laws denied Idahoans meat to feed their families. Under current bag limits a person could annually kill one elk, two deer, 1,080 each of grouse, sage hens, partridges and pheasants, 540 quail, 3,600 ducks, 3,600 each of snipe, plover and turtle doves, 600 geese and 6,600 pounds of trout plus other fish, a mountain goat and a mountain sheep.[39]

The Idaho Sportsmen's Association, led by Winfield Tatro Jr. of Boise, conducted a membership campaign in 1912 and claimed to represent 10,000 sportsmen. The association wanted to increase the influence of sportsmen and remove the game department "from the field of partisan politics and personal political activities." Ada County Rep. Charles Koelsch, a Boise attorney, sponsored the association's 1913 legislation to replace the politically appointed warden with a commission system. Three commissioners appointed by the governor would name the warden and oversee the operation of the department. The commission bill was endorsed by the House State Affairs Committee even though it was opposed by Governor Haines. A committee report said the game department had been used "to a considerable extent as a political machine" by both Democratic and Republican administrations. The

House passed the bill but it died in the Senate when an Ada County senator changed his vote. While the commission plan was lost, the sportsmen found enough legislative support to sidetrack the governor's request to put game license revenue in the state's general fund, allowing its use by other agencies. Tatro blamed the commission bill's defeat on Senators Sherman Fairchild of Ada County and David W. Davis of Oneida: "The fight against it was made solely at the behest of the state game department which wished to secure political advantage by keeping the game laws in their present condition." He said the association would make game department reform an issue in the 1914 election campaign and push for it again in the 1915 legislative session.[40]

After the legislature adjourned Warden Barber repaired relations with the association, accepting a proposal to supplement the department's force of paid deputies with unpaid sportsmen volunteers. He promised to support the commission legislation in 1915. And he began publishing a fish and game magazine as a private venture. In June 1914, Association President B.F. Walton of Boise praised Barber as "one of the most conscientious and efficient game wardens Idaho has ever had." In an article in Barber's magazine, Idaho Fish and Game, Walton laid out the case for a non-partisan game commission. He noted with satisfaction that Idaho Democrats had adopted a resolution favoring removal of the warden's office "from the field of political activity" and opposing the diversion of license fees to other uses. In the future, Walton wrote, sportsmen should support no candidate for governor or the legislature unless they pledged to support legislation backed by the association.[41]

With his mixed force of paid and volunteer deputies Barber reported that there had been 96 convictions for game law violations in 1913. But he complained that enforcement was hampered by judicial leniency. In most cases judges levied only the minimum $10 fine and the average was only $14.40. Barber cited an example: "A man whose reputation for killing game out of season is well known, who has no regard for the limit" was fined $10 after pleading guilty. "The game department had been after the man for more than a month and had actually expended $175 in getting evidence and making the arrest." Violations were fewer in communities where penalties were more severe, wrote Barber.[42]

While the law requiring screens on canals had been on the books since 1907, it had never been enforced. No warden had found a screen design that would not impede the flow of water. In 1913, Barber accepted a screen marketed by a Utah company after it was tested and received a favorable report from the state engineer. He issued an order for the installation of the screens on some southern Idaho canals. While traveling in eastern Idaho in July 1914, he learned from a newspaper that he had been fired by Governor Haines and replaced.[43]

The governor's telegram notifying him of his dismissal had failed to reach him. By the time he returned to Boise his successor, Jerel B. Gowen, was already on the job. Governor Haines had apparently been dissatisfied with Barber for some time but backlash from irrigators objecting to the $75 cost of the Johnston Self Cleaning Fish Screen may have been the last straw. Haines didn't mention screens in his letter to Barber explaining his decision but said the warden had incurred much unnecessary expense for travel by deputies and was "out of harmony with the administration." Barber responded in a lengthy open letter to the governor, denying a rumor that he was to receive a $20 kickback for each screen installed. He defended the travel costs, saying deputies were never directed to go anywhere except in response to complaints of violations. Haines had led him to believe that he supported the effort to install fish screens.[44]

"I wish to advise you that I leave the office without regret," he wrote. "Under the system imposed by law I feel that no man can conduct the affairs of the office with the degree of success expected of him by the public and that the satisfaction accruing from the holding of the position is more than overweighed by the trials and vexations that come with it." He commended Haines for his choice of a successor. "I know all too well the trials that lie before him, what criticism he shall unjustly receive, and how impotent he will be, with the means of his command, to meet the expectations of the public."

The Idaho Statesman advised readers that there was another reason for Barber's removal. The warden had wanted Haines to name him immigration commissioner or public utilities commissioner. "He was induced to accept the position of state fish and game warden but was never satisfied with the job." For months he had worked to have Haines replaced as the 1914 Republican nominee for governor, first supporting Sen. David Davis of American Falls and then M.E. Lewis of Moscow after Davis decided not to run, said the Statesman. Haines had fired an appointee who was working behind his back to prevent his re-election. (Barber would return to state government as commissioner of labor, immigration and statistics after Davis was elected governor in 1918.)

Gowen was a Caldwell businessman and community leader, founder of the city's commercial club and a former mayor. His first act as warden was to rescind the fish screen order. He announced that he was instituting a budget system, tracking monthly outlays. Gowen would serve for only seven months. Governor Haines won the Republican nomination in 1914 but lost to the Democratic nominee, former Boise mayor Moses Alexander. Haines was the victim of the Republican treasurer whose theft of $93,000 in state funds was revealed a few weeks before the election.[45]

Despite his brief tenure, Gowen made a significant contribution, initiating the first elk transplant to Idaho from Yellowstone Park and proposing the creation of a second game preserve. Elk restoration was a theme

By 1915, elk from Yellowstone Park were being transplanted to Idaho.

of his biennial report in 1915: "Of the thousands of Idaho elk that formerly ranged in our state, we now have but a few scattered bands, feeble reminders to fill us with remorse for the protection we did not give such magnificent game. If it were not for the protection given this animal by the federal government in the Yellowstone National Park and the stringent laws of the state of Wyoming, but very few elk would be found in Bannock, Bonneville, Madison and Fremont counties but on account of this protection elk are fairly numerous in these counties."[46]

Gowen cited the Payette preserve where Grandjean reported an increase in elk from 25 in 1909 to 200 in 1912. Gowen believed elk were also coming back in the northern counties where the 1911 legislature had banned elk hunting for five years. "With proper protection, within a few years our mountain ranges could be restocked with elk." With the support of Adams and Washington county residents Gowen asked the Department of Interior for 70 surplus elk from Yellowstone to restock the Weiser National Forest. Interior approved 50 on condition that Idaho protect them in a game preserve. Gowen recommended designation of a preserve in the Seven Devils Mountains adjoining the Snake River to benefit both elk and deer: "Along the Snake River is the winter range for deer and poachers and non-residents come across the river at times and kill a great many deer." The elk were transported to Idaho by train and released west of Council and at Black Lake in the Seven Devils. The 1915 legislature established the Black Lake Preserve.[47]

Like Kendall and Barber, Gowen favored reform, removing the department "as far as possible from partisan politics." He proposed having the governor, attorney general, secretary of state and a private citizen serve as a fish and game commission, appointing a warden for a 6-year term. Up to a dozen salaried deputies should be employed rather than the current three, eliminating the poorly paid part-time local wardens. "We cannot expect men to do good work unless they receive living wages and $3 per day will not pay railroad fare, horse hire and feed, and board for themselves and leave anything for salary." He proposed a rewrite of the game code with precise definitions, licensing of trappers, protection of songbirds, protection of redfish in the redfish lakes, an end to commercial fishing in Bear Lake and protection of bears as a game animal. Gowen said the grizzly bear was nearly extinct in Idaho and the black bear, which fed primarily on roots and berries, rarely killing domestic animals, could go the same way. He also addressed the fish screen problem saying it was impossible to enforce the law without giving some official the authority to install screens. "There is no doubt that as many fish are destroyed in the irrigation ditches as we plant each year in the whole state."

Encouraged by the Democratic party's endorsement of a non-political game department, Idaho Sportsmen's Association leaders anticipated success with their reform bill in 1915. The bill again provided for three nonpartisan commissioners. After the initial appointments, governors would appoint one commissioner every two years for 6-year terms. The commission would name a warden for a 2-year term and regional deputies. Sponsored by Reps. Koelsch and M.A. Kiger of Kootenai County and endorsed by the House Fish and Game Committee, the commission bill passed the House 32-24. Kiger termed the present system "an absolute failure." Opponents said the governor should have control of every department and should not be hampered by commissions and boards that could act "without his sanction." The bill was endorsed by the Senate Fish and Game Committee and passed 27-5.[48]

Sportsmen's Association leaders had only a few days to savor their success. Nine days after the Senate vote Gov. Moses Alexander vetoed eight bills including fish and game reorganization, saying the commission would remove from control of the people "one of the most important departments of the state government."[49] A frustrated E.F. Walton suggested that sportsmen forgo hunting and fishing for a year or two in protest. The Statesman termed a boycott impractical but said the veto meant the game department would continue as an instrument to propagate "votes for the reigning governor." Alexander's argument that a commission meant added expense for the public was groundless, said the Statesman. "The sportsmen pay the bill and they are clearly entitled to consideration."

The Pocatello Tribune was harsher, declaring that the real meaning of the veto statement was: "This commission is particularly objectionable (to me) because it is designed to remove still further from the control of the governor one of the most important (political) departments of the state government." The governor had criticized the game department in his campaign but now used the veto "in favor of the very thing he professed to despise."[50] Prohibition and the war in Europe, not game management, were the primary subjects on voters' minds in 1916 and Alexander was re-elected. The Sportsmen's Association gave up on game management reform and its influence waned. It would be 18 years before sportsmen were again well enough organized and motivated to push for a commission system.

Designation of the Black Lake preserve was only part of the legislature's game restoration effort in 1915. Elk hunting was closed in the entire state except in Fremont, Bonneville and Teton counties. In 1913 the legislature had declared the counties of Cassia, Twin Falls, Oneida and Bear Lake a preserve for big game. In 1915 these counties plus the counties of Bannock, Power and Franklin were declared a game preserve for five years with hunting prohibited for elk, deer, antelope, mountain sheep, mountain goat, pheasants or quail. The Lewiston Orchards area was declared a bird preserve. In 1917, three more large forest preserves were designated; the Big Creek preserve on the south side of the Salmon River east of the Middle Fork, the Selway preserve in the upper Clearwater River drainage west of the Montana border, and the Big Lost River preserve in the upper Lost River drainage. In 1919, a Pocatello game preserve was added in the Pocatello National Forest. Ten years after Emile Grandjean took the first proposal to the legislature the state had six national forest game preserves.[51]

There would also be more elk transplants. In addition to the 50 that went to the Black Lake preserve, 65 were released on the Boise River above Arrowrock dam. Sixty-five were released in Bannock County in 1915 and 1916, 21 in Shoshone County in 1919, and 58 in Kootenai County in 1925. In the 1930s there were more, in Bonner, Kootenai and Shoshone counties, another 125 in Owyhee County in 1944 and 1946, and another 40 in Bannock County in 1946.[52]

In addition to game preserves and transplants the state's strategy for restoring elk and deer included killing animals considered predators. A law passed in 1907 called for the extermination of wolves, coyotes, wildcats (lynx) and cougars. Warden Stephens reported that the game department spent $2,900 on predator killing in 1907-1908 with deputy wardens and others accounting for 522 coyotes, 19 bobcats and four badgers with steel traps and strychnine. Since not all poisoned animals were recovered Stephens believed the total killed was much higher. Acting primarily on behalf of livestock owners the legislature in 1915 directed the Livestock Sanitary Board to appoint a predatory animal inspector in every county with authority to pay bounties.

People claiming a bounty were to present the skins of animals to an inspector who would cut off the paws and send them to the state veterinarian. A tax was levied on sheep, cattle, horses and hogs to support the bounties, $2.50 for coyotes, bobcats and lynx, $10 for bears and wolves and $25 for cougars. Idaho trappers could augment their income from fur sales with bounties. By putting a bounty on bear the legislature rejected the recommendation of outgoing warden Gowen to protect bears as game animals. In 1919, the legislature directed the game department to contribute $2,500 a year to the Livestock Sanitary Board for bounty payments.[53]

The game warden carousel continued with Governor Alexander naming Leroy Jones to succeed Gowen. Jones served from 1915 to 1918 when he took a job as a U.S. Marshall. His chief deputy, W.H. Thorp, succeeded him. In his biennial report for 1917-1918, Thorp noted that the department was 20 years old, praising previous wardens for their efforts: "Our state has become famous as offering rare hunting and fishing grounds. It has ceased to be the home of the fish and game hog. Its sportsmen are worthy of the name and are numbered by the thousands. A vast majority of them are for strict law enforcement." He credited the Forest Service for helping. All forest rangers had been deputized and were "ever on the lookout for violators." The transplanted elk had "propagated until the number is much larger than originally." Thorp favored additional preserves, including one in Chamberlain Basin south of the Salmon River, an area believed to have the largest elk herd in the state, 610 based on the estimate of the Idaho National Forest, plus deer and mountain sheep. Few livestock competed with the game animals for forage, Thorp wrote, only a limited number of sheep and cattle owned by settlers. The Forest Service had issued an order to keep it that way, barring future grazing by animals from outside the area.[54]

In 1918, the state issued 51,379 resident fish and game licenses. Non-residents purchased 861 fishing licenses, 57 bird licenses and 38 big game licenses. There were 87 convictions and fines for game law violations. Fifty-nine permits were issued for private fish ponds and for commercial fishing on Bear, Pend Oreille and Priest lakes. Total income was $72,308 and outlays were $54,441. The warden's pay was $1,999.80 and the chief deputy's $1,500. Six salaried deputies, three fish hatchery superintendents and the superintendent of Heyburn State Park were paid $1,200. Another $11,334 went to pay local part time deputies. A clerk was paid $1,500 and an assistant clerk $1,070. The fish and game fund had a balance of $35,143. Rearing and planting fish continued as a major function with 10 million planted in 1917 and 1918.[55]

In 1919, Gov. David W. Davis appointed Otto M. Jones of Boise, an outdoor writer and photographer and avid hunter, to succeed Thorp as warden. Jones made no formal application, said Davis, but was chosen because of his knowledge of needed changes in the game laws and the department. By choosing Jones, said the governor, he made good his campaign pledge to take the department out of politics, rejecting 47 political applicants. The Idaho Statesman reported that Jones, "within the past two years has made a national reputation for himself as an authority on game matters and has been a regular contributor on such subjects to all the leading sportsmen's magazines. His articles on game life in Idaho have been a feature of the Sunday Statesman for more than a year." Jones was born in Montana and came to Idaho when his father purchased a sheep ranch near Boise in 1888. He attended a Virginia military academy and the Washington State University prep school. After two years in Ashland, Oregon, he returned to Boise in 1909. He and his wife were competitive skeet shooters and she accompanied him on exploring and hunting forays.[56]

The energetic Jones traveled to all parts of the state speaking to clubs and encouraging sportsmen to become more active and better organized in support of wildlife protection. He called for a new state sportsmen's organization, complaining that the Idaho Sportsmen Association did nothing but sponsor an annual trap shoot in Boise.[57] Jones put more emphasis on enforcement. He publicized all game law arrests and gave deputy wardens added duties planting fish, making stream surveys and working with local clubs. In July 1919, he personally captured 160 frogs in sloughs along the Boise River to introduce them in other parts of the state, shipping them to American Falls, Hagerman and Lewiston.[58]

In cooperation with the Forest Service in 1920, he initiated the planting of fish in mountain lakes in the Sawtooths. Many of the lakes lacked inlet streams and were barren. The fish were carried on packhorses in milk cans and by hand in cans and canvas bags. Jones persuaded the 1921 legislature to require women and children over age 12 to purchase a license to hunt or fish and to raise the license fee from $1.50 to $2. Women had been used "as a medium for exterminating game by being taken in parties principally for the purpose of claiming limits of birds and fish for each member of the party, regardless of whether they actually took part in the shooting or fishing or not. In many instances they were not suitably garbed to indulge in such work in the field but nevertheless they were accredited with their limits of fish and game," wrote Jones. The game warden's term was extended from two to six years.[59]

Jones won approval of a stronger fish screen law, giving the warden clear authority to order screens installed. Bears were declared game animals as Warden Gowen had recommended in 1915. Jones sent his fish commissioner to California in search of a better design for fish ladders. New concrete ladders were installed at Sunbeam Dam on the upper Salmon River and at Swan Falls Dam on the Snake. (Unfortunately the new ladders didn't pass salmon). Fifty-eight dams were inspected in 1921 and 1922 and 25 fishways installed. The department destroyed 11 dams that were unused, no longer needed or had owners who couldn't be found. While Jones made a start on screening irrigation canals, he proceeded with caution because of the cost of screens and hard times on the farm. With A. B. Locke of the Forest Service, Jones packed into the Middle Fork of the Salmon for three weeks to observe big game conditions. In 1922, he made a 5-week pack trip into the Lochsa and Selway country on the upper Clearwater, finding many elk and deer and few hunters.[60]

Jones nearly drowned in Redfish Lake in July 1921 but was rescued by Governor Davis and a deputy. Davis and his two sons had traveled to Redfish to observe fish planting. They joined Jones and Deputy J. N. Ansgar on a boat with a cargo of hatchery fish that were to be released near the lake inlet. When wind churned up waves on the lake, Jones took Davis and his sons to shore to lighten the load. Jones and Ansgar attempted to proceed but had trouble with the engine and the boat was swamped. Ansgar managed to swim to the shore but Jones floundered in the water. In desperation Davis and Ansgar wrenched a drifted tree loose from the shoreline and pushed it within reach of the warden.[61]

Jones published a 158-page biennial report in 1923 that included 61 photos, reflecting his skill as a photographer. It also included a lengthy response to criticism leveled at the department during the 1922 election campaign. Jones defended the women's license requirement and the $2 fee for hunting but offered a concession: let women and children under 15 fish without a license. As to complaints that the department employed too many deputies, Jones said the 40 to 45 assigned to enforcement were too few for Idaho's 84,000 square miles "a large part of which is almost inaccessible."

Because of a lack of revenue and inaction by the previous administration, Jones wrote, "our streams had been permitted to become run down or depleted, game was becoming scarcer and proper enforcement of the laws impossible without larger revenue. Today, Idaho is over the crest of a hard pull of four years in building up the fishing and hunting." It would be "a shame and a crime to drop back into the rut from which we have just pulled out." Jones wrote that critics were apparently unaware of the department's work trapping predators, destroying magpies and crows, recovering perch and bass from irrigation ditches for distribution to streams and lakes, the removal of tons of trash fish from streams and the introduction of channel catfish, Hungarian partridge and Mexican quail. Jones was troubled by complaints about the law making bullfrogs a game animal. Oregon had traded 12,000 bass for a few dozen Idaho frogs and Washington state was prepared to trade a few thousand rainbow trout eggs, Jones wrote, showing the value those states placed on frogs as a table delicacy. "In protecting the bullfrog we never dreamed that this poor insignificant member of the finny tribe would be the burning issue in a political campaign." Jones heaped scorn on game department critics, suggesting that many of them didn't buy a license. With the $2 fee, 155 citations for hunting or fishing without a license were issued in 1921. The biennial report included 26 pages naming game law violators, with charges and penalties.[62]

Jones anticipated attempts to weaken the game laws in the 1923 legislative session. And, while he was supported by organized sportsmen and by outgoing Governor Davis, his job was not secure. Gov. Charles C. Moore might be influenced by his enemies, notably the Idaho Woolgrowers Association and its president, Hugh Sproat. Sproat had conducted a relentless campaign against the game department and Jones had responded by publicly denouncing the woolgrowers and their leader. The feud began after the 1921 legislative session. According to Jones, Sproat asked him to ignore a provision in the game law requiring sheepherders who were not U.S. citizens to pay a $5 fee to carry a rifle or shotgun. The woolgrowers felt it was unreasonable since the herders needed guns to guard the sheep. Jones said it was a compromise that had been accepted by the woolgrowers, replacing a $50 fee. When he refused the request, Jones said Sproat threatened to get him and the department.[63]

Jones also riled the woolgrowers by publicly advocating reduced sheep grazing on game winter ranges. The feud erupted into public view in January 1922 when the woolgrowers adopted a resolution calling for elimination of the game department. Jones fired back saying selfish members of the association sought to annihilate anything "that in any way tends to curtail their disposition to despoil, defile, pollute or otherwise ruin certain natural resources or playgrounds that should be maintained for the enjoyment or pleasure of the community at large." Boise sportsmen called a meeting to try to defuse the conflict but Sproat added fuel to the fire. "We sprung this resolution in order to get the public interest aroused as to the fault of the game department and the game laws and to put the department on the defensive as it is now for the first time," he said.[64]

Jones responded by sending off a letter asking the Secretary of Agriculture to move sheep from Idaho game preserves to other, unused ranges. He quoted Sproat as saying Idaho sheep numbers were down by more than one million. This meant a lot of unused range was available. "The sheep can feed just as well on the open range as they can on the forest range while the big game will not venture far from the forest," said Jones. He also asked the U.S. Biological Survey to designate a game preserve in Owyhee County. District Forester Richard Rutledge met with Jones to defend sheep grazing on the preserves and Sproat issued a statement saying the Forest Service was not taking the request seriously. The woolgrowers were pleased that they had started a "conflagration," he said, and described Jones' game preserve request as a "backfire started to save the department and his job."[65]

Jones might have chosen to ignore the conflict in his 1921-22 biennial report but instead reprinted his article from Field and Stream magazine in which he said his answer to Sproat's threats was to tell him and the woolgrowers association to "go straight to hell." The woolgrowers association had no more than 75 members and if "such a handful of men" could abolish state departments or statutes "through their intimidation of state officials then we are living in a damn dangerous age." Jones also disputed Sproat's complaint that the department was doing too little to kill predators. In 1921, department employees killed more than 200 coyotes (including 71 on Sproat's summer sheep range) and 20 cougars, he wrote. (The department's killing was only part of the story. The state commissioner of agriculture reported paying bounties on 38,025 coyotes, 78 cougars, 184 wolves, 2,954 wildcats (bobcats) and 604 lynx in 1919 and 1920. And the U.S. Biological Survey also employed predator killers.) While he railed against the woolgrowers, Jones wrote that the department had operated "at all times with due regard" to essential industries; mining, agriculture, lumbering, power and grazing while still leaving game and fish "a nook in which to propagate."[66]

In February 1923, the Boise Fish and Game League hosted a gathering of 200 Idaho sportsmen. They formed a new state organization, the Idaho State Fish and Game Protective Association. They also wanted to protect Otto Jones. Word was out that he might not be retained by Governor Moore. Speaking at the sportsmen's banquet, former Gov. David Davis praised Jones. Moore said nothing about the warden in his brief remarks. The association solicited letters to Moore in support of Jones. In mid-March the Boise Fish and Game League sponsored a one-third page ad in the Idaho Statesman asking for more letters. "From all corners of Idaho letters have been directed to Gov. C.C. Moore, protesting any change in the head of the game department. Have you expressed the sentiments of your community?" C. E. Clarke of the Shoshone Rod and Gun Club was quoted as saying "we consider Otto M. Jones the most efficient game warden we have ever had, and that fish and game conditions under his administration are better than ever before."[67]

A week later, Moore asked Jones for his resignation and announced that he was being replaced by Richard Thomas of Kellogg, an assistant chief deputy, effective April 1. A resignation was needed because the 1921 game law had provided for 6-year terms for wardens. The revised 1923 game law signed by Moore restored the term to two years. It also allowed women and children under 14 to fish without a license. The $5 fee for non-citizen sheepherders to carry a rifle or shotgun was continued. Twenty-five cents of each license sold was set-aside in a separate fund for the destruction of predators. While Jones had clearly made gains in game conservation while strengthening and expanding the department his outspoken, aggressive style cost him his job.[68]

By 1923, the game department's functions were well established with emphasis on enforcement, production of hatchery fish, making war on predators, stocking big game winter ranges with salt and advising the governor and legislature on fish and game laws. With better enforcement, game preserves and elk transplants, big game populations were increasing. Estimated numbers on Idaho national forests in 1924 were 52,639 deer, 5,900 elk, 3,136 mountain goat, 1,495 antelope, 1,135 mountain sheep, 673 moose and 68 caribou. More deer and antelope roamed on public land outside the forests. The resurgence of elk was notable in northern Idaho where the devastating fires of 1910 had resulted in a tremendous increase in shrubs and grasses. A census on Grandjean's Payette preserve now showed 600 elk, 2,500 to 3,000 deer and 700 goats. The Middle Fork of the Salmon River had an estimated 6,000 deer.[69]

As in the previous decade, sportsmen and the game department supported the designation of more game preserves. A Salmon River preserve north of the Salmon in the Big Mallard and Bargamin Creek drainages was designated in 1923 along with a St. Maries preserve in the St. Joe River drainage. In 1925, came a Middle Fork Salmon River preserve replacing the Big Creek preserve, the Soldier Mountain preserve west of Fairfield, Warm Springs Creek preserve near Ketchum and an addition to the Selway preserve. Four were added in 1927, a Clearwater preserve on the North Fork of the Clearwater River, the Crooked Creek preserve in Clark and Lemhi counties and the Soda Point preserve in Caribou County. The Big Lost River preserve was expanded and the Soldier Mountain preserve's boundaries were changed. Four more were designated in 1929; the Hawley Creek preserve in Clark County on the Continental Divide next to the Montana border, Deer Creek preserve in the main Salmon River drainage in Lemhi County, the David Thompson preserve adjoining the Clark Fork River and Lake Pend d'Oreille in north Idaho and the Ada County bird sanctuary. Idaho now had 3.3 million acres in wildlife preserves, nearly all in the national forests.[70]

Richard Thomas would serve longer than any previous warden, eight years during the administrations of Moore and Clarence Baldridge. He credited Jones with improved enforcement and with strengthening the department. He engaged in no feuds. In his report he recognized that loss of habitat to settlement, wire fences and dredges was having an impact on Idaho wildlife and he supported a game preserve for the benefit of antelope in Owyhee County. He also continued to pursue increased knowledge to guide game management. One of his achievements was to substitute fingerling size fish for the tiny fry previously planted in lakes and streams. The 3 to 6-inch fingerlings had fewer natural enemies and a better survival rate. By 1930 the department and local sportsmen's clubs were maintaining 96 rearing ponds for hatchery fish. Big game numbers were still increasing. Thomas estimated that, except for moose, populations doubled from 1923 to 1930. Reports from department personnel indicated that hunters legally killed 8,709 deer, 779 elk, 140 mountain goats, 83 bear and nine mountain sheep in 1930, numbers that Thomas believed were 80 to 85 per cent of the actual totals. Thomas gave added emphasis to predator destruction. In 1924 the department employed 28 predator killers in addition to nine deputies. In 1930, the warden claimed 78 cougars had been killed on game winter ranges, along with many coyotes and bobcats.[71]

Among the leaders of the Idaho sportsmen's movement was Twin Falls jeweler Walter Priebe. In 1909, while hunting south of town Priebe and a companion, C.D. Thomas, came upon three bags of decaying sage grouse carcasses left by callous hunters. They were outraged by the wanton waste. "We were so mad we came home and the next day gave word up and down main street we were calling a meeting to organize a sportsman's club." The club was organized and Priebe became president. Eventually it would merge with a club led by Lud Drexler to form the Southern Idaho Fish and Game Association.[72] By 1925, there were sportsmen's clubs in nearly every large Idaho community. The clubs promoted ethical behavior and wildlife conservation. Some raised pheasants, maintained fish rearing ponds and worked with the state game warden to import elk.

In 1922, Priebe developed a fish hatchery in Rock Creek canyon on the edge of Twin Falls. Trout were carried to streams in milk cans on a horse drawn wagon. Priebe also developed a pheasant farm in his back yard. The Shoshone County Sportsmen's Association of Kellogg and Wallace, organized in 1916, worked with the Kootenai County Sportsmen to develop fish ponds. In 1928, the Ada Fish and Game League, claiming to have 560 paying members, reared more than 200,000 trout in ponds for release in the Boise River and tributary streams and purchased and released 92 pheasants. Members built tables and developed a free campsite at Kirkham Hot Springs on the South Fork of the Payette River and worked with farmers to reduce trespass problems.[73]

The state sportsmen's organization formed in 1923 to support Otto Jones didn't survive. But in 1926, representatives of clubs in 18 southern Idaho counties organized a regional coalition, the Southwestern Idaho Sportsmen's Association. In December 1930, the president, Claude High of Boise, welcomed 28 delegates to the second biennial convention in Gooding to consider an agenda that included reform of fish and game management. The association wanted a commission system. They agreed to give further study to the specifics and prepare a plan for the 1933 legislature. They also endorsed the Forest Service proposal for a million-acre primitive area in the Middle Fork Salmon River country.[74]

Democratic Gov. C. Ben Ross easily won a second term in 1932. During the campaign the governor told local sportsmen's clubs that he would support a commission system if it was endorsed by a majority of their organizations. After meeting with the governor in late November, Claude High said he was confident of success. "We have the governor's promise that if the sentiment of sportsmen is in favor of the commission he will sanction it." High said there was 100 percent support from the Southwest and Southeast Idaho associations representing 32 counties, and from local clubs in northern Idaho.[75] The governor's support proved to be lukewarm at best. The commission bill cleared the Senate Fish and Game Committee but was killed 28-16. It was supported by all nine Senate Republicans and seven Democrats while 28 Democrats voted no.[76]

The sportsmen returned in 1935, backing a bill sponsored by Rep. L.N. Thornburg of Shoshone County. It provided for a 5-member commission representing five geographic areas. Initial terms would vary so a governor could appoint no more than one commissioner a year. No more than three commissioners could be from one political party. A civil service system for employees would include hiring based on examination scores. "Idaho is a beautiful state with every natural resource in the world," said Thornburg. "Its fish and game should be built up and preserved for the benefit of the people.

This bill is designed for scientific supervision over fish and game in the state." The commission would gather and share with the legislature scientific information on fish culture, game conservation and stream pollution. Joining Thornburg as an advocate was C.B. Wilson, "the bewhiskered dean of Idaho Democracy" who had two game preserves named for him in Caribou County.[77]

In February, sportsmen again formed a statewide organization, the United Fish and Game Association of Idaho. Walt Priebe was named president with J.N. Haven of Lewiston vice president and C.H. Creason of Rupert secretary-treasurer. The organization included representatives of three regional associations, Southwest Idaho, Eastern Idaho and Northern Idaho. The delegates endorsed Thornburg's bill.[78] But again, there was no help from the Ross administration. The bill came out of the House Fish and Game Committee with a "do not pass" recommendation and was tabled 39-19. The Statesman's Cato the Censor reported that "heat" had been turned on Democrats and on the sportsmen's organizations and some members had written letters opposing the bill. Even C.B. Wilson defected. Once more, as in 1913, 1915 and 1933 politics prevailed over reform.[79]

Meanwhile, in Washington, D.C., J.N. "Ding" Darling was leading a movement to establish a national organization to work for wildlife conservation. Darling was a nationally syndicated newspaper cartoonist, a Pulitzer Prize winner whose cartoons appeared in 130 newspapers. Conservation of wildlife, land and water were frequent subjects of his cartoons. Darling's interest in restoring duck habitat led him to accept appointment as head of the U.S. Biological Survey, predecessor of the U.S. Fish and Wildlife Service. Darling was a Republican and no admirer of Franklin Roosevelt's New Deal but took the federal post so he could advance wildlife conservation. In 1935, Darling organized meetings in New York that led to creation of the American Wildlife Institute, a private foundation to promote conservation. At Darling's request, President Roosevelt called for a meeting of representatives of wildlife and conservation organizations from every state and Canada. The North American Wildlife Conference was scheduled for February 3, 1936, in Washington. Its primary purpose was to foster formation of a national conservation organization representing state and local clubs.[80]

Meanwhile, the United States Junior Chamber of Commerce was promoting the creation of state conservation coalitions. At the urging of State Game Warden Amos Eckert, Walt Priebe, president of the Southwest Idaho Sportsmen's Association, called for a meeting in Boise to select Idaho's delegates to the Washington gathering. Priebe and the Ada Fish and Game League worked with Dan McGrath of Burley, who represented the Junior Chamber. On January 26, sportsmen met in Boise to organize a new state coalition and select delegates to the Washington conference. This was a fresh attempt at organizing, not a continuation of the United Fish and Game Association, formed the previous February. McGrath explained that the Junior Chamber was sponsoring the gathering but would withdraw as soon as a council was organized.[81]

R.G. Cole, a member of the Ada Fish and Game League and director of the Idaho Automobile Association, was named temporary president of the new Idaho Conservation Council. Articles of incorporation said the council's purpose was to "Coordinate efforts of other organizations and associations interested in the conservation of natural resources in the state of Idaho, both organic and inorganic, and foster and promote a general and continued movement for the conservation, restoration and scientific supervision of all game, fish, fowl and other wildlife in its natural habitat in the state of Idaho, insofar as the same may be permitted by the laws of the state of Idaho." Eckert would lead a delegation to Washington that included Priebe, George Grebe of Kuna, Milton Powell of Twin Falls, George Pettibone of Grangeville and Regional Forester Richard Rutledge. The Forest Service was a sponsor of the national conference.[82]

The Idahoans were among 1,500 participants in the North American Wildlife Conference who agreed to form a national organization, the General Wildlife Federation. Among the speakers was Interior Secretary Harold Ickes who called for "a united, aggressive national conservation movement" to counter "predatory interests that would deplete our oil, forests, soil, and fish and stream resources."[83] Darling urged the delegates to get involved in elections on behalf of wildlife. "Conservationists never helped elect anybody, or as conservationists, defeated anyone." Darling, who had left the Biological Survey post, was named president of the national federation. George Grebe was named regional director for Idaho, Wyoming and Montana.[84]

Leaders of the Idaho Conservation Council scheduled a second meeting in April to follow up on the Washington conference and complete organizing work. Governor Ross welcomed 56 delegates to the Capitol. They represented 30 sportsmen's organizations from 27 of the 44 counties. After hearing reports on the Washington conference they changed the name to Idaho Wildlife Federation and voted to join the national federation, soon to be renamed the National Wildlife Federation.[85] Priebe said there was no intention of taking anything away from local organizations and no threat of control by the Forest Service or Department of Interior. "Had we had an organization like this 20 years ago to help protect our watersheds and natural habitats for wildlife we would not be in our present condition," said Eckert. Grebe said there were 36,000 organizations in the United States interested in wildlife but "the scattered groups are accomplishing very little and this proposed national federation is our chance to join in a concerted effort."[86]

Reform of wildlife management was still on the minds of federation leaders. R.G. Cole was one of a small group that gathered for Saturday lunches at Kelly's Club Cafe in Boise. They put together a reform plan along the lines of an initiative measure adopted by voters in Missouri and the 1935 Idaho commission bill. Boise attorney Homer Martin did the drafting with the help of Guy Mains, supervisor of the Boise National Forest, District Judge Charles Koelsch, legislative sponsor of the 1913 and 1915 commission bills, Cole, A.W. Weaver, a dentist and Grant Ferre, Forest Service engineer. The group had originally been convened by Mains to consider forest management.[87]

With the Kelly's Club Cafe plan, the governor would appoint a 5-member fish and game commission representing five geographic areas. Only people who had demonstrated an interest in wildlife could qualify and no more than three members could be from one political party. The commission would appoint a fish and game director and would have authority to determine game seasons and bag limits, taking that function out of the hands of the legislature meeting every two years. Employees would be hired based on merit and could not be fired without cause. They would be barred from partisan political activity. An important feature was language recognizing wildlife and game fish as valuable, to be "preserved, protected, perpetuated and managed." No existing state statute specifically recognized the value of wildlife.[88] (In 1938, Game Warden R.W. McIntyre was quoted as saying that a group of Boise poachers were trying to take his job. The Kelly Cafe group started calling themselves the Poacher's Club.)

Participants in the Idaho Wildlife Federation's second annual meeting endorsed the reform proposal in January 1937. President Cole said 90 percent of local sportsmen's clubs had joined the federation boosting membership to 10,000. "When the public is aroused you will see this great movement of conservation of our natural resources go forward with surprising results," he said. Wildlife must receive full consideration in "our future land utilization plans" rather than being subordinate to other interests. He called for a study of stream pollution by industry and municipalities "with a view toward correction." George Grebe also called attention to the importance of habitat. "The fate of wildlife is inseparably linked with the problems of soil erosion, dust storms, stream pollution, conservation and watersheds, destruction of forests, grasses and forage."[89] Federation leaders had reason for optimism when their commission bill was introduced in the legislature in February 1937. There were reports that it was favored by Gov. Barzilla Clark, elected in 1936.[90]

The House Fish and Game Committee endorsed the commission bill and, with first term Rep. Arthur Murphy of Shoshone County leading the debate, the House passed it 38-21. "It would build up an experienced and efficient force of employees and law enforcement officers within the department whose jobs would be secure regardless of their politics," said Murphy. "It would encourage fearless and impartial law enforcement by removing all outside political influence or pull. It would gratify the wishes of thousands of sportsmen and insure their greater cooperation with the fish and game department." Rep. B.F. Bistline of Pocatello spoke against the bill, describing commissions as "headless fourth branches of government." Rep. Joe Turk of Shoshone County responded saying 31 other states had game commissions and none had returned to the old system.[91]

Trouble was waiting in the Senate where Fish and Game Committee Chairman L.L. Burtenshaw of Adams County opposed the bill, saying a commission would be too costly to sportsmen. (The bill required commissioners to serve without pay and limited their annual expenses to $300). Burtenshaw's committee sent it to the Senate with a "do not pass" recommendation on a 5-4 vote. It came up on the Senate calendar late on a Saturday afternoon and the Democratic majority adopted a motion to cut off debate, allowing the sponsors only 12 minutes to present the bill. It died 28-14 with only three Democrats joining the 11 Republican supporters.[92]

The wildlife federation's legislative committee responded with a scathing condemnation of the Senate's action. "Once again the people of the state of Idaho have had their interest in fish and game crucified upon the alter of political patronage," said President Cole. "Promises made to thousands of sportsmen throughout the state that their programs would receive careful consideration meant nothing whatever. The sportsmen of this state will accept this challenge and in 1938 will give their answer in unmistakable terms."[93]

That answer would be an initiative campaign. A 1912 amendment to the state constitution allowed voters to bypass the legislature and governor, put a proposed law on the ballot and enact it by majority vote. No law had yet been passed by initiative and sportsmen fell short of the required number of signatures with an attempted commission initiative in 1936. This time they were aroused, determined and organized. Petitions went out to local clubs. Dan McGrath was hired to run the campaign. Ted Trueblood, a young Boise Capital News reporter and aspiring outdoor writer, agreed to write news releases. Sportsmen would have only seven weeks to gather 21,000 signatures of registered voters and have them certified by county clerks. On July 7, Homer Martin, McGrath and Cole delivered petitions with 24,000 signatures to the Secretary of State. Another 4,000 came in from local clubs before the deadline.[94]

Both the Democratic and Republican parties endorsed the initiative and federation leaders believed a majority would vote yes. But that might not be enough. An initiative needed a majority of the total votes cast for governor. How many voters would mark their choice for governor and pass on the initiative? In the week before the election local sportsmen's clubs sponsored meetings, handed out fliers and conducted motorcades. The Ada Fish and Game League conducted a rally at the statehouse and a parade. An auto caravan traveled to Meridian, Star and Eagle. On election day sample ballots were handed to people going to voting places.[95] Three days after the election the outcome was uncertain. Based on incomplete results Cole was hopeful that the initiative had barely passed. The final official count on November 29 gave the initiative 118,000 votes to 37,442 with majorities in every county. Twenty-five years after the defeat of the first reform proposal the 2-year-old Idaho Wildlife Federation had transformed game management. The vote was an affirmation of public support for wildlife and for more professional, scientific management.

On December 10, Lt. Gov. Charles Gossett, acting temporarily as governor, appointed the first fish and game commissioners; Walter Fiscus of Potlatch, Bird Hawley of Melba, George Booth of Burley, Stanley Easton of Kellogg and Alton R. Howell of Idaho Falls. Three of the five had been recommended by the federation. Booth was elected chairman and Hawley secretary. In March the commission named a director to succeed R.W. McIntyre, Dr. A.B. Hatch of Moscow, an instructor at the University of Idaho who had organized a January conference on wildlife management. It seemed like a good choice.[96]

Soon, however, the commission made mistakes that eroded its credibility and brought sharp criticism from leaders of the Idaho Wildlife Federation. Easton, a mining company executive, couldn't find enough time to attend meetings and resigned. Gov. C.A. Bottolfsen chose as his replacement the president of the Shoshone Sportsmen's Association, M.J. Bottinelli of Kellogg. Bottinelli joined a commission that was feuding and in revolt against Hatch who had fired the director of the Jerome game farm, creating a regional firestorm. The commission had conducted a series of meetings behind closed doors in Hawley's hotel room and minutes were not made available to the public or the governor. In late April directors of the Idaho Wildlife Federation, in a special meeting in Boise, adopted a resolution calling for open commission meetings, with minutes made available in the director's office. It said the commission had wasted time on "petty bickering, secret factional intrigue and fruitless wrangling." It had been slow to appoint a director and then hired two officers subject not to supervision by the director but by the commission. "It has demoralized the department which it was created to reorganize, harmonize and stabilize." The federation assigned primary blame to Hawley, the commission secretary and asked the governor to remove him. Hawley was accused of "inefficiency, neglect of duty and misconduct in office."[97]

The commission met the next day and voted 3-2 to ask Hatch to resign despite Bottinelli's plea to give him "a fair chance." A motion to reconsider failed on a 3-2 vote the following day and the commission approved Hawley's motion to hire Harold Harvey to replace Hatch. Harvey had been employed by the Twin Falls Chamber of Commerce and was now working for the Farmer's Home Administration in Portland. He had no game management experience but had done some writing for outdoor magazines. Gov. Bottolfsen responded to the federation petition, removed Hawley and named George Grebe of Kuna to replace him. Hawley went to court to challenge the governor's authority but his request for a restraining order to prevent the seating of Grebe was denied.[98]

After the ragged start, the commission and director settled into their work. Positions were filled based on scores earned on examinations. Harvey presented a draft of a complete revision of the game code, pointing out that there were many vague and conflicting laws. The commission named the sturgeon a game fish, banned the use of seines and snag hooks in taking salmon, designated new game reserves and bird sanctuaries, authorized an elk hunt in the Selway preserve, appointed a fish culturist and named a new director, Owen Morris of Boise, an employee of the Biological Survey's predator control branch. The commission commended Harvey for his work "during a difficult and turbulent period."

In the department's biennial report for 1939-40, Morris credited the new system with improving both game management and efficiency. In all divisions more work had been accomplished, in most instances at less cost. Arrests for game law violations increased from 350 in 1938 to 864 in 1940 and convictions were up from 342 to 844. Also significant in improving wildlife management was the Pitman-Robertson Act approved by Congress in 1937. Proceeds from a federal excise tax on sporting goods went to states for wildlife enhancement projects with a 3-1-match ratio. In 1939 and 1940, the Idaho Fish and Game Department completed or started 12 projects with a total cost of $85,000. Sixteen-hundred beaver were live trapped in agricultural areas and moved to mountain streams where their dams and pools could conserve soil and water. With the help of the Civilian Conservation Corps, 17 desert watering holes were developed from seeps and springs for sage grouse and livestock. Land purchases in Jefferson County provided hunter access and bird habitat. Land was acquired near St. Maries to improve deer winter range. Biologists were beginning a study on the Middle Fork of the Salmon River to determine why bighorn sheep numbers were declining.[99]

While Idaho now had a stronger fish and game department, less subject to political pressure, the reality was that the authority of the commission was limited. It could set seasons and bag limits but had no authority to prevent or limit destruction of wildlife habitat on 33 million acres of public land under the jurisdiction of the Forest Service and the Interior Department, on privately owned land or on two million acres of state land under jurisdiction of the State Land Board. It could only advise policy makers and land agencies on habitat issues. Similarly it had no authority to limit the loss of fish habitat to dams, mining, stream alterations or road construction. The destruction of wildlife habitat referred to by Game warden Amos Eckert at the 1936 Wildlife Federation meeting would continue. The period 1900 to 1940 brought enormous habitat losses and the pace of destruction would quicken after World War II. While some state office holders and members of Congress might express support for wildlife and woo the votes of sportsmen, their primary interest was promoting economic development. Idaho sportsmen tended to accept the notion that wildlife habitat had to be sacrificed for economic growth. It would be another 14 years before organized sportsmen would take action to limit the losses. In the meantime they would focus on such matters as bag limits and seasons.

In 1949, the Idaho Outdoor Association, sponsored legislation to have fish and game commissioners elected every two years rather than appointed for 6-year terms. The association was a reorganized version of the Idaho Trappers Association. The bill was defeated in the Senate 17-26.[100]

In 1952, controversy developed around the feeding of elk and deer on winter ranges. An estimated 500 deer and 100 elk died in Garden Valley on the South Fork of the Payette River in the winter of 1951-52. Director Tom Murray of the Fish and Game Department was accused of cutting the pay of conservation officers who fed the animals without his approval. Ada Fish and Game League members voted to ask for his removal. The Fish and Game Commission rejected a motion to dismiss him on a 3-2 vote and authorized a study of fish and game management by the National Wildlife Management Institute. Among Murray's critics was Ted Trueblood, the outdoor writer who served as publicist for the 1938 initiative. Trueblood now advocated the election of fish and game commissioners by districts with the idea of making them more accountable to sportsmen. This concept was again embraced by the Idaho Outdoor Association. The association also wanted Murray fired.[101]

Gov. Len Jordan called for action by the legislature in his 1953 message, suggesting that a change in game management was needed. "All of you are aware of the endless controversy that surrounds the management of our fish and game resources. Several delegations have come to my office and numerous petitions have been presented dealing with phases of this problem.

Because this resource is important to so many people, I recommend that this legislature try to determine what the majority of people want and that you take such appropriate action as your conclusions warrant."[102]

Statesman political columnist John Corlett reported that some legislators wanted to abolish the commission, returning to administration by a director appointed by the governor. House Fish and Game Committee chairman Robert Mills of Boise said he believed issues could be worked out while retaining the commission system.[103] House and Senate fish and game committees met as a joint committee to investigate, hearing more than 100 witnesses in 12 closed-door sessions. The legislature approved and Jordan signed the bill embodying the committee's recommendations. It abolished the existing commission, allowed the governor to appoint a new commission and gave governors authority to remove commissioners at their pleasure.[104] The initiative had allowed removal only for cause. And commissioners would now be subject to confirmation by the Senate.

With the 1938 initiative sportsmen sought to insulate the commission and department from political influence. The commission system had survived but now governors and legislators would have more power to influence wildlife management. As a result of their wrangling over Tom Murray, sportsmen had lost part of what they had worked for 25 years to win. Some of the Wildlife Federation leaders considered another initiative campaign to repair the damage but didn't pursue it. Jordan replaced three of the five commissioners including R.G. Cole, first president of the Idaho Wildlife Federation and a leader of the 1938 initiative campaign. In October, Murray was replaced by Ross Leonard, author of the Wildlife Management Institute study of Idaho fish and game management. In 1955, the federation failed in an attempt to restore language allowing removal of commissioners only for cause.[105]

Chapter 2

Streams and meadows massacred
Taking on the dredge miners

"The people have already waited too long in doing something about the ruthless destruction that dredge mining has wrought on many priceless mountain valleys and streams of Idaho." – Bruce Bowler.

By 1950, many Idahoans were becoming concerned about the destruction of streams and land and damage to fisheries by large dredge mining machines. For more than half a century these behemoths had been ripping up creeks, rivers and mountain meadows, leaving behind a desolate landscape of gravel piles. Meandering streams rich in aquatic life were converted into sterile, lifeless chutes without cooling streamside vegetation. For miles downstream gravel beds where young fish could hatch and develop were filled with silt.

Early placer miners shoveled soil and gravel into sluice boxes and rockers. The damage they left was modest in comparison to the devastation by big mechanical dredges with powerful engines. These machines could process massive amounts of soil, down to bedrock. Even minute quantities of gold or other minerals might produce a profit. But while the dredge owners might gain, the public lost with destruction of public land, streams, wildlife habitat and fisheries.

It was not just fishermen or members of wildlife organizations who were concerned. Dredge miners made enemies of cattle and sheep ranchers whose animals grazed on public land, of irrigators who saw silt from upstream dredging settle in their canals and ditches and from businesses that benefited from tourism. While sportsmen provided much of the leadership, ranchers, farmers, business owners and chambers of commerce joined in the campaign to reduce dredge mining devastation.

In 1950, a huge dredge was still tearing up the Yankee Fork, a tributary of the upper Salmon River, sending silt downstream into the Salmon. A proposal was before the Idaho Land Board to allow dredging of the upper Salmon itself in Stanley Basin. Dredging was proposed in the north and middle forks of the Clearwater River and on the lower Salmon. Interest in "rare earth" minerals and uranium was fostering new dredge projects. The Atomic Energy Commission was promoting the stockpiling of uranium bearing minerals. A dredge would soon be ripping into the ground near Big Creek south of Cascade, sending tons of silt into the North Fork of the Payette River.

The first big dredges in Idaho were greeted with enthusiasm. In June 1898, a crowd turned out to celebrate, a brass band from Idaho City played and couples danced on the deck as the New England Dredge Company prepared to begin the destruction of Mores Creek. In October, the Bedrock Dredging Company chewed up and discharged 3,000 cubic yards of gravel in 24 hours on a Grimes Creek tributary near Placerville. Historian Arthur Hart reported that large dredges operated successfully in 1895 at Warren, an early mining settlement on the South Fork Salmon River drainage. Other early dredges worked on the Snake River south of Boise. At Warren in the 1930s and 1940s dredges and draglines converted an entire mountain valley into gravel piles. On the South Fork Clearwater drainage dredges worked on Newsome Creek, Crooked River, Orogrande Creek and Red River sending tons of silt into the South Fork.[1]

Mining had a proud history in Idaho. Mining discoveries in the 1860s led to creation of Idaho Territory and later mining development helped Idaho gain statehood in 1890. Underground mines in the Coeur d'Alene River drainage were the country's leading producers of silver and lead. Tungsten provided by a mine at Stibnite near Yellow Pine helped win World War II. The Idaho Mining Association was a power in Idaho politics and elected officials tended to support mining in any form. Under the 1872 federal mining law, mining for most minerals was sanctioned and encouraged. If you believed you had found a valuable mineral on public land managed by the Forest Service or Department of Interior you could claim the mineral and sufficient land for a mining operation. Once claimed and patented the land became private property. The only public land off limits to mining was land formally withdrawn from mineral entry or land in national parks designated by Congress. Withdrawals were rare. Prospectors filed thousands of mining claims in Idaho on the national forests and public land managed by the Department of Interior. The law gave hard rock mining preference over every other use of public lands.

Streambeds and lakebeds, up to the high water mark, fell under jurisdiction of the state of Idaho. Legislation passed in 1937 authorized the State Land Board to lease the beds of navigable streams for mining. A navigable stream was one capable of floating a log four feet long and four inches in diameter. No state or federal law limited the amount of silt and debris going into streams. No law regulated or limited the destruction of streambeds. Dredge miners were not required to restore the land or repair the streams.

Visitors to today's Sawtooth National Recreation Area can observe part of the legacy of Idaho's dredge mining history a few miles east of Stanley. In 1941, a 988-ton dredge, 112 feet long and 64 feet high, powered by giant diesel engines, began work on the Yankee Fork of the Salmon River. A group of placer miners with 29 mining claims banded together in the 1930s and

Ernie Day Photo

Yankee Fork dredge piles helped generate support for a dredge mining initiative.

found a buyer for their claims, the Silas Mason Company of Shreveport, La., the contractor for the Grand Coulee dam on the Columbia River. With tests showing a potential for $16 million worth of gold, Silas Mason formed a subsidiary, the Snake River Mining Company, to operate the dredge. It was assembled in the fall of 1940 at a cost of $428,304. It was operated by 3- to 5-man shifts 24 hours a day and seven days a week. The dredge was powered by two large diesel engines and floated on a pond of water. It had 71 buckets of eight cubic feet capacity attached to a continuous circular chain to scoop up soil and gravel that was fed into a series of sluice boxes. Water washed out the gold and dumped the residue behind the dredge. The dredge could process all of the soil down to bedrock, as deep as 37 feet. During its lifetime the Yankee Fork dredge consumed six million tons of earth.

Work was interrupted during the war, from 1942 to 1946. During the 61 months that it operated between 1940 and 1952, the dredge devastated five and one-half miles of the Yankee Fork and a mile of Jordan Creek, sending thousands of tons of debris into the Salmon River. In its later years it was owned by Idaho entrepreneur J.R. Simplot, who purchased it for $75,000 in 1950. While the dredge recovered $1,023,025 worth of gold and a little silver, its operating cost was estimated at $1,076,100, suggesting that in many years of its operation there was no profit to its owners.[2]

In 1949, the Idaho Outdoor Association, a coalition of sportsmen similar to the Idaho Wildlife Federation, sponsored legislation to require operators to smooth out the dredge piles. That mild proposal was rejected. In 1950, new proposed dredging operations aroused more public concern. The State Land Board received a request to lease the streambed of part of the upper Salmon River so it could be dredged, from the town of Stanley downstream to Robinson Bar. If anyone wondered what might happen, they could take a look at the nearby Yankee Fork. This threat to the river and the scenic splendor of the Sawtooth Valley got the attention of sportsmen, civic organizations and ranchers.

The weekly Statewide's Walter Johnson wrote that "The muddy streams and wrecked landscape left by a dredge in its mucking search for treasure isn't worth all the gold that still lies hidden in Idaho's hills." George Scholer, Twin Falls dentist and president of the Associated Sportsmen's Clubs of Southern Idaho, a coalition of 19 clubs, and Rulon Bartschi of Challis, asked the State Land Board to reject the lease. So did the Idaho Fish and Game Commission and the Twin Falls Chamber of Commerce. "We feel the granting of this lease would be a shameful, inexcusable blot on our state," said a chamber spokesman. "The area in question is one of the beauty spots of the entire United States. It's God's gift to those of us now living and to all future generations." The Land Board rejected the lease request. The Twin Falls Times-News commended the protesters and supported the decision: "There is no good reason why a river so beautiful and fascinating as the Salmon should be torn up merely for mercenary purposes." The editor called for legislation providing a rigid code "to control all unnecessary damage even in those exceptional cases where dredging might be permitted."[3]

In Orofino and Grangeville the Land Board heard from sportsmen and civic leaders opposing dredging leases on the north and middle forks of the Clearwater River and on the lower Salmon. A resolution adopted by the Wildlife Federation's Second District said silt in the streambeds would mean permanent damage to fish and that recreation values exceeded potential mining profits and taxes. Also protesting the North Fork dredging were the Fish and Game Department, Potlatch Forests, the Lewiston Chamber of Commerce, the City of Lewiston, City of Orofino and the Idaho Outdoor

Association. In Grangeville, proposed leases on the Clearwater and lower Salmon were opposed by Grangeville and Cottonwood sportsmen's clubs, the Junior Chamber of Commerce, Grangeville Lions and a group of Kooskia citizens.[4]

South of Cascade the Baumhoff-Marshall Company dredge began digging into the ground near Big Creek. Owner Fred Baumhoff said it was separating monazite, limonite, zircon and garnet from the heavy sands underlying that portion of Long Valley. Sixty tons of concentrate a day were being trucked to Boise. In conjunction with the J.R. Simplot Company, a plant would be built to separate the monazite that would be shipped to Chicago for further processing. Baumhoff said the principal ingredient of monazite was thorium, a metal essential in the development of nuclear energy. He had moved the big machine from Centerville where it had been used to dredge for gold.[5]

Boise attorney Bruce Bowler, president of the Ada Fish and Game League and chairman of the Idaho Wildlife Federation's Pollution Committee, began drafting a bill to regulate dredge mining, using a California law as a model. Bowler hoped to have the draft endorsed by the federation and introduced in the 1951 legislative session. It would go beyond the Outdoor Association's 1949 version.

Bowler joined the Ada League in 1938, the year that he opened his law office. He was a recognized authority on water issues and water law. Bowler was born in Shoshone in 1911 and grew up in Gooding, the son of the Gooding County clerk. His passion for hunting and fishing developed early. With teenage friends he would ride the train to Silver Creek south of Hailey for a week's fishing. While attending the University of Idaho he packed into the Selway River country on fall elk hunts. Quiet and soft-spoken, he was a strong and persistent advocate for the public interest in land, water, fish and wildlife. While carrying on a solo law practice he gave hundreds of hours to legal research, writing and correspondence in support of conservation. While drafting a dredge mining bill in 1950, he was also working for broader water quality legislation. At that time Boise was the only Idaho city with sewage treatment and there were no limits on industrial waste discharges into streams.

Bowler believed the state had ample authority to regulate dredge mining and that regulation was constitutional. He had the benefit of a brief written by Boise attorney T.J. Martin in 1947. Pursuant to English common law, the state had a public trust duty to administer lands underlying navigable waters up to the high water mark "for the exclusive benefit of the people," wrote Martin. And it had no power to enact laws that would impair or destroy the trust. He drew a distinction between the legal status of streambeds and lakebeds and the lands granted to Idaho at the time of admission as a state. Those grant lands could be sold or leased and were managed by the State Land Board with a mandate to produce income for public schools and state institutions. There was no such mandate for streambeds and lakebeds.[6]

Bruce Bowler

While the primary goal was to limit dredge damage, Bowler wanted to put into law a broader policy statement affirming the value of streams and clean water: "It is hereby declared to be the policy of the state of Idaho to protect its streams and watercourses from destruction, and to preserve the same for the enjoyment, use and benefit of all of the people, and that clean water in the streams of Idaho is in the public interest." Dredge miners would be required to smooth over disturbed ground "reasonably comparable with the natural contour of the ground prior to such disturbance," with topsoil replaced. Watercourses were to be replaced "on meander lines conducive to good fish and wildlife habitat and recreational use." Settling ponds would be required to clarify (improve) the quality of the water before it was returned to the stream. Failure to restore the land and stream within 60 days after completion of the mining would constitute a misdemeanor and each day a separate offense. During the operation, injunctive relief could be sought in court by a city, irrigation district or canal company or by the county attorney if water was being "rendered unfit." The Department of Fish and Game could seek injunctive relief if water was being made unfit for fish and wildlife. The law would apply only to large dredges, those capable of processing 1,000 cubic yards of earth per day.[7]

Bowler advised federation members that the purpose was to limit the damage, not to stop dredge mining. But he believed the cost of compliance would discourage marginal dredge projects. Federation members endorsed the draft at their December meeting and Sen. Seth Burstedt of Challis introduced it in the 1951 legislature. Burstedt was a rancher, banker, vice president of the Idaho Cattlemen's Association. The federation bill was opposed by dredge miners and by the Idaho Mining Association. It was also opposed by the Idaho Outdoor Association on grounds that it went too far. The bill died with Senate approval of Valley County Sen. Harry Nock's motion to postpone consideration indefinitely. Nock said the bill was aimed at the monazite sand dredging near Cascade. Burstedt opposed the motion: "You all know how these dredges leave nothing but desolation and waste behind them. This bill would just require dredging companies to level off gravel they leave behind and to establish settling ponds." Bowler concluded that there was little chance of success in the legislature. He began drafting an initiative. The Idaho Wildlife Federation had bypassed the legislature to reform fish and game management in 1938. Perhaps it could do the same with dredge mining.[8]

A flurry of new dredging proposals generated more concern. There was also a harvest of anti-dredging newspaper opinion. Even The Idaho Statesman, which was almost always pro-development in its comments on land, water and wildlife issues, published an editorial wondering "whether the state ever benefits from such transactions, when approved, or whether the net result is not more of a loss. Certainly there can be no quibbling with the fact that the monster dredges can, in a very short time, turn what was once a beautiful mountain river of great scenic attraction into a flowing channel of muck, killing off fish which once provided outdoor recreation, and leaving in their wake a ghastly pile of rubble." Noting that the state received a royalty of only 2.5 percent on streambed leases the Statesman wondered further "if any kind of royalty arrangement can justify a continued wholesale plundering of areas of the Idaho outdoors as yet unspoiled." This editorial was written by the paper's weekday editorial page editor, not by Jim Brown, the general manager and author of most of the paper's editorials on resource issues.[9]

Another proposal was before the Land Board to dredge part of the upper Salmon River, downstream from the segment proposed for dredging in 1950. The board conducted a hearing on the request of Kate Finch of Fairfield to renew her 1941 lease on 89 acres of riverbed 18 miles below Stanley. Her husband, Claude Finch, said the river could be dredged to a depth of 20 feet for monazite sand without damaging habitat for fish.

Fifty people turned out to oppose renewal of the lease including Fish and Game Department Director Tom Murray, legislators from Custer County, the Custer County attorney, spokesmen for the Fairview Grange of Buhl and the Stanley Basin Cattlemen's Association. Petitions opposing dredging were presented by the Twin Falls Chamber of Commerce, Kiwanis Club of Twin Falls, Lemhi and Custer County residents and by the fourth district of the Idaho Wildlife Federation. Senator Burstedt said recreation and grazing were continuing sources of income: "Dredging takes out all the money in a short time, leaving the ground a tremendous loss." Challis hotel owner Don Crawford asked: "If the part of the state you lived in was being defaced and turned into a gravel bar...would you as a man take it sitting down?" State Rep. Glenn Brewer of Stanley said that in 1949 the state received only $1,600 in revenue from all dredge operations and all but two operated at a loss. (In his biennial report for 1946-48 State Land Department Director Ed Woozley wrote that none of the leases issued by the Land Board since 1939 had paid a royalty.) Two weeks later the Land Board rejected the request saying it was "against the best interests of the state as a whole."[10]

On the same day as the Salmon River hearing, the Land Board received a lease request for the South Fork of the Payette River in Garden Valley. The Idaho-Canadian Dredging Company proposed to dredge for gold, silver, rare earths and radioactive minerals from the Garden Valley ranger station to the river's juncture with the North Fork. Protests were submitted by the Idaho Wildlife Federation, Idaho Outdoor Association and the Fish and Game Department. No one was more passionate about dredging than editor Lewis Hower of the Emmett Messenger: "Under favorable conditions nature requires a thousand years to make one inch of soil. Man can build it no faster. Neither can man restore a stream that has had its food producing capacity utterly destroyed by the insidious silt of dredging." Two days before the scheduled hearing the lease application was withdrawn.[11]

Meanwhile Ada Fish and Game League members were up in arms about possible dredge mining in Bear Valley, a glacier carved valley 95 miles north of Boise. Porter Brothers Corporation filed claims on 11,500 acres of national forest land, expecting to remove minerals of strategic value. Test drilling by the U.S. Bureau of Mines revealed uranium, columbian, tantalum, thorium, titanium and monazite in the sand and gravel underlying the valley. Porter Brothers applied for a federal loan that was potentially available for extracting minerals used in arms production. Bear Valley Creek, a meandering headwater stream of the Middle Fork of the Salmon River, drained Bear Valley. With miles of gravel streambeds and crystal clear water, it was one of the most productive salmon streams in the middle fork drainage. Salmon were so numerous in spawning season that it was difficult to find a place to cross with a horse. The valley was an important elk calving area. And it provided forage for 1,600 cattle. For many Idahoans this was sacred ground, "one of the few great mountain meadows left in Idaho undestroyed by placer mining operations." Bear Valley was outside the Idaho Primitive Area and vulnerable because a forest road provided easy access for heavy equipment. A State Mine Inspector's report explained that the deposits of the uranium metal euxenite in the sands underlying Bear Valley resulted from the blocking of Bear Valley Creek by a glacier during the late Pleistocene era.[12]

The Ada Fish and Game League adopted a resolution opposing dredge mining in Bear Valley. If there were strategic minerals sufficient to justify it, said the League, the operators should pledge to keep silt out of the stream, to restore the streambed as work progressed, to level the ground behind the dredge, save and return all topsoil, and restore vegetation: "It is now clear that the people of the western states have lost uncounted thousands of acres of its best livestock and game range to the destructive dredging of meadows and stream bottoms. It is obvious that the self-renewing productivity of these areas would have been far more valuable to the people of the country than any amount of placer gold that has been taken out of them. It is time this foolishness stopped. It has been the custom in past years to point to our antiquated mining laws and make helpless speeches. It is time we stopped this, too." The League called for letters to Gov. Len Jordan and to Idaho's senators and congressmen asking them to oppose dredging in Bear Valley.[13]

The Idaho Fish and Game Commission weighed in with a resolution declaring that the dredge operators would be held "fully accountable" for any injury resulting to fish and game as a result of their operation. The commission said it was prepared to "seek and apply every remedy available," declaring that "within established legal principles" no one had a right to destroy any water course or render it unfit for beneficial use. It also offered to work with the miners and cooperate "in studies, plans and technical information." The commission declared that its duty was to "protect, in the public interest, the welfare of fish and game and its habitat in Idaho." This public declaration was an unusually bold action for the commission. In declaring that it had a duty to protect wildlife habitat the commission relied on language in the 1938 initiative.[14]

Bowler enlisted the help of Congressman Hamer Budge to clarify the role of the Atomic Energy Commission (AEC) in the Bear Valley mining. The AEC's Jesse Johnson advised Budge that the commission had contracted with the Bureau of Mines to investigate thorium deposits in the United States. Under this contract the bureau drilled in Bear Valley, furnishing the results to Porter Brothers. The AEC was interested in negotiating a contract with Porter to purchase uranium concentrates.[15]

Three dredges were now tearing up land near Cascade, sifting out "the radioactive black sand called monazite." Monazite was a combination of minerals including one used in the production of titanium, a harder than steel metal used in jet engines. Interruption of imports from India in 1950 stimulated interest in Idaho monazite and contributed to a rash of dredging proposals. The Valley County dredges were sending debris into the North Fork of the Payette River, covering the stream bottom and destroying habitat for fish. Dr. D.B. Patterson, John Eaton and Art Smith of the Cascade Rod and Gun Club appealed to sportsmen statewide for a renewed effort to generate public support for legislative action: "We do not ask nor contemplate any legislation that will eliminate mining activity but we do hope for future laws that will allow adequate control and prevent the destruction of lands, watercourses, fish, fowl and recreational facilities." They said the Payette River "from Cascade downstream is completely polluted by mining waste."[16]

On September 1, 1951, Bowler sent members of the IWF water pollution control committee and President Ted Wegener a preliminary draft of a proposed initiative: "It will be noted this is merely the preliminary draft and is patented after Senate Bill 148 which we tried to get passed by the last session of the Legislature. It is my personal conclusion that there are too many conflicting factors to ever get a suitable bill of this kind through the Legislature." Bowler believed an initiative would be approved and that the federation could "readily obtain" the 18,000 to 20,000 signatures needed to put it on the ballot.[17]

Because Idaho law limited initiatives to years when governors were elected, there could be no initiative vote until 1954. Federation members decided to proceed with an initiative but they would try again in the legislature in 1953. Bowler asked members to seek the support of their legislators. Frank Cullen of the Coeur d'Alene Wildlife Federation advised him that Sen. John Rasor and Rep. Grant Potter "know the feeling of our membership and will go all out for your bill." Pierre Pulling, professor of biology at Idaho State College, was assured of support by Bannock County's senator, Dr. Ray J. Davis, the Republican majority leader. He described Davis as a "very broad-minded legislator, as well as highly capable scientist and educator. Few people in the Senate have more power." Pulling praised Bowler's drafting: "Everyone I have heard discuss your work in the preparation of these bills (the dredge mining bill and a water pollution control bill) has been most complimentary. This pollution business is the biggest single and apparently easily solvable problem in the natural resources field. Idaho is well out there in natural resources but pretty primitive in handling them."[18]

At the urging of Senator Burstedt the Senate Fish and Wildlife Committee introduced the federation bill in early February 1953. Burstedt said such legislation should have been enacted a generation ago to prevent the "ruthless wasting" of recreational areas. "My county and others as well have lost valuable recreational grounds from this abuse. A horrible example is the Yankee Fork area of the Salmon River, one of the most attractive pleasure spots in Idaho and now a horrible mass of boulders that can never be restored."[19]

The bill was sent to the Senate Mining Committee where dredge operators testified that they couldn't live with it. Bowler wrote federation members urging them to contact legislators: "The people have already waited too long in doing something about the ruthless destruction that dredge mining has wrought upon many priceless mountain valleys and streams of Idaho. Interest in the current legislature over this measure is high and its chance of passage appears to be directly dependent upon what the legislators hear from their own communities. The opposition is working hard, and support for the law is urgently needed if it is to pass this session... Don't let this opportunity pass, and a few days may be too late for this session. Then it will be two more years of destruction until we can try again."[20]

This time the federation bill had the support of the Idaho Outdoor Association. Citing past destruction and current proposals, including the dredging of Bear Valley, the association's David Brazil of Boise described the situation as an emergency. Public support and the threat of an initiative were having an impact. Rather than simply opposing the federation's bill, the Idaho Mining Association proposed a weaker substitute along with an interim legislative study. The Senate Mining Committee held the federation bill and reported out the substitute. The Senate rejected Burstedt's motion to pull the federation bill from committee. Bowler advised federation members that the substitute was a "miners protection" bill. It left out language declaring that clean water was in the public interest, that stream courses must be replaced on meander lines or that water quality must be clarified before being returned to a stream. It put enforcement with the State Mining Inspector rather than the Land Board, gave the inspector no authority to write regulations and it eliminated bond requirements.[21]

The federation managed to get its version introduced in the House with the help of legislative leaders on the Ways and Means Committee. An indignant Harry Marsh of the Idaho Mining Association said federation members believed they "can stop the Russians by hitting them in the face with a fish." He said their bill would throttle dredge mining and the production of minerals used in defense and in the nuclear power industry. Marsh said the miners were willing to smooth over dredge piles, use settling ponds and go further "if we can find it economical."[22]

The Senate passed the miner's bill 32-3 despite Burstedt's assertion that it had no teeth, rejecting his plea to wait for the House bill. He suggested that both bills could be passed, letting Gov. Len Jordan choose between them. Sen. John Albertini of Shoshone County said the federation bill might hamstring monazite dredging, "one of the greatest new industries in Idaho history." The next day the House passed the Senate-approved miner's bill 49-7 and then passed the federation bill 40-17, setting up the possibility that both bills might go to the governor. But time was running out and next day's 25-16 Senate vote to suspend the rules and consider the House bill fell short of the two-thirds majority needed. If the federation wanted something better than the toothless miner's bill it would have to proceed with an initiative in 1954.[23]

Gathering enough signatures to put an initiative on the ballot would test the dedication of federation members and their allies. The dredge miners would say they were smoothing over disturbed land and were attempting to limit the amount of silt going into streams with the existing law and nothing more was needed. Also, dredging was producing important defense minerals and minerals for the atomic energy program. Fred Baumhoff, president of the Idaho Dredge Operators' Association, said the initiative "is designed to eliminate dredging and discourage industrial production of Idaho's resources." State Mine Inspector George McDowell said his office had issued six permits under the 1953 law and dredge operators "were sincerely trying to comply." State Auditor N.O. Nelson chimed in, saying the initiative wasn't needed and questioned whether the state could regulate dredging on federal land. When a letter writer questioned the patriotism of initiative supporters, Gordon Lucky of Boise responded, saying he had easily gathered 60 signatures on his street because people "are sickened to see the beautiful countryside of Idaho laid waste by a few money-hungry individuals who care nothing for the rights of many."[24]

R.G. Cole, chairman of the initiative committee, set signature targets for each of the wildlife federation's five districts. The Idaho Outdoor Association, Grange and Woolgrowers Association gave their support. Local clubs competed for signature honors with the Ada Fish and Game League and

Capitol City Sportsmen each gathering more than 4,000. Cole said Ernie Day and Norm Tague "couldn't be stopped." Dr. Al Klotz of the Public Health Association secured several hundred names. Dr. George Scholer led the south central Idaho campaign that yielded nearly 5,000 signatures. Heber Smith of Grace headed the effort in the Pocatello area and Cy Davis in the upper Snake River area. The two northern districts contributed 2,500 signatures. Among the volunteer signature gatherers was Bethine Church, wife of a young Boise attorney, Frank Church.[25]

On July 1, Idaho Wildlife Federation President Ted Wegener reported that 20,641 signatures had been delivered to the Secretary of State's office. This was barely enough but another 3,000 were mailed in or delivered before the deadline bringing the total to 23,576, or 3,097 more than the required number. Four other proposed initiatives failed to make the ballot. In November the initiative won majorities in every county and passed by more than a 5-1 margin, 174,377 yes to 30,102 no. Idahoans had overwhelmingly declared their support for protection of streams, mountain meadows, fish and wildlife. And, for the first time, Idaho sportsmen had organized to put in place a law to protect fish and wildlife habitat.

With this decisive vote initiative supporters hoped the State Land Department would move quickly to enforce the law. They would be disappointed. Even with deep snow, the Porter Brothers dredge began work in Bear Valley on January 21, 1955, operating 20 hours a day in two shifts. Fish and Game Department biologist Forrest Hauck took water samples and found 1,200 pounds per million of solids, more than enough to kill all of the salmon and steelhead fry living in the stream gravel and enough to smother any remaining unhatched eggs. Hauck said the stream bottom could be clogged for 20 miles below the dredge. Action was needed but Hauck said the initiative was flawed. It provided no specific standard for the quality of water returned to a stream, saying only that it should be "reasonably clarified." The Fish and Game Department asked the attorney general to prepare a request for a court injunction to stop the dredging and also filed a criminal complaint against the dredge operators, relying not on the initiative but on an older law making it a misdemeanor to dump any material into a stream that would destroy or drive away fish. Hauck called for public support of the department's stand: "If the salmon fry still survive, every 24 hours is now critical."[26]

Porter Brothers shut down the dredge, saying operations would resume in the spring with better provision for settling and clarifying the water. In April, a Valley County jury found the operators not guilty of dumping material tending to destroy fish. A disappointed Hauck said there might be no game fish in Bear Valley Creek in 10 years. Lewis Hower of the Emmett Messenger had gone to Bear Valley in February, snow shoeing to the dredge site. He published an account of what he saw along with the department's appeal for public support. With the Cascade verdict Howe suggested "the dredge operators now apparently have unlimited license to kill all the fish wherever they choose to operate."[27]

Three months after the initiative became law the Land Department's mining engineer, O.T. Hansen, said it had not yet been put into practice. Hansen called a meeting of representatives of the dredging companies, Fish and Game, the Land Department and the attorney general's office to discuss implementation. He questioned whether the law could be enforced in Bear Valley because the dredging was all on federal land and under contract with the Atomic Energy Commission. Bowler's language applied the law to dredging in any location and the state clearly had jurisdiction over streams and water quality. "We want to strike a medium between sportsmen and dredge operators," said Hansen. "We don't want to drive the dredges out of operation." In his opinion the only way the law could be enforced "is by public opinion," as if there had been no expression of public opinion by the voters.[28]

Meanwhile, the Messenger's Hower was describing the North Fork of the Payette as still "darkly ugly with dredge offal." The dredge act was a spontaneous "grassroots" demand of the people but was not being enforced, he wrote. Hower interviewed Arthur Wilson of the Land Department and what he heard was disappointing. "Well, he said, it isn't very good law. It might work a hardship on dredge operators and he thought it might be difficult to enforce." Were the dredges operating under permit and filing surety bond of $300 per acre as required? "Oh, no, they couldn't be expected to tie up capital in performance bonds." How about putting in settling ponds and restoring stream courses? "Well, we decided if we don't crowd the operators they will work something out on that." Hower called on Gov. Robert Smylie to see that the law was enforced.[29]

Initiative supporters would continue to be frustrated by weak enforcement. In 1955, District Two Wildlife Federation members tried to persuade the Land Board to shut down Claude Finch's Clearwater Dredging Company operation on Crooked River, tributary of the South Fork of the Clearwater. Frank Roberts of Lewiston advised Arthur Wilson of the Land Department that nothing was being done to clarify the water. All of Crooked River was being diverted into a pond supporting the dredge and silt was discoloring the South Fork as far as Kamiah 50 miles downstream. After an inspection trip O.T. Hansen told federation members that the muddy appearance of the stream was not sufficient evidence of damage to fish. The Land Department policy was to attempt to persuade operators to correct problems and it often worked, he said. Eleven months later the Land Board revoked the dredging permit and Finch said he would test the law in court.[30]

The upper St. Joe River was threatened by an application for a streambed lease by the Lewis and Clark Uranium Company of Kamiah. And mining claims were filed on national forest land along 35 miles of the river's course. Charles Scribner and Charles Moody of St. Maries and Morton Brigham of Lewiston went to work organizing opposition. Brigham wrote that the proposed dredging threatened an unroaded area where the St. Joe meandered through alpine meadows, yielding cutthroat trout "of size and abundance unequalled on any tributary of the Clearwater River." The Shoshone County Sportsmen gathered signatures on petitions. The lease request was denied. But there would be recurring dredging threats on the St. Joe.[31]

In May 1956, a Fish and Game conservation officer found that two weeks after dredging resumed for the season in Bear Valley, no attempt was being made to keep muddy water out of the creek. Silt was clogging salmon spawning beds. The Third District of the Wildlife Federation headed by Ernest Day and the Ada Fish and Game League appealed to Gov. Smylie to intervene. As evidence they submitted Day's aerial photo showing the murky water in Bear Valley Creek. Smylie promised to conduct a "complete investigation."[32]

The initiative did not stop all dredge pollution of streams but some miners did smooth over dredged land. While the federation's 1951 bill called for restoration of topsoil, that provision was omitted from the 1953 bill and the initiative. The absence of a specific water quality standard was used by the Land Department as an excuse for lax enforcement. Another weakness was the exclusion of smaller dredge and placer operations. Bowler limited the initiative to machines capable of processing 500 tons of earth a day, believing that the big dredges were the prime destroyers and that regulating smaller placer operators would mean more opposition.

Further mining threats to the St. Joe River resulted in a second initiative campaign in 1968, led by Coeur d'Alene attorney Scott Reed and St. Maries Gazette publisher Bob Hammes. The signature drive fell short but resulted in legislation in 1969. The law was extended to all placer mining operations with equipment capable of moving more than two cubic yards per hour. Miners were now required to level and restore the land to its original condition "insofar as is reasonably possible" with topsoil and planting of grass and trees. Water quality language was tightened requiring use of settling ponds or filtration processes "fully adequate" to meet state water quality standards then in place. The bond requirement was increased. In 1970, Gov. Don Samuelson signed legislation banning dredge mining on Idaho rivers included in the national Wild and Scenic Rivers system. In 1972, Gov. Cecil Andrus persuaded the legislature to pass a Stream Protection Act requiring permits from the Department of Water Resources for stream alterations.[33]

One of the dredges operating near Cascade capsized and sank in 1953 when a pontoon filled with water. The equipment was salvaged. The other two shut down in 1955, when the market for monazite collapsed. The Bear Valley dredge continued operation through 1958, destroying part of Bear Valley Creek and leaving 900 acres of gravel piles. A new stream channel was carved at the edge of the dredge piles. In 1957, the Idaho Wildlife Federation and the Idaho Fish and Game Department supported a proposal by the U.S. Fish and Wildlife Service to withdraw from mineral entry 31,000 acres drained by the upper Salmon River and tributaries and part of the Middle Fork drainage including Bear Valley Creek downstream from the Porter mining.

Speaking at the hearing in Boise, the federation's Homer Martin asked: "Are these values worth saving for future generations or shall they be destroyed as many have been destroyed before them?" Frank Cullen of Coeur d'Alene said: "No streams remain unexploited unless they are set aside and protected." The Izaac Walton League's Rollin Bowles of Portland said 70 percent of the Northwest's salmon spawning areas had been lost to dam construction and development. Mineral withdrawal was also supported by Regional Forester Floyd Iverson. It was opposed by the Idaho Chamber of Commerce, Idaho Mining Association and State Mining Inspector George McDowell. He said Governor Smylie's investigation of Bear Valley dredging in response to "overzealous sports groups" had proven that mining could be carried on without harm to fish life. No action was taken on the proposed withdrawal because part of the proposed acreage had been included in an earlier withdrawal application by the Bureau of Reclamation. The question arose again in 1974 after the Bureau relinquished its application. Withdrawal was now blocked because of opposition by the Forest Service.[34]

In 1979, Bear Valley Associates of Houston, Texas applied for a state lease on four miles of Bear Valley Creek below the earlier dredging, along with more than a mile of Casner Creek. Inspections of the area showed that the man–made stream channel was sloughing off sediment and the streambed was clogged with silt for six miles below the dredged area. The silt was only gradually being carried out by the slow-moving stream. Forest Service biologist Bill Platts said Bear Valley Creek couldn't handle further stress. The lease request was still pending before the Land Board in 1980, when President Jimmy Carter signed the River of No Return Wilderness bill. Thanks to the efforts of Scott Reed and Sen. Frank Church it included a provision banning dredge mining in the entire Middle Fork Salmon River drainage.[35]

The proposed Bear Valley lease was only part of a surge of streambed lease applications in 1979 and 1980. Included was a proposed lease of 28 miles of the South Fork of the Boise River. The State Land Board was finally persuaded to adopt regulations to enforce provisions of the Dredge Mining Act, 26 years after the initiative was passed.[36]

Chapter 3

Salmon and steelhead lose habitat to dams

"Such is the fortune of the mighty Snake. For ages it has been flowing through its dark canyons, a useless stream...Human genius has triumphed and hereafter the rolling waters will be at the beck and call of science and enterprise to aid in the work that the race has undertaken in this western region." – Idaho Statesman, 1901.

With the coming of spring, snow melted on the flanks of the mountains and in the high meadows, sending water surging into creeks and rivers. Young salmon began a massive migration. Carried by the current and facing upstream, they traveled toward the Pacific to begin another stage in their life's journey. At the mouth of the great Columbia River they passed into the ocean going from fresh water to salt water. With the ocean's bounty of plant and animal life they gained size and strength. After two to five years, the fish found their way back to the mouth of the Columbia.

With fierce determination, pushing through rapids, leaping over barriers, they retraced the route of their seaward journey. In two or three months they arrived in the stream where their lives began. There, females paired with males and began a life-renewing ritual. The female used her tail to clear out a trough in the gravel, occupied the trough and released her eggs. The watchful male moved in quickly to fertilize them. Then the female moved upstream and stirred gravel to be carried by the current to cover the nest. Their life's mission now complete, both the male and female would soon die. Nutrients provided by their bodies benefited the stream's plant and animal life. In a few months the young would emerge from the gravel. For seagoing trout the cycle was similar to that of the salmon except adults lived on after spawning and some would make another journey to the sea.[1]

Over millions of years natural forces had fashioned a perfect environment for salmon and steelhead, pushing up mountains that caught the moisture moving in from the Pacific, storing it as snow for spring delivery. Glaciers carved depressions that became meadows and lakes. The meadows, lakes and forest vegetation helped maintain a year-round flow of cool water in the streams.

Before the 19th century more than two million of the seagoing fish returning to the Columbia were bound for the Snake River and its tributaries including the Clearwater, Salmon, Boise, Payette, Weiser and Bruneau in Idaho, Washington's Tucannon and Oregon's Grand Ronde, Imnaha, Powder, Owyhee and Malheur. Northwest Indians took thousands with nets, traps and spears, drying fish for year-round use and for trade. For the Indians the seagoing fish were spiritually important as well as a vital source of food. The Pacific Fishery Management Council's estimate of more than two million fish for the Snake included 1.4 million chinook, 200,000 coho, 150,000 sockeye and 340,000 steelhead.[2]

There were two runs of steelhead, one going to the Clearwater River drainage and one to other Snake tributaries including the Salmon River. Some salmon entered the Columbia in the spring, some in summer and some in the fall. The big fall chinook were the only fish that spawned in the Snake River. Other salmon and the steelhead found their way to tributary streams. The sockeye spawned in lakes. The Salmon River and Clearwater River drainages were the most productive with hundreds of miles of tributaries providing ideal spawning and rearing habitat. Salmon and steelhead migrated as far upstream in the Snake as Shoshone Falls (near today's city of Twin Falls) where the river plunged 210 feet in a scenic display rivaling Niagara.

Forty miles downstream were the upper and lower Salmon Falls, favorite fishing places for Shoshone, Bannock and Paiute Indians. A few Indians were still fishing there in the 1880s and 1890s when commercial fishermen, using large nets, were pulling tons of salmon and steelhead from the river. Liberty Millet lived on an island below the Upper Salmon Falls. At the foot of the falls, just above the island, was a spawning area of about 1,000 by 600 feet. Millett reported catching as many as 200 fish in a single sweep across the spawning bed with his 300-foot seine. His 1892 catch was between seven and eight tons. E.E. Sherman leased the operation from Millett and hauled in eight tons in 1893 and seven tons in 1894. Six miles downstream was lower Salmon Falls. Robert Conner reported that for four or five years after his arrival in 1882 he could observe 1,000 salmon at a time in a chute on the south side of the falls.[3]

A representative of the U.S. Fish Commission who interviewed Millett, Sherman and Conner in 1894 also reported that there was commercial salmon fishing downstream at Glenns Ferry. The greatest concentration of commercial fishing on the Snake was 100 miles from Salmon Falls below the mouth of the Boise River. William O'Brien fished four miles downstream from Weiser on the Oregon side with a 350-foot by 12-foot seine and a crew of three. The seine was deployed from a rowboat while the shore end was held fast. The seine was then pulled downstream by the boatman and by a horse on shore. After the boat end was pulled to shore the fish were captured and put into a pond where they could be kept alive indefinitely. O'Brien sold his fish to farmers, peddlers and hotels in Weiser. He also shipped some by express to such places as Pocatello and Butte. Farmers could buy a fish for 25 cents while others paid four cents a pound. The total September and October 1894 catch for eight of the commercial fisheries between Ontario and Huntington, Oregon, including O'Brien's, was 2,935 salmon and 3,966 steelhead.

Idaho Historical Society Photo No. 73-51.21C

Swan Falls Dam, completed in 1901, locked salmon out of 140 miles of their former Snake River habitat.

Based on his interviews, Evermann believed the Snake River salmon runs had declined. Certainly there had been a dropoff in the sockeye salmon ascending the Payette River to Payette Lake. Evermann was told that two large commercial fishing operations were carried on between 1870 and 1880 with one of them, Hughes and Bodily, shipping as many as 75,000 pounds in one year and that Louis Fouchet had salted and shipped 30,000 to 40,000 pounds a year to mining camps. Evermann quoted W.C. Jennings who lived in the area: "Formerly the redfish were very abundant...there were millions of them. Very few in recent years."[4]

The decline of Snake River sockeye and spring, summer and fall chinook was related to the robust commercial fishing industry on the Columbia River. The output of Columbia canneries peaked at 43 million pounds in 1885 but was still averaging 33 million pounds in the 1890s. Ocean trollers were taking additional Columbia salmon.[5]

Another threat to Idaho's seagoing fish was the loss of habitat that began with the first gold strikes. Silt from placer mining operations settled in salmon spawning beds. An Indian fishing at Salmon Falls in 1894, Camas Joe, believed silt from placer mining along the river was affecting the salmon. With mining and farming came dams that blocked upstream movement of salmon, steelhead and resident trout. In 1875, the territorial legislature declared that any dam blocking any fish run was a public nuisance and was to be destroyed by officers of the law. Legislators soon realized that such a prohibition conflicted with mining and irrigation. It was replaced by a law requiring dam owners or operators to provide fishways or ladders for upstream migrants.[6] This would prove to be a difficult policy to enforce and the fishways, when they were built, often failed to work. Even if adult fish were able to pass, the dams took a toll on juvenile fish headed downstream.

Six years after E.E. Sherman took seven tons of salmon and steelhead at Salmon Falls the seagoing fish of the Snake River suffered their first great calamity. Near Swan Falls, 100 miles downstream from Salmon Falls, the Trade Dollar Consolidated Mining Company blocked the river with a rock and concrete power dam. Completed in 1901 at a cost of $250,000 the Swan Falls dam had four generators that provided power for the company's mines and mills at Silver City, 27 miles to the south, replacing steam generated by stripping the mountains of trees. Surplus electricity was sold at wholesale.

The Idaho Statesman published a special section in its January 1, 1901 issue boasting of the state's economic achievements and potential for further development. Idaho had 161,000 people, more than a million acres of land under cultivation, including 535,000 acres that was irrigated, and mines that produced $14 million worth of minerals in 1900. There were 1,250 miles of railroad. Three million sheep grazed in pastures and on public land. There was "lots of land, lots of water with unexcelled opportunities for homeseekers." Evidence of the state's economic progress was Swan Falls dam, "a magnificent accomplishment of engineering skill," and "one of the greatest water power plants in the country. Such is the fortune of the mighty Snake. For ages it has been flowing through its dark canyons, a useless stream... Human genius has triumphed and hereafter the rolling waters will be at the beck and call of science and enterprise to aid in the work that the race has undertaken in this western region."

With Swan Falls dam, salmon lost access to 140 miles of the Snake River and were shut out of the Bruneau River, Rock Creek and Salmon Falls Creek. A fish ladder was installed, as state law required, but few fish were able to use it. State Game Warden W. Van Iorns inspected the wooden structure in 1903 and found that "salmon can go up it scarcely at all."[7] The ladder provided a series of pools for ascending fish but these were only a foot long, not long enough for a salmon. At the request of Game Warden Otto Jones, Idaho Power Company installed a new concrete fishway with better design in 1922. Jones described it as one of the best in the state. But it worked no better than many other fish ladders of the era. There was no revival of salmon runs above the dam although some steelhead managed to use the ladder.

In 1907, an irrigation diversion dam blocked fish runs on the Payette River three miles below Horseshoe Bend. This cut off the Payette Lake

Idaho Department of Fish and Game Photo

Sunbeam Dam on the upper Salmon River was a barrier to salmon until Idaho Game Warden Amos Eckert had the south end dynamited in 1934.

sockeye as well as most of the salmon and steelhead that formerly ascended the north, south and middle forks of the Payette. The dam had a fish ladder but few fish were able to use it. Frank Clarkson of Horseshoe Bend recalled seeing fish attempting to jump the dam. A plank apron below the spillway prevented the fish from getting a good start for their jump. Clarkson said fish congregated by the hundreds in a pool at the foot of the ladder but would not enter the ladder. He was hired to make repairs and alterations but the fish still would not use the ladder.[8] Clarkson, who came to the area in 1881, remembered big runs of salmon and steelhead before the dams with many salmon in Shaffer and Harris creeks. Soldiers came from Fort Boise to shoot salmon in the Payette at Horseshoe Bend. Settlers caught salmon in willow fish traps in the creeks and sold them in the Boise Basin mining camps. William Talley, who served as a deputy game warden, said both salmon and steelhead spawned in the Middle Fork of the Payette and there was a big steelhead spawning area between Donnelly and Payette Lake on the North Fork.[9]

The irrigation dam was followed by a power dam at Horseshoe Bend built by the Idaho-Oregon Light and Power Company. The next blow to Payette River salmon and steelhead was the Canyon Canal Company's Black Canyon irrigation dam near Emmett. In 1924, the original dam was replaced by a 90-foot concrete dam built by the Bureau of Reclamation. There was no fish ladder. Before the Black Canyon dam, salmon could be observed in the Payette near Emmett "thick as cord wood" in August and September. "Many people speared them at night." Indians and settlers speared salmon in the riffles near Montour. In the 1890s and early 1900s, Indians camped on the banks of Squaw Creek and caught and smoked large quantities of salmon. Al White of Emmett said that for two or three years after completion of Black Canyon dam salmon by the hundreds jumped at the base of the dam attempting to get over.

Large salmon and steelhead runs in the Boise River continued even after a 6-foot high irrigation dam went in near Caldwell about 1885. In 1905, the Barber dam north of Boise, built to provide power for the Barber sawmill, blocked salmon. The fish ladder didn't work for salmon and only a few steelhead continued to make it past the dam. The final blow to Boise River salmon and steelhead came in 1915 with completion of the 348-foot high Arrowrock dam 20 miles north of Boise.[10]

The Salmon River did not escape the dam builders. In 1910, the Sunbeam Consolidated Gold Mining Company built a 30-foot high power dam on the upper Salmon, just above the mouth of the Yankee Fork, to provide electricity to operate its mill on Jordan Creek. The fish ladder didn't work and seagoing fish, chinook, sockeye and steelhead, were locked out of the upper Salmon River, its tributaries and lakes. Sunbeam Consolidated fared no better than the fish. The power plant was in operation for only one year. In June 1911, the mine closed and the company was placed in receivership because of a trespass lawsuit by another mining company, debts incurred for construction of the dam and power plant and the purchase of additional milling equipment. The power plant and equipment were sold at a sheriff's auction.[11] While it generated no power, the dam continued as an obstacle to the sockeye salmon that migrated to Redfish, Alturas, Stanley, Pettit and Yellow Belly lakes, and to chinook salmon and steelhead that spawned in the upper river and its tributaries in the Stanley Basin.[12]

Soon complaints were reaching the state game warden. In 1913, Warden Frank Kendall reported it was impossible for salmon to pass Sunbeam dam. A fish ladder had been built and was accepted by the previous warden but it was "absolutely useless" and should be replaced.[13] In 1915, Warden J.B. Gowen proposed that the game department pay for and build a new ladder.[14] But nothing was done until 1920 when the Sunbeam Dam Company, at the request of Gov. David W. Davis, installed a concrete fish ladder in cooperation with the game department. Despite the optimistic report of Deputy Warden John

Pearson, it didn't work. But some fish were able to pass through the old power tunnel near the base of the dam.

In 1930, Gov. Clarence Baldridge received a letter from Ben Anderson of the Aztec Mining and Milling Company of Pocatello asking that the state remove the dam. Baldridge referred the question to the Commissioner of Reclamation, who advised Anderson that the state had no authority to remove the dam or to compel the owners to remove it. He suggested that the state game warden attempt to persuade the owners to install a new ladder.[15] In 1933, Gov. C. Ben Ross, responding to citizen complaints, asked the Commissioner of Reclamation to investigate. Because the water was muddy from placer mining the commissioner reported that he couldn't determine if the dam was obstructing fish. He didn't favor Game Warden Amos Eckert's proposal to blow it out but suggested construction of a new ladder.[16]

Eckert asked the dam owners to pay half of the estimated $1,300 cost to construct a bypass channel next to the dam. Acting through attorney Chase Clark, the Sunbeam-Holden Company offered to pay only $200. Eckert fell back to a less costly approach, contracting to have an opening blasted at the south end of the dam. In 1934, four boxes of dynamite opened a gap that allowed fish to pass.[17] The Idaho Recorder at Salmon quoted Eckert as saying the new "fishway" would allow salmon and steelhead to return to the lakes and streams above the dam.[18] While claiming success, Eckert was not fully satisfied with the dynamite work and the game department got a $200 refund on the $749.82 it had paid. Salmon and steelhead regained access to the upper Salmon, and its tributaries and sockeye returned to Redfish Lake. In 1942, a U.S. Fish and Wildlife Service survey team observed 200 spawners in Redfish Lake and in 1954, 996 were counted passing a newly installed weir.[19]

The Clearwater River drainage, 9,000 square miles, was second only to the Salmon River and its 14,000 square miles as a source of Snake River salmon and steelhead. Its north fork provided abundant spawning gravel for large numbers of steelhead. Both salmon and steelhead ascended the Lochsa and the Selway. The south fork had many miles of tributaries meandering across grassy meadows, ideal spawning habitat for salmon. In 1905, citizens advised the state game warden that the Dewey Mine Company's dam on the South Fork near Grangeville was preventing salmon from reaching their spawning waters. Deputy Game Warden M.H. Harbough inspected the dam and provided plans for a fish ladder, receiving assurance that it would be installed immediately. When no ladder appeared citizens renewed their complaints, threatening to carry their protest to Gov. Gooding. The mine manager said the company had no money to build a ladder and had no alternative but to blow out the dam with dynamite. In September the Spokane Spokesman-Review reported that Harbough was en route to blow out the dam, after conferring with the county attorney.[20]

In 1903, the Grangeville Electric Light and Power Company put a dam across the south fork constructed of log cribs filled with rock. In 1918, a concrete dam replaced the log dam. It had no fishway. In 1920, Deputy Game

Warden John Pearson provided the company with a plan for a rock and concrete ladder similar to the one that had been constructed at Sunbeam dam. This ladder apparently worked no better than the one at Sunbeam. In 1935, a wooden fishway was built. It washed out in 1949.[21]

In 1927, the Inland Power and Light Company built a concrete dam across the Clearwater at Lewiston, just above its juncture with the Snake. The dam's fish ladder allowed steelhead to pass but salmon were lost from the entire Clearwater drainage. This was the worst disaster yet for Idaho's seagoing fish.

In 1932, the U.S Bureau of Reclamation completed its largest structure to date, a 417-foot high, 800-foot wide dam near Adrian, Oregon that blocked access by salmon to the Owyhee River and tributaries in Idaho, Oregon and Nevada. Before the dam, fish traveled up to 900 miles to spawn in the Owyhee. No fish ladder was contemplated or installed. Owyhee dam took its place with Arrowrock on the Boise River and Black Canyon on the Payette as federally sponsored destroyers of Snake River seagoing fish. At the time it was built, the Owyhee dam was the highest in the world. It provided irrigation water for 120,000 acres of land in Oregon and Idaho at a cost of $6 million.

In the first 32 years of the 20th century Idaho salmon and steelhead had been eliminated, or virtually eliminated, from the Snake above Swan Falls and, from the Bruneau, the Boise, Payette and Owyhee. Salmon had been lost and the steelhead run reduced on the Clearwater. Salmon were now shut out of nearly half of their previous Snake River habitat.

With the end of World War II, progress was again on the march. Federal planners and their political allies would renew their efforts to harness the energy of western rivers for electricity. Private power companies would seek to build their own dams and feed an expected surge in demand for electricity. One of the great prizes of the power planners was the Snake River in Hells Canyon on the Oregon-Idaho border. There snow from mountains in Wyoming, Idaho, Nevada and Oregon delivered a huge volume of water through what was believed to be the deepest canyon on the continent. The planners saw a tremendous dam site in the narrow space between the canyon walls just above Hells Canyon Creek, 60 miles above the Snake's juncture with the Salmon River. The proposed Hells Canyon high dam was part of a grand design of the U.S. Bureau of Reclamation and the Army Corps of Engineers for multiple dams on Columbia Basin rivers including the Snake, the Salmon and the Clearwater. The 750-foot dam would store up to 3.5 million acre-feet of water in a reservoir extending 93 miles upstream with turbines that could generate 1,400 megawatts of electricity. Part of the revenue from power sales would be used to finance the Bureau of Reclamation's Mountain Home project, bringing irrigation water to 400,000 acres of Idaho desert land. The high dam would also provide power for phosphate fertilizer processing plants in the Pocatello area.[22]

In 1950, the Idaho Power Company filed an application with the Federal Power Commission (FPC) for a license for a much smaller dam 10 miles upstream from Hells Canyon Creek at the Snake River's Oxbow. There the river abruptly veered to the east for two miles, then turned back to the west before continuing its northerly course, leaving a narrow strip of land. Idaho Power's 115-foot Oxbow dam would block construction of the high federal dam. The filing touched off a prolonged political battle between the advocates of private and public power that divided Idahoans while attracting national attention.

Private power supporters blocked Senate legislation to authorize the high Hells Canyon dam in 1950 despite aggressive lobbying by the Truman administration and public power advocates. As the battle progressed Idaho Power responded to the complaint of high dam advocates that its puny dam would generate too little power and "waste the river." The company proposed to build three dams; one 30 miles upstream from Oxbow at the site of the former Brownlee ferry, one at Oxbow and the third 10 miles downstream near the proposed federal dam site just above Hells Canyon Creek. The three smaller dams would produce half as much power as the high dam while storing one million acre-feet of water in 90 miles of reservoirs.[23]

Idaho Power was able to generate spirited opposition to the federal dam in southern Idaho, warning irrigators that it would threaten their water rights and limit future irrigation development. Idaho Power promised to make the water rights for its dams subordinate to future upstream diversions. Supporters of a federal high Hells Canyon dam pointed out that authorizing legislation included a similar guarantee. But Idaho Power won the argument with the irrigation establishment and with Republican office holders including Gov. C.A. Robins and his successor, Len Jordan.

What about the seagoing fish, the big fall chinook that spawned in the Snake below Swan Falls dam and the spring chinook and steelhead that migrated to the Weiser River and other tributary streams above Hells Canyon Creek? The fish didn't get much attention in the FPC hearing process but the Idaho, Oregon and Washington fish and game departments weighed in with comments. Idaho Director Tom Murray supported the Idaho Power dams on condition that the FPC require the company to finance for four years a Grand Coulee approach, trapping adult fish below the dams, taking eggs for a hatchery and transplanting hatchery-raised fingerlings in other drainages, the Clearwater or Salmon. Murray didn't believe fish ladders were feasible for the 300-foot Brownlee and Hells Canyon dams proposed by Idaho Power and was willing to accept the loss of the salmon and steelhead habitat above Idaho Power's proposed Hells Canyon dam. Washington's game department took a similar position. Oregon's department said the FPC should require preservation of the fish but offered no advice on how to do it. What about fish and the 750-foot high federal dam? No specific plan was proposed but $4 million was to be used for fish preservation. While the Federal Power Act required fish passage facilities in dams licensed by the Federal Power Commission, there was no such requirement for federal dams.[24]

Idaho Power Company's Hells Canyon Dam.

Some members of the Idaho Wildlife Federation supported the high dam and some favored the smaller Idaho Power dams but the federation took no position. The prevailing view was that there would either be a high dam or three smaller dams. Having no dam was not an option. No Northwest conservation organization attempted to speak up for salmon and steelhead as interveners in the Federal Power Commission proceedings.

Dwight Eisenhower's election as president in 1952 improved Idaho Power's prospects. Eisenhower began his campaign with a speech in Boise advocating private development and opposing the federal dam. In 1955, the FPC granted a license to Idaho Power and in 1956, the U.S. Supreme Court rejected an appeal of the licensing decision. Public power advocates weren't giving up and in 1956, voters sent more public power backers to the U.S. Senate. One was Frank Church. In 1957, the Senate approved Hells Canyon dam authorization with Church making the case for the high dam in his first Senate speech. But Idaho Rep. Gracie Pfost's House version of the bill died in committee with a successful motion by Pennsylvania Congressman John Saylor to strike the enacting clause.

Idaho Power Company's victory meant that the company would be responsible for passing salmon and steelhead past its dams. The plan that was adopted included a fish trap to capture the adults migrating upstream. They would be hauled in trucks and released in the reservoir behind Brownlee dam so they could continue their journeys to spawning gravels upstream in the Snake or in tributary streams. The juveniles heading downstream would be collected near the surface of the reservoir with the help of a 2,800-foot by 120-foot net that would steer them toward three traps and prevent them from going through the power turbines. This "skimmer net" was an unproven system but power planners were hoping it would work and could be used with other dams not yet built.

By 1962, the verdict was in. The skimmer system was a disastrous failure. In the fall of 1958, thousands of fall chinook were lost after the trap at the Oxbow washed out. The widely publicized "Oxbow Incident" (see Chapter 4) was only part of the story. Many adults that were collected and trucked to Brownlee reservoir never survived to reach the spawning beds. Some of the returning juvenile fish were lost in the 53-mile long reservoir. Some swam under the net and were lost in the turbines. The numbers of returning juveniles plummeted. Rather than providing a model for successful fish passage at high dams, the Oxbow-Brownlee experiment demonstrated that the engineers had no answers, that high dams still meant destruction of seagoing fish.

With the support of state and federal fishery agencies, the skimmer experiment was abandoned and the Federal Power Commission and Idaho Power agreed to a substitute plan. Adult salmon and steelhead would be trapped below Hells Canyon dam and juveniles from their eggs would be reared in hatcheries and released in the Salmon River drainage. Idaho Power financed the construction of a hatchery on Rapid River, a tributary of the Little Salmon River near Riggins. Spring chinook, the offspring of fish trapped below Hells Canyon dam, were reared there by the Idaho Fish and Game Department and released in Rapid River, beginning in 1966. In 1968, more than 2,000 adults found their way back to Rapid River. Steelhead were reared in a Fish and Game hatchery at Niagara Springs and released in the Pahsimeroi River, a tributary of the upper Salmon near Challis.[25] The big fall chinook run, the 20,000 fish that formerly migrated up the Snake to spawn below Swan Falls, were written off.

Chapter 4

Fighting for the Clearwater

"Each barrier in the river disrupts the migration of salmon and, despite fish ladders, you can't teach the salmon new tricks."– Joseph Blackeagle, Nez Perce tribe.

"This dam would cost the taxpayers an estimated $200 million, flood a beautiful valley, drown out range needed for one of the finest herds of elk and deer in North America, ruin a fine steelhead and trout stream for all time, and destroy a beautiful free flowing stream." – Morton Brigham.

Rising in the Bitterroot Mountains along the Idaho-Montana border, draining an area of 2,400 square miles, the North Fork of the Clearwater River flowed for 135 miles to its confluence with the main Clearwater near Orofino. Salmon and steelhead migrated from the sea to deposit their eggs in the abundant spawning gravels of the north fork and its many tributaries. There were also good populations of cutthroat and rainbow trout. Thousands of elk, white-tailed deer and mule deer wintered in the lower canyons.[1]

It was near the confluence of the north fork and the Clearwater that the Lewis and Clark party emerged after their difficult trek over the Bitterroots in 1805. The Nez Perce Indians befriended them and gave them food and assistance. The seagoing fish of the north fork were important to the Nez Perce. Each fall they gathered at a large eddy they called Tee-mee-mup to take steelhead. "The women wove cedar bark into panels that were placed in the river to trap fish. The men speared the fish from platforms built out over the river. The women cleaned and boned the steelhead and hung the flesh on racks to dry."[2]

Fifty years after the Lewis and Clark expedition the U. S. government recognized the Clearwater country as part of the land of the Nez Perce under terms of an 1855 treaty. A horde of gold seekers moved in during the 1860s after Eliason Davidson Pierce, trespassing on Nez Perce land, found gold on Orofino Creek. Eventually the Nez Perce lost 90 per cent of the land granted in the 1855 treaty though they retained the right to fish and hunt in the land that was once theirs.

The former Nez Perce land became public land under jurisdiction of the U.S. Government. Thousands of acres went into private ownership in the late 19th and early 20th centuries with the Timber and Stone Act and grants to the Northern Pacific Railroad. Part of the land in the north fork drainage was purchased by timber magnate Frederick Weyerhaeuser and his associates. In 1927, they built a large mill at Lewiston, described as the largest white pine mill in the world. Starting in 1928, logs were collected and floated down the north fork and then 40 miles down the Clearwater to the mill in huge log drives.[3]

In 1928, the 70-foot high Lewiston Dam was built on the Clearwater near its juncture with the Snake to generate power for the mill. The dam had a fish ladder but few salmon were able to use it. The Lewiston Dam virtually eliminated salmon and reduced steelhead runs in the 9,000-square-mile Clearwater River drainage which included the north fork, middle fork, south fork, Lochsa and Selway.[4] Before dams the Clearwater ranked second only to the Salmon River among Snake River tributaries as a producer of seagoing fish.

In an effort to improve fish passage, a second ladder was added in 1938. In 1947, the Fish and Game Department started an experimental project to restore salmon to the Clearwater. The goal was to determine whether spring chinook from spawn in another drainage would return to the streams in which they were released. Eggs were taken from Middle Fork Salmon River fish and juveniles were reared at the Mullan hatchery and released in the Little North Fork, a north fork tributary. Progress was slow but results were promising. Only nine adult salmon returned to the Clearwater in 1950 but in 1953, the number was 62. Steelhead numbers were rising steadily, from 4,202 in 1951 to 10,604 in 1953. The South Fork was blocked by a power dam and some spawning beds were clogged with silt from dredge mining but the north fork, middle fork, Lochsa and Selway might produce thousands of seagoing fish. The north fork and its tributaries had more than a million square yards of gravel suitable for salmon and steelhead spawning.[5]

But federal planners saw great potential for high dams in the canyons of the Clearwater, dams that would generate power for the Northwest and reduce downstream flooding on the Columbia. Clearwater dams had been on the U.S. Army Corps of Engineers list of possible Columbia River Basin projects since 1943. With the failure of Congress to authorize the high Hells Canyon dam on the Snake, there seemed to be greater reason to dam the Clearwater. In 1953, the Corps was ready to move, proposing two high dams. Bruces Eddy on the north fork two miles above its juncture with the main Clearwater would be 570 feet high, would flood 11,000 acres and create a 50-mile reservoir. Penny Cliffs dam would rise 590 feet on the middle fork just upstream from the village of Kooskia. It would back water for 68 miles, flooding 40 miles of the middle fork plus 20 miles of the Lochsa and 28 miles of the Selway. The reservoir would reach six miles into the Selway-Bitterroot Primitive Area. It would require relocation of part of the Lewis-Clark highway then under construction. The decision to recommend Congressional authorization of Bruces Eddy and Penny Cliffs was formally revealed Nov. 20, 1953 at a public meeting in Orofino conducted by the Corps and the Bureau of Reclamation. It was known before the meeting that Bruces Eddy and Penny Cliffs were being considered along with smaller dams on the north fork and the Selway.[6]

Ten days before the Orofino meeting. Idaho Fish and Game Director Ross Leonard issued a statement warning that Bruces Eddy and Penny Cliffs would "most certainly block and annihilate all runs of salmon and steelhead above the point of construction. In fact it may well be that the salmon and steelhead will be almost completely annihilated from the entire Clearwater River drainage since there is only a very small portion of the river below the dam sites that is suitable for spawning purposes." Leonard also said elk and deer winter range would be lost to the reservoirs behind the dams. The Clearwater drainage provided excellent elk habitat and accounted for nearly half of the 9,000 elk taken by Idaho hunters in 1952.[7] The Lewiston Tribune responded to Leonard's statement with an editorial questioning the possibility of serious damage to big game.[8]

Along with the Clearwater dams the federal agencies recommended a high dam on the Snake River, Mountain Sheep, to be built by the Bureau of Reclamation above the mouth of the Salmon and below the mouth of Oregon's Imnaha River. The Bureau's plan included an 8-mile diversion tunnel to carry Salmon River water to the reservoir behind Mountain Sheep, adding storage and power generation. The Bureau and the Corps had agreed to divide the Snake River drainage; the Bureau would build the dams above the Salmon and the Corps the dams below. The plan was leaked to The Idaho Statesman's John Corlett before the Nov. 20 meeting. He reported in a column published in Boise and in Lewiston that Bruces Eddy, Penny Cliffs and Mountain Sheep dams were being promoted as the Eisenhower administration's substitute for the federal high Hells Canyon dam, the proposed dam that the President opposed and that Congress had so far refused to authorize. Corlett claimed that the three-dam combination would provide more power, more storage and more flood control than Hells Canyon dam.[9]

The Orofino meeting was billed as both a forum for disclosure of the Corps and Bureau proposals and a public hearing. It turned out to be a rally for Bruces Eddy and Penny Cliffs. The 27 speakers favoring construction of the two big dams included representatives of the Nez Perce and Idaho County commissioners, cities of Orofino and Lewiston, villages of Kamiah and Kooskia, the Orofino, Lewiston, Grangeville, Riggins, Idaho Falls and Spokane, Wash. chambers of commerce and Idaho Outdoor Association chapters in Orofino, Kooskia and Pierce. Qualified support came from the Hells Canyon Association, Inland Empire Waterways Association, Potlatch

Forests and the Lewiston Central Labor Council. State Reclamation Engineer Mark Kulp and Gov. Len Jordan also voiced support: "The way to stop floods is to tame these wild rivers," said Jordan.[10]

Joseph Blackeagle of the Nez Perce tribe was one of only five speaking against the Clearwater dams: "Each barrier in the river disrupts the migration of salmon and despite fish ladders, you can't teach salmon new tricks," he said. If the Nez Perce had to give up historic hunting and fishing grounds, they should at least be compensated. Col. F.S. Tandy, head of the Walla Walla District, said the Corps would cooperate "if competent legal authority" found an obligation to the Nez Perce. Frank Cullen and Frank Evans of the Coeur d'Alene Wildlife Federation and Oregon Game Commissioner C.J. Campbell also spoke for elk, deer and fish. Ross Leonard repeated his warnings about loss of salmon and steelhead and winter range for big game. Leonard said the Clearwater salmon and steelhead could not be transferred to other streams because there were no suitable streams left unobstructed.

While the Clearwater was to be sacrificed, the Salmon River would be temporarily spared. Tandy said two potential dams on the Salmon were not recommended for authorization "at the moment" because of the fish problem; no adequate system had yet been devised to pass fingerlings downstream past high dams.

With the outpouring of support, Tandy said the Corps would ask Congress to authorize the Clearwater dams. Wildlife Federation members were frustrated and angry. The Corps had obviously given pro-dam forces advance word of its recommendations and had ignored likely fish and wildlife losses, not even consulting the U.S. Fish and Wildlife Service (FWS). The FWS representatives learned of the Bruces Eddy and Penny Cliffs decision at the hearing. Also anti-dam witnesses believed they were treated unfairly by the hearing moderator, Mayor A.B. Curtis of Orofino, an ardent dam booster.

Six weeks after the Orofino meeting, delegates to the Idaho Wildlife Federation's annual convention in Boise voted to "forcefully oppose" the Clearwater dams and Mountain Sheep. A companion resolution decried the "deadly violation of democratic procedures" at the Orofino hearing. Morton Brigham of Lewiston, president of the Lewis and Clark Wildlife Club, described Bruces Eddy and Penny Cliffs as "the worst possible example of butchering fish and game on the alter of power." Frank Cullen asked: "How far can you trust the engineers? They said they would protect the wilderness areas in the Clearwater drainage and now they are ready to tear it to pieces." Boise attorney Bruce Bowler said he had been misled by Corps press releases suggesting that reservoir pools would be below big game winter ranges. "This so-called power and reclamation development of the Northwest is going to make wildlife resources a dead loss," he said.

The anti-dam resolution passed despite go-slow comments by Federation President Ted Wegener of Boise and a warning from Dr. W.R. Jacobs of Lewiston that by opposing the dams, rather than just speaking for consideration of fish and wildlife, they risked being branded obstructionists. The federation had never before opposed construction of an Idaho dam. It opposed neither the proposed high federal Hells Canyon dam on the Snake nor Idaho Power Company's smaller dams. The federation had not joined Oregon and Washington conservationists fighting the proposed Ice Harbor dam on the lower Snake River in Washington State, the first of four federal dams being sought to bring slackwater navigation to Lewiston. While resolving to defend the Clearwater, delegates also voted to proceed with a dredge mining initiative. The federation had crossed a threshold. It would now act aggressively to defend habitat for fish and wildlife.[11]

These decisions came after decades of fish and wildlife habitat destruction, with salmon and steelhead locked out of 40 per cent of their historic Idaho spawning grounds, with thousands of acres of game range flooded in reservoirs behind dams, with streams and mountain meadows ravaged by dredges, with rivers poisoned by untreated sewage from cities and industrial plants. Led by Bruce Bowler, the federation had been working for water pollution control legislation since 1950 only to be disappointed by legislative inaction. Federation leaders were not against development or economic growth. But they were determined to defend the Clearwater and Salmon rivers, their wildlife and seagoing fish, and to limit the damage by dredge mining.

For nearly a century Idaho office holders had been working to develop and populate the state and that was still their primary goal. The rugged geography of the Clearwater country held back the forces of progress, preventing construction of a railroad across the Bitterroots and down the Lochsa and Clearwater. The long contemplated highway linking Lewiston to Montana was still under construction. Lewiston's dream of slackwater navigation on the lower Snake and Columbia was stalled by opposition to Ice Harbor dam. For the Lewiston and Orofino chambers of commerce and their allies the Clearwater dams were part of a design for economic development that included seaport status for Lewiston and the Lewis and Clark Highway.

Advocates like A.B. Curtis believed Bruces Eddy, nearly as high as Hoover dam on the Colorado, would be a great tourist attraction. Wildlife Federation leaders saw it differently as reflected in these comments by Jack O'Connor of Lewiston: "This wilderness and assets we have here in climate, scenery and opportunities for hunting, fishing and other outdoor activities are about the most valuable things this area has and they shouldn't be thrown away willy-nilly." The dams "would help turn north Idaho into a forest of concrete," declared outdoor writer Jim Parsons of Sandpoint.[12]

The anti-dam resolution brought immediate reaction. Statesman columnist John Corlett chastised the federation for its heresy, accusing it of acting contrary to "the welfare of the state. The several industries have a greater stake in Idaho than the sportsmen. Were it not for industry, including agriculture, there would be no sportsmen." Corlett suggested that the resolution was adopted only because of resentment over the treatment of anti-dam witnesses at the Orofino hearing. He declared that the federation was now "uncompromisingly opposed to dams and dredges," and was acting "like a spoiled child who has not yet learned to live with the people surrounding him."[13]

The Potlatch Corporation, Morton Brigham's employer, supported Bruces Eddy. Company managers hoped to cut costs by eliminating the colorful spring log drives on the north fork and instead floating logs on the tranquil reservoir, then dropping them over a chute at the edge of the dam. The Corps projected annual saving of $500,000 a year to Potlatch. Brigham's remarks at the federation convention were reported in the Lewiston Tribune. The day after returning from Boise he was fired. "They wanted to write my speeches," he said in a 1977 interview. "I wouldn't put up with that so we parted company. I don't see how you could have anything to do with conservation issues and keep it secret. These are all public issues."[14]

Morton Brigham

Brigham had hunted and fished in the Clearwater country for 20 years, logging hundreds of miles on foot and horseback. He was raised on a farm near Genesee, the son of a pioneer settler, J.W. Brigham, legislative sponsor of the 1888 bill establishing the University of Idaho and a delegate to the 1889 convention that wrote the Idaho Constitution. Childhood polio reduced the muscle capacity in Brigham's back and one leg. To help rebuild his strength he took a summer job manning a Forest Service lookout. After earning a degree at the University of Idaho in 1939, he was employed as an engineer with Potlatch. After being fired by Potlatch he became a sawmill consultant, speaking and writing as he pleased. He would be the most active foe of Bruces Eddy and Penny Cliffs and the greatest champion of the natural quality of the Clearwater country.[15]

Private utilities were also interested in the power potential of the Clearwater River. Washington Water Power Company, the Spokane based utility serving eastern Washington and northern Idaho, in 1953 formed a partnership with Pacific Power and Light, Portland General Electric, Mountain States Power Company and Montana Power Company to build dams on Northwest rivers, sharing costs and power. In December 1954, the combine filed a request with the Federal Power Commission for a preliminary permit for Bruces Eddy and Penny Cliffs. President Kinsey Robinson of Washington Water Power told an Orofino Chamber of Commerce audience that if the results of engineering studies were favorable they hoped to begin construction by the fall of 1956. The utilities had discussed their plans with the Corps, the Department of Interior and the Federal Power Commission and had "advance approval" of the Jordan administration. Robinson said they hoped to avoid any "formidable opposition" that could cause delay. In that event they would look at other sites.[16]

Now the Clearwater needed defending on two fronts, in Congress and before the Federal Power Commission (FPC). Bruce Bowler drafted a petition to the FPC protesting the request for a preliminary permit. It was submitted in early March on behalf of the Idaho Wildlife Federation's 80 affiliates and 20,000 members, in defense "of the public interest involved in the wildlife and its habitat." The petition said reservoirs behind Bruces Eddy and Penny Cliffs "would flood and destroy critical winter range and migration routes of great amounts of elk and deer, and particularly the elk inhabiting the Selway River and Lochsa River drainages which are among the best and greatest elk populations in the world, supplying extensive recreational hunting benefits annually to more than 11,000 persons from many states." The dams would block salmon and steelhead, with loss of important spawning areas, said the petition. With water levels fluctuating 143 to 205 feet, the deep, narrow reservoirs would be of little value for fish and wildlife habitat or recreation. "Extensive areas of unique wilderness that have very great scenic and recreational values to the people of the United States" would be diminished and destroyed with commercial development facilitated by the dams. Other sites for power and flood control dams were available "that would not destroy such gems of nature as the Selway and Lochsa rivers courses and their attendant fish and wildlife resources which the higher public interest would require retention for future generations to know and enjoy." Bowler sent copies of the petition to the power companies.[17]

Leaders of the utility coalition, now formally organized as the Pacific Northwest Power Company, had second thoughts. Kinsey Robinson said they were giving up on Bruces Eddy and Penny Cliffs because they believed the fight with the wildlife interests would be too long and bloody. While retaining the preliminary permit on the Clearwater dams they decided to look elsewhere, applying for and receiving a preliminary permit to study sites on the Snake River above the mouth of the Salmon. Their first choice was Pleasant Valley. It was 20 miles above the Salmon and could provide nearly as much power as Bruces Eddy and Penny Cliffs at less cost.

Dr. E.M. Wygant told District Two Federation members in November 1954 that the Clearwater battle, once a rout, was now a stalemate. It was not won. Dam boosters would continue their efforts and the result could be either a federal dam or a "partnership" dam with the government sharing construction costs with private utilities. The partnership concept was being pushed by the Eisenhower administration. District Two reaffirmed its opposition to the Clearwater dams while declaring support for the proposed Libby Dam on the

Kootenai River in Montana and a dam on the Middle Snake.[18] While no dam site was specified, the statement could be interpreted as lending support to Pleasant Valley. The virtue of Pleasant Valley was that it would foreclose the possibility of losing Salmon River salmon and steelhead to a high dam on the Snake below the mouth of the Salmon at a site called Nez Perce. Having endorsed other dams, District Two could now shed the obstructionist label. The Lewiston Tribune's Bill Johnston applauded the shift from "a negative to a positive approach on river development" moving from "unqualified condemnation to qualified endorsement of dams."[19]

While Orofino mayor A.B. Curtis led the Bruces Eddy and Penny Cliffs campaign as spokesman for the Clearwater Dams Association, Morton Brigham led the opposition on behalf of The Committee for the Preservation of the Clearwater. He marshaled information, solicited donations to pay for brochures and postage, reached out to potential allies and wrote countless letters to members of Congress. The National Wildlife Federation joined the fight along with the Federation of Western Outdoor Clubs, Izaac Walton League of America, National Audubon Society, National Parks Association, Oregon Wildlife Federation, Sierra Club, Wilderness Society, Outdoor Writers Association and the Wildlife Management Institute.[20] The national organizations were able to generate letters to Congress from all parts of the country. Some were also fighting the proposed Echo Park dam on the Colorado River in Utah's Dinosaur National Monument. Echo Park would be defeated in 1956.

Brigham kept Bruce Bowler informed, providing this update in November 1956: "Jack O'Connor and I have gone from one place to another raising money, a few dollars here and a few there, for the Clearwater battle. During the last session of Congress we spent something over $500. The last round cost us over $300. Many individuals and groups footed their own bills. After mountains of work, people across the country are becoming aware of the Clearwater threat, and if Dworshak gets work started on dam construction on the Clearwater in the near future, he won't do it without a fight."[21]

The primary political champion of the Clearwater dams was Idaho Sen. Henry Dworshak, former publisher of the newspaper at Burley in southern Idaho. Dworshak was elected to Congress in 1938, serving four terms before winning a special Senate election in 1946. In 1948, he was defeated by Democrat Bert Miller. When Miller died after only five months in office, Republican Gov. C.A. Robins appointed Dworshak to succeed him. He was re-elected in 1954, telling voters he favored maximum development of Idaho water.

Clearwater dam authorization died in committee in 1954 and the Clearwater defenders were able to keep a request for $100,000 in planning money out of the public works appropriation bill in 1955.[22] In 1956, Dworshak tried to get both dams included in the multi-project Omnibus Rivers and

Harbors bill. He got Bruces Eddy with language authorizing its construction and committing an initial $25 million.[23]

When the bill came up for a Senate vote, Oregon Senators Richard Neuberger and Wayne Morse proposed an amendment to delete Bruces Eddy, touching off a spirited debate. They warned that the dam would eliminate North Fork Clearwater steelhead, damage the largest remaining elk herd in the U.S. and would inevitably be followed by Penny Cliffs. The two dams would "wipe out a considerable portion of the largest unspoiled primitive territory anywhere in our country," said Neuberger He had hiked and camped there and considered it "one of the most marvelous regions in our nation."

Neuberger and Morse were sponsors of the 1956 Hells Canyon dam bill that the Senate rejected 51-41 and they linked Bruces Eddy to the Hells Canyon issue. Neuberger said he had warned in 1955 that without the power and flood control provided by the high federal dam on the Snake, it was more likely that dams would be built on the Clearwater and the Salmon. Now Bruces Eddy was being promoted as a partial substitute for Hells Canyon. Neuberger cited the Idaho Fish and Game Department's 1953 statement on the Clearwater dams. Senator Dworshak said he was unaware of any opposition by the Fish and Game Commission. But, in any event there would be two years of study of fish and wildlife issues and opportunity for opponents to make their case before Congress decided whether to proceed. In the meantime, engineering studies should go forward. He provided a statement by the Corps saying an average of only 33 salmon and 9,000 steelhead passed Lewiston dam from 1950 to 1955, describing the Fish and Game Department's salmon restoration effort as a failure. Sen. Robert Kerr, the Oklahoma Democrat who chaired the Public Works Committee supported Dworshak, saying he believed Bruces Eddy would enhance fish and wildlife. The Senate rejected the Neuberger-Morse amendment on a voice vote with only seven dissenters.[24] But the north fork was temporarily saved when President Eisenhower vetoed the omnibus bill on grounds that some of the projects had received insufficient study.

In 1956, Bruce Bowler volunteered to help in the U.S. Senate campaign of Frank Church. Bowler believed the 32-year-old Boise attorney would be a friend of sportsmen and a defender of wildlife habitat. So did photographer Stanley Burns, a friend of Church since childhood and, like Bowler, a member of the Ada Fish and Game League.[25] Campaign manager Carl Burke put Bowler to work placing radio, television and newspaper ads in advance of the August primary.[26] Church won the Democratic nomination by 171 votes over former Sen. Glenn Taylor, allowing him to challenge Republican Sen. Herman Welker. Church campaigned primarily as a champion of economic growth, claiming that Idaho lagged behind other states and needed a more vigorous and more effective senator.[27]

While Church was supported by Bowler and other sportsmen who opposed the Clearwater dams, his campaign also had the backing of dam supporters including Orofino attorney Ray McNichols, keynote speaker at the 1956 state Democratic convention, Tom Boise of Lewiston, prominent Democratic power broker, labor organizations, Lewiston Tribune publisher A.L. Alford and editor Bill Johnston.

The only Idaho U. S. Senate candidate on record with a public statement opposing both Bruces Eddy and Penny Cliffs in 1956 was Herman Welker. In an interview with Boise outdoor writer Lea Bacos, Welker questioned the construction of high dams on the Clearwater: "Before the winter range of the Selway elk herd is destroyed, and the run of salmon and steelhead stopped, there had better be a more paramount interest in flood control than I can now see. Especially when, at least in my view, flood control can be completely effective with upstream low dams and not high downstream storage dams." Welker's comments were quoted with approval by outdoor writer Ed Zern in Sports Illustrated magazine.[28] In a memo to the Committee to Save the Clearwater the National Wildlife Federation's Stewart Brandborg said Idaho conservationists should commend Welker for his stand. Welker, however, declined requests from Clearwater defenders to ask the Senate Public Works Committee to delete authorization for Bruces Eddy. He was in Idaho campaigning and not present to vote on the Neuberger-Morse amendment.

Morton Brigham wrote to Church in September asking his position on the Clearwater dams and Carl Burke asked Bowler to draft a response.[28] In his letter to Brigham, Church said Penny Cliffs should never be built but more study and planning were needed to determine if Bruces Eddy "could be justified in the public interest." He added that some consideration should be given to a low head dam on the Clearwater system for flood control and power.[29]

On the plus side for Clearwater defenders Church was saying no to Penny Cliffs. And he was not committing to Bruces Eddy, supporting more study. Bruces Eddy opponents believed studies by the Idaho Fish and Game Department and U. S. Fish and Wildlife Service, then in progress, would support their position and that the studies should be completed before Congress considered authorizing the dam.

The Church campaign managed to acquire the names and addresses of all Idaho fishing and hunting license holders and Bowler drafted a letter for Church soliciting their votes.[30] There was no mention of Clearwater dams or other specific Idaho resource issues but Church indicated that he was on the side of sportsmen and favored more consideration of fish and wildlife: "I have a genuine appreciation for the basic fundamentals of our environment and believe that the care, preservation and improvement of our land and water is essential to the present and future welfare of our civilization. I believe that the federal government has important responsibilities in furthering these objectives and we should always regard fish and wildlife as an important part of our national heritage, worthy of equal status to other multiple use purposes involved in river development programs.

"All projects utilizing our rivers for irrigation, power, transportation or flood control should be carefully planned and integrated so as to preserve and improve the fish and wildlife values, which I consider essential to the general welfare of the people of Idaho. The objective of public lands administration should be protection and preservation of the public domain for public use and benefit and not for exploitation. Yet, my opponent Herman Welker has consistently supported measures in Congress to give special and superior rights to private livestock grazing and lumber interests in our national forests." With Church's victory over Welker, leaders of the Idaho Wildlife Federation believed they now had an ally in the Senate.

By December, federation members were concerned about a possible threat to Salmon River salmon and steelhead as well as the potential disaster on the Clearwater. The Hells Canyon Association, the public power coalition lobbying for the high Hells Canyon dam, was now promoting construction of a high dam at the Nez Perce site on the Snake, downstream from the mouth of the Salmon. Bruce Bowler wrote the association's attorney, Evelyn Cooper, warning of the likely loss of Salmon River seagoing fish with a Nez Perce dam, sending Brigham a copy of his letter. Brigham advised Bowler that he had written repeatedly to association leaders George Taylor and Lloyd Tupling, with no success: "I think we must face the fact that power groups in general and public power groups in particular have little concern for any values that can't be measured in acre feet or kilowatt hours." Brigham felt, however, that only "a small noisy group" was promoting Nez Perce and it was not yet a serious threat. The most imminent threat, except the Clearwater dams, was the plan for four low dams on the Snake between Lewiston and Pasco, Washington. The promoters had gained a breakthrough with authorization of the first dam, Ice Harbor. If the four were built, warned Brigham, "the anadromous fish of the Salmon, Clearwater, Grand Ronde, Imnaha and Middle Snake are as good as lost. In such an event, construction of Nez Perce would surely follow."[31]

Church heard from both supporters and opponents of Bruces Eddy after taking office in January 1957. A.B. Curtis wrote: "The time for Idaho to step forward is long past and I am sure that with your energy and ability we have an opportunity to start along the road to progress."[32] Morton Brigham provided a three-page summary pointing out that Bruces Eddy would provide much less power and flood control than a high Hells Canyon dam. There had been only two floods on the Clearwater since record keeping began in 1894, in 1933 and 1948, with the north fork contributing only 30 per cent of the water in the 1948 flood. A recent Fish and Game Department survey showed 28,600 small steelhead moving downstream on the north fork. In addition to its value for steelhead, it provided the best cutthroat trout fishery among the Clearwater's branches. In the previous winter the Fish and Game Department counted 5,300 elk and several hundred deer in the drainage. "Why should we sacrifice recreational streams, scenery, big game range, the wilderness values when we could store more than three times as much water, enhance waterfowl habitat and lose mostly cactus and rocks at Hells Canyon where nearly three times as much power can be produced in one dam?" Brigham asked. He was not deceived by Dworshak's claim that money for Bruces Eddy engineering would not assure construction, that the project could be stopped after engineering studies were complete.[33]

A staff memo advised Church that the issue was "emotion packed, politically charged," suggesting that the conservationists had the better part of the argument. Church was deluged with telegrams from North Idaho wildlife clubs urging him to ask the Public Works Committee to delete authorization for Bruces Eddy. Church went before the Public Works Rivers and Harbors Subcommittee and asked that authorization of Bruces Eddy be delayed until studies then underway by the Idaho Fish and Game Department and the U.S. Fish and Wildlife Service were completed. While plans for a dam had been discussed for 15 years, he said, no authoritative report had yet been provided on its impact on fish and wildlife. Clearwater defenders were delighted with Church's effort. Brigham credited him "for your courage and interest in this problem." But Church knew that Bruces Eddy authorization would remain in the bill. Senator Kerr was incensed with the 1956 veto and was determined to send the President the same bill with no changes. Church advised dam opponents that he was apprehensive because most of the committee members had been "committed on this bill long before I came to Washington" and intended to report the same bill so there could be an early Senate vote without extended committee hearings.[34]

Sen. Warren Magnuson of Washington had some thoughts on Bruces Eddy. He advised Church that he and Sen. Henry Jackson believed it would be difficult to gain enough votes to delete it and it would also be politically unwise. If it was omitted, the administration might muster the votes to substitute the private-public partnership project it had recommended or Pacific Northwest Power might pursue its application with the FPC. As an alternative Magnuson suggested that Church take the lead in proposing a Senate amendment specifying that no money could be appropriated for construction until wildlife studies were complete.[35] Church accepted the suggestion and the amendment was approved. With the amendment he voted for the omnibus bill and did not support Neuberger's attempt to delete Bruces Eddy.[36]

Church received a scorching letter from Dr. E.M. Wygant of Lewiston chastising him for his vote and for not supporting Neuberger's amendment: "It was very largely through the efforts of Bruce Bowler who assured us that you would be a supporter of conservation that you received a great many of your votes in this part of the state. We now feel that both you and Bruce have let us down."[37] Church responded, saying he had gone before the Public Works Committee, "the forum that offered the only real chance of affecting change in the bill. Bruces Eddy had been included in the omnibus bill that was approved in the last Congress. It was included again in this year's bill, owing to commitments made long before I came to Washington." Church claimed credit for the wildlife study language. "This in my view, and the view of wildlife groups, represented a net gain." Church scolded Wygant for criticizing Bowler "after the years of dedicated selfless service he has rendered conservation."[38]

Bowler approved of Church's effort and his response to Wygant: "I feel certain that his observations are not typical and you handled the situation beautifully." Some North Idaho federation leaders also praised Church.[39] Brigham was less generous, saying that if the omnibus bill passed the House and was not vetoed "conservationists will simply be beaten."[40] Lewiston attorney Eli Rapaich complained that Church had gone back on his campaign position on Bruces Eddy and sat on his hands while the Neuberger amendment was debated. An exasperated Church responded at length. He had never said during the campaign that he opposed the dam but that wildlife studies should be completed and considered before it was authorized. His committee testimony had resulted in helpful language. He was presiding over the Senate when the Neuberger amendment was debated and Neuberger himself had voted for the bill. He feared some conservationists weren't really interested in what the wildlife studies would show and "rabid conservationists" did not help their cause.[41]

The pro-dam Lewiston Tribune said Church's position was not much different than that of Senator Dworshak who was saying wildlife studies should be completed before construction proceeded.[42] On the other hand, the Statesman's John Corlett, in a column datelined Orofino, accused Church of opposing Bruces Eddy, saying he had received "a terrific spanking from Democrats in this area and since then he has been quiet on the subject."[43] Among the Orofino residents voicing displeasure was florist Shearl Lomax. He had voted for Church thinking "you were a good and intelligent man for the good and progress of the state of Idaho," but now he regretted his vote because Church had aligned himself with the extremist, minority "wildlifers."[44] The criticism from both sides illustrated the difficulty Church faced in addressing Bruces Eddy.

Bruces Eddy supporters were pleased and opponents disappointed when the Fish and Game Department released a report on its 1955-56 winter count of big game in the proposed Bruces Eddy pool area. It showed only 112 elk, 12 mule deer and 55 white-tailed deer in the area below the reservoir high water mark.[45] The Lewiston Tribune said the figures "virtually demolish" the claims by wildlife advocates of heavy elk losses.[46] The game department's Ross Leonard conceded Bruces Eddy would do less damage to elk than "some people thought a few years back." There had been no count yet for Penny Cliffs, which was expected to be "a much greater deterrent" to elk. Dam opponents still hoped that the yet to be completed wildlife studies would support their position but this was a setback.

Ross Leonard wrote Church with updated numbers, disputing the Corps assertion that Clearwater salmon restoration was a failure, cited by Senator

Dworshak in the 1956 Bruces Eddy debate. Since 1947, 254,167 Salmon River fry had been released in the Little North Fork, a north fork tributary, and 171 adults had returned from the ocean, wrote Leonard. "This does not appear to be a very high return, yet successful spawning of these adults (40 per cent of which would be females and average 5,000 eggs each) coupled with good water years and low mortality could produce as many fry as were originally planted. The important point is that adult chinook salmon, have been returning to the Clearwater, have been observed spawning and young chinooks observed at Lewiston dam, ocean-bound apparently." Leonard said the results showed salmon could be restored in the Clearwater drainage. Church inserted the letter in the Congressional Record.[47]

With Senate passage of the omnibus rivers and harbors bill the opponents shifted their efforts to the House Public Works Committee and succeeded in getting authorization of Bruces Eddy omitted from the House bill. Bruce Bowler wrote committee members thanking them for voting to spare the valley of the north fork, "a priceless heritage" and "one of the few remaining natural Rembrandts of America." He hoped the Senate-House conferees would do the same, recognizing there were better places for dams for power and flood control.[48] They did, but Dworshak was not done. He was able to persuade the Senate to include $500,000 for Bruces Eddy planning in the $884 million public works appropriation bill. When conferees met to resolve differences in House and Senate bills the House chairman objected, pointing out that Bruces Eddy had not been authorized. Dworshak prevailed, using a fairness argument; $2 billion had been spent on Colorado River storage and nothing on the Clearwater which had an average flow of 10.4 million acre feet of water per year, nearly as much as the Colorado's 12.3.[49] Bruces Eddy supporters were still celebrating four days later when the House voted 363 to 23 to eliminate the Dworshak amendment from the conference report. With the overwhelming House vote, the Senate capitulated but not before Dworshak vented his frustration, calling Senator Neuberger a saboteur working in collusion with the National Wildlife Federation and "hypocritical groups" to block the project.[50]

In 1958, Dworshak again got Bruces Eddy included in an omnibus bill authorizing new water projects. Bruce Bowler and Morton Brigham wired the President urging his veto. They were not disappointed. Eisenhower said some of the projects in the $1.5 billion bill were wasteful and some were not accepted by executive agencies.[51] But five months later he signed a $1.1 billion appropriation bill that included $500,000 for Bruces Eddy planning and money to start work on or plan 115 other Army Corps and eight Bureau of Reclamation projects. While he believed some were irresponsible, Eisenhower said the bill included "essential funds" for continued work on river and harbor and reclamation projects started in prior years.[52]

The camel's nose was now under the tent. In November the Corps awarded a $79,000 contract for drilling to help determine the specific site for Bruces Eddy dam.[53] A.B. Curtis was the Republican nominee for Congress.

He emphasized his work for Bruces Eddy and faulted Rep. Gracie Pfost for doing too little to help the cause. It didn't help him. Pfost easily won re-election to a fourth term.

On the day the President signed the bill putting work on Bruces Eddy in motion, a fish disaster was developing on the Snake River, a debacle that would raise new doubts about passing seagoing fish past high dams. When the Federal Power Commission granted a license to Idaho Power Company for the Brownlee, Oxbow and Hells Canyon dams in 1955, it directed the company to provide passage for seagoing fish in cooperation with the Idaho and Oregon fish and game departments and the Oregon Fish Commission. A run of about 20,000 fall chinook, the largest of the Snake River salmon, ascended the Snake in September and October to spawn in the river between Marsing and Swan Falls dam. The river corridor was also used by spring chinook and steelhead that spawned in Snake River tributaries above the Idaho Power dam sites, including the Weiser River.[54]

Fish ladders hadn't been successfully used at dams as high as Brownlee's 295 feet or Hells Canyon's 318 feet. The plan favored by Idaho Power and accepted by the U.S. Fish and Wildlife Service and the Idaho and Oregon wildlife agencies included no ladders. Returning adults were to be captured in a trap below the dams, loaded on trucks and hauled upstream for release above Brownlee dam. The young downstream migrants were to be stopped short of Brownlee's turbines by a huge net barrier and lured by moving water into three traps near the surface of the reservoir. Water moving through a large rubber pipe would carry them to trucks for transport to the river below the dams. Having won Federal Power Commission approval in the battle against public power and the high dam, the company was willing to accept the considerable cost of this mechanized fish transportation system. The whole operation would be an experiment to determine the feasibility of passing salmon and steelhead past high dams. The Federal Power Commission was betting that the system would work and could be used with other proposed dams.[55]

In the fall of 1957, returning adult salmon were trapped below the newly constructed Brownlee dam, loaded in trucks and released above the dam in an operation described by the Fish and Wildlife Service as "reasonably successful." In 1958, work was in progress 12 miles downstream at the Oxbow. There, the river turned to the northeast and then looped back forming a bow before continuing north. In 1906, the Oregon-Idaho Power Company cut a tunnel through the half-mile wide neck of the bow for a power plant. The plant had ceased operation years before but the tunnel remained. This tunnel was now being used to carry the river's flow while a temporary cofferdam blocked the river channel above the construction site. A fish trap was in place below the tunnel in preparation for the large run of fall chinook expected in September and October.

In August a Bureau of Commercial Fisheries team found that water flowing under the trap had nearly washed away its foundation. Idaho Power reduced the river flow from Brownlee to allow repairs. When the flow was restored the trap's foundation washed out again. With the salmon now expected to arrive within days, Idaho Power had the contractor, Morrison Knudsen, blow a hole in the cofferdam, allowing the river to flow past, so the flow through the tunnel could be stopped, allowing the trap to be rebuilt. Adult fall chinook began arriving in large numbers, attempting to ascend the rapids below the breached cofferdam. Idaho Power deployed a crew with large dip nets to catch the fish and installed a temporary wooden trap. Finally, with the trap below the tunnel repaired the river was re-routed through the tunnel and the cofferdam was restored, cutting off the river flow over the dam. The salmon in the 2-mile oxbow section of the river were expected to drop back below the now repaired trap. Instead they were stranded in pools with too little oxygen. Some were saved when oxygen was pumped in with drill compressors but thousands died. Final estimates of the number of dead fish varied from 2,700 to 4,000. The total loss was much greater. Half the 14,000 chinook that were netted or trapped and trucked to Brownlee reservoir did not survive to spawn, the Fish and Wildlife Service reported, because of "rough handling during the emergency."[56]

The well-publicized "Oxbow incident" generated a barrage of criticism of Idaho Power. Oregon Gov. Robert Holmes described the loss as catastrophic, scalding the company for taking more than a month to repair the trap.[56] Idaho Power officials said only 600 fish had died but Idaho Fish and Game Director Ross Leonard said thousands were lost. Fish and Game employees salvaged and cleaned several hundred 20 to 30 pound salmon, trucking them to Boise for cold storage and distribution to charitable organizations. Salvaged salmon were also given away in Oregon communities. Both Leonard and Oregon Fish and Game's P.W. Schneider termed the fish kill a disaster and Schneider said it illustrated the "extremely critical problem created by the erection of massive structures astride the main migration routes of important salmon runs."[57]

While the trap and net experiment continued there was increasing skepticism within federal and state fishery agencies about its ultimate success. The Oxbow fiasco called into question the theory that biologists and engineers could find ways to let salmon survive high dams, that they could indeed teach salmon new tricks. It helped spark interest in designating the Snake River below the Idaho Power dams, the Salmon and Clearwater and some remaining Oregon and Washington rivers as dam-free salmon sanctuaries.[58] In March 1957, District Two of the Idaho Wildlife Federation had endorsed the idea of making the Salmon River a fish sanctuary, while reaffirming its opposition to the Clearwater dams.[59]

By 1958, the Federal Power Commission was considering rival applications for high dams on the Snake River downstream from the Idaho Power complex. Pacific Northwest Power Company wanted to build Mountain Sheep dam just upstream from the mouth of the Salmon. Public power forces supported the application of the Washington Public Power Supply System for Nez Perce dam five miles below the Salmon. Either dam would back water nearly to Idaho Power's Hells Canyon dam. Nez Perce would also flood 60 miles of the Salmon River. In October 1958, Interior Secretary Fred Seaton asked the power commission to defer licensing of any additional dams on the Snake "pending solutions to the problem of fish passage."

Wendell Smith was hired as Idaho Power's first fish biologist as a result of the Oxbow incident. He described the many difficulties encountered in a 1960 report titled Progress of Fish Handling at High Dams. Since salmon were accustomed to moving water, some of the upstream migrants "wandered" in the 57-mile Brownlee reservoir and never reached the spawning area 120 miles above the dam, he wrote. Summer heat raised reservoir water temperature to 70 degrees as far down as 135 feet and many downstream migrants swam under the 120-foot net, perishing in the turbines. An unforeseen problem developed as one million trash fish showed up at the Oxbow trap. They were separated from the salmon and steelhead and killed, a time-consuming process that slowed the truck transport. It wasn't possible to separate the thousands of trash fish entering the downstream traps at Brownlee and they were hauled and returned to the river with the young salmon and steelhead. Smith emphasized the experimental nature of the operation and didn't claim success, only "progress," including recognition of problems yet unsolved.[60] The experiment continued, with declining returns of salmon and steelhead. In 1959, only 150,000 downstream migrants passed Brownlee dam in comparison to the one million expected. In 1960, there were only 50,000 and in 1961, 20,000.[61]

Not everyone saw the Oxbow incident as evidence against high dams on salmon streams. In 1959, Senator Dworshak was able to get an additional $770,000 in planning money for Bruces Eddy, saying that the Brownlee skimmer demonstrated that ocean-bound fish could be passed over high dams. The added money won Senate approval despite committee testimony by Eli Rapaich of Lewiston, District Two Wildlife Federation president, citing the Oxbow debacle as evidence that the fish passage problem remained unsolved.[62] Morton Brigham wrote Bruce Bowler complaining "nobody back there from Idaho lifted a finger in opposition."[63]

The much-anticipated Fish and Wildlife Service report on Bruces Eddy was released in June 1960, bolstering the position of the opponents. By this time the Corps had revised its plans, proposing a 60-foot higher dam, 631 feet, with a 53-mile reservoir submerging 17,000 acres. The wildlife report was based on the earlier plan. It said 60 per cent of all Clearwater steelhead spawned in the north fork. Bruces Eddy would eliminate 717,000 square yards of spawning habitat for salmon, steelhead and resident trout in the pool area and block or impede access of salmon and steelhead to another 813,000 square yards upstream from the pool. The spawning areas to be lost were sufficient to accommodate 109,000 steelhead and Chinook salmon redds. The sport catch of salmon and steelhead downstream in the Clearwater, Snake and Columbia would be reduced.

There would also be a significant loss to commercial steelhead fishing in the lower Columbia. While the Corps was proposing to include fish passage facilities, there was no assurance that they would work. Even if they did, allowing fish access to spawning areas above the reservoir pool, the 717,000 acres of spawning habitat in the pool area would be lost, said the agency. North fork elk, numbering 11,000 to 15,000, would be "substantially reduced" and 40 per cent of the deer would be lost. The 15,000 acres of habitat to be inundated along 69 miles of streams at low elevations received the least amount of snowfall in the watershed, said the agency. Its elimination would displace many animals, pushing them into higher, less desirable range with extensive damage to vegetation and further loss of carrying capacity. Delay was recommended pending development of fish passage facilities permitting losses no greater than were occurring with the smaller dams on the lower Columbia. Of course no one could say with certainty that such facilities would ever be developed. If the dam was to be built the Fish and Wildlife Service called for investments to reduce the damage including $15 million in fish passage facilities plus $3 million in hatchery facilities for seagoing fish and $900,000 for a resident trout hatchery to stock the reservoir. Another $2 million was recommended to acquire 26,000 acres of land to be managed for elk and deer, partly offsetting the winter range loss to the reservoir.[64]

A.B. Curtis disputed the estimates of fish and game losses and questioned the need for $15 million in facilities to move salmon and steelhead past the dam. The Clearwater Tribune's R.D. Werner ridiculed the report, saying while the Fish and Wildlife Service seemed to be resigning itself "to the inevitable conclusion that the dam will be built," it was recommending over $20 million "to salve the wounds of the sportsmen."[65]

Despite the conclusions of the Fish and Wildlife Service, and even though he had said he would base his ultimate stand on the wildlife report, by mid-1960 Senator Church was moving toward support of Bruces Eddy. He had steered a careful course, giving both supporters and opponents hope that he would ultimately side with them. Following up on a meeting with Tom Boise in Lewiston, Church wrote on August 13: "I know how important this project is to you, and I would like to find a way to resolve the difficulties which have beset it so far." With the planning money approved in 1959, Senator Dworshak was not pushing for authorization in the 1960 omnibus bill. Since the fish studies and the adverse report by the Fish and Wildlife Service had not been reviewed by Congress, Church wrote, authorization was unlikely even if Dworshak wanted to pursue it. "I have this matter under intensive consideration and I have some thoughts for resolving the conflicting interests."[66]

Western water development was a theme of Democratic campaigns in 1960. Speaking at the Idaho Jefferson-Jackson Day Dinner in March, Sen.

John F. Kennedy called for more irrigation dams, saying the Eisenhower administration had "halted and hamstrung" water development projects.[67] In Idaho's Second District a young potato company executive, Ralph Harding, pummeled veteran Rep. Hamer Budge for his failure to win authorization of the Burns Creek dam on the South Fork of the Snake River. Harding was elected. Church had been pushing for Burns Creek from the beginning of his Senate service. The dam would provide 100,000 acre-feet of storage that could be used for irrigation in a short water year. It was strongly supported by the upper Snake River irrigation establishment. Utah Power Company, which served most of eastern Idaho, opposed Burns Creek, seeing it as a public power project.

In March 1961, Church disappointed Bruces Eddy opponents, announcing that he and Rep. Gracie Pfost would support construction of the dam. After reviewing the fish and wildlife studies he had concluded; "On balance, the benefits that can be derived from the Bruces Eddy project definitely outweigh the objections to it." To make the dam more acceptable, the authorization bill they were drafting would prohibit any other dams on the Clearwater drainage (no Penny Cliffs), reserve half the power for use in Idaho and require users of log chutes to pay a fair share of the cost of installation and maintenance. The Corps plan included a chute to drop logs over the dam after they were moved down the reservoir.[68]

The Church announcement was a crushing blow to Morton Brigham and others who had fought for eight years to save the north fork. They would continue the fight. But chances of success were greatly diminished with Church and Pfost joining Dworshak in working for the dam. Church's decision was driven by political considerations as he approached the 1962 election as well as by his assessment of the jobs and economic benefits the dam would provide versus the wildlife losses. He was already under fire in Idaho for his support of the Wilderness Act in the Senate Interior Committee. Opposing Bruces Eddy while supporting the Wilderness Act could result in his defeat in 1962. His support for the dam was welcome news to influential Democrats including Tom Boise, Ray McNichols and the Lewiston Tribune's A.L. Alford and Bill Johnston. Church had won high marks from Idaho conservationists by standing with them on the Salmon River and its seagoing fish and they applauded his support for the Wilderness Act. But he disappointed them on the Clearwater. From the beginning he had opposed Penny Cliffs but the threat of a high dam on the middle fork had declined. Construction of the long-awaited Lewis-Clark Highway was nearing completion and a Penny Cliffs dam would inundate many miles of the roadway, requiring costly and time-consuming relocation.

Art Manley advised Church of the "keen disappointment" felt by Coeur d'Alene Wildlife Federation members and asked that he reconsider. Maurice Harland of the White Pine Sportsmen's Association wrote that every businessman in his town of Troy had signed a petition against the dam. The

Idaho Historical Society Photo

Floating logs down the North Fork of the Clearwater.

reservoir would cover "Floodwood Creek, Breakfast Creek, the Little North Fork and many miles of the North Fork." It was the only river in that part of the state that still had "the large, beautiful cutthroat trout in good numbers." In his reply to Manley, Harland and other Bruces Eddy opponents, Church said his legislation would protect the other Clearwater tributaries for fish rehabilitation. The reservoir would give the area a "lake size" body of water while providing needed power and flood control: "We cannot lock up our resources for the sole benefit of the sportsman any more than we can dissipate them for the sole benefit of industry and payrolls." As to the fish passage problem, Church was supporting Interior Secretary Udall's push for a "crash" program to find an answer, believing "it is likely we can resolve this problem and get on with harnessing our rivers to bring progress and increased prosperity to Idaho." Church was one of many victims of wishful thinking on high dams and fish.[69]

In late August 1962, Tom Kimball, executive director of the National Wildlife Federation, advised Bruce Bowler that authorization of Bruces Eddy was likely. He suggested that conservationists propose a compromise, agreeing not to continue a nationwide fight against Bruces Eddy in exchange for legislative language prohibiting Federal Power Commission licensing of dams on the Middle Fork of the Clearwater or on the Salmon. Bowler questioned whether such a deal would be accepted, saying he preferred "to go down fighting for what is right." He felt the Lewis-Clark Highway would deter Penny Cliffs while a good case had been made for protection of the Salmon in the FPC's current consideration of the rival applications for Mountain Sheep and Nez Perce dams on the Snake.[70]

Senator Dworshak's unexpected death on July 23, 1962 left Church as the primary congressional advocate for Bruces Eddy. Gov. Robert Smylie named former Gov. Len Jordan to fill the position temporarily. There would now be two Idaho U.S. Senate contests with Boise attorney Jack Hawley challenging Church and Jordan facing Rep. Gracie Pfost. Church's re-election might hinge on his effort to win authorization of Bruces Eddy. In September he was able to get it included in the Senate's omnibus public works bill despite the efforts of Idaho conservationists. Morton Brigham, Bruce Bowler and Ernie Day wrote Sen. Robert Kerr opposing authorization.[71] Brigham had written Church in March, urging delay pending results of Idaho Power's fish passage experiment, adding that if Bruces Eddy was approved it appeared that conservationists had no choice "except to commence a war or stand idly by while the country is ruined." Church reminded Brigham of his politically risky leadership on the wilderness bill adding that conservation was not served by "unqualified opposition to progress."[72] While Bruce Bowler continued to fight Bruces Eddy, he remained loyal to Church, writing a campaign fund raising letter to fellow conservationists.[73]

On Sept. 27, Church proudly reported that the Senate Public Works Committee had voted to authorize construction of Bruces Eddy and five other Idaho dam projects with a projected cost of $332 million, "the first step toward our biggest breakthrough in the development of our river resources." Included were two low elevation dams on the Snake, Asotin above Lewiston and China Gardens a few miles below the Snake's juncture with the Salmon, Burns Creek on the South Fork of the Snake, Ririe dam in eastern Idaho and improvements for the Blackfoot dam. The next day Church reported that the Senate Appropriations Committee had approved $2 million in the public works appropriation bill to begin Bruces Eddy construction. The Senate passed both bills.[74] But the dam's opponents continued to find friends in the House and Bruces Eddy was not included in the House public works authorization bill.

After House members of the conference committee refused to accept Bruces Eddy, a desperate Church announced that he would carry on a one-man filibuster in the Senate, holding the floor "as long as God gives me strength to stand."[75] He was prepared to tie up the Senate and delay the adjournment of Congress, frustrating members anxious to go home and campaign. He said he had the support of the Senate leadership and the White House to let the public works authorization bill die in the Senate if House conferees would not accept Bruces Eddy. After two days of deadlock the conferees reached agreement.

Bruces Eddy was included but eight other Senate-approved projects were omitted including China Gardens and Burns Creek. Authorization of Asotin was approved along with the Ririe dam and Blackfoot dam improvements.[76] Bethine Church helped break the impasse. At Church's request, she called a friend, the wife of Rep. Clifford Davis, a House Public Works Committee member, who persuaded her husband to help Church on Bruces Eddy.[77]

A triumphant Church, along with Senate candidate Pfost and Rep. Ralph Harding, claimed credit for getting authorization of five Idaho water projects with total projected construction costs of $292 million. With Bruces Eddy approved, it appeared that Church's re-election was assured. Orofino attorney Ray McNichols, co-chair of Church's re-election committee and Bruces Eddy booster said Clearwater Valley residents were elated. McNichols said the dam would not only provide power and flood control but would open large areas of private, state and federal timber lands to harvest with reduced transportation costs.[78] Tom Boise wired his congratulations: "You are entitled to and deserve the unending appreciation, loyalty and support of all people of this area for your magnificent achievement yesterday. Bruces Eddy, with Snake River dams, unlocks the economic potential we have been seeking for many years. Congratulations."[79] Church was re-elected while Senator Jordan edged Gracie Pfost in the other Senate race.

The Bruces Eddy authorization did not include the provisions Church had requested barring other dams on the Clearwater, requiring that Idaho receive half the power or requiring payment for a log chute. Responding to a query from Lewiston attorney Wynne Blake, Church wrote that "It took a desperate struggle to obtain authorization for the Bruces Eddy dam on any terms and I was not in a position to press for special provisions of any kind in the bill."[80]

Church embraced the suggestion of Senator Jordan to name the dam for Senator Dworshak, recognizing his leadership in getting it built. The name Bruces Eddy was believed to have originated when a Northern Pacific engineer, Bruce Lipscomb, identified the site as a potential dam location in an 1887 railroad survey. The Corps advised Church that it would address the fish passage issue. Salmon and steelhead returning to the North Fork would be trapped below the dam and then lifted 670 feet in an elevator and dropped into the reservoir. Based on studies conducted at another dam, the Corps believed downstream migrants could survive passage through the power turbines.[81] This improbable plan would be rejected by wildlife agencies in favor of construction of a large steelhead hatchery below the dam.

Bruces Eddy opponents did not give up. In August 1963, their hopes were revived when Potlatch President Benton Cancell dropped a bombshell, warning company directors that Bruces Eddy would jeopardize the continued operation of the company's sawmill and plywood plants in Lewiston. Rather than reducing log transportation costs, the reservoir would greatly increase costs while inundating 5,000 acres of company timber land. After supporting the construction of Bruces Eddy for years the Clearwater Valley's largest employer was now describing it as an economic liability. Cancell said the company had not pushed for construction of the dam and recent analysis resulted in the revised view.[81] Morton Brigham forwarded copies of the Lewiston Tribune story to Church. Conservationists were hoping Congress would now refuse to provide further construction funds.[82] But dam advocates suggested Cancell was exaggerating, looking for a better price for the company timber land that would be submerged. Preliminary work continued and the main contract for construction was awarded in 1966.

While the North Fork of the Clearwater was lost, the campaign to save it helped focus attention on the destruction of free flowing rivers by federal and private dams. In 1964, Interior Secretary Stewart Udall proposed that Congress protect some rivers and river reaches in a national system that would include the Middle Fork of the Salmon, the Selway, the Lochsa and the Middle Fork of the Clearwater. Frank Church became the primary Senate sponsor of the Wild and Scenic Rivers Act. In 1967, with the rivers bill still hung up in Congress, Church called on the Corps to deny reports that it was considering conducting hearings on Penny Cliffs.[83] The Corps didn't conduct Penny Cliffs hearings but was proceeding with a study of a re-regulating dam on the Clearwater below Dworshak. The Corps wanted to build a 70-foot dam at Lenore to smooth out fluctuating flows from Dworshak. A Lenore dam would allow installation of three more generators at Dworshak with greatly increased power output. This dam had been in the Corps plans all along but was not included in the 1962 authorization language.[84]

The prospect of losing another 11 miles of flowing river heavily used for steelhead fishing aroused a storm of protest. The Corps faced a hostile audience of 350 at a Lewiston hearing in November 1970. Eighty witnesses spoke, all opposing the dam except representatives of the Bonneville Power Administration, Federal Power Commission and the Northwest Public Power Association. Also opposed was the Corps plan for peaking operation at Dworshak with rapid changes in downstream river flows. Monte Richards of Idaho Fish and Game said the irreversible, tragic losses for fish and wildlife with Dworshak should not be compounded. Leroy Smith of the Nez Perce tribe received cheers and applause when he said: "This is one time the cowboys and Indians can get together and fight the cavalry." William Jollymore of the Lewiston Chamber of Commerce's fish and wildlife committee said "the most dangerous and detrimental organization operating in the United States today is the Army Corps of Engineers." Sen. James McClure said there was no record of congressional authorization of more than three Dworshak generators, echoing the position of Senator Church that additional generators and a re-regulating dam were not authorized in the 1962 legislation. Opposition was voiced also by representatives of the Idaho and national wildlife federations, Northwest Steelheaders and the Idaho chapter of the Wildlife Society. It was a rout and the Corps retreated. There would be no Lenore dam.[85]

Army corps of Engineers Photo

Dworshak Dam nearing completion in 1971.

Construction of Dworshak dam began in 1967. A 40-foot diversion tunnel was cut through the left abutment of the canyon to carry the river flow during construction. The tunnel was closed in September 1971 and the reservoir began to fill. Bruce Bowler and son Bert made a fall hunt near the pool area and Bruce killed a large buck deer. A Moscow citizen's group that included University of Idaho faculty members asked Gov. Cecil Andrus to seek a court injunction to delay the filling of the reservoir to allow an independent economic analysis. Their own analysis showed that costs far exceeded benefits. The Corps had ignored the increased costs of log transport with the reservoir, had subtracted nothing for the loss of river related recreation, for the recreation value of land to be flooded, for the losses to the Nez Perce tribe or for the loss of game winter range or fisheries. Most of the claimed flood control benefits had been eliminated with construction of other dams on Columbia River tributaries. Power could be provided by adding generators to existing dams. While they made a powerful case, Andrus wasn't willing to battle against a completed dam.[86]

White-tailed deer ventured onto the thin ice covering the rising reservoir in the winter of 1971-72 and more than 100 died. Photos of deer with the ice breaking around them provided evidence that the dam's opponents had been right about what would happen to big game. The Corps blamed the losses primarily on coyotes chasing deer on the ice. A Fish and Game Department marksman shot some of the coyotes from a helicopter but the basic problem was the reservoir. A wildlife mitigation plan called for intensive management for elk of a bloc of land near the upper end of the reservoir and the junction of the North Fork and Little North Fork. The Corps purchased 5,000 acres of private land but the Idaho Land Board balked at using state land for elk rather than for timber harvest and the mitigation acreage fell far short of the 26,000 acres sought by the wildlife agencies. What was described as the world's largest steelhead hatchery replaced the Northwest's best steelhead stream. At a cost of $500,000 the hatchery was soon producing three million steelhead smolts a year along with 2.5 million trout and kokanee for the reservoir.[87]

At the dedication ceremony in June 1973, Governor Andrus called Dworshak dam a tribute to community tenacity while predicting that it would be the last of its kind in the Clearwater basin, a conservative prediction since the Middle Fork of the Clearwater, the Lochsa and the Selway were now in the wild and scenic river system. The Corps described Dworshak dam at 717 feet as the highest straight axis concrete dam in the world and the largest ever built by the Corps. It was 525 feet wide at the base and 3,287 at the crest. Its three generators with 400 megawatts of capacity would produce enough energy to power a city the size of Boise. Senator Dworshak's widow unveiled a plaque with the senator's picture and Nez Perce dancers performed.[88]

While salmon and steelhead had lost access to the North Fork of the Clearwater, access to the south fork was restored. In 1960, the Idaho Fish and Game Department began negotiating with Washington Water Power for removal of the Grangeville dam. The company agreed and in August 1963, five tons of dynamite obliterated the dam in a single blast. The historic removal of a salmon and steelhead-killing dam reopened many miles of spawning habitat in meandering tributary streams.[89]

The Lewiston dam was removed in 1978, also with the help of dynamite. Lower Granite dam, under construction 53 miles below Lewiston, was going to back water into the dam's pool area and reduce the power output. The Corps of Engineers, Potlatch Corporation and Washington Water Power reached an agreement on removal of the dam and construction of a dike to protect the Potlatch mill property from flooding by the Lower Granite pool. The Lewiston dam would no longer obstruct salmon and steelhead entering the Clearwater.[90] But now there was a greater problem – the cumulative effect of the downstream dams on the Snake and Columbia. Those dams and reservoirs were now recognized as a deadly combination threatening the survival of all Snake River salmon and steelhead.

Chapter 5

Designation of the Idaho and Selway-Bitterroot primitive areas

"The development and settlement of the west leaves few places where the demand for a wild undeveloped area may be met, but owing to the natural features making this section suitable to such use and the lack of values for development purposes it is particularly adapted to such a purpose." – S.B. Locke, regional game supervisor for the Forest Service, 1924.

In 1879, the U.S. Army conducted a campaign in the rugged mountain country of central Idaho adjoining the middle fork, south fork and main Salmon rivers. The soldiers traveled more than 1,200 miles in six months, finally gaining the surrender of 51 Sheepeater, Bannock and Weiser Indians. Two soldiers were wounded in an ambush in the narrow canyon on lower Big Creek and one was killed in a skirmish in the same area. Many mules and horses were lost to fatigue and tumbles down the slopes. General Oliver Otis Howard, commander of the Army's Pacific Division, declared that, "there is not a rougher or more difficult country for campaigning in America."[1]

The campaign was generated by the murder of five Chinese miners on Loon Creek, spreading fear in nearby mining camps. After their surrender, the Indians denied killing the Chinese. It was the Army's last campaign against Indians in Idaho, coming two years after the pursuit of the Nez Perce into Montana and a year after hostilities with the southern Idaho Bannocks.

The Sheepeaters (Tukuarikas) were also known as the Mountain Shoshoni. Small bands occupied the Sawtooth Mountains, Stanley Basin and the Middle Fork Salmon River country, living on deer, mountain sheep, elk, salmon, trout, roots and berries. They were skilled hunters and proficient in the preparation of animal hides for clothing. They hunted in the mountains in summer, trapped, speared and dried salmon in the summer and fall and wintered in the warmer lower canyons. They were never very numerous.[2]

By the 1870s, miners were increasingly moving into the country that the Sheepeaters and their predecessors had occupied for centuries. Minerals were found in many locations. In 1901, reports of discoveries in the Monumental

Idaho Historical Society Photo No. 3475

Harry Shellworth

Creek drainage east of Big Creek attracted swarms of miners. But the excitement had subsided by 1907. Many claims were filed along the main Salmon, the middle fork and other streams but most involved small placer operations.

Homesteaders claimed meadowland along the middle fork and on some of the creeks and brought in livestock. But ranching was hampered by harsh weather, isolation and long distances to markets. Some land claims were abandoned. The middle fork country remained primarily the realm of wildlife. By the 1920s, it was attracting sportsmen who had the time and money for prolonged wilderness hunts with the opportunity to take bighorn sheep and mountain goats as well as deer, bear and elk.

Among the hunting enthusiasts was Harry Shellworth of Boise, agent for the Boise Payette Lumber Company. Shellworth came to Idaho from Texas with his family in 1890. At age 13 he showed exceptional enterprise, working as a telegraph messenger, selling newspapers on the streets and working as a page for the first state legislature. At 17 he left home and found work with a steamship line out of San Francisco. With a friend he joined the gold stampede to the Klondike in 1897, a venture that ended when they were mugged and robbed on the trail. In 1898, he joined the Idaho Spanish American war volunteers who were sent to the Philippines and helped suppress a Filipino revolt. He returned to maritime work, serving on an Army transport ship. After returning to Boise to marry he was hired in 1905 as a timber cruiser for the Payette Lumber Company. The company merged with the Barber Lumber Company of Boise in 1913 to form Boise Payette.[3]

Shellworth made numerous hunting trips into the Big Creek area, often in the company of eastern businessmen. He organized the trips, arranging for packers, guides and horse wranglers. In 1924, Shellworth organized a trip for Frederick Weyerhaeuser of the Weyerhaeuser timber empire, Charles Speed of Evanston, Ill., vice president of the Evanston Railroad, Claude Fordyce of Falls City, Neb., associate editor of Outdoor Life magazine, and a prominent Denver physician. Fordyce's 1925 article said Idaho was a hunting paradise with bountiful game in hundreds of square miles of primitive forests, inaccessible with few trails, yet untouched "by the mania of destruction which characterizes modern America." It had more game and fish than any other state.[4]

Idaho Historical Society Photo No. 61-96.9

Gov. Clarence Baldridge

Idaho game wardens and the Forest Service recognized that the middle fork country had exceptional value for wildlife. In 1917, the legislature established a game preserve in an area south of the Salmon River and east of the middle fork, the Big Creek Preserve. It was not named for the Big Creek that flowed into the middle fork but for the Salmon River tributary on the preserve's eastern boundary that was later renamed Panther Creek.[5] In 1919, Warden William H. Thorp recommended designation of the Chamberlain Basin area south of the Salmon River and west of the middle fork's Big Creek as a game preserve. The Idaho National Forest estimated the elk population at 610 and there were also many deer and mountain sheep.

The area had few settlers and the Forest Service had closed it to livestock grazing for the benefit of wildlife, except "for the few sheep and cattle belonging to settlers in the region."[6] In 1925, acting on the recommendation of Warden Richard Thomas, the legislature replaced the Big Creek Preserve with a Middle Fork Preserve along both sides of the river for 60 miles from Marble Creek to Big Creek. The basic idea was to protect deer on their winter range along the river and in the lower canyons of the tributaries. The 250,000-acre preserve left most of the middle fork country open to hunting and trapping, including the Big Creek area and Chamberlain Basin.[7]

By the 1920s, some people in and out of the Forest Service were entertaining the idea of setting aside some not yet roaded or developed national forest areas as wilderness, to be left in their natural state. The middle fork country, with its rugged topography, large wildlife populations and few settlers, was recognized as a candidate for wilderness management, a place to preserve a part of the west as it was before settlement. An early advocate for a Salmon River wilderness was Fredrick Ransom, a Clarkston, Wash. fruit grower, a frequent visitor to the area and sometimes hunting companion of Salmon River miner Robert G. Bailey. Ransom wrote Forest Service officials and office holders urging the creation of a Tukuarika wilderness area, named for the Sheepeaters.[8]

In 1924, S.B. Locke, regional game supervisor for the Forest Service, led a party that included the Salmon and Idaho forest supervisors and a deputy state game warden on an 8-day inspection of deer winter range conditions on the middle fork. A related purpose was to help determine Forest Service management policy. Locke's report described the country as particularly suitable for "the wilderness area idea." It had high value for recreation and a "lack of development values." Locke stopped short of "specific recommendations" but said, "it is desirable to have the (wilderness) matter receive consideration." It was unlikely "that any development inconsistent with such use will take place in the near future."

There could be no doubt about his opinion: "The settlement and development of the west leaves few places where the demand for a wild, undeveloped area may be met, but owing to the natural features making this section suitable for such use and the lack of values for development purposes it is particularly well adapted for such a purpose. There are offered recreation features, hunting, fishing, the study of wild life and camping in a section which has many natural features and a past history which adds much to its interest." The few ranches were limited to strips along the rivers and were difficult to operate at a profit. "It is so far from settlements or shipping points and so rough that the grazing values are very low." Locke suggested that forest grazing should be limited to stock fed on hay on area ranches during the winter and that ranch land should be acquired by exchange or state purchase.[9]

As Locke's report suggested, the idea of managing some areas for wilderness values was percolating through the Forest Service. Weeks after Locke's middle fork visit a district forester designated a 574,000-acre Gila Wilderness in New Mexico, as advocated by a forester named Aldo Leopold. Chief Forester William O. Greeley in 1926 endorsed further wilderness designations.[10] The Forest Service did not follow up on Locke's report in 1925 or 1926. But the concept had another champion, Harry Shellworth. He had talked about it with companions on his middle fork hunting trips including Game Warden Otto Jones and taxidermist Robert Limbert. Shellworth was a capable advocate, well connected in the business world and in the Idaho Republican party.[11]

Another key figure was Richard Rutledge, regional forester in Ogden, Utah, an Idaho native who had joined the Forest Service as a guard in Long Valley in 1905. Like Shellworth, he believed the middle fork country was well suited to the wilderness concept. In October 1927, Shellworth organized and led a large hunting party into the area. It included Stanley Easton of Kellogg, manager of the Bunker Hill and Sullivan mine, Boise photographer Ansgar

Johnson, Boise attorney Jess Hawley, Rutledge and the governor of Idaho, Clarence Baldridge. In addition to hunting, fishing and having a good time, the purpose of the trip was to show Baldridge the country and to promote the idea of an Idaho Primitive Area.[12] Baldridge was a Parma merchant and community leader. Before his election as governor in 1926 he had served four terms in the legislature and four years as lieutenant governor.

The party mounted horses for a ride that took them down Big Creek to the Dave Lewis ranch where they pitched their tents. "Uncle Dave Lewis," also known as Cougar Dave, had lived alone for years on his 66-acre land claim, far from any settlement, earning a livelihood as a trapper, hunter and guide. He was known as Idaho's premier cougar hunter, claiming to have killed hundreds of the big cats with the help of his three dogs. Lewis helped guide the 1924 Shellworth party and had won notoriety with write-ups in The Idaho Statesman and mention in Outdoor Life, the Portland Oregonian, Denver Post and the Nashville Banner. Lewis was 72, an Oregon native who had joined the mining migration to Idaho in the 1860s. At age 24 he served the Army as a packer in the Sheepeater campaign and was present when Pvt. Richard Egan was fatally wounded near Big Creek a few miles from the location of the Lewis ranch. Through his efforts a monument to Egan had been erected on Soldier Bar where he died.[13]

The country's rugged geography and the abundance of wildlife impressed Baldridge. At one time 460 deer were counted on the slope across from the Lewis place. The governor was receptive to Shellworth's campfire conversation about the virtue of keeping the middle fork country as it was, with no improved roads or autos, where people could experience raw nature with exceptional hunting and fishing. Shellworth would credit the campfire talk on this trip with setting in motion the events that resulted in designation of the Idaho Primitive Area. Gaining Baldridge's backing was a big step in marshalling political and public support. Rutledge now had more reason to gather information and develop a plan.

If the forester wanted further reason to proceed he got it in 1929 when the Forest Service adopted its L-20 regulations that officially authorized the designation of primitive areas "to maintain primitive conditions of transportation, subsistence, habitation and environment to the fullest degree compatible with their highest public use." The Forest Service policy was consistent with a report that resulted from President Calvin Coolidge's sponsorship of a National Conference on Recreation in 1924 and 1926. Conferees called for a series of studies. The wilderness study by the American Forestry Association and National Parks Association, identified more than 12 million acres as suitable for wilderness preservation "free of the ubiquitous motor." Three of the areas were in Idaho, the middle fork, 1.2 million acres, plus the Selway and the Owyhee, one million acres each.[14]

After being advised by Rutledge in April 1930 that study of a central Idaho primitive area was underway, Shellworth suggested in a letter to R.E. Shepherd of Jerome, president of the State Chamber of Commerce, that the governor should name a committee including office holders, sportsmen and foresters to consider the proposal. He shared his letter with a number of legislators, Forest Service officials and Idaho Game Warden Richard Thomas.[15]

The Forest Service plan came into public view in mid-November 1930, when The Idaho Statesman and Boise Capital News reported on a Boise meeting by Rutledge with regional foresters and their decision to proceed toward designation of a million-acre Idaho Primitive Area. Participants, in addition to the Idaho, Boise, Salmon, Challis and Payette forest supervisors, included State Rep. Cowles Andrus, a Challis rancher, and three sportsmen representatives, Harry Shellworth, Game Warden Thomas and Ada Fish and Game League President Frank Martin Jr.[16]

While in Boise, Rutledge took the plan to Governor Baldridge who promised to convene a committee to consider it. On December 1, Baldridge named Shellworth to head the committee. It would represent all interest groups including sportsmen, mining, timber, farming and livestock grazing. Shellworth was the timber industry's member. Some of those named by the governor were people recommended by Shellworth who were already acquainted with and favored the proposal including mining representative Henry Easton. Four were Republican legislators: Cowles Andrus; Rep. C.M. Hatch, Victor merchant; Sen. Roscoe Rich, Burley rancher and president of the Idaho Woolgrowers Association; and Sen. E.G. Van Hoesen, Mesa fruit farmer. Others were Cascade farmer Robert Coulter, Democratic representative and state party chairman; W.B. Mitchell, Parma attorney and president of the Dairymen's Cooperative Creamery in Parma; and Idaho Forest Supervisor S.C. Scribner, Shepherd and Game Warden Thomas. Meanwhile, Rutledge had written the regional foresters, asking them to solicit favorable letters from sportsmen's groups in their area. On December 15, the Southwest Idaho Sportsmen's Association, meeting in Gooding, adopted a resolution expressing "hearty accord" with the Forest Service plan. The association represented 10,000 sportsmen in 18 counties.[17]

The governor's committee met in the House caucus room of the statehouse on December 20. All were present except Shepherd and Easton. Baldridge led off, describing the 1927 trip, saying the primary purpose was to investigate the feasibility of a large primitive area to be left in nearly a natural state as possible for future generations. The few ranches would be acquired at a fair price by the state or the federal government. Mining could proceed. The area had timber but commercial development was unlikely for many years. All those with existing rights would be protected and the designation would not "sew the matter up" so no one could "break in in the future."

Idaho Forest Supervisor Scribner provided more detail. The area had an estimated 13,000 deer, 475 elk, 475 mountain sheep, 425 mountain goats and 700 bears. He believed the elk, sheep and goat estimates were conservative. The few small ranches supported only 130 cattle and 45 horses, he said. Many attempts at homesteading had failed and lands previously listed as available had been recalled. He said it would be desirable to acquire private lands, which totaled 4,395 acres, for winter game range. There was no grazing by domestic sheep and no demand for it, he said. The area had 1,195 acres of patented mineral land and there would be no interference with mineral development or prospecting. Scribner said the yellow pine and other timber had no market value because of the area's inaccessibility and long distances to markets.

Coulter raised questions, saying he had received many letters of protest from prospectors. They would probably be "hit the hardest" because they would have to build their own roads and trails. Rutledge responded, saying the Forest Service planned to build low standard roads for fire protection, would put in more trails and would improve existing trails. R.G. Cole, secretary of the Southwest Idaho Sportsmen's Association, presented the association's resolution and was added to the committee. The primitive area was acceptable to Rich because there was presently no sheep grazing. Mitchell said farmers valued a primitive area in the headwaters of streams as beneficial for a water supply. Hatch felt that the area was "splendidly adapted" for primitive status. Andrus said it would be an asset with increasing value over time, would be recognized nationally and would attract hunters from out of state. He could see nothing that would prevent the development of any mining claim. Rutledge said it was an ideal area for game with both summer and winter range. He cited economic benefits, estimating that hunters taking 1,000 deer a year would pay $2,000 in license fees and spend $15,000 on equipment.

A 5-member committee named by Shellworth drafted a resolution that won unanimous endorsement by the full committee, favoring the primitive area and directing Rutledge to submit the plan for approval by the Forest Service. "Since it is the intent, by the proposed primitive area, to designate approximately one million acres of rough mountainous land in central Idaho to uses for which it is best adapted, since this will involve no change in the legal claims of the prospector or of the mining industry, nor will it interfere with present Forest Service policy of cooperation in the construction of mining roads, since all agricultural, livestock, mining and other interests are being and will be given proper consideration, since no action taken by this committee, at this meeting, shall be interpreted as encouraging infringement on the rights of private interests through establishment of similar areas in other parts of the state and since all fish and game and fur bearing animals are recognized by this committee to be the property of the state and shall be kept under state control, therefore be it resolved that this committee approves the plan to establish the Idaho Primitive Area. That the report of the regional forester be submitted to the Forest Service and that this committee be called at a later date by the chairman to consider whether any funds should be raised for acquiring any private lands that are for sale in this area and to take whatever action that may be desirable."

On December 28, The Idaho Statesman published Watson Humphrey's enthusiastic account under the headline: "They Would Keep the State's Wildest Beauty Unspoiled. The Story of Idaho's Proposed "Primitive Area." Humphrey had been thoroughly briefed. He credited Shellworth with originating the proposal and described the 1927 campfire discussion with Baldridge on Big Creek as the catalyst that put the plan in motion: "In the spring of 1930, an exchange of correspondence among prominent Idahoans, foresters, United States congressmen and eastern millionaires added to the enthusiasm for the primitive area and helped bring about the success of the scheme."[18]

No other area in the U.S. had such variety and numbers of big game, wrote Humphrey. It was "probably the outstanding hunter's paradise in the nation" and offered exceptional fishing. The only development consisted of trails, telephone lines and a few trapper's cabins and shelters. No improvements were contemplated except a few bridges across the middle fork, Big Creek and the main Salmon, horse trails, lookout structures and low standard motorways for fire protection, mainly on ridge tops. There would be no improved roads for tourists and no automobiles. The committee had been told that the ban on roads would not interfere with the possible construction of a road along the Salmon River from Salmon to Riggins. A federal withdrawal was in place for a possible dam or dams on the main Salmon. Otherwise water storage projects would be barred except for mining.

The topography, described in the Forest Service report, ranged from high rolling plateaus and undulating ridges in the Chamberlain Basin, Cold Meadows and Thunder Mountain regions to steep canyons and precipitous bluffs "as one descends to the Salmon River and the middle fork." There were about 50 lakes of one to 100 acres "Hundreds of small streams head in the high country and fall rapidly in tortuous channels to the river below."

Rough and rocky bluffs impede travel in the higher altitudes, and as streams tributary to the middle fork descend from mountain goat habitats, open meadows and beautifully timbered bars offer camping sites to visitors, wrote Humphrey. Further downstream, deep, narrow canyons are formed. Precipitous cliffs block traffic of both men and animals. “One forest trail is routed down the middle of a creek so near are the canyon walls.” In ascending from the river to the crest of high plateaus it was sometimes necessary to climb 6,000-7,000 feet in a distance of eight or 10 miles. Elevations ranged from Mount McGuire’s 10,700 feet at the head of Roaring Creek to 2,500 feet on the lower Salmon River. A number of peaks topped 9,000 feet.[19] Humphrey quoted the report further: “The physical characteristics of the area as a whole are not more marvelous than can be found in many other parts of the Rocky Mountain region. Probably its strongest appeal is the immensity of the area and its isolation.”

Even before the committee’s decision the Boise Capital News had warmly embraced the plan, saying the primitive area “may be in the due course of time become the most unique thing in the country.”[20] But there were dissenters. The Statesman quoted Idaho Mine Inspector Stewart Campbell, as saying anyone interested in the state’s further growth and prosperity should oppose the primitive area. Mining was the only industry “in which any great expansion is possible and this proposal forces any miner or prospector to build roads in this region without any state or federal aid.” The 1,840 square miles was all potential mining ground and much of it was so recognized in the Thunder Mountain, Big Creek and Crooked Creek mining districts, said Campbell. He feared that once the primitive area was established, it would be but a short step to have mining excluded.[21]

Merle Wallace of Warren, a former Forest Service ranger and now a Big Creek rancher, responded to the Humphrey story. While the Forest Service had described the proposal and invited comments at several public meetings, these occurred so late in the fall and with such short notice that it was impossible for people in the back country to attend, he wrote. Wallace disputed the Forest Service view that the area had limited potential for ranching. The absence of irrigation costs, low taxes and grazing fees and splendid range made it possible to produce beef at half the cost of places more accessible to markets, he wrote. It was true that some homesteads had been abandoned but, in at least four instances, this was due to the death of the head of the family with no sons able to carry on. “In some instances the homesteader was of a type who would fail to make good anywhere” or was a “packhorse tramp” that moved in to get an easy living off game and moved on when living became too arduous. Wallace feared the Forest Service would restrict grazing to get a better price from the landowners. He suggested that the area would be a playground “for a few millionaire sportsmen” at the expense of mining and ranching.[22]

Members of the governor’s committee had talked about the possibility of further meetings to take public comment but there were no further meetings.

Chief Forester R.Y. Stuart approved Rutledge's recommendation and signed the report designating the 1.1-million-acre Idaho Primitive Area on March 17, 1931. By that time Idaho had a new governor, Democrat C. Ben Ross. Clarence Baldridge was a lame duck governor completing his second two-year term when he convened the Shellworth committee. Baldridge's role in creating the Idaho Primitive Area, one of the last acts of his administration, would be recognized as one of his best achievements.

Harry Shellworth continued to lead hunting parties to Big Creek and the middle fork. When the Civilian Conservation Corps (CCC) was created in 1933, Governor Ross named Shellworth as his personal representative for CCC work in Idaho. Idaho had more camps than any other state except California, 163. The CCC workers cut forest trails, built roads and bridges, constructed campgrounds and fought fires.[23]

In 1933, the legislature abolished the Middle Fork Game Preserve, recognizing that deer were overpopulating the winter range. In 1936, Rutledge proposed and Chief Ferdinand S. Silcox approved a 145,000-acre addition to the Idaho Primitive Area in the Pistol Creek and Indian Creek drainages. A year later Rutledge went to Washington to head the newly organized Taylor Grazing Service, bringing regulation of livestock grazing to public lands managed by the Department of Interior. The Fish and Game Department purchased some of the primitive area ranch properties. Cougar Dave Lewis continued at his Big Creek place until a few days before his death June 18, 1936, riding out only when he was fatally ill. He had sold his place to Jess Taylor and it became known as the Taylor Ranch. Dave Lewis Peak at the head of Soldier Creek was named for the mountain man. In the 1960s, the University of Idaho purchased the Lewis homestead from Taylor for a research station.[24]

In the mid-1930s, the middle fork began attracting adventurers for float trips on its almost continuous rapids. It would gain recognition as one of the premier white water rivers in the country. In 1935, a National Geographic Society trip down the main Salmon River generated publicity and stimulated further interest in the river and adjacent wild country. Unmentioned in the Forest Service's 1930 report on the Idaho Primitive Area was the significance of the many middle fork tributaries as spawning and rearing habitat for salmon and steelhead. This habitat would become more significant as dam construction locked salmon out of other Snake River tributaries.

The designation of the Idaho Primitive Area was part of a flurry of Forest Service primitive area decisions. By May 1932, Chief Forester Stuart had approved 48 areas totaling 8,410,986 acres, mostly in the western states. The Idaho Primitive Area was by far the largest in the west but was exceeded by the 1,268,538-acre Superior Primitive Area in Minnesota's Superior National Forest.[25]

North of the Salmon River was another large expanse of mostly unroaded mountain country. The Lewis and Clark party's 1805 crossing of the Bitterroot Mountains was the most difficult part of their journey to the Pacific. They struggled for 11 days across a maze of seemingly endless mountains and canyons, through brush and fallen timber with steep climbs and descents, suffering from cold and hunger. On the fifth day they climbed from the river (the Lochsa, a branch of the Clearwater) to a mountain ridge where they camped for the night, using snow water to cook the remains of the colt they had killed the day before. "From this mountain I could see high rugged mountains in every direction as far as I could see," wrote Clark in his journal.[26]

Along much of their route they followed the Lolo Trail, used by the Nez Perce for annual forays to hunt buffalo east of the Bitterroots. It was the route used by the Nez Perce in their flight from the pursuing U.S. Army in 1877. The trail passed over high ridges on the divide between the North Fork of the Clearwater and the Lochsa. To the south was another trail used by the Nez Perce to reach the buffalo country and by 1860s miners to reach the mines around Virginia City, Montana. The Selway drainage and part of the Lochsa remained mostly unroaded and undeveloped, little changed since the time of Lewis and Clark. Its rugged geography turned back railroad builders, and the mountainous terrain, thin soils and harsh winter weather limited settlement. The area attracted trappers and hunters and the Nez Perce continued to hunt, fish and visit historic religious sites but there were few year-round residents. By the 1930s, a road from Montana reached down the Lochsa to the Powell Ranger Station and further construction along the north side of the Lochsa was contemplated. (An all weather road linking Montana and Lewiston would not be completed until 1962.)

In its 1924 survey for the forestry and national parks associations, the Forest Service had identified a potential million-acre Selway wilderness north of the Salmon River. In July 1936, the Forest Service designated the country's largest primitive area, the 1.8-million-acre Selway-Bitterroot, including the peaks of the Bitterroot crest on the Idaho-Montana border, reaching from the Lochsa River on the north to the Salmon, including much of the Selway River drainage, part of the Lochsa, part of the Salmon and part of the Bitterroot. It included 1,585,000 acres in Idaho and 290,000 in Montana.[27]

Designation of the Selway-Bitterroot was the result of persistent lobbying of the Forest Service by forester Bob Marshall. By 1936, Marshall had emerged as the country's leading wilderness advocate. He was recognized as an authority on forest recreation, had earned a doctorate degree, and had written a book celebrating the lives of natives and prospectors in a remote village in Alaska's Brooks Range. He had also written extensively for national journals on the value of wilderness. With other wilderness enthusiasts he had founded The Wilderness Society and was tapping his personal wealth to support it.

Wilderness Society Photo

Bob Marshall

Marshall was born in 1901, the son of a prominent and wealthy New York City lawyer. His enthusiasm for wilderness was fueled by his passion for hiking and mountain climbing. The Lochsa, Selway and Salmon River country ranked high on his list of areas deserving protection.[28] From 1925 until 1928, he was assigned to the Forest Service's Northern Rocky Mountain Research Station in Missoula, Montana, working much of the time at Priest River, Idaho, on a study of the regeneration of conifers after logging and fires.[29] This allowed him to explore nearby wilderness areas in Idaho and Montana. After a winter hike on the Lochsa in 1926, he referred to the surrounding country as "the greatest forest wilderness left in this country."

In 1930, Marshall laid out his arguments for preserving wilderness in articles published in the magazine Scientific Monthly: "Wilderness As a Minority Right" and "The Problem of Wilderness." Marshall defined wilderness as a region without permanent inhabitants, offering no possibility of mechanical conveyance and large enough that a person crossing it must sleep out. "The dominant attributes of such an area are: first, that it requires anyone who exists in it to depend entirely on his own effort for survival; and second, that it preserves as nearly as possible the primitive environment. This means that all roads, power transportation and settlement are barred. But trails and temporary shelters which were common long before the advent of the white race, are entirely possible."[30]

Marshall believed that some forest areas should be left without roads to serve people who found physical, emotional and spiritual renewal in wilderness. "There is just one hope of repulsing the tyrannical ambition of civilization to conquer every mile of the whole earth. That hope is the organization of spirited people who will fight for the freedom of the wilderness."[31]

In 1932, Marshall compiled a list of areas that he believed the Forest Service should give primitive area status, including the Selway. He submitted the list to L.F. Kneipp who headed the Forest Service's primitive area system. Kneipp passed it on to regional foresters but their reaction was mostly negative. Marshall wrote to Meyer Wolff, an assistant regional forester in Missoula: "I do wish you would hurry up and get that entire country from the Locksaw River to the southern border of Region One (the Salmon River) set aside as wilderness before some damn fool chamber of commerce or some nonsensical organizer of the unemployed demands a useless highway to provide work for hotdogs and gasoline."[32]

Marshall was a recognized authority on forest recreation, contributing three chapters on that subject to a lengthy Forest Service report on forest management. In 1933, he was named chief of forestry of the Bureau of Indian Affairs, part of the Department of Interior. While working for reform of Indian land policy and practice, he continued his wilderness hikes and his advocacy. In January 1935, he and other wilderness enthusiasts organized The Wilderness Society. It was to be a national organization working continuously for recognition and protection of wilderness areas.

In May 1935, Marshall submitted to Forest Service Chief Ferdinand Silcox a memo describing remaining national forest areas he believed should be designated primitive areas, saying the Selway was the greatest of all. Silcox passed the memo on to regional foresters and invited Marshall to address them at their annual meeting in Washington in November. The foresters accepted only one of the 12 areas on Marshall's list, the Selway.[33]

Assistant Regional Forester Elers Koch prepared proposed boundaries in March 1936. In May, Silcox wrote Regional Forester Evan Kelley asking for the region's report on the area, suggesting that no further road or truck trail construction should be done in the meantime. Meyer Wolff wrote the report describing the proposed Selway-Bitterroot Primitive Area and plans for its management. It encompassed "a very rough mountainous country lying mostly west of the spectacular crest of the Bitterroot Range which here forms the Idaho-Montana border. This range is one of the roughest of all mountain areas, alternating deep, sharp, narrow canyons with high barren peaks. This extreme topography very gradually gentles toward the west until rapidly running short mountain creeks give place to slower moving rivers. The scenic Salmon River canyon forms part of the southern boundary."[34]

Evan Kelley submitted the report on June 22 and on July 3, acting Forest Service Chief Earle Clapp designated the nation's largest primitive area. With the Idaho Primitive Area south of the Salmon, Idaho now had the west's two largest primitive areas with continuous designated wilderness reaching from south central Idaho to the Lochsa River on the north.

As with the Idaho Primitive Area, the Selway-Bitterroot was recognized as having high value for primitive recreation, including hunting and fishing. Wolff's report said: "Recreation is entirely of 'wilderness' character and will always remain so." Fires in 1910, 1919 and 1934 burned over large areas, leaving openings that fostered the growth of shrubs and grasses, enhancing the range for elk. Elk and other game animals were protected in part of the area, the Selway Game Preserve established in 1917. With game surveys showing an increasing elk population, hunts were authorized in the preserve in 1936 and 1937.

Wolff's report said the Selway-Bitterroot had no significant mining activity. In any event prospecting and mining would not be prohibited. Timber included pine, fir, spruce and larch but it was "all permanently inaccessible on account of low stands per acre, extremely rugged topography causing expensive logging in place and long distances to market points." Settlement was limited to three small ranches. Livestock grazing was also limited with 10,000 sheep and 250 cattle on allotments partly inside the primitive area boundaries. Grazing was to be reduced over time. The plan recognized a high risk of lightning caused fires. Ten existing truck trails built to aid fire fighting would remain but further construction would be limited to 19 miles of extensions for six of them.

The report said there had been "no general pressure" for establishment of the area, meaning there was no groundswell of public or political support as there had been for the Idaho Primitive Area. The Selway-Bitterroot was entirely the result of Bob Marshall's advocacy and the initiative of the Forest Service. There was also little opposition except for the city of Salmon. Wolff's report said this was based on fear the primitive area would prevent construction of a road through the Salmon River canyon. The Selway-Bitterroot plan specifically authorized construction of the road. Before construction was interrupted by World War II, Civilian Conservation Corps crews had extended both the east and west ends of the road, leaving about 75 miles unroaded.[35]

In 1937, Bob Marshall left the Indian Bureau to accept appointment by Silcox as director of the Forest Service's newly created Division of Recreation and Lands. In that role he drafted new regulations for better management of primitive areas. Policies had varied with the regions retaining considerable discretion. With the new U regulations drafted by Marshall and adopted in 1939, primitive areas were to be reviewed and areas of 100,000 acres or more designated "wilderness" and areas under 100,000 acres as "wild." Road construction and logging would be barred. The new policy also required the

Martel Morache Photo

Rocky stretch of the lower Selway River

Forest Service to give public notice and conduct public hearings before establishing, changing or abolishing the primitive areas.

Bob Marshall died unexpectedly while traveling from Washington to New York by train on Nov. 10, 1939. He was 38. Chief Forester Silcox asked regional foresters for proposals to honor Marshall. Evan Kelly suggested that his name be given to the Selway-Bitterroot Primitive Area. Renaming the area for Marshall was endorsed by the Washington staff in March 1940. In May, Silcox advised Region One that the decision had been made to call it the Bob Marshall Wilderness Area and asked for a new report with an updated map. Regional Forester Kelley, who had proposed the name change, had second thoughts. He suggested that the 625,000-acre South Fork Primitive Area in Montana's Flathead National Forest had better scenic quality and would be a better choice to honor Marshall.

Kelley contended that the Selway-Bitterroot "as a whole" lacked distinctiveness "except for the monotony of color, character of topography, burned over land, hot canyons, poor soil and lack of grass and lakes." Its claim for recreational distinction, he wrote, "rests almost entirely on size related to lack of roads." Also the landing of private planes was allowed at three airstrips. "This practice was always objected to by Bob Marshall yet such permission could not be revoked and shouldn't be." Kelley's view would prevail and three Montana primitive areas were combined in the Bob Marshall Wilderness in August 1940.[36]

Wilderness lost
Citizens organize to save the upper Selway

"Our group now has the backing of thousands of aroused citizens and the means to bring its viewpoint to a much wider public. Assuredly you will be hearing from us." – Doris Milner to Agriculture Secretary Orville Freeman March 1965.

It was not until 1954 that the Forest Service began to seriously consider reclassification of the Selway-Bitterroot Primitive Area as wilderness under the U regulations. Because the regulations barred roads, it was recognized that there would be boundary adjustments. Also the Magruder Road might become the new southern boundary with the Salmon River portion of the primitive area south of the road designated a separate wilderness – a change that had been endorsed by Bob Marshall in 1939 before his death. The Magruder Road was a primitive road across the primitive area connecting Elk City, Idaho and Darby, Montana, completed by the Civilian Conservation Corps in the 1930s.[37]

Director Howard Zahniser of The Wilderness Society was intensely interested in the Selway-Bitterroot reclassification and accepted a Forest Service invitation to visit the area in August 1955 and hear Region One's ideas on boundary changes. Zahniser and seven other Wilderness Society members skirted part of the area by car, rode horseback along Moose Creek and camped at Indian Lake. Zahniser recognized the Selway-Bitterroot, with its lofty peaks, tranquil lakes, rushing streams, abundant wildlife and great size as one of the most valuable wilderness areas in the country. At the Wilderness Society annual meeting in Moose, Wyoming in September 1955 the organization's governing council agreed that the Magruder Road would remain and supported designation of a separate wilderness south of the road to become part of the Idaho Primitive Area. The society wanted to keep the wilderness as large as possible.[38]

The Forest Service didn't release its proposal until August 1960. It reflected the timber industry's increased interest in the area's potential saw timber and the Forest Service's desire to boost the supply for Montana and

Martel Morache Photo

Good salmon-steelhead spawning areas in Whitecap Creek, a tributary of the Selway River

Idaho mills. Demand for timber and the volume taken from national forests had increased dramatically after World War II. With the proposed Selway-Bitterroot Wilderness a total of 523,000 acres of the primitive area would lose wilderness protection. Most of the excluded acreage would be in the upper Selway drainage, 310,000 acres north and south of the Magruder Road. The wilderness's northern boundary would be moved back from the Lochsa River to the ridge tops, excluding the southern side of the canyon, a reduction of 71,000 acres. Also lost to wilderness management would be 73,000 acres around White Sand Creek on the Lochsa, an area penetrated by roads. The eastern boundary in Montana would be modified to exclude roads into the Bitterroots, a change accepted by wilderness advocates. The 188,000-acre

Salmon River portion, including the north side of the Salmon River canyon, would be detached and renamed the Salmon River Breaks Primitive Area. Its future wilderness status would be determined by the Forest Service's Region Four in conjunction with its pending review of the Idaho Primitive Area.[39]

Howard Zahniser sent a memo to Wilderness Society members and allies urging testimony at Forest Service hearings and letters opposing the upper Selway and Lochsa canyon exclusions. More than a fifth of the acreage of the existing primitive area would be lost, he wrote, warning of soil erosion and silted streams with roads and logging.[40] Potlatch Forests wanted another 300,000 acres excluded and sent a memo to employees advising them that existing mills would need the additional timber from that acreage within a few years to maintain the present level of production. Employees were asked to speak at hearings, and write to the regional forester, Senators Church and Dworshak and Rep. Gracie Pfost in support of the timber industry position.[41]

At the first hearing in Missoula, Montana, Stewart Brandborg of The Wilderness Society said the organization opposed the acreage reductions. There was also support for retaining most of the primitive area acreage from residents of the Bitterroot Valley including Guy Brandborg, former supervisor of the Bitterroot National Forest and father of Stewart Brandborg. The older Brandborg recalled that he had worked with Bob Marshall in drawing proposed boundaries for the primitive area. He said the area offered exceptional opportunity for a wilderness experience that could not be equaled elsewhere in the national forests or national parks.[42] George Marshall, brother of Bob Marshall, speaking for the Sierra Club, also asked that most of the acreage be retained.[43]

In Lewiston, 18 of 46 witnesses supported the Wilderness Society position. Among them were Ernie Day of Boise, president of the Idaho Wildlife Federation, Bruce Bowler of Boise, Morton Brigham of Lewiston, Art Manley and Frank Evans of Coeur d'Alene and Gertrude Maxwell of Elk City. Others, including a spokesman for the Idaho Chamber of Commerce, agreed with Royce Cox of Potlatch Forests in calling for exclusion of another 300,000 acres. Some supported the Forest Service proposal. Al Teske of the Idaho Mining Association wanted a decision delayed pending a mineral survey of the area.[44]

Bruce Bowler said the test should not be whether anyone else wanted the land or if it was potentially useful for minerals or timber. "It is highly desirable that some of the good environment be preserved in an undeveloped state for future generations."[45] Idaho Fish and Game Commissioner Frank Cullen said the commission wanted the upper Selway in wilderness to protect cutthroat trout and steelhead. "These species have remained in healthy condition primarily because the Selway River watershed has remained in pristine condition." Supporters of a smaller wilderness were in the majority in the final hearing in Grangeville. The Grangeville Chamber of Commerce endorsed the Forest Service plan. Grangeville Mayor George Klein wanted less wilderness. So did the Northern Pacific Railroad and the Idaho Association of Highways.[46]

Wilderness supporters were disappointed when Agriculture Secretary Orville Freeman announced the Forest Service's decision Jan. 11, 1963. Most of the excluded acreage was still excluded in a Selway-Bitterroot Wilderness of 1,239,840 acres. A total of 418,000 acres lost wilderness protection including 230,000 acres of the upper Selway drainage north and south of the Magruder Road and 32,830 acres of the upper Bargamin Creek, a tributary of the Salmon River. Freeman's order said the value for logging in the excluded areas outweighed the wilderness value. The Forest Service proposal had been modified to reduce the upper Selway exclusion by 37,380 acres to include in wilderness an area along the river north of the Paradise Ranger Station with Crooked Creek, Eagle Creek, Grouse Creek and several miles of Running Creek and 12 miles of the Selway. Also retained was 15,870 acres along the Selway south of Fogg Mountain with seven miles of the Selway River Canyon. Another 42,700 acres in the upper Selway was left in primitive area status as part of the 216,000-acre Salmon River Breaks Primitive Area. An area of 4,740 acres on the Lochsa face south of the Lochsa ranger station was retained as wilderness. Another 42,700 acres south of the Lochsa was still excluded but was to be managed primarily for scenic and recreational values.[47]

The Bitterroot Forest immediately began making plans to increase its timber output with logging of the upper Selway. The plan included improvement of the east end of the Magruder Road for logging trucks. Both Idaho and Montana conservationists recognized that roads and logging could fill creek and river gravel beds with silt, interfering with salmon and trout reproduction. Forest Service plans included a 20-mile extension of the Magruder Road along the Selway. Among those most concerned were Hamilton, Mont. residents Guy Brandborg, the former Bitterroot Forest Supervisor, and Doris and Kelsey Milner, who had enjoyed family vacations on the Selway.

In September 1964, they organized the Save the Upper Selway Committee to rally public support to stop the logging, appealing to Secretary Freeman to intervene and seeking the aid of Montana and Idaho members of Congress.[48] Joining in the effort was the North Idaho Wilderness Committee headed by Morton Brigham of Lewiston. Brigham fired off letters to the Forest Service and members of Congress pointing out the damage done to the North Fork of the Clearwater and other streams by roads. All of his favorite cutthroat trout holes along 31 miles of the north fork had been "blown full of rocks" as a result of road construction. The same thing had happened on the Lochsa, he advised

Regional Forester Neal Rahm.[49] Bruce Bowler wrote Freeman describing the devastation of South Fork Salmon River salmon as a result of roads and logging. Gravel spawning beds had been covered with sand for many miles. "The contrast is plain and convincing. The Upper Selway still shows wonderful quality water and gravel formation for optimum spawning for salmon and steelhead," wrote Bowler.[50] Outfitter Vern Haslett of Shoup wrote Senator Church that "expecting a destructive logging operation and recreation to co-exist in this area is like asking a mouse to live in a box with a snake."[51]

The citizen's campaign had two objectives; to stop the Forest Service's logging plans and to win wilderness status for the area by act of Congress. Congressional action would be necessary because, with the passage of the Wilderness Act in September 1964, the Forest Service no longer had authority to add excluded areas to the Selway-Bitterroot Wilderness or to designate any other wilderness area. The Selway-Bitterroot now had statutory protection as wilderness but the exclusion would be permanent unless Congress intervened.

The Forest Service persisted with the logging plans. Bitterroot Forest Supervisor Harold Anderson estimated a potential cut of 12 million board feet a year.[52] Brigham, who made his living as a sawmill consultant, advised upper Selway defenders and the Forest Service that this amount would supply a small mill for only 12 weeks a year and a large mill for two weeks.[53] Secretary Orville Freeman ordered a two-year delay in timber cutting but the Forest Service went ahead with surveys for logging roads. In 1966, the Selway defenders persuaded Sen. Lee Metcalf of Montana to agree to introduce a bill to add the area north of the Magruder Road to the Selway-Bitterroot Wilderness.[54] This helped Metcalf and Senator Church win Freeman's agreement to authorize a study of the Forest Service plan by an independent committee. Freeman specified that the committee's task was to evaluate the Forest Service plan, not to revisit the wilderness issue.[55]

Freeman named George Selke to head the committee. Selke was a former chancellor of the Montana university system, a former aide to Freeman when he was Minnesota governor and was currently acting as a consultant for the Department of Agriculture. Other members were Dr. James Meiman, Colorado State University professor of watershed management; Dr. Kenneth Davis, professor of forest management at the University of Michigan; William Reavley, western field representative for the Idaho Wildlife Federation; Dr. Donald Obee, chairman of the Division of Life Sciences at Boise State College; and Daniel Poole of the Wildlife Management Institute. The committee visited the area and in December 1966 conducted public hearings in Missoula, Grangeville and Boise.

Upper Selway defenders turned out to speak for the watershed, the fisheries and wildlife. Among them were spokesmen for the Idaho and Montana wildlife federations, and the Idaho Fish and game Department as well as the Save the Upper Selway Committee and the Federation of Western Outdoor Clubs. The committee received more than 1,000 letters and statements with approximately two-thirds opposing roads and logging.[56]

The Selke Committee's 58-page report, released in June 1967, called on the Forest Service to give more consideration to protecting the streams and recreational values of the Magruder Corridor (the excluded upper Selway areas north and south of the Magruder Road) with "a reduction or elimination of timber management activity on at least a substantial part of the area" classified as suitable for logging. The committee said there should be no further road building pending further studies: "The construction and maintenance of roads in the topography and soils of the Corridor is difficult, expensive, conducive to erosion and stream sedimentation, and in total, the most critical consideration in the development and management of the area."

The committee noted the significance of the Selway for Columbia River salmon and steelhead with its excellent spawning conditions, pointing out that the soils in this area of steep terrain were extremely fragile and subject to massive erosion. The report called for the preparation of a new management plan recognizing: one, the area's value as a strategic watershed involving both water supply and fish resources; two, its value as a historic connecting route between Idaho and Montana; and three, its value for recreation, particularly in providing access to the surrounding wilderness and primitive areas.[57]

Secretary Freeman accepted the Selke recommendations and directed the Forest Service to implement them. The Forest Service went to work preparing a new plan for public review and comment. While the Selke report was a victory for the corridor's defenders, it did not fully resolve their concerns. The Forest Service might manage an area outside a wilderness primarily for watershed values and primitive recreation but there was no long-term certainty that it would. The effort to win wilderness status for the excluded areas north and south of the Magruder Road continued. Senator Metcalf introduced a wilderness bill in 1970 and Senator Church joined him as a co-sponsor in 1972. Also the Forest Service was beginning a review of the Salmon River Breaks and Idaho Primitive areas, preparing to submit a recommendation to the Department of Agriculture and the Congress. Some of the excluded acreage could potentially be restored as part of the Salmon River wilderness that might be established by act of Congress.

Chapter 6

Club women campaign for Sawtooth national park

"Should one scale one of these Sawtooth peaks and look off over Idaho's illimitable glory, one would see misty mountain masses, peaks in crenulated complexity, gaunt canyons falling sheer and deep; then an opulence of beauty with sun lighted splendor, lakes in the Alpine regions, shadowy forests, silver flashing water falls, vast and boundless stretches of mountains, and always the overpowering sense of the stupendous grandeur of Idaho." – Jeanne Conly Smith.

"The magnificent and rugged peaks, the beautiful lakes, of fresh water, clear as crystal, located in the fastness of the mountains, the bracing and invigorating air, will make that section one of the most popular national playgrounds in the entire United States." – Congressman Addison Smith.

Travelers entering central Idaho's Stanley Basin from the south in 1910 followed a wagon road from Ketchum in the Wood River Valley, climbing to the 8,700-foot Galena Summit. From the summit they looked down on a valley flanked on the left by a long line of jagged peaks, the Sawtooths. Forty-two of the peaks rose more than 10,000 feet. In depressions left by glaciers were 500 lakes. The mountain chain reached 30 miles to the north and was about 20 miles wide. Hidden from view behind glacial moraines were five large lakes at the base of the peaks.

A small stream flowed down the slope on the left, the beginning of the Salmon River. This small stream was joined by creeks flowing from the mountains on the right and left and from the large lakes. By the time the Salmon reached the tiny village of Stanley, 40 miles down the valley, it was a substantial stream, gathering volume and power on its 424-mile course to the Snake River on the Idaho-Oregon border. The Sawtooths also fed the Middle Fork of the Boise River and the South Fork of the Payette. Just to the north of the Sawtooth peaks other mountain streams joined to form the headwaters of the Middle Fork of the Salmon. The middle fork would join the main Salmon after 106 turbulent miles.

Idaho Historical Society Photo No. 75-130.2 by S.B. Brown

In 1912, three Columbian Club members accompanied Boise National Forest Supervisor Emil Grandjean on a 15-day trek in the Sawtooths. From left, Jeanne Conly Smith, Grandjean, Margaret Keenan, Phyllis Morrow and unidentified ranger. Woman in background is also unidentified.

Winters in the Sawtooth Valley, at 7,000-foot elevation, were long and cold. Year-round residents were few, mostly ranchers, ranch hands, trappers and miners. Mining camps at the south end of the valley, Vienna and Sawtooth City, had flourished for a time in the 1880s but now mining activity was limited. Occasionally Idaho newspapers carried accounts by members of hunting and fishing parties dazzled by the area's splendor. In 1875, three years after Congress established Yellowstone Park, an Idaho judge, Alanson Smith, suggested that the area merited consideration for a national park. "He fairly revels in the wonderful mountain scenery and the lakes containing the red fish," said The Idaho Statesman. But nothing was done to advance the idea.[1]

Jeanne Conly Smith, a nature lover and a member of Boise's Columbian Club, had seen the Sawtooths, exploring and camping on the west side, and gathering specimens in pursuit of her study of birds. She was enchanted by the stately peaks, the lakes and streams, the wildflowers and the diverse animal life. In 1911, she persuaded club members to support her plan for a Sawtooth National Park. She said a park would protect an area of exceptional beauty while attracting visitors from eastern and other states. It could also foster road improvements to provide easier access to the Sawtooth country.

Smith came to Boise from Salt Lake City in 1895 with her husband, George, an agent for the Pacific Express Company. The Columbian Club was a social club dedicated to personal and community improvement and social reform. It was organized in 1893, provided furnishings for the Idaho exhibit at the Columbian Exposition in Chicago and established Boise's first public library. The club was affiliated with the Idaho Federation of Women's Clubs, a statewide coalition that was active on many fronts including women's property rights, an 8-hour day for working women, regulation of child labor and civil service for government employees. The Idaho Federation was part of a national coalition, the General Federation of Women's Clubs.[2]

In October 1911, Conly Smith presented her plan to representatives of 12 southwestern Idaho clubs meeting in Mountain Home. The women of the Second District of the Idaho Federation of Women's Clubs adopted a resolution saying the Sawtooths should become a national park and appointed a committee, headed by Mrs. Smith, to work for its creation.[3] A few days later The Idaho Statesman published, under Conly Smith's byline, her exuberant description of the proposed park: "This wonderful piece of Idaho scenery the club women of the state propose to make either a state or a national park, where the beauties may not only be preserved but where it may be thrown open to the tourists of the world." It was a land of "unscaled peaks, deep dark canyons, mountain meadows, innumerable lakes, numerous waterfalls, hot mineral springs having a temperature of 175 degrees, alpine flora, and birds both rare and beautiful… Except for the forest rangers who patrol this region against fire, it is silent and undisturbed, as in primitive times."[4]

Smith described the approach to the mountains, galloping past many colorful wildflowers "until the glory of wonderful peaks burst into sight – the Sawtooths. Now, having chosen a path beside a twisting, swirling stream by which to ascend the mountain, a fine bridal veil spray sparkles in the sun as the stream leaps from its course, forming one of the numerous waterfalls for which these great park-like gardens will be famous." It was a land of deer, elk and mountain goats, many small mammals and a great variety of birds with "deep and blue" mountain lakes.

Idaho was known for its large acreage of virgin land to be reclaimed, potatoes, apples, Senators Borah and Heyburn and as a state where women vote, wrote Smith, but few people knew about these wonderful mountains "which only the Alps equal." Accompanying Smith's story was a map showing the possible boundaries of a park. It would include the 220,000-acre Payette Game Preserve on the west side of the Sawtooths, the peaks and an area on the east side embracing the large lakes.

Elk were increasing in the preserve, Smith wrote, and a park would protect them on the east side of the mountains as well as the west. She described the abundant redfish found in the large lakes: "Fishing in these lakes cannot be excelled and is carried on both for pleasure and business." Large quantities of redfish had been taken in the 1880s and 1890s for sale in mining camps. Fish were speared with pitchforks and thrown onshore. The redfish included both the resident kokanee that spawned in streams feeding Redfish, Stanley, and Alturas lakes and the larger sockeye salmon that migrated 800 miles up the Columbia, Snake and Salmon rivers to spawn along the lake shores. The Sunbeam dam built on the Salmon River ten miles below the village of Stanley in 1910 would block the sockeye and lock them out of the lakes. But there were still large numbers of kokanee. In a later article Smith wrote that the redfish needed protection in a park because no Idaho fish law protected them. "These fish cannot be caught by bait but are taken by means of grab hooks, dipped up in buckets and numerous other ways to such an extent that they are becoming depleted."[5]

In June 1912, the Idaho Federation of Women's Clubs, meeting in Boise, embraced Smith's proposal, voting to send a memorial to Congress favoring a Sawtooth national park. Mrs. Smith served as the Second District conservation chairman and was a member of the national federation's conservation committee. She was a capable writer and speaker and a determined and persistent advocate. She campaigned tirelessly for the Sawtooth park, gaining favorable publicity in newspapers, speaking to civic clubs and showing slides. Her daughter, Josephine, recalled coming home from school one day in 1911 to find the living room "literally plastered" with pictures of the redfish lakes and the Sawtooth peaks.[6]

The Sawtooth proposal was part of the Idaho Federation's campaign to promote recognition and protection of Idaho's scenic natural landscapes. The April 1912 issue of the federation's magazine, the Idaho Club Woman, included photos and articles on Shoshone Falls and Payette Lake as well as Conly Smith's article on the proposed Sawtooth park. Before endorsing a Sawtooth park the Second District club women heard reports on Shoshone Falls and Twin Falls, Coeur d'Alene Lake, the Trinity Lakes, the Henry's Fork area in eastern Idaho and the ice caves near Shoshone. During their 1912 meeting, the women helped organize a See Idaho First Association. Speaking at the organizing meeting, Gov. James Hawley said Idaho had scenery equal to the scenic attractions of the old world that might become a commercial asset if it were accessible. He urged the club women to lobby the legislature and counties for road improvements.[7]

Conly Smith added to her knowledge of the Sawtooth country on a 15-day pack trip led by Emil Grandjean, supervisor of the Boise National Forest, in August 1912. The 6-member party, including three club women and photographer S.B. Brown, set off from Atlanta, following a trail up Mattingly Creek "passing over the divide into the Redfish lake country." After 10 days of

Royce Williams Photo

Redfish Lake in the Sawtooth Mountains

exploring and fishing around Alturas, Pettit, Redfish and Stanley lakes, they followed a trail up Stanley Lake Creek to a summit, and then made a steep descent to the South Fork of the Payette. From there they climbed to a divide on a route that crossed snow fields and descended to the Middle Fork of the Boise River. At times Grandjean let Smith take the lead so she could say she was the first white woman to see the country. Smith described this expedition in the October issue of the Club Woman. She reported that they had seen a grizzly bear feeding on a mountain goat, and elk and deer at a Forest Service salt lick. They had covered 200 miles on horseback and hiked 10 hours a day.[8]

While Conly Smith initiated and led the campaign for a Sawtooth national park, Emil Grandjean played an important role. He recognized the beauty and recreation potential of the Sawtooth country and its importance as habitat for wildlife. In a 1909 report to the Forest Service, he said the grandeur of the mountains "cannot be excelled," describing them as "the Alps of America: The sunsets in this high mountain region are something wonderful, changing from fiery red to a dark purple nearly black." Grandjean in 1909 persuaded the legislature to designate Idaho's first game preserve, providing a 220,000-acre sanctuary for elk, deer, mountain goats and other wildlife on the west side of the Sawtooths. Grandjean provided information that helped Conly Smith prepare the park proposal and invited the club women to join him on the 1912 pack trip. He allowed his rangers to help Conly Smith gather signatures on petitions in support of the park. And he served as the first chairman of the See Idaho First Association.[9]

Conly Smith wrote Congressman Burton French and Sen. William E. Borah asking them to introduce park bills. French advised her to demonstrate public support with more publicity and a petition campaign, suggestions that she embraced. In February 1913, French introduced a bill for a 230,000-acre park, including the peaks, part of the game preserve on the west side and an area on the east side around the large lakes. Sheepmen, represented by the Idaho Woolgrowers Association, objected because a national park would exclude grazing. Most of the state's two million sheep grazed on public lands and the woolgrowers were a potent force in Idaho politics. In response to the woolgrowers, Conly Smith and the Columbian Club scaled down the park proposal to 145,000 acres, moving the western boundary to the crest of the mountains and adjusting the eastern boundary to avoid interfering with stock driveways.[10]

She advised French that it would be "absolutely necessary to exclude grazing of all kinds of stock from the park" except animals used by the government, campers, tourists, sightseers and other park visitors. "By reducing the area of the park, the objections of the stockmen cannot interfere, since only about 5,100 head of sheep are using or have been using this territory for grazing purposes. I believe that the Forest Service will transfer the sheep to other parts of the forest." Smith said the Forest Service would be asked to build and improve roads to the park. Based on information provided by Smith, the Boise Capital News declared that "forest reserve officials are in sympathy with the purposes of the park and heartily join in the request for its creation." Following Smith's instructions, French introduced a bill for a 145,000-acre park, excluding the sheep.[11]

While Emil Grandjean had helped Smith advance the park plan, his Forest Service superiors wanted no Sawtooth park and no transfer of land to the jurisdiction of the Interior Department. Forest Service Chief Henry Graves instructed district foresters to follow a strategy of delay, opposing all park proposals in the absence of an agency to run national parks and criteria for their creation. The National Park Service would not be established until 1916.

In a report to the House Public Lands Committee on French's Sawtooth bill, the Secretary of Agriculture said the proposed park included grazing lands, timber and minerals and would complicate forest management in the area. "It may be said that there are proposals for at least 20 national parks," he declared, but there was no policy on how many should be established, their distribution, and features justifying their creation, how large they should be or how boundaries should be drawn. The Secretary of Interior supported the Sawtooth bill with changes to conform to existing national park policies but the Agriculture Department prevailed and the bill died in committee.[12]

In October 1913, George Smith was transferred to Lincoln, Nebraska, and Idaho lost the Sawtooth park's principal advocate. But Jeanne Conly Smith continued as a leader of the campaign, writing, speaking and generating favorable press comments. Her Sawtooth park articles continued to appear in The Idaho Statesman, other papers and magazines. Other Idaho club women picked up the banner and the park plan won the support of local commercial clubs and the Idaho League of Women Voters as well as Idaho Game Warden J.B. Gowen. The National Federation of Women's Clubs, meeting in San Francisco, endorsed a Sawtooth park.[13]

There was no action in Congress in 1914 but in March 1915, the Idaho Legislature unanimously adopted a resolution favoring Burton French's 1913 bill for a 145,000-acre park. Sponsored by Sen. Irvin Rockwell of Ketchum, the resolution echoed themes developed by Conly Smith: The proposed park encompassed the most scenic area in Idaho, unmatched in the intermountain West in the grandeur of its mountain and lake scenery. There were few private land holdings within the proposed boundaries, preservation of the forests would protect the watershed and serve the interest of downstream irrigators. The park would provide a valuable game refuge in conjunction with the adjoining state game preserve and would allow protection of the redfish. It would protect the unusual flora and abundant fauna while providing a natural recreation ground for present and future generations, attracting people from all parts of the country, allowing them to learn about "the vast resources of the state." While livestock grazing would be barred, this would eliminate only a very few grazing permits with no injury "to any material degree" to the sheep industry. No sheep trails were included, densely wooded areas were inaccessible to sheep and forage production was low.[14]

Rockwell was a first term state senator, a former Chicago businessman who purchased and reopened the Minnie Moore silver mine at Bellevue in 1901. He also owned an interest in a Wood River electric power company and was a friend of Sen. William E. Borah and Congressman Addison Smith. He had campaigned for improved roads and was a strong advocate for the Sawtooth park. In the 1920s, he would gain further stature for leadership in rescuing the Bureau of Reclamation's American Falls dam project after it had been shelved by Interior Secretary Albert Fall.

At the request of assistant Interior Secretary Stephen Mather, R.B. Marshall, chief geographer of the U.S. Geological Survey and a USGS geologist, examined the Sawtooth area in the summer of 1915. They traveled by train to Ketchum and from there by auto. Marshall found the Sawtooth range "unusually striking in mountain sculpture," a composite of the Rocky Mountains in Colorado, the Sierra in California and the Cascade range in Washington. The lakes were "rare in their brilliant transparency, reflecting the mountains and the black pine forests fringing their edges." He recommended a much larger park than proposed by French in 1913, 330,000 acres including areas both west and east of the peaks. "A national park must be accessible on all sides" and most of the population of southern Idaho would naturally prefer to enter on the west side via the existing 75-mile wagon road from Boise to Atlanta, he wrote.

Marshall believed existing roads accessing the area from Boise, Mackay and Ketchum were "fairly good for present purposes" but the road from Ketchum to Stanley required improvement around the Galena summit. It was so steep and dangerous for about three miles on either side that "small pine trees were cut at the summit and tied to the rear of the machines for additional brakes." He also proposed an extension of the Atlanta road to allow visitors to make a complete circuit of the park without retracing their route. Mather recommended no restriction on mineral exploration or development in the park, noting that no deposit of commercial value had been found. He also proposed no ban on livestock grazing or water power development. The small amount of commercial timber, found in strips about six miles wide on either side of the peaks, should be preserved for its beauty and protection of the watershed, he advised. Public lands outside the park boundaries should be exchanged for the small amount of private holdings.[15]

Both Congressman Addison Smith and Sen. William E. Borah visited the Sawtooth country in 1915. Smith told the Hailey Commercial Club that he was enthusiastic about a park and would introduce legislation. In January 1916, Smith and Sen. William E. Borah introduced bills for a 330,000-acre Sawtooth National Park, accepting Marshall's boundaries and management policies but rejecting his recommendation to change the name to Idaho National Park. Marshall had dismissed "Sawtooth" as a "common name applied to some

Ernie Day Photo

One of the 500 high mountain lakes in the Sawtooths.

portion of almost every mountain range." Acting Interior Secretary Andreius Jones endorsed the Smith bill in a report to the House Public Lands Committee: "It could be readily visited by tourists from the Yellowstone National Park, and furthermore, would constitute a most important link in a chain of national parks, located as it is between the Yellowstone and Mount Rainier national parks."

But Secretary of Agriculture D.F. Houston objected, saying the area was not of national park caliber. Parks should be "truly notable scenic marvels" such as the Grand Canyon, the falls and gorges of Yosemite, the glaciers of Glacier National Park, the geysers of Yellowstone, the giant trees of General Grant or the natural bridges of southwestern Utah, he advised the House committee. "Where such wonders exist," it would be worthwhile to dedicate an area for visitors and sightseers and preserve it from changes caused by lumbering, grazing, mining and agriculture. Except for timber cutting, Smith's bill would not provide such protection but would make the park "to all intents and purposes a national forest in everything but name." It would take an area from three national forests, surrounded by national forest land, to "give jurisdiction to another department." Houston said a "fuller and more substantial use of all the resources of the area may be secured by retaining them in the national forest and carrying out a specific plan for their development."

While Addison Smith's bill specifically allowed continued livestock grazing, Houston nevertheless declared that with a park "it will be necessary to find other range for about 20,000 sheep." This part of his statement was at odds with his complaint that the bill allowed most existing uses, including grazing, to continue. Newspaper accounts of his statement in Idaho focused on the fictional loss of grazing for sheep.[16]

The Idaho Woolgrowers adopted a resolution asking the Idaho congressional delegation to oppose a Sawtooth park, saying it would deprive cattle and sheep of range that was already much restricted and would also protect predatory animals. In the face of this opposition, Addison Smith redrew the boundaries, including only the east side of the peaks and the large lakes. His revised 145,000-acre bill was similar to the French bill of 1913 except it allowed continued sheep grazing. He issued a statement saying there was no reason for the sheepmen to oppose the bill: "The boundaries of the proposed park have been redrawn in a way to exclude nearly all the grazing land that was included in the first limits suggested. Moreover, as it stands sheep and cattle may be grazed on what little land is included in the park." But the woolgrowers continued to object. In an appearance before the League of Women voters of Boise President Hugh Sproat said the bill would eliminate grazing for 15,000 sheep. The woolgrowers trusted the Forest Service but feared a park managed by the Interior Department. The headline on the Statesman's story on Sproat's encounter with the women voters declared: "Sawtooth Park Appears to be Dead."[17]

State Sen. Irvin Rockwell recognized that the park bill could be lost. He composed a blistering critique of the woolgrowers and sent it to Idaho newspapers: "The sordid ruthlessness of the 'master of the flocks' was never better illustrated than in this appeal to close all opportunity for a great national playground and art gallery within our state." The grasses for the sheep would be "as succulent and abundant" under one regime as the other, declared Rockwell "but he objects and the Department of Agriculture objects with him." Idaho spoke unanimously to Congress in the 1915 legislative resolution favoring a park, Rockwell maintained. "Idaho wanted it then, she has wanted it for 30 years, she wants it now, regardless of the owners of 15,000 sheep." Rockwell asked if the women of Idaho, who had worked so earnestly for the park for five years, would "stand for this riot of selfishness in high places?" The battle was half won, he declared, pleading for letters and telegrams to Idaho's members in Congress.[18]

The Idaho Statesman chided the sheepmen in an editorial, suggesting their fears were groundless: "Might not the public be given the benefit of this park, thereby preserving as a playground one of the west's most choice bits of natural scenery without any disadvantage accruing to the sheep industry?" After all, sheepmen had bitterly opposed the forest reserves but had benefited from their creation. Hugh Sproat replied to both Rockwell and the Statesman, still maintaining that the Smith and Borah bills would reduce sheep grazing. Sproat said the woolgrowers wanted only the area suitable for grazing, meaning the area on the west side of the mountains. This area had already been excluded from Addison Smith's revised bill.[19]

Well known Colorado naturalist Enos Mills had written Addison Smith in support of the Sawtooth park. Now he sent a statement to the Statesman chastising the Forest Service for its "unworthy opposition." Mills said scenery was a valuable resource with benefits best realized by making scenic places into parks. A Sawtooth park would not only bring travelers who would spend money but would bring people who would become Idaho residents and investors. A national park offered "the least expensive and most effective way of building up a western state."[20]

In May, the National Federation of Women's Clubs and other conservation-minded groups could rejoice as President Woodrow Wilson signed the bill establishing the National Park Service. It included a provision allowing the agency to permit livestock grazing in national parks.[21]

Despite the objections of the woolgrowers and the Forest Service, the Committee on Public Lands reported the Sawtooth bill to the House with a favorable recommendation in January 1917. The bill included a provision saying present grazing privileges would not be curtailed. Addison Smith wired the good news to the presidents of the Idaho Federation of Women's Clubs and the Columbian Club. The women were now hopeful that the Sawtooth park would soon become a reality.[22]

But the Forest Service was working behind the scenes to persuade key park supporters in the Wood River Valley to switch sides. If they would withdraw their support for a park, the Forest Service would improve the Ketchum - Stanley road. Irvin Rockwell told the story at a public meeting in 1936: "The representatives of Blaine County were given their choice between a national park or a road over Galena Summit. A road was essential and therefore Congress was wired to withdraw the park bill."[23]

The bill died when Congress adjourned in February and was not reintroduced in the following session. In April 1917, the Forest Service reported that work would soon begin on improving 12 miles of road around Galena Summit, a project that was completed in 1919. The Forest Service also helped finance improvements on the road between Stanley and Salmon and put crews to work on a road through the South Fork Payette River canyon from Garden Valley to Lowman.[24]

The favorable House committee report of 1917 represented the high water mark for the Sawtooth park campaign initiated by Jeanne Conly Smith. Idaho still had no national park to attract visitors but many more Idahoans now knew about "this wonderful piece of Idaho scenery." In 1922, Rep. Addison Smith again introduced a Sawtooth park bill but again encountered objections from sheepmen. Smith didn't give up until 1926, but the bill never came to a vote in the House. In 1924, Sawtooth Forest Supervisor M.S. Benedict advised District Forester Richard Rutledge that continued efforts to establish a park were inevitable because of the area's scenic quality and because, in fact, it had little value for grazing, timber or minerals. He proposed that the Forest Service prepare a management plan demonstrating its commitment to recreation use. The Park Service was not then working actively for a park but was still interested.[25]

In 1926, a committee representing both agencies visited the area to consider the merits of Park Service versus Forest Service management. Rutledge was ready with a Sawtooth management plan oriented to scenic protection and recreation. It would bar timber cutting next to Alturas, Redfish and Stanley lakes and keep livestock out of lakeside camping areas and the high lake basins. There would be new campgrounds at the large lakes, more mountain trails and improvements to the Galena, Bear Valley and Salmon roads accessing the area. The committee sided with the Forest Service, recommending no further consideration of a Sawtooth park.

Four years after the woolgrowers and the Forest Service scuttled Addison Smith's Sawtooth park bill, another Idaho national park proposal emerged. This time the campaign was initiated and led by Robert Limbert of Boise. A native of Minnesota, Limbert carried on a taxidermy and hide tanning business, using as an advertising message: "Let us mount your head and tan your hide." Limbert pursued interests in photography, wildlife and landscapes. He designed the Idaho exhibition for the 1915 Pacific International Exposition in San Francisco. In May 1920, Limbert and Walter Cole of Boise made a

17-day, 80-mile hike exploring part of the vast and little known area of lava flows, craters, fissures and caves between the Pioneer mountains and the Snake River west of Arco. Limbert recorded his impressions, took 200 photos, mapped the route and christened the area "moon valley." He shared his adventure and pictures in lectures to civic and commercial clubs, suggesting that this strange, forbidding area with its unusual features and surprising beauty should become a national park.

In April 1921, The Idaho Statesman published three pages of Limbert's photos and text. Limbert described "a miniature replica of the moon country, a vast expanse, silent, dead, except for an occasional bird, a country with cold volcanic mountains, numberless 'sputtercones,' bottomless pits, frozen lakes and rivers and waterfalls of stone, hillsides of flaming red, cliffs of cobalt blue, cones striped with yellow and green, a riot of color and fantastic shapes so unearthly as to make one believe himself on another planet." A national park would be a "fitting tribute to the volcanic forces which built the great Snake River valley." The park would attract tourists now passing nearby on their way to and from Yellowstone Park while protecting archeological sites and geologic features.[26]

In June, Limbert led another exploring expedition sponsored by The Idaho Statesman. The party of 10 included a naturalist sent by the U.S. Biological Survey and Arco newspaper publisher C.A. Bottolfsen. They spent nearly two weeks exploring and mapping 800 square miles. More than 200 area residents turned out and the Arco high school band played at a picnic celebrating the expedition's return. The Arco Chamber of Commerce had promoted the area as a tourist attraction and had joined the park campaign. Limbert found more audiences, eventually enlisting the support of 150 organizations that signed on to petitions. In 1923, a Craters of the Moon National Park Association was organized with a membership that included Gov. Charles C. Moore. The campaign encountered little opposition because the area was considered almost useless for livestock grazing, farming or mining.[27]

The Idaho Automobile Association's H.W.L. Niemeyer of Nampa suggested a national park including both a Sawtooth and craters division. But he found no sponsor for such a bill. Backers of a craters park eventually shifted focus, seeking a national monument designated by presidential order rather than a park approved by Congress. Rep. Addison Smith supported the monument approach. Limbert's accounts and photos impressed Park Service Director Steven Mather who asked for a report from Harold T. Stearns of the U.S. Geological Survey. Stearns found that the area was geologically unique in the continental United States, the result of a "fissure eruption" rather than eruptions from a single volcano. The Park Service sent its recommendation to President Calvin Coolidge for a Craters of the Moon national monument and Coolidge signed the proclamation on May 24, 1924. The monument included 53,000 acres, too little in Limbert's opinion. But the protected area would ultimately be enlarged to more than 700,000 acres under both Park Service and Bureau of Land Management jurisdiction.[28]

While Idaho now had a national monument administered by the Park Service, there was continuing interest in a Sawtooth park. In 1935, Democratic Sen. John Pope introduced a Sawtooth National Park bill, attempting to revive the issue at a time when the state was struggling to emerge from the depression and desperately in need of new jobs. Pope soon received objections from sheepmen. In December, Pope and Addison Smith advised park supporters in the Wood River Valley that, with opposition by sheepmen and the Forest Service, there was little chance of success.[29]

Pursuant to New Deal legislation that encouraged states to prepare plans to promote economic development, Gov. C. Ben Ross appointed an Idaho State Planning Board. The board recognized that Idaho, with millions of acres of mountain and desert scenery and abundant fish and wildlife, had great potential for increased tourism. Interest in capitalizing on recreation visitors was also spurred by the Union Pacific Railroad's plans to develop a winter resort at Ketchum to be called Sun Valley. By the summer of 1936, work was underway on the Sun Valley Lodge that was to have 75 guest rooms. The resort was expected to open for the Christmas holiday season. The Planning Board scheduled a 2-day conference on recreation in Hailey in late August. It would bring together representatives of state and federal agencies, office holders, interest groups and Union Pacific executives to talk about what might be done to bring more visitors to Idaho.[30]

A month before the conference R.G. Cole, manager of the Idaho Automobile Association and president of the recently organized Idaho Wildlife Federation, launched a new campaign for a Sawtooth park. He sent letters to Idaho's senators and congressmen asking them to sponsor the association's park plan, emphasizing the potential to promote Idaho tourism. Cole's proposed park looked much like Burton French's revised bill of 1913 and Addison Smith's revised bill of 1916. It included only the east side Redfish Lake area with a western boundary along the crest of the peaks and with the eastern boundary at the Salmon River. Cole left the determination of management policies to the congressional sponsors. His proposal made a splash with a full-page layout in The Idaho Statesman including the map and photos under the headline: "Idaho Wants a National Park."

Feature writer Dick d'Easum described the area as a "camper's delight" with a jagged line of peaks up to 11,000 feet offering perpetual scenery and unlimited mountain climbing, scores of lakes and some of the best fishing in the west. Cole said tourism was now "a mass movement that follows certain logical routes dominated by national parks. People go from one to another and see as many as they can on their vacation days." While visiting Glacier, Yellowstone, Mt. Rainier, Crater Lake, Yosemite and the Grand Canyon they "circle entirely around Idaho," which could provide "the best national park of all." Cole claimed tourism was already Idaho's third or fourth ranking industry

Ernie Day photo

Some of the 42 peaks in the Sawtooths that rise above 10,000 feet.

with more potential for enhancement than agriculture, mining or timber. While Cole was president of the Idaho Wildlife Federation, the park plan was advanced as a proposal of the Automobile Association not of the federation.[31]

"Sawtooth National Park Is Given a Great Boost," proclaimed the Hailey Times, crediting Cole and the Statesman with reviving the issue while reprinting every word of d'Easum's article. The Hailey Chamber of Commerce named a committee to promote the park and, in a follow-up story the Times asserted that "All Idaho Is Stirred Over New Park." Cole reported receiving messages of support from a number of chambers of commerce and citizens. He said the association only wished to start the movement, expecting other organizations to work for the park. Cole hoped to conduct a Sawtooth area tour in advance of the recreation conference.[32]

Responding to speculation that the Planning Board was promoting the park, Chairman Will Simon said this was not the case. The board was going to Hailey to "get all information possible," anticipating that there would be further study and possible consideration of the subject at a later conference. "There are good arguments on both sides of the question and the matter is not ready to be settled," he said. Both the Statesman and the Boise Capital News told readers that the park issue was sure to dominate the recreation conference.[33]

The agenda included three Forest Service speakers. Assistant Regional Forester C.J. Olson described the virtue of national forest primitive areas. Responding to public sentiment favoring the preservation of areas with "paramount inspirational and educational character and significance," he said, the agency had designated 67 primitive areas totaling 10 million acres including the 1,087,744-acre Idaho Primitive Area and the recently established (July 3) Selway-Bitterroot Primitive Area with 1,580,000 acres in Idaho. "All of these primitive areas are roadless. Within them are no hotels or dude ranches, no hot dog stands or gasoline pumps," he said in a not so subtle jab at national parks. Olson made no mention of any plan for a Sawtooth primitive area as an alternative to a park but some in the audience of 100 must have recognized such a possibility. In fact, Regional Forester Richard Rutledge and the Boise, Challis and Sawtooth forest supervisors had already drafted a proposal for a 200,000-acre primitive area including the Sawtooth peaks and high lakes.[34]

Speaking for the park, R.G. Cole emphasized the "cold dollars and cents angle." He cited estimates that 300,000 cars carrying recreation visitors entered Idaho in 1929 contributing an average $11 a day, adding $7 million in "new money" to the economy. It would be more like $10 million in 1936 but Idaho was not getting "anywhere near its share" of the Northwest tourist business, he said. The Sawtooth area was equal to any on the continent but was practically unknown and visited by few people. The balance of Cole's statement was defensive. He said he had been accused of promoting a park without regard to other users and was told the sheepmen were "loaded for me."

Cole said he had stated in his letter to the congressional delegation that he was "merely opening this question for intelligent discussion." Development of the area for greater use was imperative whether "through a national park, a primitive area or such other designation," he said.[35]

National Park Service consultant John B. Williams said nothing for or against a Sawtooth park but described Park Service standards and policies. Parks were for recreational use and scientific study with preservation of plant and animal life and management leaving them "unimpaired" for the future. Mining, timber cutting and grazing were not permitted and the Park Service opposed reservoirs. The area must be accessible to people and, if necessary, wilderness areas might be made "excessively accessible" so recreation use could equal the economic potential for timber and mining.[36]

In a statement by Regional Forester Rutledge, delivered by Boise Forest Supervisor Guy Mains, Forest Service management was credited with protecting watersheds, reducing flooding and putting livestock grazing and timber removal on a "sustained yield" basis. The Forest Service had always recognized recreation as important, said Rutledge, and improved roads, cheap cars and shorter working hours now made it possible for "all classes of people to participate." Southern Idaho forests served 775,000 recreation users in 1935, triple the 1924 number. Wide open areas best fit "the needs of our people," said Rutledge, implying that a park would bring fees and restrictions. "Some enthusiasts would have us forget other uses and devote large parts of our forests exclusively to recreation use or even turn it into national parks," he said, while others "would devote large areas to game production to the exclusion of the livestock industry."[37]

Park backers might have entertained hopes that the Union Pacific Railroad would side with them. The Northern Pacific had promoted the creation of Yellowstone Park and a Sawtooth park could generate rail passenger business. In his Capital News story in advance of the conference, reporter Ted Trueblood had identified the Union Pacific as a park supporter. But E.C. Schmidt, assistant to the Union Pacific president, speaking on the railroad's promotion plans for Sun Valley and the value of advertising to attract visitors, made it clear that the railroad opposed a park. Schmidt said there was a lot in a name and the term "primitive area" had "lure" while the term park suggested a children's playground. Union Pacific General Manager H.J. Plumhoff framed the issue in a different way. There were already enough national parks. "We now want areas left open for the material development of cattle, minerals, etc." Idaho didn't need a national park because, with advertising of the Idaho Primitive Area and the forests, "visitors will be attracted quite as much as otherwise." The Union Pacific was siding with its livestock shippers rather than the park advocates.[38]

J.E. Shepherd of Jerome, president of the Idaho Chamber of Commerce, and Harry Shellworth, a leader in establishing the Idaho Primitive Area, helped shape the Union Pacific position. In July, at the request of Shepherd,

Shellworth had helped arrange a central Idaho visit for Union Pacific executives including President Carl Gray, Schmidt and Plumhoff. They visited the large Sawtooth lakes with Shellworth serving as host. He described the virtue of the Idaho Primitive Area including its fabulous hunting. Shepherd also arranged for sheepmen to meet with the Union Pacific party in Ketchum to voice their opposition to a park.[39]

Also speaking against a Sawtooth park was W.W. Deal of the Idaho State Grange, representing farmers, and J.M. Lambert, attorney representing Boise Valley irrigators. A group of irrigation promoters was trying to persuade the Bureau of Reclamation to prepare a plan to tunnel through the Sawtooths and send water from Redfish Lake to the Payette River drainage, allowing the irrigation of additional desert land east of Boise. While the pending Sawtooth park bill (Senator Pope's) had a clause saying the U.S. Bureau of Reclamation could make water diversions for irrigation, similar language in the Rocky Mountain National Park bill "didn't work," said Lambert. "Any national park bill that places the water users under such restrictions is opposed."[40]

While no votes were taken and no resolutions were considered at the conference, a consensus emerged. The park proposal had been decisively rejected. The Statesman reported that, with the position of the Grange and the irrigators, "sentiment grew in opposition to a park." Some of Boise's returning delegates reported "almost unanimous sentiment in keeping the area under the jurisdiction of the Forest Service." The Forest Service, meanwhile, was publicizing plans for campgrounds at Redfish and Alturas lakes that would be available with no fee and small log cabin shelters at some of the lakes reached by trail. The Twin Falls Evening Times, which had opposed Cole's plan, predicted that there would be "no further agitation" for a park and the Hailey Times did not renew its park advocacy. Still, Senator Pope had not given up and in February 1937 introduced a Senate resolution asking for another Sawtooth study by the Park Service. But when woolgrowers and the Shoshone Rod and Gun Club publicly denounced the Park Service for promoting a park, Pope backtracked. He issued a statement saying he was demanding an investigation of the Park Service.[41]

In May 1937, Regional Forester Rutledge unveiled the Forest Service's proposal for a 200,000-acre Sawtooth Primitive Area embracing the peaks and high lakes, at the first meeting of the newly organized Idaho Frontier Club in Shoshone. It was part of the agency's vision and plans for the Sawtooth and Salmon River country. His audience included 150 delegates from 11 counties. Rutledge asked that they form a committee to cooperate with the Forest Service in its planning. Because the Sawtooths now had national significance, access roads would be improved and campgrounds would be added, with the help of the Civilian Conservation Corps, to accommodate an expected surge of visitors to the lakes east of the peaks, said Rutledge.

That area would become the playground "for the masses of people who cannot penetrate into the more remote reaches of the Salmon River," Rutledge said. It would also be the doorway to the Idaho Primitive Area and surrounding territory. "We have here in Idaho something which no other state has, a vast area of several million acres of unspoiled territory," said Rutledge. "If we are wise enough we can hold and maintain for our children and grandchildren a frontier condition which our forefathers met, with its freedom of use, with its freedom from artificiality, with its inspirational qualities unblemished. A bit of the old west, the last frontier." He said a decision on the Sawtooth Primitive Area would be made after "all affected interests had a full opportunity for expression."[42]

In August, the Idaho Planning Board named a 19-member committee including representatives of timber, grazing, mining, irrigation, railroads, chambers of commerce, sportsmen and the Frontier Club to consider the Forest Service's Sawtooth primitive area plan. The committee's report was favorable and, after a hearing in Boise on September 10, the Planning Board endorsed primitive area status for 200,942 acres in the Sawtooths. The proposal also had the support of the Idaho Game Department.[43]

The day before the Planning Board's meeting Second District Congressman D. Worth Clark reported that the chief of the Forest Service had approved the plan and an order would be forthcoming. Clark was undoubtedly aware that the Planning Board decision was not in doubt. Clark also reported on highway work, promising completion of the Idaho City-Lowman road in 1938 and more work on the Grandjean-Stanley road. Clark said designation of the Sawtooth primitive area would not change present grazing, hunting or mining rights but "will act as an advertising feature to bring tourists to the area."

"Idaho's famous Sawtooth Range of jagged peaks, hidden jewel lakes and pristine wilderness has now come into its own," declared the Lincoln County Journal after Chief Forester Ferdinand A. Silcox issued the order on November 5, 1937. The peaks had "stood silently guarding the headwaters of the Boise, Payette, Salmon and Wood rivers. Their serrated outlines have served as a magnet drawing and holding those who would come and admire. Now this hub of south Idaho's mountains will remain roadless, primitive and dedicated to wilderness."[44]

The Forest Service described the area as "in as near a wilderness state as possible" with no roads, few trails and no human habitations. Emphasis would be on preserving wilderness values and on regulating and protecting the "fine herds of wild animals" which included 1,000 elk, 4,000 mule deer and 650 mountain goats. The Forest Service would cooperate with the Idaho Game Department and hunting would be permitted in the area outside the Payette Game Preserve. No public roads would be built. And no buildings except simple log structures for fire protection, administration or sanitation and, perhaps, simple overnight shelters and corrals for riding and pack animals.

About 30 percent of the area was used for summer grazing by 5,680 sheep and that would continue. Timber cutting was not barred but the timber was not of commercial quality. Continued mineral exploration was permitted and roads built by miners for access were not ruled out but the area showed "no evidence of mineral value." The Sawtooth Primitive Area had an average elevation of 8,000 feet with 3,000 acres of lakes, 150,000 acres of forest and 354 acres of grassland. The Forest Service estimated that 750 people visited the area in 1936, most with pack animals.[45]

Twenty-six years after Jeanne Conly Smith and the Idaho club women began their campaign for a Sawtooth national park the high peak area had gained official recognition and some protection for its natural quality. The interest in the Sawtooths stirred by repeated park proposals and the park campaign had resulted in a defensive strategy by the Forest Service and designation of the primitive area. While Boise Forest Supervisor Emile Grandjean played an important role in the initial Sawtooth park movement, Regional Forester Rutledge had been a leader in the primitive area designation, just as he had been with the Idaho Primitive Area. With the primitive area established, Senator Pope gave up on the park, withdrawing his resolution. In 1938, Pope would lose his bid for re-election as D. Worth Clark defeated him by 7,000 votes in the Democratic primary.

Idaho park opponents and the Forest Service believed that designation of the primitive area ended the threat of Park Service management of the Sawtooths. It didn't. Interior Secretary Harold Ickes had favored a Sawtooth park and in 1939, he proposed bringing national forest areas of park quality under Park Service jurisdiction with the Antiquities Act, the law that allowed a president to declare areas of historic or geologic interest as national monuments. Ickes directed the Park Service to draft monument proclamations for candidate areas including the Sawtooths.

But the plan ran into a roadblock within the Interior Department, opposition by the Bureau of Reclamation. Responding to Boise Valley irrigation promoters, the Bureau in 1937 filed land withdrawals in Stanley Basin for a project that would irrigate thousands of acres with Salmon River water. A tunnel through the Sawtooths would send water from Redfish Lake to the Boise River drainage. Also contemplated were dams and reservoirs on Bear Valley and Marsh creeks, headwater streams of the Middle Fork of the Salmon, with a tunnel to the Payette River's Warm Springs Creek. Boise attorney J.M. Lambert had raised the same objection to a Sawtooth park at the 1936 recreation conference.

Using Salmon River water had been suggested repeatedly since 1902 in connection with various irrigation schemes. Spearheading the current effort was the Southwestern Idaho Water Project, a group headed by Harry Morrison of the Morrison-Knudsen Construction Company. Their first goal was construction of the Bureau's proposed Anderson Ranch dam on the South Fork of the Boise River. The Sawtooth tunnel project would follow some time in the future. The Park Service opposed irrigation reservoirs in national parks or monuments but the Forest Service's primitive area would be no obstacle if Congress could be persuaded to authorize and fund the project.[46]

There were still Idahoans who yearned for a Sawtooth park. One of them was Grace Barringer, a member of the Columbian Club, who voiced her sentiments in the Boise Capital News in November 1937. The primary motive for the primitive area "was the sidetracking of a national park," she wrote. "I believe in primitive areas (in certain locations) but surely so remarkable and so striking a region as the Sawtooth Mountains should not be locked up in such a manner." It would be accessible primarily to people of "heavy pocketbook" while the Park Service would accommodate "every degree of income" providing roads and trails for access, she wrote.

Forests were managed for commercial purposes while national parks preserved nature's handiwork "exactly as nature made it." The primitive area would "let down its bars" to grazing sheep but would exclude the rest of mankind (except for our wealthy eastern visitors who are able to afford guides and pack trains). Sheep were "hooved locusts, devouring every leaf in sight," she wrote, quoting naturalist John Muir. Citing Regional Forester Rutledge's statement: "We wish to preserve an air of romance and mystery – inspirational qualities unblemished," she wrote, "I prefer my romance and inspiration sans sheep." In spite of the obstacles (Chamber of Commerce, Planning Board, Union Pacific, Forest Service) "there they stand – the majestic Sawtooths – evidence sufficient for any man! It is unbelievable that these mountains should have a part in anything else except a glorious future. As a matter of pride, if for no other reason, they should be immortalized in a national park."[47]

Chapter 7

Frank Church and the Wilderness Act

"This could well be some of the most important legislation of our age." – Bruce Bowler to Frank Church, June 22, 1958.

"The wildernesses must be set aside or they simply will not exist." – Lyle Stanford to Frank Church, October 2, 1958.

In the 1950s, the Forest Service was continuing a review of primitive areas started in 1939, reclassifying them as wilderness or wild, sometimes with boundary changes and acreage reductions. With increasing demand for timber in national forests, wilderness advocates feared that part or all of the Idaho primitive areas might be lost. High on the unwritten agenda of conservation leaders like Morton Brigham, Bruce Bowler, Ernie Day, Ted Trueblood and Art Manley was keeping the Idaho primitive areas wild.

After engaging in multiple struggles to defend existing wilderness areas and national parks, leaders of national conservation organizations embraced a bold strategy proposed by Howard Zahniser of the Wilderness Society. They would take the offensive, asking Congress to put into law a declaration that wilderness was a national asset worthy of protection, securing "for the American people of present and future generations the benefits of an enduring resource of wilderness." The wilderness advocates recognized that with increasing demand for timber and minerals and with a growing population, pressures to reduce or eliminate existing wilderness was growing. Meanwhile, the value of wilderness for recreation, scientific study and habitat for wildlife was increasing as the country became more urbanized.

Bills were introduced in the Senate and the House in June 1956 providing that the 14 million acres of national forest wilderness, wild and primitive areas designated by the Forest Service since 1928 would all be declared wilderness with continued Forest Service management. Prohibitions on roading, motorized travel and timber cutting would continue while mining, livestock grazing and dams, all permitted with existing law and policy, would be banned. The Secretary of Agriculture could add national forest wilderness areas and the Secretary of Interior would be authorized to designate wilderness areas in national parks and monuments, wildlife refuges and Indian reservations. Either house of Congress could veto additions to the system. A 6-member wilderness commission would offer advice but would have no decision-making authority. Minnesota Democrat Hubert Humphrey and nine co-sponsors including Oregon's Wayne Morse and Richard Neuberger, introduced the Senate bill. Pennsylvania Republican John Saylor and five co-sponsors sponsored an identical version in the House.[1]

From the beginning, leaders of the Idaho Wildlife Federation embraced the concept, hoping a Wilderness Act would result in permanent protection for the nearly three million acres in the four Idaho primitive areas – the Idaho, the Salmon River Breaks, the Selway-Bitterroot and the Sawtooth.

The National Wildlife Federation's Charles Callison provided input on the original bill and the national federation endorsed wilderness legislation at its March 1957 annual meeting, joining the Wilderness Society, Sierra Club, Audubon Society, Izaac Walton League and many regional and local organizations in a campaign for a wilderness act.

Spokesmen for the timber and mining industries, livestock grazers and water development lobbies ripped into the bill in Senate and House Interior committee hearings in June 1957. And the Forest Service's Richard McCardle said he couldn't support a bill recognizing the value of forest wilderness until Congress passed a law giving statutory recognition to other uses. National Parks Director Conrad Wirth said the parks were already protected and needed no wilderness designations. It was apparent that the bill had no chance in Congress and Zahniser began considering changes.[2]

As a member of the Senate Interior Committee, Frank Church was deluged with letters on both sides. It was a politically sensitive issue for him since so much of Idaho's economy was based on access to the national forests for mining, timber cutting and livestock grazing. While he embraced the wilderness concept, as on Bruces Eddy, he would be cautious. He rashly considered co-sponsoring the original bill when Humphrey re-introduced it in February 1957, but reconsidered and declined invitations to co-sponsor the revised bills introduced in 1958 and 1959.[3]

Opposition in Idaho was fierce, eventually including the Idaho Chamber of Commerce, North Idaho Chamber, many local chambers, Potlatch Forests, the Idaho Mining Association, Idaho Farm Bureau, Idaho Cattlemen's Association, Idaho Woolgrowers, Idaho Reclamation Association, Idaho Power Company, J.R. Simplot Company and the Idaho Legislature. State Aeronautics Director Chet Moulton generated a flood of letters from backcountry pilots fearing that primitive area airstrips would be closed. Potlatch Forests urged employees to write, advising them that jobs were at stake. Custer County Democratic Sen. Dennis Donahue wrote: "Frank, I hope that wilderness bill can be knocked in the head."[4]

Church also heard from many Idahoans who liked their primitive areas and wanted them kept wild. "We have the greatest primitive state in the nation

Martel Morache Photo

Cathedral Rock and Yellowjacket Lake, Idaho Primitive Area

with its mountain grandness, its beautiful lakes and streams," advised Mr. and Mrs. Calvin Hazelbaker of Lewiston. Nancy Mae Larson of Coeur d'Alene shared with Church her letter rebuking Sen. Henry Dworshak for saying land shouldn't be set aside only for the scenery or for millionaires to enjoy: "I am a low salaried Idaho school teacher and I know of no one who enjoys the wilderness more than I do. I get a lift, and I can almost say a renewed life from a few days hiking trip into the mountain lake area of the Clearwater-St. Joe divide." Gertrude Maxwell of Elk City asked Church to support wilderness adding, "we are still trying frantically to save the Meadow Creek country as part of the (Selway-Bitterroot) wilderness area." Mrs. Elaine Kilgore of Pocatello said her family, including her 78-year-old grandmother, had enjoyed the wilderness for years with twice yearly 3-week trips into the Selway-Bitterroot: "Fishing, backpacking, camping hiking are all necessary vitamins to our daily existence."[5]

Bruce Bowler recognized the Wilderness Act's significance, praising Sen. Humphrey and Rep. Saylor for their leadership while sharing his thoughts with Church.[6] The Idaho senator also heard from Ted Trueblood, Morton Brigham, College of Idaho biology professor Lyle Stanford, Sun Valley doctor

George Saviers, Idaho Wildlife Federation Vice President Don Samuelson and Salmon River guide Andy Anderson asking him to support the Wilderness Act. Russell Mager of Orofino invited Church to join the Mager family on a horse trek into the Selway-Bitterroot Primitive Area.[7]

In June 1958, Humphrey and Saylor introduced Zahniser's watered-down bill. It empowered the President to permit prospecting, mining and dams in wilderness areas if he found it was in the "national interest." Livestock grazing and use of aircraft and motorboats, where already established, could be allowed to continue. The supremacy of state water law was explicitly recognized. The changes won more congressional support but did little to soften the opposition of timber, mining, grazing and water development interests at hearings in Salt Lake City, Albuquerque, Phoenix, Seattle and Bend, Ore. in 1958 and 1959. Wilderness supporters also turned out in large numbers, suggesting that public support was increasing.[8] The Idaho Wildlife Federation adopted a resolution favoring the bill in November 1958.[9]

Senator Church supported the wilderness bill but was not revealing his position in his correspondence with most supporters and opponents. In August 1959, however, he hinted at support for the bill in a letter advising Bruce Bowler that he expected the Interior Committee to act, after considering amendments, before the end of the congressional session in 1960. The committee did not act, however, and the bill remained stalled in committee in 1960. It was still hung up after being endorsed by President John F. Kennedy in a special message to Congress on resource issues in March 1961. Church opposed crippling amendments favored by timber and mining industries, sponsored by Colorado Senator Gordon Allott and backed by Idaho Senator Henry Dworshak. Allott wanted to leave decisions on national forest primitive areas to Congress rather than the Forest Service. With his amendment, primitive areas could not be designated wilderness without legislation approved by the Senate and House and the President. And there would be no protection of wilderness values pending recommendations from the Forest Service and action by Congress.[10]

In an effort to end the impasse Church in March 1961, proposed milder amendments drafted by the Forest Service at his request. The amendments responded to timber and mining industry opposition and Church believed they might allow the bill to clear the committee. The amendments would also help him explain his support for the bill to wilderness opponents in Idaho.

The bill before the committee allowed Congress to reject a presidential wilderness decision for a primitive area but only by concurrent resolution of both houses. With Church's amendments either the House or Senate could reject it. And any primitive area would lose wilderness management protection if no Forest Service recommendation was submitted in 15 years. Mineral prospecting would be allowed in wilderness areas "if it would not do violence to the wilderness concept." Introducing his amendments in the Senate, Church said they were needed in Idaho and other western states where extensive areas were proposed for inclusion in the wilderness system: "Wilderness designation is desirable only on condition it does not stifle those basic industries upon which the growth and prosperity of our states and region depend." In a press release Church said there was great concern in Idaho about proposals to "lock up in a wilderness system" three million acres in present primitive areas.[11]

Idaho wilderness advocates reacted with shock and anger. Even Bruce Bowler, among Church's most devoted supporters, was taken aback: "I think you have bought the bill of goods of the wrong people," he wrote, referring to the Forest Service. But he added: "You can count on me for continued support of the wilderness concept." Morton Brigham was appalled. With Church's congressional veto language, "I would expect this to amount to the abolition of nearly every acre of wild country in Idaho," he wrote. Ernie Day, current president of the Idaho Wildlife Federation, felt the same way: "They (the amendments) will mean that here in Idaho we will never have one square foot of wilderness in the system." President Kennedy had fine ideas on conservation and wilderness, wrote Day, but Idaho was represented by "not one but two reactionary senators" who didn't share the president's conservation ideals. Ted Trueblood was also disappointed but not critical. He recalled how proud he had been when Church introduced the Salmon River sanctuary bill. He urged Church to show courage, to help "leave to our children as good an America as our forefathers left to us." He added: "Surely if New Mexico can elect a Clinton Anderson, then Idaho can elect a Frank Church who takes a vigorous far-sighted stand in the public interest on resource legislation."[12]

Church responded to wilderness supporters, saying his amendments didn't imperil the bill's basic objectives and were the minimum required to win Interior Committee approval. "Much more drastic amendments are being proposed, with strong support, that would emasculate the bill." Church's amendments won praise from Potlatch Forests and from the Idaho Woolgrowers but the Idaho timber and mining industries and livestock grazers continued to oppose the bill.[13]

The committee adopted the Church amendments and reported the bill out in July 1961, ending five years of congressional stalemate and inaction. Church won praise for his efforts from Sen. Clinton Anderson, the principal sponsor of the wilderness bill and chairman of the Interior Committee. Anderson credited Church with showing skill and courage in opposing damaging amendments, recalling Church had advised him during a recess "that you would stand with me in ditching the whole bill rather than report to the Senate a butchered version of what was already somewhat of a compromise."[14]

Church had been stung by criticism of his amendments by Howard Zahniser and now expressed his frustration. He sent Zahniser a copy of Anderson's letter and of John Corlett's Idaho Statesman column with its blistering criticism. "I anticipate that my support of the Wilderness Bill will be one of the main issues used against me in Idaho in the coming election," wrote Church. "This will be damaging to me among the mining, lumbering and grazing industries in my state, the hard bitten foes of the bill. Ironically, many wildlife and conservation groups have been led to believe, on the basis of information supplied them through your offices, that I was an opponent of effective wilderness legislation. It is this kind of experience that leads one to conclude that the course of prudence would have been to continue to hide behind the stalemate on the wilderness front, rather than to try to make headway in establishing a much needed Wilderness System."[15]

Three weeks before sponsoring the wilderness amendments Church had disappointed Idaho conservation leaders by breaking his silence on Bruces Eddy, endorsing construction of the dam. Now he had disappointed them again with his Wilderness Act amendments. And, as he advised Zahniser, Church's committee support for the Wilderness Act brought a storm of criticism in Idaho. Republicans were now more confident that he could be defeated in 1962. Yet when Senator Anderson was sidelined for surgery on the eve of the Senate vote, Church accepted his request to fill in as floor sponsor of the bill. This would mark him not only as a supporter of the Wilderness Act but as one of its primary advocates. While it would enhance his stature with conservation supporters, it could make him a one-term senator. Anderson chose Church as his substitute because of the junior Idaho senator's skill in debate, knowledge of the issues and his commitment to the cause.

As debate began Church laid out the case for the Wilderness Act with eloquence and logic, describing the reasoning behind each provision, the history of the bill and why it was needed while responding to every argument that had been used against it. If it became law, he said, "we will have preserved for now and for generations unborn areas of unspoiled pristine wilderness accessible by a system of trails, unmarred by roads or buildings but open to the considerable use and enjoyment of hikers, hunters, fishermen, mountain climbers, and all of those who find in high and lonely places a refreshment of the spirit and life's closest communion with God." The people of the west would benefit most: "The vanishing wilderness is yet a part of our wilderness heritage."

Church said most of the 500 witnesses at Senate hearings and most of the committee members agreed that the nation must preserve some of its wild scenic lands in their natural unspoiled state "while we still can." Because the areas embraced by the bill were already set-aside in their primitive state, the wilderness system could be established "with no adverse effect on anyone." The land was already excluded from timber cutting. Mining, where rights were established, could continue, as could non-motorized exploration. The President could authorize new mining operations and dams. There were only six existing mining operations on wilderness lands. Livestock grazing could continue where already established. State water law was recognized and state fish and game management would continue.[16]

Primitive areas would have be reviewed by the Forest Service within 10 years and "those portions found to be more suitable for timber cutting, mining or (motorized) recreation" would revert to ordinary forest lands, said Church. Areas recommended for wilderness would be reviewed by Congress and subject to veto by either the House or Senate. After 10 years no new areas could be designated except by affirmative action of Congress. The bill would return to Congress "its rightful supervision and control over our public lands." With existing law, "areas may now be created, their boundaries altered and new tracts added by administrative decision alone without need of any review or approval by Congress." Resource users would benefit, said Church, with greater stability in the management and classification of public lands. Church rejected the argument that only the rich could afford access to the wilderness. Most of the thousands of visitors to the Idaho primitive areas were not the wealthy but "ordinary farmers, ordinary working people, ordinary hunters and fishermen from the farms and cities of Idaho." And the visitors from other states were "good business."

The Senate rejected 53-32 Senator Allott's amendment to require Congressional legislation to designate any primitive area as wilderness. Sen. Allen Ellender's motion to send the bill to the Agriculture Committee for further study was defeated 41-32. After two days of debate the final vote was 78-8 with 14 absent or not voting. Sen. Henry Dworshak voted no. Church won praise for his handling of the bill from Senators Morse, Humphrey, Gruening, Moss, Jackson and Kuchel. Utah Sen. Frank Moss credited him for his courage: "The wilderness bill has not been well understood in the mountain states and interests there have brought great pressure on their congressional representatives."

While Idaho wilderness opponents now mounted a shrill anti-Church campaign, Idaho conservationists who had criticized his amendments showered him with praise. Bruce Bowler wrote: "We appreciate your good work. The wolves are howling with pack leaders like Dworshak, Corlett, Teske, Derr and Cox but the quiet good of real wilderness will absorb the sounds and something great can remain for America of this little bit of wilderness. Thanks." Morton Brigham thanked him. Ernie Day praised him for his courage and statesmanship. When The Idaho Statesman lashed Church saying the purpose of the wilderness bill was to drive the livestock, timber and mining industries "out of the hills and preserve them exclusively for recreation," Ted Trueblood defended Church in a letter to the editor: "Frank Church is the only Idaho senator I can remember who has shown a sincere interest in conservation." In Washington John Carver Jr., his former assistant, congratulated him for "a magnificent job in handling the bill, adding that he, more than most people, 'realize the political courage' that was involved." Howard Zahniser wrote Church praising him and asking for a photo.

Columnist Jack Anderson credited Church with uncommon political courage. Frank Church was now a national as well as an Idaho conservation hero.[17]

Martel Morache Photo

Middle Fork Salmon near Tappan Falls.

Church recognized that he needed to counter what he considered a scare campaign in Idaho. In press releases, newsletters and personal appearances he emphasized that the Senate bill would provide congressional control over decisions on the primitive areas, reducing the authority of the executive: "It won't cause anyone to lose his job; it won't close a single road; it won't shut down a single mine; it won't take one cow or sheep off grazing on public lands; it won't reduce our annual timber cut by a single tree; it won't create another agency or cost the taxpayers an additional dime; it won't even add one acre of new wilderness."[18]

The bill required a review of the primitive areas which were "hastily withdrawn by the Forest Service in the first place" to "restore tracts of merchantable timber and other parts found to be suitable for multiple use," said Church. The remaining parts – "the remote uplands having little or no commercial value, but great scenic and recreational value – would then be preserved as wilderness..." With Congress adjourned, Church embarked on a

2-month Idaho courthouse tour that allowed him to address the opposition campaign. He told a Kellogg audience that "the big mine owners" opposed him because he refused to take orders from them. But he had always supported "the legitimate interests of the mining industry," citing his bill, signed into law, providing a subsidy to small producers of lead and zinc, his success in stripping from the foreign aid bill a provision allowing stockpiling of strategic metals and his protests against sale by the Treasury of silver reserves.

Those efforts brought no statements of appreciation from the companies, he said, but "the newspapers are filled with half-page ads and the airwaves are crowded with paid propaganda programs against me because of my support of the wilderness bill."[19] Even before his Kellogg appearance State Rep. Naomi Steffens of Wardner advised him that he was "making hay" with the wilderness bill. "The common people want our wilderness areas preserved," she said. After Church spoke to the Orofino Chamber of Commerce, Ray McNichols reported that reaction on Main Street was positive with everyone he talked to saying they were impressed. "Several indicated they now felt they had the wrong idea about the wilderness bill" while others "felt you were certainly sincere and your motives were proper."[20]

While Idaho conservationists were awaiting Senate action on the wilderness bill they were reacting with alarm and disappointment to the Forest Service's proposed decision on the Selway-Bitterroot Primitive Area. The 1,875,000-acre primitive area would be pared by 523,000 acres. The proposal called for a Selway-Bitterroot Wilderness of 1,163,555 acres with 188,796 acres on the north side of the Salmon River assigned to a new Salmon River Breaks Primitive Area. It would be studied in connection with the pending study of the adjoining Idaho Primitive Area south of the river. A large part of the upper Selway River drainage, 310,000 acres, was to be opened to roads and logging. The timber industry wanted another 300,000 acres sliced from wilderness management. Potlatch Forests advised its employees that this acreage contained 1.7 billion board feet of timber. The Idaho Mining Association wanted no wilderness.

While supporting the Wilderness Act, Idaho conservationists were also rallying to oppose the Forest Service's proposal for the Selway-Bitterroot. Frank Church kept hands off the Selway-Bitterroot issue but in letters to wilderness opponents he cited the Forest Service proposal for 1.1 million acres of wilderness as evidence of the need to return wilderness decisions to Congress as provided in the Wilderness Act.

Idaho Rep. Gracie Pfost scheduled an October hearing on the Senate bill in McCall before her Public Lands Subcommittee of the House Interior Committee. The Senate committee had conducted no hearings in Idaho and this would be a significant test. In a column in advance of the hearing John Corlett advised readers that more was at stake than wilderness. Since the bill was first introduced in 1956, he wrote, "the Idaho users of the public domain have seen it as the beginning of the end for them." They anticipated that, if the wilderness bill became law, the exuberant wildlifers "will move to wipe them off the other portions of the public domain." The issue was multiple use of the public domain versus "single, recreation and non-productive use." The Forest Service, he wrote, had bitterly fought the wilderness bill for two years but capitulated under the Kennedy administration. The Fish and Wildlife Service grew bolder and had "turned in adverse reports" on Bruces Eddy dam and the proposed Guffey dam in southern Idaho, a key part of the plan to irrigate the Mountain Home desert. Corlett blamed the influence of liberals in the Interior Department, specifically Church's former aide John Carver, Jr.[21]

On the first day Rep. Pfost's committee heard testimony for 12 hours with 20 speaking for the bill and 50 against. A.M. Derr, Richfield superintendent of schools and former Democratic candidate for governor, said wilderness was based on a false philosophy, "costly to taxpayers and a violation of the laws of God and man." Twin Falls County Assessor Russell Larsen said the state couldn't afford it. Royce Cox of Potlatch, speaking for the Inland Empire Multiple Use Committee, said no more wilderness was needed since 20 million acres were in national parks and seven million in already designated wilderness areas. John Edwards of McCall, speaking for the Idaho Resort Association, said the bill would create "an untouched, beautiful, famous but deserted" wilderness in a large part of Idaho. The bill was opposed by Emmett and Council sawmill workers, the Idaho Chamber of Commerce, the Idaho Reclamation Association and the Idaho Outfitters and Guides Association.[22]

Ted Trueblood spoke for the Boise Valley Natural History Society: "Our remaining undisturbed wild areas are the museums of nature. They are the libraries of God's work," he said. Ernie Day of the Idaho Wildlife Federation said the issue was whether "to chew up every acre" with roads and commerce or to stop a little short of that. Pierre Pulling said most people favored wilderness, labeling the Idaho Chamber of Commerce "public enemy number one." Bruce Bowler said the losses to the people occurred, not with wilderness, but when commercial enterprise was permitted to take for individual gain "wonderfully unique, perpetual natural assets that truly belong to all the people of this nation."[23] Heber Smith of Grace, a director of the National Wildlife Federation, said areas designated as wilderness, roadless and primitive were serving "their highest and best use." Lyle Stanford of Caldwell spoke for consideration of the prevailing national sentiment in favor of the bill. Commissioner Frank Cullen said the Idaho Fish and Game Commission endorsed the wilderness concept "in order to maintain a high quality of hunting and fishing for the present and future people of Idaho" but made no recommendation on the bill.

Opposing witnesses in two days of testimony outnumbered supporters 78 to 28 but the committee had received 113 written statements for the bill and 34 against for a total of 141 in favor and 112 against. Rep. Pfost said the committee would take no action before January 31, the expected date of the report of the Outdoor Recreation Review Commission.[24] Bruce Bowler was encouraged, advising Church that while much remained to be done to "truthfully inform" the people of Idaho he was hopeful that Church's position would be sustained. To help inform people and encourage Rep. Pfost to support the bill Bowler and Day mailed 9,000 fact sheets to First Congressional District residents on behalf of the Wilderness Users Committee of Idaho. Pfost reported that her Idaho mail was evenly divided on the wilderness bill while the national mail was running ten to one in favor.[25]

Martel Morache Photo

Upper Middle Fork Salmon Canyon

Wilderness advocates were encouraged when the Outdoor Recreation Review Commission endorsed a system of wilderness, recommending additions to the acreage currently designated.[26] They hoped that Rep. Pfost would resist the industry-backed campaign to require Congressional approval of wilderness status for primitive areas. But In August 1962, she endorsed and her subcommittee recommended a substitute bill drafted by Interior Committee Chairman Wayne Aspinall providing that primitive areas could be designated wilderness only by legislation, as the timber and mining industries demanded. The existing wilderness, wild and canoe areas totaling 6.8 million acres, would be subject to review every 25 years. Wilderness areas would be closed to new mining claims after 10 years but mining would continue in the interim.[27] Once again Idaho wilderness supporters were disappointed. President Art Manley of the Coeur d'Alene Wildlife Federation wrote Pfost describing the substitute as "complete surrender to the timber-mining-cattle interests and not representative of the will of the people of Idaho."[28] After the House Committee reported the bill out with a provision barring floor amendments House action was stalled. There would be no vote before 1963.

With the death of Senator Dworshak in July 1962, Rep. Pfost was preparing to run for the Senate. The Republican nominee was former Gov. Len Jordan. Church's opponent was Boise attorney Jack Hawley who framed the campaign as a contest between Church's pro-government views and Hawley's stand for free enterprise and limited government. Church emphasized his efforts to help Idaho farmers, ranchers, miners, loggers and irrigators and his success in winning authorizations and appropriations for federal dams. While Republicans still hoped the wilderness issue would hurt him, his success in winning authorization of the Bruces Eddy dam was credited with restoring support in the Lewiston and Orofino areas. And the concern of wilderness opponents had been softened with the amendments to the House bill. After a 44-county pre-election tour, John Corlett wrote that Church had been in trouble in north Idaho in 1961 because of the wilderness issue but was now a likely winner.[29]

When the votes were counted it was apparent that Church's advocacy for the Wilderness Act did not hurt him. Clearwater County gave him a three to one margin. In Nez Perce County it was 8,229 to 3,090, in Idaho 2,895 to 1,707. Despite the mining industry's 1961 campaign against him he won in Shoshone County, 3,934 to 3,194. His large margin north of the Salmon River allowed him to win the election by 24,528 votes. Despite her impressive showing in the North, Pfost lost to Jordan by 4,881 votes.

In 1963, Church again steered the Wilderness Act through the Senate 73-12, adding an amendment to prohibit acquisition of privately owned land by condemnation. In the House, Rep. Aspinall was still insisting upon requiring Congressional approval for wilderness designation of primitive areas or parts of national parks or wildlife refuges, a provision still unacceptable to Senator Anderson. Finally, in 1964, the wilderness supporters gave in, accepting the Aspinall language but with a provision providing for continued protection of primitive areas pending congressional action. Mining would be allowed in wilderness areas for 25 years. This version passed the House 374-1 in July 1964. Idaho wilderness supporters were again disappointed. Brigham advised Church that it could be worse than no bill at all "as we would stand to lose the Sawtooth and Idaho primitive areas."[30] In the Senate-House conference committee, Church accepted the House provisions but with mining in wilderness areas for 19 years rather than 25. "This is a good bill in which we can all take pride," Church advised Idaho wilderness backers. "It does not contain all the provisions you or I would like to have but it is far stronger than we had any reason to expect several months ago."[31] Anderson, Aspinall, Church and Stewart Udall were present when President Lyndon Johnson signed the bill on September 3, 1964. Also there was Alice Zahniser, widow of Howard Zahniser who had died on May 5.

The 8-year struggle for a Wilderness Act was over. Idaho conservationists had played a major role, supporting Church's politically risky leadership and helping him win re-election. But, while the debate seemed to have increased public support for wilderness in Idaho, the Wilderness Act had also reduced the prospects for continued protection of the Idaho, Salmon River Breaks and Sawtooth primitive areas. The 1.1 million acre Selway-Bitterroot Wilderness, designated in 1963 by Secretary of Agriculture Freeman, received statutory protection with the Wilderness Act, as did other national forest areas previously classified as wilderness. Those areas now had better protection. But Idaho conservationists recognized that more than 400,000 acres of the former primitive area, including much of the upper Selway River drainage, were now at risk for roads and logging.

Chapter 8

Must the Salmon River die?
Sportsmen fight to save seagoing fish

"The construction of high dams in the Salmon River or in the Snake below its confluence with the Salmon would strike a shattering blow to the Columbia Basin fisheries." – Idaho Fish and Game Director Ross Leonard.

"It is something we want to continue to happen, the phenomena of these salmon and steelhead that traverse upwards of 1,000 miles to return to the headwaters of their birth to spawn. We feel there is something more in this than merely today's economic value of the fish taken." – Bruce Bowler.

The first great Snake River public versus private power battle had not ended when a second began. In its 1947 report to Congress the U. S. Army Corps of Engineers identified four possible sites for a high dam on the Snake downstream from the Hells Canyon dam site – Pleasant Valley, Appaloosa, Mountain Sheep and Nez Perce. After giving up on Bruces Eddy on the North Fork of the Clearwater, a coalition of four private power companies, Pacific Northwest Power, filed an application with the Federal Power Commission to build a 600-foot dam at the Pleasant Valley site, 40 miles below the Hells Canyon dam site and 20 miles upstream from the mouth of the Salmon River and of Oregon's Imnaha. The public power coalition that had lobbied unsuccessfully for the federal high Hells Canyon dam intervened, opposing the license application, declaring that a dam at Pleasant Valley would block the construction of a dam at Nez Perce, a superior site that would store more water and generate more power.

A 700-foot Nez Perce dam three miles below the Salmon River's junction with the Snake would impound water of three rivers, inundating 63 miles of the Snake almost to Idaho Power's Hells Canyon dam, 60 miles of the Salmon and 10 miles of Oregon's Imnaha. Nez Perce was the worst nightmare of the Idaho Wildlife Federation and the Idaho Fish and Game Department. It would lock salmon and steelhead out of the 14,000-square-mile Salmon River drainage, the source of 40 per cent of salmon in the Columbia River Basin. With hundreds of miles of salmon and steelhead habitat lost to earlier dams and with the Clearwater under siege, the Salmon was the last great stronghold of seagoing fish in Idaho.

The Corps had also identified potential sites for 700-foot dams on the Salmon. A Lower Canyon dam three miles above the river's juncture with the Snake would back water 70 miles and store 2.5 million acre feet of water while generating 447 megawatts of electricity. A Crevice dam upstream from Riggins, 99 miles from the river's mouth, would drown 65 miles of the Salmon and 10 miles of the south fork. With it would come a 200-foot Freedom dam near White Bird, regulating flows from Crevice.

Recognizing that no way had been found to pass downstream migrants over high dams, the Bureau of Reclamation and the Corps had recommended construction of Mountain Sheep dam just above the mouth of the Salmon rather than Nez Perce in 1953, and in 1958 had deferred recommending congressional authorization of Lower Canyon or Crevice on the Salmon. But the Federal Power Commission (FPC) was not so concerned about seagoing fish. In November 1957, the FPC rejected Pacific Northwest Power's license request for Pleasant Valley, endorsing construction of a dam at Nez Perce: "Any combination of projects which includes Nez Perce is consistently superior to any project which does not include Nez Perce." The commission brushed off the fish passage issue, terming it: "an engineering problem no greater than many others that must be solved in connection with any project the size of Nez Perce." With the rejection of Pleasant Valley, Pacific Northwest Power filed for a permit for Mountain Sheep, which would generate more power than Pleasant Valley.[1]

Bruce Bowler kept Sen. Frank Church informed on the threat to seagoing fish posed by a possible Nez Perce dam. And Church met with Franklin Jones of the Idaho Wildlife Federation and representatives of the Idaho Fish and Game Department and Fish and Wildlife Service who emphasized the importance of Idaho salmon and steelhead. In 1959, Church joined with Washington Sen. Warren Magnuson in proposing a 5-year moratorium on licensing further dams on the Middle Snake, allowing time to seek an answer to the high dam fish passage problem. But he soon backed away from the moratorium. Instead, Church embraced the suggestion of the Izaac Walton League and the Idaho Wildlife Federation's Second District for legislation to make the Salmon River a "fish sanctuary," off limits to high dams. Bruce Bowler wrote Church encouraging him to pursue the sanctuary concept: "There will be some mighty grateful people in the world in the next and succeeding centuries if such could be accomplished now."[2]

In August 1959, Church and Sen. Richard Neuberger of Oregon introduced a bill barring the licensing of dams on the Salmon higher than the smaller dams already in place or authorized downstream on the Snake and the Columbia until the high dam fish passage problem was solved. In his Senate remarks introducing the bill, Church was almost apologetic about proposing that Congress limit the authority of the Federal Power Commission to license

Steelhead catch

dams on any river. He cited the significance of the Salmon River drainage with its many tributary streams where salmon and steelhead spawned.

The sanctuary bill was Church's first legislative initiative backed by leaders of the Idaho Wildlife Federation and the senator received mostly positive comments from his Idaho constituents. The bill was referred to Senator Magnuson's Interstate and Foreign Commerce Committee and a hearing was scheduled in Lewiston in November. The committee also heard testimony on Magnuson's bill for a 5-year moratorium on further Middle Snake dams and Oregon Sen. Richard Neuberger's bill to ban dams without fish passage plans approved by the U. S. Fish and Wildlife Service. Most of the witnesses opposed Magnuson's moratorium. It was supported by public power backers who hoped that delaying an FPC licensing decision on High Mountain Sheep would lead to a fish passage breakthrough, enhancing the prospects for a Nez Perce public power dam.

Bruce Bowler was convinced that northwest salmon advocates should support the licensing of High Mountain Sheep to insure that there would be no Nez Perce dam. Both Bowler and Ernie Day testified in support of licensing Mountain Sheep, against the moratorium and for the Salmon River sanctuary. While most witnesses endorsed Church's bill, a notable exception was Idaho Fish and Game Director Ross Leonard who said it was well intentioned but flawed because it barred only high dams and not smaller dams. Church responded, accusing Leonard of letting down "the fish and wildlife groups he represents," saying Leonard's approach was "a totally unrealistic plan for solving the fish-dam conflict."[3] Nevertheless Church proposed to amend the bill in 1960 with language barring any dams on the Salmon.[4] He reintroduced it with that language in 1961, this time with Sen. Maureen Neuberger as a co-sponsor. She had taken the Oregon Senate seat after her husband died.

Despite the support from Idaho sportsmen, the sanctuary bill had little chance of success because of the opposition of the Washington State Grange, electrical unions, Oregon and Washington public utility districts, Pacific Northwest Power, Senator Magnuson and the Federal Power Commission. The commission was adamant. Chairman Jerome Kuykendall sent a memo to members of Congress complaining that Church's bill would "halt all non-federal multiple purpose development on the Salmon River." Without dams the Salmon's water might be "wasted for most purposes."[5]

In March 1960, a coalition of 16 Northwest public utility districts, organized as the Washington Public Power System (WPPS), filed for a license for Nez Perce dam as an alternative to Pacific Northwest Power's application for Mountain Sheep. Now there was an active, immediate threat to Salmon River salmon. And the decision was to be made by a Federal Power Commission that had already endorsed Nez Perce as the best site for a Middle Snake dam while brushing off the high dam salmon passage issue as an "engineering problem" that could be solved. That opinion had preceded the Oxbow incident and the increasing evidence that Idaho Power Company's skimmer experiment at Brownlee was a failure. But the FPC's primary concern was kilowatts, not fish, as evidenced in Chairman Kuykendall's comments on the Salmon River sanctuary bill.[6]

Bruce Bowler believed that Northwest fish advocates should all get behind the licensing of High Mountain Sheep dam. Many were already on board but some wanted neither dam. "I think the fish and wildlife people who oppose High Mountain Sheep are making a big fat mistake, and if it helps to contribute to eventual construction of Nez Perce, we can only rate them as damn fools," Bowler wrote Portland attorney Rollin Bowles. "The Middle Snake is already clobbered up with the Idaho Power licenses, and while the experiments for fish passage should certainly be continued and improved for that area, it's my conviction that high dam fish passage problems should be confined to the Middle Snake and no risk permitted for dams below the confluence with the Salmon." He added: "We are not going to get fish to the exclusion of all dams."[7]

Other leaders of the Idaho Wildlife Federation agreed with Bowler. The directors voted unanimously to intervene in the Federal Power Commission licensing case, favoring a license for High Mountain Sheep dam and opposing Nez Perce. Bowler volunteered to do the legal work including the preparation

Martel Morache Photo

Floating the Main Salmon River at Salmon Falls Rapids.

of briefs at no cost to the federation, an offer that made intervention possible. Bowler had met with Pacific Northwest Power executives and described the company as "a real ally, financially able, substantial and sincere," recognizing the value of salmon in applying to build Mountain Sheep rather than Nez Perce. "They stuck their necks out to get High Mountain Sheep dam when they could just as easily have applied for Nez Perce." Bowler said he believed the FPC "would grant in 30 minutes" a license to any private power company applying to build Nez Perce.[8]

The federation also renewed its support for Church's Salmon River sanctuary bill "as permanent insurance to save our salmon run." The sanctuary bill would not block a Nez Perce dam but would prevent the licensing of the Lower Canyon or Crevice dams on the Salmon. The plan of the Army Corps called for Lower Canyon as a companion dam with Mountain Sheep as the alternative to Nez Perce. Pacific Northwest Power was not applying for Lower Canyon at this time but the threat of a dam at that site would remain if the power commission approved Mountain Sheep.

Ernie Day

Ted Trueblood

Some Northwest conservationists wanted Church to include a ban on Nez Perce in his sanctuary bill. Bowler disagreed, recognizing that opposition by the public power lobby could assure the bill's defeat. And since a license application for Nez Perce was pending before the FPC, a ban on Nez Perce would set up a conflict between the executive and legislative departments. Rather than attempting to use the sanctuary bill to block Nez Perce, Bowler believed Northwest conservationists should do all they could to pass the sanctuary bill as it was.[9]

In the October 1960 issue of Field and Stream magazine, Americans across the country were reading Ted Trueblood's article "Must the Salmon River Die?" Trueblood began by telling readers how he was awakened in his tent on a July night in 1939 by the sound of salmon struggling through riffles on Sulphur Creek. Trueblood was there with his wife, Ellen, on a month-long backcountry honeymoon. He described the valiant 700-mile journey of the spring chinook to renew the cycle of life in the stream where they were born: "Leaving tidewater in the spring, they had fought their way up the mighty Columbia, turning unerringly into the Snake River at its mouth, then into the Salmon. From the main Salmon River they had swung, guided by an ancient instinct, into the Middle Fork. After surmounting its brawling rapids for 70 miles and passing many tributary streams en route, they had come at last to the mouth of Sulphur Creek."[10]

A Nez Perce Dam would end forever the migration of salmon and steelhead to the Salmon River, he declared. "Salmon spawned in the Salmon River in Idaho are caught off the Aleutian islands. They help provide a livelihood for commercial fishermen all up and down the west coast and they bend the rods of thousands upon thousands of anglers in the states of Oregon, Washington and Idaho." Ted asked readers to help by sending letters to Bowler who was to represent the federation before the Federal Power Commission. The response was overwhelming. Letters poured into Bowler's office from across the country, 3,000 letters. A lot of people wanted to save the Salmon River and its seagoing fish. Some also wrote in support of a larger cause, retaining some of the country's wild natural environment not yet damaged or destroyed by the forces of development:

"You in the West are, figuratively speaking, a few years behind. You have space as yet uncluttered, clean lakes and rivers, timber areas without fence or barrier. In many areas you can fire a rifle shot and have it heard by only yourself. You can cast a fly without being molested by a powered watercraft. A disease referred to as 'prosperity' is crawling, walking, flying, and digging its way westward. I pray that it meets many deterrents in its path." – Joe Hermann, Plainview, Texas.

"It is my opinion that advancing civilization should refrain from ruining the most beautiful, sincere and serene part of the earth, namely the wilderness with its unaltered, unadulterated and unpolluted waters. There are few places left in the U.S.A. where there is even an inkling of what would be called wilderness."– Richard Parch, Rochester, New York.

"As you can see I am in the armed forces. I like to think that I am serving my country so that we can have some of its natural beauty preserved along with peace. Someday my children will want to hunt and fish. What would I tell them? 'It's been destroyed because someone didn't take the time to figure out a better solution'. " – Daniel T. Klonoski

"In 1953, I spent 15 glorious days of leave on the Salmon prior to leaving for an overseas assignment. The memory of the cutthroat trout caught and the salmon and steelhead hooked but not landed have sparked many a conversation and filled much reverie. I hope to fish the Salmon and some of its tributary creeks at the first opportunity that I can, military assignments permitting. PS: I'd like my sons to have the opportunity, too!" – Walter L. Richey, major USAF

"Reading Ted Trueblood's article, "Must the Salmon River die?" in the October issue of Field and Stream left me with a feeling akin to the death of a close friend. I have never been in the Northwest and may never get there, although I hope to. Therefore, I speak as a citizen who would like to see an end to the practice of blocking all the natural spawning grounds with these concrete monuments to progress."– James A. Cain Jr., Atlanta, Ga.

"The Salmon River is a national treasure, not to be tampered with by either the so-called 'Corps' or the public power grabbers. It is time these

people were stopped. The Federal Power Commission has a duty that goes beyond the mere granting of a license to one or the other of the contending applicants in this case or others like it." – Harry G. Dennis, Seattle, Wash.

"The wanton destruction of the Columbia River salmon runs cannot be permitted. No small group of men can have the moral right to destroy forever such an important esthetic and economic resource."– Ray C. Hallberg, Portland, Ore.

"It seems to me we have already lost enough of our wilderness and great streams to satisfy anybody. For the sake of all that is good in this world, Nez Perce must not be built." – Leroy Harring, Little Valley, New York.

"It seems to me that some people will sacrifice anything for the sake of so-called progress. Congratulations on your fine and noble interest and may I wish you the most success." – Pfc. Thomas Kulczynski, Fort Bliss, Texas.

"I attended the university at Moscow but I was never lucky enough to see the Salmon. Unless the unforeseen happens, I never will. Still I like to know there is a Salmon River with all its wild country, unmarred by any large man-made structure and especially by a dam."– Robert Ferris, Sulphur, Okla.

"I am only 17 years old, but when I grow up, I want to be able to see a river running instead of a great cement monster of a dam."– Jon Buelendorf, Pasco High School, Kansas City, Mo.

"I've never seen the Salmon River, never seen a salmon on a spawning bed, never been west of the Dakotas. Don't let it be spoiled by a power hungry few who don't seem to see that within our lifetime solar and atomic power will make waterpower as obsolete as a horse and rig. The same factions are forever grasping for the last remnants of unspoiled streams in Wisconsin also. Don't give up the fight." – Jerry Condon, Sr., Mosinee, Wis.

Roy Roark of Caldwell, age 50, wrote that he had "lived to see the pressure that dams have brought against the run of salmon migrating to Idaho." He cited the loss of the Boise River runs to Barber and Arrowrock dams, the loss of Snake River fish above Swan Falls and the demise of Payette River salmon with Black Canyon dam. He cited the 1958 losses at the Oxbow. "I, for one, had personal contact with an employee who worked on the Oxbow dam and who informed me that so many salmon were lost in one run that a detail of men had to be directed to bury dead salmon in large quantities."

Federation Secretary Kenneth Reynolds of Pocatello got off a letter asking all local clubs to contribute $25 or more to send Bowler and Day to Washington to present the federation's case: "This notice of intervention is a very costly project. If the work that will represent the Idaho Wildlife Federation had been done professionally, it would have cost us over $25,000. Through the joint efforts of Bruce Bowler, Ernie Day, Franklin Jones and others, this project was completed at no cost to us. The project that they have completed is something that every sportsman in Idaho should see. It will absolutely be the first time testimony from us 'fish folks' has been heard by the Federal Power Commission, and if it doesn't open their eyes as to how we regard our salmon fishing in Idaho, nothing else will."[11]

Proceedings before the FPC involved the presentation of written testimony by "expert" witnesses with cross-examination by opposition attorneys and by the FPC staff or commissioners. Ernie Day was the federation's expert witness, describing the importance of salmon and steelhead fishing to the people of Idaho, their economic value and the significance of the Salmon River for rearing and spawning. Accompanying his testimony were his photos of salmon and steelhead fishermen on the main salmon, the middle fork and the south fork. Attached to Day's testimony was Trueblood's "Must the Salmon River Die?" along with 26 of the letters received in response.

The Idaho sportsmen would not be alone. The fish and game departments of Idaho, Oregon and Washington had also intervened in support of Salmon River salmon and steelhead. So did Oregon and Washington conservation organizations, representatives of ocean and Columbia River commercial fishing and the Chinook, Cowlitz, Cayuse and Makah Indian tribes. Nearly all supported a license for Mountain Sheep as an alternative to Nez Perce, assuming that one or the other would inevitably be licensed. But the Columbia River Salmon and Tuna Packers opposed both dams.[12]

Speaking at a pre-hearing conference in Portland, Boise attorney Thomas Jones presented the position of the Idaho Fish and Game Department in a statement also endorsed by Oregon and Washington fish and game agencies. Assuming that a dam was going to be licensed, Mountain Sheep would do less damage than Nez Perce, said Jones. Snake River runs above the Mountain Sheep site had already been severely damaged with Brownlee dam, and runs above Idaho Power's yet to be built Hells Canyon dam might be lost entirely. The Salmon River runs were enormously valuable and could be destroyed by Nez Perce.

"The fishery agencies do not have the answer to fish passage at high dams and we do not believe that anyone else has the answer," Jones said. Since it appeared that a dam would be constructed with losses and possible destruction of seagoing fish, the choice should be the dam that would cause the least damage, he said. That was Mountain Sheep. The loss of Salmon River runs would be the worst blow to Columbia River fish since Grand Coulee dam, he said. Grand Coulee was the high federal dam completed in 1941 that shut seagoing fish out of 500 miles of the upper Columbia and 900 miles of its tributaries.[13]

Washington Public Power's attorneys moved to strike most of Ernie Day's testimony along with his photos of fishermen with their catches and photos of spawning salmon, contending that he was not an expert, not a fisheries biologist. Bowler responded with a brief asserting that Day was qualified based on his experience in fishing for salmon, his observation of other fishermen and his knowledge of the economic value of salmon and steelhead fishing on the Salmon and its tributaries. As to Day's comments on the threat posed by a Nez Perce dam, Bowler declared "no witness needs to be qualified as a biological expert to know the experience of the loss of anadromous fish at high dams." Bowler also opposed the motion by FPC attorneys to strike the Trueblood article and letters, saying these were permissible exceptions to the commission's rule against hearsay testimony. The Day testimony and most of the photos were accepted but Hearing Examiner William Levy excluded the Trueblood article and the letters.[14]

As usual, The Idaho Statesman's Jim Brown was unsympathetic to sportsmen's concern about salmon: "Fish problems badger every dam in the Northwest. They have cost millions of dollars at Brownlee dam and will cost millions more," he wrote. Why hadn't sportsmen opposed the proposed high Hells Canyon dam?[15] Brown's editorial mistakenly identified Nez Perce as a private power project and accused sportsmen of opposing it for that reason. Ted Trueblood set the record straight in a letter to the editor: "The Statesman apparently regards the sportsmen of Idaho as a gang of insidious public power schemers, using migratory fish as a lever with which to upset the tower of private enterprise."

The Wildlife Federation was opposing the public power dam, he pointed out, while supporting the private power Mountain Sheep. With Mountain Sheep, 51,000 salmon and steelhead migrating up the Snake might be lost but Nez Perce would mean the loss of 172,500 that returned to the Salmon River. The Wildlife Federation had never supported the federal Hells Canyon dam, he wrote. Some member clubs and some individuals backed it but a majority did not. At its annual meeting in January 1956, the federation endorsed the dams for which Idaho Power had been granted a license, while the controversy continued with renewed attempts to win congressional authorization of the federal high dam. The National Wildlife Federation's 1952 resolution opposing a high Hells Canyon dam had been placed in the record of a House committee hearing by the Idaho Reclamation Association, said Trueblood. He concluded by inviting the Statesman to help avoid "a tragedy for Idaho and the entire Northwest" by supporting the federation's stand.[16]

In November 1960, Acting Interior Secretary Elmer Bennett asked the Federal Power Commission to delay any license decision in view of the unsolved fish passage issue and the recent completion of a Columbia River treaty with Canada. No decision would be needed for at least five or six years in view of the added power that would be available from Canada and from other Northwest projects as a result of the treaty, a minimum of 1,686 megawatts of prime power, said Bennett. Also, Canadian storage, plus storage at the proposed Libby dam on the Kootenai River in Montana, would end the threat of Columbia River floods and this needed to be considered in determining the benefits of the proposed Snake River dams. Bennett spoke for the soon to be replaced Eisenhower administration but he made a compelling case for delay, reflecting the concern of the Fish and Wildlife Service about dams and Columbia River salmon. Bennett cited the difficulties experienced with Brownlee and Oxbow and described as unproved the plans of Pacific Northwest Power to maintain Imnaha River runs with a 17-mile canal that was to bypass the lower end of Mountain Sheep reservoir.[17]

Washington Public Power System's Owen Hurd responded to "Must the Salmon River Die?" He sent Ted Trueblood a lengthy description of plans for fish passage at Nez Perce. WPPS was prepared to spend $28 million on facilities based on "successful biological and engineering experience gained over the years at various locations," he wrote. Trueblood sent a copy of the letter to Bowler hoping that it could help him in the FPC proceeding.[18]

The primary challenge for fish advocates was to convince the commission that salmon and steelhead were unlikely to survive the proposed Nez Perce fish passage system. Bowler kept in touch with Hugh Smith, Pacific Northwest Power attorney. He drafted six pages of questions for Smith to use in his cross-examination of William R. Martin, the engineer who designed the system. He also sent questions for Washington Public Power System's fish biologist Harlan Holmes. With the Washington Public Power System (WPPS) fish plan upstream migrants were to enter a "pressure lock" device at Nez Perce after ascending a 200-foot fish ladder. The pressure lock would prepare them for the greater pressure to be encountered after being moved through the dam and released in the reservoir 360 feet below the surface.

Among Bowler's questions: How much pressure would the fish experience in the pressure lock? How many fish could be passed through the dam per day? What would be the pressure on the juvenile downstream migrants that were to be dropped through a 600-foot spiral chute after being collected at a 100-foot barrier dam on the Salmon near White Bird and loaded on barges for a 60-mile reservoir ride to the dam?[19] Opposition fish biologists testified that the upstream migrants would have insufficient oxygen when released deep in the reservoir. Survivors would become confused, unable to find their way to the stream of their origin in a reservoir that mixed water of different temperatures from three rivers, the Snake, the Salmon and the Imnaha.

Idaho Fish and Game's Forrest Hauck testified that only a fraction of the expected number of downstream migrants were showing up at Brownlee Reservoir. Even WPPS biologist Holmes admitted that he could not vouch for the success of the Nez Perce fish passage plan. The system's designer, William Martin, said further studies were needed to confirm the value of the plans, including a study of the effect of pressure in the pressure lock.[20]

With its fish passage plan decimated, WPPS announced that it would amend its application, asking the FPC for permission to seek a license to build Mountain Sheep. Owen Hurd said directors still believed Nez Perce was the best project but fish passage questions threatened to delay a license decision for further studies. Hugh Smith wrote Bruce Bowler that the move was "an admission that they can no longer hope to win the case for Nez Perce on its merits." While fish advocates were encouraged, they understood that the fight was not over. WPPS was still pursuing a license for Nez Perce while saying that if the commission would not approve Nez Perce, it wanted to build Mountain Sheep. It cited the provision in the Federal Power Act giving a preference to public power for construction of hydroelectric dams.[21]

The FPC had ignored the November 1960 request of the Eisenhower Interior Department to delay a license decision in favor of further fish passage studies. On March 15, 1961, the Kennedy administration's Interior Secretary, Stewart Udall, made a similar request, asking the FPC to suspend further hearings while the Fish and Wildlife Service conducted a 4-year "crash study" to try to find an answer on high dam fish passage. The next day in a Salt Lake City press conference Udall said he had received information that the Brownlee fish passage facilities were "a very sad failure" and this was one of the reasons for his request.[22]

An alarmed Bruce Bowler wrote Udall advising him that it would not be possible to prove the success of any fish passage plan in such a short time, "before many more 4-year (fish) cycles." Bowler wanted no delay in the licensing decision, believing that a good case had been made for Salmon River salmon and steelhead and that the FPC would rule for Mountain Sheep.[23] The commission wanted no delay either and proceeded with hearings. The case was apparently completed in April 1962 with the filing of final briefs. The next step would be a recommendation by Hearing Examiner Levy.

In June, Udall stepped into the case with both feet, asking the FPC to recommend construction of High Mountain Sheep dam as a federal project rather than granting a license to either Pacific Northwest Power or Washington Water Power. He advised the commission that Fish and Wildlife Service studies to date "show little promise of a sudden major breakthrough which could produce a satisfactory solution to the fish problem at the Nez Perce site by the end of 1964." If the FPC accepted Udall's request, construction of a dam would be delayed pending a request for Congressional authorization and congressional action. Udall said federal construction would assure that every effort would be made to protect the fish runs. Udall's eleventh-hour request was opposed by the FPC staff, Pacific Northwest Power, Washington Water Power and most of the interveners. They filed opposition briefs.

As fish advocates had hoped, Hearing Examiner Levy recommended that the FPC issue a license to Pacific Northwest Power for High Mountain Sheep. It could be built "without delay, without risk to the major fishery resource of the Salmon River and without adding substantially to the existing problem of maintaining the major fishery resource of the Snake River." Conditions had changed since 1958 when the commission rejected PNP's license application for Pleasant Valley, identified Nez Perce as a superior site and said Idaho Power's plans offered a "promising outlook" for passing fish at high dams, wrote Levy. "The 'promising outlook' at Brownlee has not materialized" and "the record of this proceeding does not support an optimistic outlook for the success of the proposed Nez Perce facilities."

Levy did not endorse PNP's fish passage plan for High Mountain Sheep either, but emphasized the significance of Salmon River runs in comparison to the numbers passing the Mountain Sheep site – 200,000 versus 64,200 based on the best estimates of the Idaho and Oregon fish and game departments. He quoted Bruce Bowler: "The failure of successful fish passage at Brownlee is supplying now some of the negative answers from experimentation. To keep the experiments above the mouth of the Salmon for many years is paramount." Levy cited a joint statement by the fishery agencies describing the Nez Perce plan as a combination of untried and untested elements "piling risk upon risk to the extent that no biologist, including that of WPPS, will predict it will work."[24]

Levy found that the Mountain Sheep "plan of development" provided more power and more flood control than Nez Perce. This conclusion was based on the eventual construction of the companion dam on the Salmon, Lower Canyon. Levy said that with the licensing of Mountain Sheep, Lower Canyon could be deferred pending further Interior Department fish studies, further site exploration and until it was required for power. Levy's comments made it clear that the licensing of Mountain Sheep would not end the high dam threat for Salmon River seagoing fish. Church's salmon sanctuary bill was still languishing in committee.

Levy rejected both the WPPS request for a license for Nez Perce and Udall's proposal for federal development, saying it would delay construction of a dam, noting that the secretary had submitted no request to Congress. Two months later Udall asked the FPC to let him intervene in the case, a move that was opposed by all the participants including the Idaho Wildlife Federation. Udall was not allowed to intervene but was granted "limited participation" including participation in oral arguments.[25]

In February 1964, the FPC issued a license to Pacific Northwest Power for High Mountain Sheep dam. The commissioners were unanimous in favoring the High Mountain Sheep site but divided three to two on who should have the license. Commissioners unanimously rejected Udall's request to endorse federal construction. The commission said the High Mountain Sheep plan permitted earlier construction of a dam without endangering "the important fish resource on the Salmon River." It might take years, perhaps 15 to 20 according to the Corps of Engineers, to resolve the fish problem and allow construction of Nez Perce. Like Examiner Levy, the commission envisioned the eventual construction of Lower Canyon dam, declaring that the Mountain Sheep plan with Lower Canyon would provide more benefits than Nez Perce.[26]

The Idaho Wildlife Federation and the other fish advocates had won an important victory. Nez Perce dam was apparently dead and the Federal Power Commission had made a decision based on the value of seagoing fish. Tim Vaughan, fish biologist for Pacific Northwest Power, wrote Bruce Bowler saying that PNP had been getting congratulations from all quarters but "I say you are the one to be congratulated." He quoted the commission order: "The record and contentions of the fisheries' interests make it clear that conservation of the fish is an important public end, and we so find." The history making recognition by the FPC that fish were "a beneficial public use," wrote Vaughan, was "due in large measure to the fine work you did for the Idaho Wildlife Federation." The decision was praised by Idaho Gov. Robert E. Smylie, declaring that it meant the Salmon River could remain forever a sanctuary for salmon and steelhead.[27]

Pacific Northwest Power hired an engineering company to begin preliminary work on the dam. But the contest was not over. After being denied a rehearing by the FPC, both Udall and WPPS appealed the decision to the U.S. Court of Appeals in Washington. Bruce Bowler drafted the Idaho Wildlife Federation's petition to intervene, declaring that Pacific Northwest Power had shown "the utmost good faith" toward the anadromous fishery and should have the license for High Mountain Sheep. Also intervening were the fish and game agencies and the other organizations that had opposed Nez Perce dam before the FPC. Bowler did not file a brief, deferring to the briefs filed on behalf of other interveners.

The Court of Appeals unanimously upheld the FPC decision, rejecting both Udall's arguments for a federal dam and Washington Water Power's claim for preference. Now the question was whether the Supreme Court would accept the Udall or WPPS requests to review the decision. Bowler was hoping it wouldn't. He agreed with Hugh Smith who advised against filing a brief on behalf of the Idaho Wildlife Federation. Smith was concerned that "the more parties who now appear tend to lend greater weight of importance to the case." The only issue before the court was whether the case was "sufficiently important" for review. And a brief for other fish advocates opposing review had been filed by Seattle attorney Joseph Mijich.[28]

The Supreme Court decided the case was indeed worthy of review. The primary questions to be considered were Udall's plea for federal construction of a dam and the WPPS claim for preference. Nez Perce dam was no longer an issue. Nevertheless, Bowler believed the Idaho Wildlife Federation should intervene in support of a license for Pacific Northwest Power, recognizing that "we owe much to the Pacific Northwest Power Company for bringing about the result that now exists." Also, if the license for High Mountain Sheep went to WPPS there would be a serious threat of a Lower Canyon dam on the Salmon as an eventual companion to Mountain Sheep.

In the brief filed by the Idaho Wildlife Federation, Bowler asked the Supreme Court to confirm PNP's license. He cited Kinsey Robinson's FPC testimony for Pacific Northwest Power declaring that the commission should consider the Salmon River as a fish sanctuary until methods were found, tested and proven to pass migrating salmon. Washington Public Power had taken no such position, meaning that if it won the license for High Mountain Sheep, the Salmon River's seagoing fish would still be in jeopardy. WPPS had been willing to sacrifice the fish with Nez Perce and had taken no position against construction of Lower Canyon dam. Neither had Secretary of Interior Udall. "The Lower Canyon dam will destroy the Salmon River anadromous fisheries as effectively (as) would Nez Perce."[29]

It would be June 1967 before the Supreme Court handed down its decision, a decision that would surprise and shock the Federal Power Commission and the litigants. It would open the door to a new chapter in the history of Hells Canyon and the Snake River.

Chapter 9

Rivers wild and free

"Nowhere in America are there left such jewels among our remaining wild rivers as the Salmon and Clearwater systems." – Sen. Frank Church

While the Idaho Wildlife Federation was battling to save the Clearwater and Salmon rivers and their seagoing fish from dams, other Americans were engaged in similar struggles. Free flowing rivers were disappearing with remarkable speed before the onslaught of dam construction.

Even the rivers most prized for scenic quality, water quality and fish and wildlife habitat were threatened. In June 1962, while he was thinking about his re-election and preparing to wage an all-out push for Bruces Eddy dam, Sen. Frank Church met with Interior Secretary Stewart Udall to talk about Udall's ideas for protecting some of the nation's remaining undammed rivers. Udall followed up by sending Church the text of the 1961 recommendation of the Senate Select Committee on Natural Resources for a national protected rivers system and the Outdoor Recreation Review Commission's 1962 endorsement of the concept. The Commission said some rivers should be off limits to dams licensed by the Federal Power Commission if natural values outweighed their value for development.[1]

Also in 1962, President John F. Kennedy approved an administration policy statement, suggested by Udall and Secretary of Agriculture Orville Freeman, declaring that in some instances wild river segments should be "maintained and preserved as a proper use of rivers." In 1963, the Interior and Agriculture departments surveyed 100,000 miles of rivers and tributaries averaging a flow of 550 cubic feet per second or more and found that "only a few may be classified as wild or relatively unspoiled." The team identified 67 possible candidates for protection and made detailed studies of 17. By 1965, Udall and Freeman were ready to proceed with legislation. President Lyndon Johnson called for protection of some of the country's rivers in his January message to Congress and in a special message on natural beauty.

In March, Church and Sen. Henry Jackson of Washington, the Interior Committee chairman, introduced the administration's bill. It would protect six rivers, providing the nucleus for a wild rivers system while authorizing study of seven others for possible future designation. Topping the list of rivers

Ernie Day Photo

Lower Middle Fork of the Salmon River.

considered worthy of immediate protection were segments of the Salmon and the Clearwater in Idaho totaling 400 miles.

Included were 150 miles of the main Salmon from the mouth of the north fork to Riggins, along with the Salmon's entire middle fork, which drained the Idaho Primitive Area and adjacent wild country, 106 miles. The Clearwater's middle fork would be protected for 22 miles from Kooskia upstream to Lowell along with 69 miles of the Lochsa and 90 miles of the Selway.

Also receiving immediate protection would be parts of Oregon's Rogue River, the upper Rio Grande in New Mexico, the Green in Wyoming and the Suwanee in Georgia and Florida. The bill would prohibit the licensing of dams by the Federal Power Commission. Dams could still be constructed with Congressional authorization. Backers of the legislation recognized that Congress would be unlikely to approve a dam on a protected river but Church and other advocates could say that dams could still be built if a future Congress decided that development was more important than river protection.

"From our national beginnings rivers played a major role in our expansion and development and in our way of living. Early explorers used the rivers as pathways into the wilderness," Church told the Senate. "They were followed by hunters, trappers and traders who boated and rafted these natural arteries, soon to become avenues of trade and commerce. Since then the waterways have been harnessed for power, water supply, navigation, flood control and used for disposal of wastes. We are still in this latter process of comprehensive river development. And now, suddenly we have awakened to the realization that only a few rivers remain untamed, that a part of our scenic and cultural heritage is threatened with destruction. Unless we take immediate steps, the generations which wait at our threshold may never know the excitement of white water, fish in crystal clear rivers or a leisurely float down blue streams which meander between tree-covered banks. Even as our rivers disappear, our need for this type of recreation escalates."

Church said the wild rivers bill would accomplish for Salmon River salmon what he had attempted to do with his sanctuary bill. And that Dworshak dam, now under construction on the North Fork of the Clearwater, lent emphasis to the need to leave the other forks unobstructed. The Idaho rivers to be protected flowed almost entirely through public land, much of it in wilderness or primitive areas with few private inholdings, he said. "To designate them as wild rivers will insure their unspoiled beauty for the pleasure of future generations, that their waters remain pure, and that these major spawning grounds continue to supply both the sportsman and the commercial fishing industry."[2]

While the wild rivers bill was a "necessary companion measure" to the wilderness bill enacted in 1964, said Church, it would be less restrictive. There was no prohibition on road construction next to designated rivers. Grazing, timber cutting and mining on public land along the rivers could continue, subject to regulation to protect wild river values. Private land holdings adjoining the rivers could be acquired by purchase but emphasis would be given to purchase of scenic easements. When Sen. Milward Simpson complained that Wyoming's governor had been assured that the Green River would not be included Church said the bill would, of course, be subject to revision. And he pointed out that most rivers would remain open for development.

Church had been one of the Senate's foremost dam promoters. His first Senate speech in 1957 was in support of a federal high Hells Canyon dam. He had repeatedly pushed for appropriations for the four lower Snake River dams that would bring barge transportation to Lewiston: Ice Harbor, Lower Monumental, Little Goose and Lower Granite. He had threatened a filibuster in 1962 to get Bruces Eddy and had secured authorization of Asotin dam on the Snake upstream from Lewiston. In 1964, he persuaded Congress to authorize a Bureau of Reclamation dam on the Teton River and Ririe dam on Birch Creek in eastern Idaho. He had repeatedly sought authorization of Burns Creek dam on the South Fork of the Snake.

Church sought to serve both his river development and river protection constituencies. While he had broken the hearts of Bruces Eddy opponents, he had always opposed Penny Cliffs dam on the Middle Fork of the Clearwater. And he sponsored the Salmon River sanctuary bill, recognizing the significance of the Salmon and its tributaries for seagoing fish. Now he was leading the way in challenging the doctrine of unlimited river development just as he had led the Senate debate for the Wilderness Act.

Leaders of the Idaho Wildlife Federation were delighted with the rivers bill but recognized a glaring weakness. It omitted the lower 70 miles of the Salmon, leaving the door open to Federal Power Commission (FPC) licensing of a Lower Canyon dam. Federation leaders and members sent off a flurry of letters to Church and Jordan supporting the bill and asking inclusion of the lower Salmon. Church prepared an amendment to include it. The federation distributed a fact sheet saying the rivers bill "represents our best – and possibly our last – chance to preserve the steelhead and salmon runs in the Salmon and Clearwater rivers."[3]

Bruce Bowler worried about Sen. Len Jordan, an ardent champion of irrigation development and, like Church, a member of the Senate Interior Committee. Jordan believed that not enough unclaimed water remained in the Snake River for all of the desert land that might be irrigated in southern Idaho. Ultimately, he envisioned augmenting the water of the Snake with Salmon River water. Bowler heard that Jordan would oppose the wild rivers bill and the lower Salmon amendment. He asked S. Eddie Peterson, mayor of Idaho Falls and a federation member, to use his influence with Jordan.[4]

The Idaho Wildlife Federation raised $400 from local clubs to send Ted Trueblood to speak for the rivers bill at the Senate Interior Committee's April 25 hearing in Washington, D.C. For many years, he said, protection of the Salmon River had been the number one priority of the federation with its 85 local affiliates and 20,000 members. In all the years of the nation's development, with claims filed for land, timber, mines and dams, said Trueblood, "nobody staked a claim in the name of the people of America."

The wild rivers bill would do that, he said, allowing Americans to enjoy protected rivers "forever in their unspoiled state." He cited the 3,000 letters received in response to his 1960 plea for the Salmon River salmon in Field and Stream magazine, some from every state, and quoted a Kansas City high school student: "I am only 17 years old but when I grow up I want to be able to see a river running." Those words made a deep impression, said Trueblood, "I have thought of it hundreds of times." He said he was thrilled with the bill's immediate protection of the Middle Fork of the Salmon: "I have been along every foot of the middle fork from its headwaters to its confluence with the main Salmon. My wife and I spent our honeymoon on the Middle Fork of the Salmon River. I have floated it in a boat. I have ridden a horse along the trail above it. I have walked the shore ice in winter carrying a pack."

Trueblood asked inclusion of the lower Salmon, the 30 miles below Riggins skirted by Highway 95 and the last 40 miles through a wild canyon. The Salmon and Clearwater were little changed since explorers Lewis and Clark saw them in 1805, he said. "The sparkling water, trout, salmon and steelhead, the bighorn sheep and Rocky Mountain goats, the towering cliffs and snow-clad peaks are there. The high ridges still lay one beyond the other as far as the eye can reach until they fade in the blue haze of distance."[5]

Idaho Gov. Robert E. Smylie endorsed the rivers bill in a statement delivered by Fish and Game Commissioner Frank Cullen. Smylie said his statement reflected the position of the commission, the State Forester and the reclamation commissioner. Since Smylie's election in 1954, Fish and Game Director Ross Leonard had been keeping him informed about the value of Salmon River and Clearwater River seagoing fish. Smylie backed the commission in its support of Mountain Sheep dam on the Snake as a less damaging alternative to Nez Perce. He had opposed the Wilderness Act but now his endorsement would give the rivers bill and Church a significant boost. Smylie had pushed for legislation establishing a state park system and was promoting Idaho tourism, recognizing the economic significance of hunting and fishing.

One of Smylie's strongest supporters was Ernie Day, past president of the Wildlife Federation, now serving as a member of the State Parks Board. Another endorsement of the rivers bill came from Pacific Northwest Power's John Burke. While PNP had a license for Mountain Sheep dam it had no intention of filing for the potential companion dam, Lower Canyon, he said, and in view of the immense value of the salmon fishery and "with what we have been able to learn regarding fish passage around high dams," no dam should be built on the Salmon River.

The Ada Fish and Game League paid travel expenses for Boise printer Franklin Jones who described family trips to the Salmon River beginning when he was 12: "I have a picture of my father and me holding a big salmon we took in 1920, hanging from a pole across our shoulders. Its tail touched the ground." Jones said the Salmon River excursions were the family's most enjoyable events and he was now taking his 80-year-old mother to some of the same camping spots. Senator Jordan hosted Jones and Trueblood at lunch in the Senate dining room and Jones got the impression that Jordan would support the bill.[6] Most of the witnesses at the Washington hearing favored the rivers bill.

Responding to Senator Jordan's request, for an Idaho hearing and a similar request for Wyoming, Church scheduled hearings in Rock Springs and Boise before his Public Lands Subcommittee. Testimony in Rock Springs was mostly negative with most witnesses opposing protection of the Green River. At the Boise hearing Church said the bill had generated a tremendous volume of mail from Idaho, overwhelmingly favorable, with many asking inclusion of the lower Salmon.

The leadoff witness, Governor Smylie, repeated his endorsement: "I am pleased that the Congress of the United States is contemplating through the Wild Rivers Act the preservation of the values inherent in our Idaho rivers. I agree that legislation is necessary to lend permanence to the free-flowing status of the Salmon, the Middle Fork of the Clearwater, the Lochsa and the Selway as they are today." Smylie asked for inclusion of the lower Salmon and for more specific language to assure continued timber cutting, grazing and mining on public land adjacent to wild rivers. He was satisfied with the protection given present and future water rights. The governor cited the Fish and Game Department's estimate of the value of hunting and fishing in the Salmon and Clearwater drainages, $12 to $15 million a year.[7]

Smylie's position was not shared by Edson Deal of Nampa, president of the Idaho State Chamber of Commerce and former lieutenant governor. The chamber favored delaying the legislation pending a report of the Public Land Law Review Commission expected in 1969. The language authorizing regulation to protect river values in streamside corridors could result in "arbitrary regulation" by land managers of timber cutting, grazing and mining, said Deal, and it usurped congressional authority. Senator Jordan told Deal he shared his concerns while Church invited him to submit language on timber, grazing and mining.

Also opposing the bill were the familiar Wilderness Act foes: the Idaho Mining Association; Idaho State Reclamation Association; the cattlemen's and woolgrowers associations; the Associated Taxpayers of Idaho; the Southern Idaho Timber Association and the Associated Industries. State Sen. Cecil Andrus, Orofino Democrat, had some concerns. He opposed including the lower Salmon River because language saying it was to remain "free flowing" might conflict with construction of China Gardens, the low dam on the Snake below the mouth of the Salmon that was to regulate water releases from Mountain Sheep dam. China Gardens would back some water into the

Martel Morache Photo

Protecting the Salmon River was a primary goal of the Idaho Wildlife Federation.

mouth of the Salmon. Regulation of flows from Mountain Sheep dam with China Gardens would be needed, Andrus said, both for added power generation and for the port of Lewiston. He also feared that regulation authorized by the rivers bill could stifle mining development. Church promised to look into the China Gardens question, noting that the intent was only to keep dams off the Salmon.

Outdoor writer Annette Tussing of Clarkston, Wash., asked: "How dare a few men or agencies commandeer for their own devices the waterways that belong to all Americans and to the future," noting that the Inland Empire Waterways Committee was currently meeting in Washington, D. C. and lobbying for 89 Corps of Engineer and 10 Bureau of Reclamation projects. Tussing spoke both for herself and the North Idaho Wilderness Committee headed by Morton Brigham.

She introduced Brigham's statement suggesting a different name, "scenic river system" rather than "wild rivers system" to avoid confusion over including some wild rivers and some with streamside development in the same bill. Brigham suggested that rivers in wilderness country should be classified as wild with tight restrictions on development, rivers with some road access but essentially primitive conditions as semi-wild and rivers with adjacent development as developed rivers. (The legislation would eventually be revised to provide for wild, scenic and recreational river sections.) Most of the 54 witnesses in Boise supported the rivers bill with inclusion of the lower Salmon. When the results were tallied, including written statements submitted for the record, 141 of 173 favored the bill.[8]

The legislation also won positive editorial comments in the Lewiston Tribune, Idaho Falls Post-Register, Pocatello's Idaho State Journal and The Idaho Statesman. The Statesman had new management with Jim Brown's sale of the paper to a small Michigan based chain, Federated Publications. A new publisher, Eugene Dorsey, brought a more balanced approach to editorial comment. The Statesman would no longer chastise sportsmen for supporting wilderness or river protection or scald Church for his conservation efforts. Church inserted the Statesman editorial in the Congressional Record. The writer, Bob Anderson, quoted from Supreme Court Justice William O. Douglas in his book, "A Wilderness Bill of Rights." Douglas urged protection of remaining wild and unpolluted rivers including the Salmon's middle fork, which he had floated. In another favorable development the rivers bill was unanimously endorsed by directors of the Lewiston Chamber of Commerce, even though the North Idaho Chamber opposed it.[9]

A more formidable opponent would soon emerge, the newly organized Idaho Water Resource Board. The director of the Los Angeles Department of Water and Power had advanced a proposal in 1963 to supplement the southwest's water supply by diverting "surplus" Snake River or Columbia River water through hundreds of miles of aqueducts. Alarmed Idaho office holders declared that there was no surplus water to divert. Remaining unclaimed Snake River water would be needed to irrigate more land.

In response to the diversion threat, Governor Smylie called a special session of the legislature in 1964 to propose an amendment to the state constitution establishing a water resource board. The board was to prepare a plan for Idaho water, demonstrating that none was available for export. Voters approved the amendment overwhelmingly in November 1964. The legislature passed authorizing legislation in 1965 and Smylie appointed the 8-member board, four Republicans and four Democrats as the law provided. Elected as chairman was George Crookham of Caldwell, owner of the Crookham Seed Company, the country's leading producer of seed corn. Like Senator Jordan, Crookham favored the maximum use of Idaho water for irrigation development. Crookham and most of the other board members did not agree with Smylie on the rivers bill, the first issue the board chose to consider. While no formal vote was taken, in late August Crookham revealed that a poll showed six of the eight members opposed the bill.[10]

When the Senate Interior Committee took up the bill in September, Senator Jordan proposed an amendment to exclude the Salmon and the Clearwater from protection, putting them in the study category. Ultimately, said Jordan, the salmon problem would be solved. Either there would be "no salmon at all in the upper reaches" or a means would be found to pass fish over high dams. When Jordan spoke of "no fish in the upper reaches" he was suggesting that the runs might be entirely lost because of the eight dams in place or authorized on the Columbia and Snake below Lewiston.

Evidence was emerging of severe losses to the downstream dams. Idaho fishermen caught 39,000 salmon in 1957 and 24,000 in 1958 but only 8,000 in 1964. With fewer salmon returning to the spawning beds, in 1965 the Fish and Game Department closed the season, the first salmon fishing closure in the state's history. Jordan said he was not advocating dams on the Clearwater and the Salmon but Idaho should not be denied the right to "evaluate the economic potential of two great rivers." Jordan believed the Water Resource Board would determine that Salmon River water was needed for irrigation development and might decide that more flood control was needed on the Clearwater. Jordan also argued that Idaho should be receiving a share of power revenue from federal dams in the Northwest to support irrigation development.

Church responded, saying the purpose of the Jordan amendment was to allow dams on the Salmon and Clearwater. It would "cut the heart out" of the proposed wild river system "and leave the bill a shambles." After a spirited debate by Jordan and Church, the committee rejected the Jordan amendment and sent the bill to the Senate on an 11-5 vote with Democrats voting with Church and the Republicans with Jordan. Jordan opposed the bill even with his amendment establishing a National Wild Rivers Review Board that he said would make it possible to change the status of rivers in the future. Republican members of the committee also joined Jordan in a minority report that opposed immediate protection of the Idaho rivers, emphasizing his argument for further study of the economic benefits of dams.[11]

With the bill moving toward a Senate vote, the Idaho Water Resource Board intervened, scheduling its own hearing on the bill in Lewiston and asking Church to delay action to allow the board to determine its position. Church knew the bill would pass easily and delay meant there would be no Senate vote until 1966. He also knew that the purpose of the hearing was to delay a vote, provide a forum for supporters of the Jordan amendment and block protection of the Salmon and Clearwater. Nevertheless Church asked Senate Majority Leader Mike Mansfield to defer consideration of the bill.

At the Lewiston hearing, Church said he had delayed a Senate vote "in deference to this board and in order that every possible opportunity be extended to Idahoans to be heard." He delivered a passionate defense of the bill and the Salmon and Clearwater while describing in detail his record of support for dams including his current sponsorship of the Bureau of Reclamation's proposed 500,000-acre Southwest Idaho project. Without the rivers bill, he said, no rivers would be spared from dams. Without it, once a license application was submitted the Federal Power Commission alone would decide the fate of the Salmon and Clearwater, not the board, not the people of Idaho and not the Congress: "You may be satisfied to leave it that way. I am not."

Church questioned the need for further study. "For 50 years we have been accumulating exhaustive data on the whole Columbia-Snake River drainage. We have the complete record of the river flows, year by year, of the salmon runs, the flood cycles and the navigational, irrigation and hydro-electric capacity of every navigable river in the Northwest." The issue should not be dodged, he declared, "on the flimsy pretext that more facts are needed." Citing Smylie's position, he said the bill enjoyed broad, bi-partisan support in Idaho. And he noted that it had received overwhelming support at the April hearing in Boise. Church said that, like Jordan, he supported the idea of a Columbia Basin account, giving Idaho a share of power revenue from federal dams to help pay for irrigation development. But "obstruction of the rivers bill is not going to bring us a basin account." And he said wild rivers designation for the Salmon and Clearwater would be evidence that Idaho had no surplus water for export. Church also chided board members for taking a position on the bill "before these hearings were called, before any testimony was taken," adding that "if I were accused of murder and six of my eight judges had announced to the press, prior to my trial, that they believed me guilty, I wouldn't be very optimistic about my chances of being acquitted in their court."[12]

Smylie didn't testify but State Forester Roger Guernsey did, reminding the board of Smylie' position. For himself Guernsey said he believed "in preserving some land, some forests and some streams in their natural state because of the special recreational and aesthetic values to be derived therefrom." Louise Shadduck, director of the state's economic development agency, gave the bill a lukewarm endorsement, saying the ultimate use of the Salmon and Clearwater should be determined by the board's studies. Fish and Game Commissioner William Durbin of Moscow reiterated the commission's support and Bruce Bowler and Ernie Day spoke on behalf of the Idaho Wildlife Federation.[13]

The first three witnesses opposed or raised questions about the bill. Col. Frank McElwee, district engineer for the Army Engineers, said three potential dams on the Salmon, Lower Canyon, Freedom and Crevice, along with Penny Cliffs on the Clearwater, would provide 7.1 million acre feet of storage and protect Lewiston from floods while producing 12 billion kilowatt hours of energy per year. The Corps estimated that potential economic benefits of $58 million per year would be given up with the rivers bill. (He didn't say that in calculating the benefits of dams the Corps subtracted nothing for the loss of flowing rivers, river recreation, fisheries or wildlife habitat.) Dr. T.R. Walenta of the University of Idaho's Water Resources Research Institute, argued against protection of the lower Salmon, saying it wasn't suitable for wild river management. J.L. Colbert of the U.S. Geological Survey said Idaho had 46 developed power projects and 269 undeveloped water power sites, a great many in the Salmon and Clearwater basins.[14]

The featured speaker in the hearing's second day was Senator Jordan who repeated his arguments for putting the rivers in the study category. Total runoff of the Salmon and Clearwater was greater than that of the Colorado River, he said. Potential power output was also greater and exceeded the output of Grand Coulee. Senator Church wasn't present to hear Jordan. He had gone fishing with a guide on the Clearwater and returned briefly to the hearing later in the day to show off his five-pound steelhead.

A Democratic state legislator, Rep. Herman McDevitt of Pocatello, shocked the board and startled the audience, accusing the board of acting as a political tool of Senator Jordan. McDevitt said the board was established to promote use of Snake River water "before someone else does" and shouldn't be concerning itself with the Salmon and Clearwater. "Name me a river anyplace that belongs more in this bill." McDevitt was chastised in a Statesman editorial and by John Corlett for questioning the integrity of the board and its statewide water-planning mandate. The Lewiston Tribune's editorial by Bill Hall offered no comment on McDevitt's charge but questioned the board's judgment. If it couldn't support protection of the Salmon and Clearwater it should at least "bow out of the wild rivers dispute."[15]

Church knew that he could get the bill through the Senate despite Jordan's opposition and the Water Board's objections. But continued conflict with Jordan and the board would make it more difficult to gain approval in Wayne Aspinall's House Interior Committee. Aspinall had already declared his opposition. It made sense to seek a compromise with Jordan. A Water Board committee headed by George Yost of Emmett helped bring the Idaho senators together. Jordan agreed to support the bill if it was amended to say that a wild river designation could be set aside if the National Review Board found that reclamation would better serve the economic interests of a state. With the amendment adopted by the Senate, Jordan voted for the bill as it passed 71-1 on January 18, 1966. The Cacopon River in Virginia and portions of the Shenandoah were added to the five previously included for immediate protection – the Salmon, Clearwater, Rogue, Rio Grande and the Eleven Point in Missouri. The list of rivers to receive further study was increased from seven to 17.[16]

In his closing Senate debate, Church referred to likely trouble from Aspinall: "Every indication I have is that the House Interior Committee will not proceed with haste." It didn't proceed at all. Aspinall refused to consider the bill and it died when Congress adjourned. Church got no help from Idaho's congressmen. First District Rep. Compton I. White, a Democrat, took no position on the bill and Republican Second District Rep. George Hansen opposed it.

When Church re-introduced the bill with 38 co-sponsors in 1967 he no longer had an ally in the Idaho governor's office. State Sen. Don Samuelson of Sandpoint upset Smylie in the 1966 Republican primary and then won a four-way general election race for governor. Samuelson was a long-time member of the Idaho Wildlife Federation, a former director and the 1962 vice president. He had written Church in support of the Wilderness Act and the rivers bill. But as governor he would not champion river protection, deferring to the Water Resource Board.

Senator Jordan declined Church's invitation to co-sponsor the 1967 bill and the Water Resource Board formally adopted a position, opposing protection of the Salmon and the Clearwater pending further study. George Crookham spoke for the board at a Senate Interior Committee hearing in April and Jordan proposed an amendment putting the Salmon and the Clearwater in the study category while barring construction of dams until studies were complete.

Jordan had voted for the bill in 1966 but now said he had changed his position because of information developed by the board. The board was now thinking about future diversion of water from the upper Salmon near Stanley for irrigation as well as use of water from the lower Salmon. The Lewiston Chamber of Commerce withdrew its support of the bill, endorsing study status for the two rivers. Meanwhile, the Corps of Engineers was actively promoting Penny Cliffs dam on the Clearwater, hosting Water Resource Board members on a tour of the dam site. Statesman columnist John Corlett weighed in with a column strongly supporting the Water Board and endorsing diversion of water from the upper Salmon. Even Church seemed to be wavering in view of the Water Board's opposition. Outdoor writer Ferris Weddle described the developments in an Intermountain Observer column under the headline "Wild Rivers In Trouble."[17]

In late July, with the rivers bill scheduled for consideration by the Interior Committee, Church and Jordan worked out a compromise. The Clearwater and the Middle Fork of the Salmon would receive immediate protection but the main Salmon River would not. It would be placed in the study category with dams prohibited for five years. The Water Resource Board could pursue study of the use of Salmon River water for irrigation. If the bill passed the House, there would be no Penny Cliffs dam on the Clearwater but the Salmon would still be in jeopardy. Statesman Washington correspondent Cleve Corlett, John Corlett's son, reported that Church and Jordan had worked out their deal in a 2-hour closed door session. "The stalemate in the committee (between himself and Jordan) has been broken without a bitter partisan split," said Church. "We can now go forward with a wild rivers bill which should command the support of a united Senate. A serious division in the Senate would have fore-doomed

Martel Morache Photo

Big Mallard Rapids on the Salmon River.

whatever chances there are for favorable action in the House of Representatives." The amended bill now included nine instant rivers. It designated 26 for study with 5-year protection from dams. Rivers could be classified as wild or scenic. The scenic river provision had been borrowed from the rival administration bill backed by Udall and rejected by the committee.

Cleve Corlett wrote that political observers credited the agreement to Church and Jordan's mutual respect and personal rapport. He noted that Jordan had not supported a right-wing recall movement against Church earlier in the year and that Church had given only token support to Ralph Harding in his campaign against Jordan in 1966. Corlett suggested that Jordan would probably give the same treatment to Church's Republican opponent in 1968.

By ending the Idaho battle over the rivers bill, Church helped prospects for his re-election. But he again disappointed his Idaho conservation supporters. After losing a long struggle to save the North Fork of the Clearwater, the Idaho Wildlife Federation, with the help of hundreds of hours of legal work by Bruce Bowler, had carried on a successful 7-year fight against Nez Perce dam. It had supported Church's Salmon River salmon sanctuary bill and marshaled support for the Wilderness Act and the rivers bill. President Art Manley voiced his frustration in the federation newsletter, declaring that after five years the Salmon would be "wide open to the dam builders and water diversionists." Bruce Bowler had written Church saying, "Reclamation should not be the sacred cow of water." But the gospel of maximum irrigation development still prevailed in Idaho.[18]

The Senate gave unanimous approval to the Wild and Scenic Rivers bill 84-0 after Church described its history, major provisions and refinements. Rivers or segments designated as wild included the Middle Fork of the Salmon, the Middle Fork of the Clearwater, the Lochsa and the Selway. Twenty-seven rivers were to receive study with protection from dams for five years. Road building, timber harvesting and livestock grazing along the rivers could continue. So could mining of existing claims but mining of claims located after the effective date of the act could be regulated. States would be encouraged to establish their own protected river systems and there would be no change in water rights. Private land could not be acquired by condemnation in states with 50 percent or more public land ownership but condemnation could be used to acquire scenic easements. Church had inserted the 50 percent public land provision to bar any condemnation purchases in Idaho. In states where condemnation was permitted no more than 100 acres per mile could be acquired on both sides of the stream. River corridors could include no more than 320 acres per mile.

Attention shifted to the House where five wild river bills were introduced, including Rep. Aspinall's scaled down version giving immediate protection to only four rivers. Perhaps because of Aspinall's power on resource issues, Udall endorsed his bill on behalf of the Johnson administration. Rep. John Saylor of Ohio, ranking Republican member of the committee, introduced a more robust version with protection of 16 rivers and study of 50. It had a more refined classification system, defining three classes of scenic rivers – Class 1, wilderness, accessible only by trail; Class 2, primitive, and Class 3, accessible in places by road.

In July 1968, the House Interior Committee approved a rivers bill that was based on the Church bill but gave the land agencies more condemnation authority, protected study rivers for eight years rather than five and eliminated the review board. Among the co-sponsors were Idaho Reps. James McClure and George Hansen. Rep. Saylor acted as House floor sponsor. The bill came to a House vote with a procedural rule barring amendments and requiring a two-thirds majority. It failed because of objections by a Pennsylvania congressman to inclusion of parts of the Susquehanna River in the study category. A disappointed Church said the bill might be dead for the current session.

But Chairman Aspinall was persuaded to ask the Rules Committee to bring it back with a rule allowing amendments and it passed 265-7. McClure said it would "prove more productive over the years than almost any other measure in the parks and recreation field." George Hansen was in Idaho campaigning against Church but left a "pair" supporting the bill. Both congressmen said they had backed the effort to give the bill a second chance. House and Senate conferees accepted the more limited land acquisition authority preferred by Church and accepted the House decision to eliminate the review board.

There would be three categories of protected rivers: wild, scenic and recreational with the designations determined by the land management agencies, the Forest Service and Bureau of Land Management. The final bill had 27 study rivers including five in Idaho, the Salmon from the north fork to its mouth, the Priest, the Moyie, the main St. Joe and the Bruneau. The agencies would have 10 years to complete the studies and submit recommendations. Dams would be prohibited for five years. States were invited to participate in the studies and to establish their own protected rivers systems.[19]

It was apparent in the House and Senate votes that river protection was hugely popular nationally and enjoyed strong public support in Idaho. The Church-Jordan compromise left the Salmon in jeopardy but made it possible for the bill to clear the House Interior Committee with the support of Idaho's two Republican congressmen. It was an unusual display of bi-partisanship and it came during an election year that featured a battle between Church and George Hansen. This time Church was not challenged on land or water issues but was under attack by Hansen for his criticism of the Vietnam War. It was a year of national turmoil with riots in major cities, anti-war demonstrations, President Johnson's decision not to seek re-election and the assassination of

Robert Kennedy. Church would win re-election by 59,000 votes, with majorities in 38 of Idaho's 44 counties.

There would be no Penny Cliffs dam on the Clearwater but the Salmon River and its seagoing fish were still at risk, including those that returned to the middle fork. But the middle fork was off limits to dams and its status was enhanced. Over the years it had gained a reputation as one of the country's premier white water rivers, passing through a spectacular wilderness canyon with great fishing for cutthroat trout. Visitors were likely to see bighorn sheep and mountain goats. After World War II the advent of rubber rafts made it possible for river guides to carry visitors over the many turbulent rapids in relative safety and float traffic was increasing. In 1968, the Forest Service counted 1,600 floaters. More people were also hiking trails in the middle fork country and growing numbers were flying into airstrips to fish, hunt and explore.[20]

The Selway would also gain increasing favor with floaters as a high quality wilderness river. While Dworshak dam would close the North Fork of the Clearwater to seagoing fish, the rest of the drainage was intact. Steelhead and salmon numbers had been increasing in the Clearwater drainage and the Idaho Fish and Game Department and the Fish and Wildlife Service were expecting a further increase.[21]

In 1969, Idaho Atty. Gen. Robert Robson questioned the authority of the Forest Service to prevent the state from issuing leases for dredging the beds of wild rivers. Robson was defeated in 1970 but others pursued the issue. In 1974 the Republican controlled legislature passed a bill calling for federal compensation for beds of streams in wild and scenic rivers. The Idaho House voted to override the veto by Gov. Cecil Andrus but the 21-14 override vote in the Senate fell short of the two-thirds required.[22]

Chapter 10

Church's 1960 Sawtooth Park bill stalled by opposition

"There is no scenic grandeur anywhere in the United States that exceeds the jagged peaks of the Sawtooth Mountains." – Frank Church.

As he struggled with the politically troublesome Bruces Eddy issue in January 1960, Sen. Frank Church attempted to revive the movement for a Sawtooth National Park. He had earlier proposed legislation to protect the Salmon River from salmon-killing high dams. Now he announced that he was thinking about asking for a Park Service study of a Sawtooth Wilderness National Park. Up to this time the first-term senator had concentrated on economic development issues in support of Idaho miners, irrigators, loggers, farmers and livestock grazers. Now he proposed to bolster Idaho tourism by giving the state a national park. The Salmon River bill was his first proposed Idaho conservation legislation and the Sawtooth proposal was the second.

"There is no scenic grandeur anywhere in the United States that exceeds the jagged peaks of the Sawtooth Mountains," he said, announcing that he was considering asking for a study of a possible national park. "A national park would preserve the natural beauty and the wildlife of this lofty wilderness, while at the same time enabling many more people to come and witness it." The park would act as a magnet for tourism with no harm to other land users, he said. "The high, rocky ground won't support grazing, nor will it yield commercial timber. Furthermore there are no mining operations within the proposed study site." Church's map of the potential park included most of the 201,000-acre Sawtooth Primitive Area plus Alturas and Redfish lakes.[1]

Church's park initiative came as a surprise to both potential supporters and opponents. While the 1911 park proposal was initiated and promoted by Idaho clubwomen, this time there had been no groundswell of popular support. The Forest Service had blocked the earlier park proposals and responded to Church's proposal by stirring up opposition with chambers of commerce and civic groups. The past Sawtooth Forest supervisor said three operators would lose grazing for 25,000 sheep, 10 million board feet of timber in the proposed park would go uncut, and minerals that might be needed for national defense would be off limits. Privately owned cabins might be torn down and ranch

Ernie Day Photo

One source of the Salmon River high in the Sawtooths

land in the Sawtooth Valley might be taken by condemnation.

Since there was currently no timber cutting or mining in Church's proposed park area, only 9,600 sheep grazed there and privately owned Sawtooth Valley land would be outside the suggested boundaries, the potential impact was greatly exaggerated. But the Forest Service campaign was effective in generating opposition in Custer County, the Wood River Valley and the Twin Falls area.[2]

The Stanley Cattlemen's Association, Challis Cattlemen's Association and the Central Idaho Rod and Gun Club of Challis issued a protest. They were soon joined by the Twin Falls Chamber of Commerce, the Idaho Mining Association and the Idaho Reclamation Association. Stanley Basin property owners formed the Stanley Basin Association to fight the park. It was opposed by the Northside Communities, Inc. representing seven south central Idaho counties and, because hunting would be excluded from a park, by the 11-county Fourth District of the Associated Sportsmen.[3] And while the Lewiston Tribune, Idaho State Journal and Arco Advertiser supported a park study, the Twin Falls Times-News and Idaho Statesman denounced the idea. Democratic State Sen. Don Frederickson of Gooding warned Church that a park bill could be political suicide for him while also damaging the Democratic Party. Idaho Falls Post-Register political editor Ben Plastino advised Church that it was "generally harmful to you." As the Arco Advertiser pointed out, Church had made a strategic mistake in not consulting constituents in Custer and Blaine counties before announcing his proposal.[4]

An anti-park resolution was introduced at the annual meeting of the Idaho Wildlife Federation. Bruce Bowler managed to head it off with a motion calling for further study of the issue. Bowler wrote Church offering his help, citing the opposition of the Forest Service and asking for information on boundaries and park policies. In his reply Church acknowledged that his proposal had "stirred up a hornet's nest as I knew it would." The attitude of the Forest Service came as no surprise, he wrote, because "the Forest Service regards the Park Service as its implacable enemy."[5]

Ernie Day, responding to Church's request, sent some of his Sawtooth photos for the senator's use to promote the park. Day said he was happy to help, adding that the fragile high lakes and meadows must be protected. "Let's channel the macadamized mobs through the lower valleys and around the larger, more accessible scenic lakes and preserve the alpine country as much as possible." Day wrote that he had spent a great deal of time in the Sawtooths and "love this area more than any other part of our state." In reverence for the Sawtooth high country, Day was the Jeanne Conly Smith of his generation. He and his family spent many days at a summer home south of Stanley. Day had hiked all of the Sawtooth trails, taking black and white photos reminiscent of the work of Ansel Adams. He would wait for hours for the best light conditions to dramatize the majesty of the mountains.[6]

One of the most enthusiastic park supporters was Glenn Brewer, owner of the Rod and Gun Club Cafe in Stanley, a former state representative who had supported curbs on dredge mining. Brewer had written the Park Service in 1949 asking for a Sawtooth Park study. Now he wrote to Church supporting the park proposal. "Just when I was feeling that the whole Sawtooth range had fallen in on me, you reached out and extended the hand of a friend," Church said in his reply. Brewer went to work organizing a Proposed Sawtooth Park Association to promote the park.[7]

To counter the many "rumors and distorted stories" being used against his proposal, Church mailed a newsletter with a map and description to 50,000 households along with a postcard inviting constituents to tell him whether they supported the Sawtooth park study and his legislation to bar high dams on the Salmon River. The response was both surprising and encouraging. By early March, he had received more than 8,000 replies with 6,483 favoring the park study, and 1,860 opposed. More favored than opposed the park in every county except Custer. The postcard poll also generated many favorable letters. Bolstered by the response, Church introduced his bill calling for a park study to be conducted jointly by the Forest Service and Park Service. The agencies might submit separate recommendations. Church noted that the Idaho Legislature had memorialized Congress for a Sawtooth Park in 1915 and park bills had been sponsored by Reps. Burton French and Addison Smith and by Senators William Borah and James Pope.[8]

Bowler had some good news, advising Church that the Ada Fish and Game League had endorsed his park study. And Bowler's speech in support of a park was well received at the annual Sportsmen's Jamboree hosted by the Bonneville Sportsmen's Association. Bowler said he had been making summer trips into the area for 30 years. "It is a grand and glorious region that nature has wrought and can stand against the wonders of the world," he said. While the Sawtooth Primitive Area with Forest Service management was open to timber cutting, mining and grazing, park status would provide permanent insurance against such commercial encroachment, said Bowler. It would also provide far more material benefits to Idaho. Bowler believed sportsmen should be willing to forego hunting in the area in view of the benefits of park administration.

Sawtooth Forest Supervisor Floyd Iverson also spoke, saying the Forest Service planned to continue to manage the Sawtooth Primitive Area for wilderness recreation without roads or the use of motorized vehicles. Hunting would continue. While half of the area was still in Emil Grandjean's Payette Game Preserve, the Fish and Game Commission had opened the preserve to hunting. For the other 1.1 million acres in what the Forest Service defined as the Sawtooth region, there were ambitious plans for much more timber cutting, more roads and more campgrounds to accommodate rapidly increasing recreation use. There might also be more mining since the Bureau of Mines said the area was highly mineralized.[9]

Harry Caldwell, associate professor of geography at the University of Idaho, had written a thesis on Idaho tourism. He advised Church that an Idaho national park would be equal to adding a new industry with a payroll of 500. The Idaho State Intertribal Council endorsed both a Sawtooth park study and the Salmon River bill. Michael Throckmorton of Boise, a park supporter, said the loss of deer and elk hunting in the mountains would be negligible but favored a provision allowing special hunts to avoid overuse of the game range. Parley Rigby of Idaho Falls supported a park but said people were wary because of excessive charges by private concessionaires in Yellowstone. C.W. Mulhall, Idaho Falls realtor, wanted an end to sheep grazing in the Sawtooths. He believed the mineral potential of the area was limited, having put much money and time into exploration and finding only small pockets of ore. A number of business men and women in the Ketchum area signed a letter for the park saying the opposition was limited to the Forest Service, a few livestock groups and chambers of commerce influenced by the Forest Service.[10]

Kathryn Young of the Triple H Ranch in Stanley Basin made the case for continued Forest Service management. The area was seeing startling growth in visitors without park status, she wrote. Some were refugees from the over development in national parks described in a critical article by Devereux Butcher in Atlantic magazine. The parks "no longer even pretend to foster the conservation practices for which they were set aside," wrote Young. The Butcher article attracted much attention, forcing Parks Director Conrad Wirth to defend his Mission 66 program that included more motels, hotels and ski resorts in the parks.[11]

Even with the postcard results Church recognized that the vocal opposition by important interest groups offered an element of danger for his re-election in 1962. And he was alone, without support from other members of Idaho's congressional delegation. He decided not to press the issue. In February 1961, he advised Glenn Brewer that "before we can move forward on this project, there must be developed an increased awareness, not only in Idaho, but throughout the nation, on the need for such a park." A few months later he agreed to act as Senate floor sponsor for the Wilderness Act, generating a furious backlash in Idaho and damaging his re-election prospects.

The Sawtooth park issue would be set aside until after the election. In February 1962, he advised A.D. Greene of Boise that with many chambers of commerce, timber and mining groups on record opposing a study and without united support from the congressional delegation, there was no chance for his study bill. "I am hopeful, however, that Idaho's supporters of a park will continue their activities and that a stronger consensus for it will develop in the state. Now that a national park has been authorized for Nevada, Idaho is the only western state that doesn't have one." Church had asked Interior Secretary Stewart Udall if the Interior and Agriculture departments could conduct a study without legislation. John Carver Jr., Church's first natural resource adviser, had moved to Interior as an assistant secretary. He advised Church aide Ward Hower that Interior had a man in the area, not a government employee, quietly making inquiries and gathering data, and Hower told Church: "John says he believes you want no initiative on this from the Park Service or anyone else until after you are re-elected."[12]

Church did not pursue the Sawtooth park proposal in the months immediately following his 1962 re-election. In February 1963, the Forest Service seized the initiative, announcing that it proposed to establish a Sawtooth Wilderness of 192,402 acres in place of the 200,942-acre primitive area. The wilderness proposal was part of the agency's review of primitive areas. Just as the primitive area served as the Forest Service answer to a Sawtooth park in 1937, the wilderness designation could now be an answer to the renewed threat of a park.

Church saw the Forest Service wilderness proposal as helpful rather than hurtful to his park concept. The question would no longer be national park versus multiple uses because "commercial uses other than recreation would be barred or severely limited in either case." He released to the press a letter to Agriculture Secretary Orville Freeman asking for hearings in Idaho, acknowledging the secretary's power to establish wilderness areas by "the stroke of a pen" and reminding constituents that he favored limiting this authority to Congress in the proposed Wilderness Act. In May, Church asked Sen. Len Jordan, Second District Rep. Ralph Harding and First District Rep. Compton I. White to join him as Sawtooth Wilderness Park sponsors. White had succeeded Rep. Gracie Pfost. Church provided "two thick files" of his Sawtooth correspondence. Overall response had been highly favorable, he told them, with "serious pockets of resistance." He believed some of the opposition had dissipated and the Forest Service's wilderness proposal "should add further to the argument for a national park."[13]

Among Idahoans urging Church to pursue a park was Challis rancher and banker Seth Burstedt, the former Custer County state senator who had championed dredge-mining regulation. Church was delighted since Custer County was a hotbed of opposition. Church asked Burstedt to contact Jordan and White who still had reservations. "Ralph Harding unqualifiedly favors the idea," Church said. Harding was anxious to move and had a park bill drafted for him by the Park Service. It was not the wilderness park Church envisioned. He advised Harding that it was "essential to have a bill that will not necessarily displease the many individuals and groups in Idaho who are inclined to favor the Forest Service wilderness proposal."[14]

Inevitably both the proposed Sawtooth Wilderness and the wilderness park concept were addressed at the Forest Service's September hearing even

BSU Albertson's Library Archives Photo

Frank Church in the Sawtooth Mountains

though the park proposal was not on the agenda and the bill was not yet introduced. Church was the only member of the congressional delegation supporting a Forest Service wilderness, believing it was compatible with a wilderness park. Rep. Harding said the Sawtooth wilderness "could kill forever the dream of a Sawtooth National Park." Rep. White endorsed the park concept and opposed the wilderness designation as contrary to "multiple use." Senator Jordan said no changes should be made in land classifications until Congress updated the land laws, following a study proposed by House Interior Chairman Wayne Aspinall. Jordan's position mirrored the view of the Associated Industries of Idaho, a coalition that included the state's largest corporate businesses.[15]

As Church's mail had indicated, Idaho Wildlife Federation leaders enthusiastically favored a Sawtooth wilderness but many were lukewarm or hostile to a park. Bruce Bowler, Ernie Day, Ted Trueblood, Stanley Burns, Franklin Jones and Phil Fairbanks spoke for the Forest Service wilderness at the hearing, asking restoration of the deleted acreage plus the addition of 13,300 acres. They were joined by representatives of the Sierra Club and the Wilderness Society. While Bowler and Trueblood supported Church's park proposal and Day was willing to accept it, their primary goal was permanent wilderness status for the Sawtooths with or without a park. Idaho Wildlife Federation President Kenneth Reynolds of Pocatello had written Harding supporting a Forest Service wilderness and opposing a park.[16]

While livestock, mining and farm groups backed the designation of the Sawtooth Primitive Area in 1936, the Idaho Mining Association, Idaho Farm Bureau and Idaho Woolgrowers now wanted no wilderness. Timber industry spokesmen favored it, recognizing that the area had little potential timber. State Rep. Vard Chatburn of Albion, chairman of the House Resources Committee, favored the wilderness, as did Democratic Rep. Vernon Ravenscroft. Park advocates included Challis minister Paul Kreuzenstein, the Idaho Motel Association and Glenn Brewer's Proposed Sawtooth Park Association.

In late September, Church, Harding and White introduced identical Sawtooth Wilderness National Park bills in the Senate and House. The park would include a wilderness embracing the Sawtooth Primitive Area, a northern extension including McGowan Peak and 34,000 acres of non-wilderness around the large lakes. Church emphasized the economic benefits of increased tourism. His bill would "equally preserve the upland wilderness while more effectively developing the recreation potential of the adjacent base lands." Sheep grazing by existing permit holders would continue. Mining of existing valid claims was not prohibited but the language suggested that new claims were barred. Church's park wilderness would be nearly the same as the proposed Forest Service wilderness except that the Park Service would administer it, new mining claims might be barred and there would be no hunting.[17]

The Park Service drafted the bill following Church's instructions but didn't like the wilderness designation. "We provide in the national parks only such development as may be required for the public use and enjoyment of the park consistent with its preservation in the natural state," Interior Assistant Secretary Max Edwards advised Church. In other words, the Park Service should be trusted to preserve the wilderness without direction by Congress. The sponsors hoped that the bill's introduction would launch a Park Service study. But Church assistant Verda Barnes advised him that the agency would probably drag its feet because of a "non-aggression pact" between Interior and Agriculture, particularly if Congress didn't act on the wilderness bill that was hung up in Wayne Aspinall's House Interior Committee.[18]

Jordan declined Church's invitation to become a sponsor, objecting to the wilderness designation: "I am sure most of the area will always be wilderness as God made it, but I would prefer that parts of it be opened by roads for greater enjoyment by more people." Jordan was inclined to favor a Forest Service scenic area designation, allowing roads to prominent points. Gov. Robert E. Smylie advised Church that he supported a national park but opposed the wilderness concept because it would deny visitors "real access to the area within the time usually available to the ordinary man." Smylie's support for a Sawtooth park was consistent with his administration's promotion of tourism.[19]

The Twin Falls Times-News published a scathing editorial chastising Church for introducing his park bill without benefit of the Forest Service Sawtooth Wilderness hearing record. Church wrote Publisher Jack Mullowney expressing amazement at the paper's hostility to a park since it would help Magic Valley area businesses. Mullowney was apologetic, saying he had been "booby trapped by some of the pack trip boys in the newsroom." City Editor O.J. Smith had previously written Church applauding his advocacy of the Wilderness Act but asking him to reconsider a Sawtooth park. Smith supported the proposed Forest Service wilderness designation but feared a park would inevitably spur efforts to open the Sawtooth high country to greater recreation use.[20]

Robert Wing of Lewiston, a Church supporter and one-time summer Park Service employee, saw it the same way. At first he favored a Sawtooth park but his opinion changed: "Our parks are now becoming areas of congestion to equal the downtown areas of large cities at the changing of the shifts. Even the footpaths through some of these parks are posted with one-way signs." He didn't believe Church's park wilderness "could withstand the assault of time and increasing numbers."[21]

The Senate and House Interior committees took no action on the park bills in 1964. Both the Agriculture and Interior departments asked for delay while they conducted a joint study to be completed in 1965. The Forest Service marked time on its proposed Sawtooth Wilderness and when President Lyndon Johnson signed the Wilderness Act in September 1964 authority to act on national forest primitive areas shifted to the Congress. The Forest Service would be limited to an advisory role, submitting recommendations to the President. In November 1964, park advocate Ralph Harding was defeated by Republican George Hansen.[22] Church re-introduced his Sawtooth Wilderness Park bill in February 1965. He was delighted when the previously hostile Idaho Statesman endorsed a park. Church had been in touch with publisher John Scott and associate publisher Eugene Dorsey, hoping to win kinder treatment from the state's largest newspaper under its new management.[23]

The Sawtooth study produced competing options. The Forest Service proposed, in lieu of a park, a Forest Service managed National Recreation Area. It would emphasize recreation values but would be less restrictive than a national park. The Park Service proposed a park but provided little information on how it would be managed, suggesting a lack of enthusiasm. By contrast, the Forest Service developed a detailed plan for its national recreation area.

Both proposals addressed a growing concern about visual pollution in the Sawtooth Valley, subdivisions that were springing up on some of the 22,000 acres of privately owned land, marring the pastoral landscape that provided the foreground for views of the mountains. The study's authors proposed to include the privately owned valley land within the boundaries of the proposed park or the National Recreation Area (NRA). It would be subject to purchase in a park. With the NRA the Forest Service proposed to encourage regulation with county zoning. Also included in both the park or NRA would be more than 100,000 acres of national forest and 30,000 acres of public land managed by the Bureau of Land Management that was not included in Church's earlier park legislation. Emphasis in the NRA would be on recreation, fishery and wildlife values but livestock grazing and timber cutting would not be prohibited.

The study suggested that the area should be withdrawn from further mineral entry. This would mean that mining of existing claims might proceed but new claims would be barred. With a national recreation area the Forest Service would ask Custer County to adopt a zoning ordinance in line with Forest Service rules for the location of buildings, lot sizes and building standards. If no ordinance was adopted the agency would have authority to acquire property by condemnation.[24]

Forest Service Chief Ed Cliff counseled Church's resource assistant, Porter Ward, on the virtues of the Forest Service's alternative. Ward composed a memo to Church: "I believe the report sets out a favorable balance of assets for the National Recreation Area against a park; it accomplishes your objective of saving the Sawtooths and the valley, at the same time giving them national recognition as a tourist attraction... Politically it is certainly more palatable to the state and particularly to the area involved. Your feeling that the Forest Service will help sell the idea is solid, and I am sure we can encourage this." In a letter to Feature Editor O.A. (Gus) Kelker of the Times-News, Church indicated that he was leaning toward the NRA. It would retain the multiple use concept and would not involve the acquisition of much private land.[25]

Senator Jordan continued to oppose a park but was willing to support the less restrictive NRA with Forest Service management. In April 1966, Church introduced another Sawtooth National Park bill and he and Jordan jointly introduced a Sawtooth National Recreation Area bill. Both encompassed a much larger area than the previous Church bills, 380,000 acres for the park and 350,000 for the NRA. The park bill included the 22,000 acres of privately owned land in the Sawtooth Valley. This land was excluded from the proposed NRA but would be subject to local zoning with Forest Service oversight. Idahoans were invited to testify on both bills at a two-day hearing in Sun Valley in June before the Senate Subcommittee on Parks and Recreation.

Neither bill designated the Sawtooth Primitive Area as wilderness as recommended in the joint study. Church was confident that Congress would eventually make it wilderness, following procedure prescribed in the Wilderness Act. But the omission troubled Ernie Day, who wrote wilderness supporters urging them to speak for immediate designation of a Sawtooth Wilderness in the park or NRA bills. Day also offered a "personal opinion" that in spite of its "obvious weaknesses" the NRA "would best preserve the wilderness jewel of the Sawtooths. Probably less people would be attracted to the area and less pressure would be brought to road up the high country."[26]

Commercial interest groups that opposed a park were willing to accept a Forest Service national recreation area as an alternative. Among them were the Idaho Cattlemen's Association, Idaho Farm Bureau, Idaho Woolgrowers, Idaho Associated Industries, and the Southern Idaho Forestry Association. The Idaho Mining Association favored the NRA with deletion of land south of Alturas Lake and around Atlanta. The NRA bill did not include the mineral withdrawal proposed in the joint study and new claims would be allowed in the primitive area until 1983, if it became wilderness under the Wilderness

Act. The Idaho legislature, which had previously gone on record against a park, unanimously endorsed the National Recreation Area.

Ernie Day photo

Ice-carved peak in the Sawtooth Mountains

Testimony at the Sun Valley hearing conducted by Senators Church, Jordan and Frank Moss of Utah, with Rep. White sitting in, was overwhelmingly in favor of the NRA. Many of the witnesses spoke of the need for early action to protect the scenic quality of the Sawtooth Valley. Most wanted the ranch operations to continue and opposed their acquisition by the Park Service. "As the motorist travels along the highway in Sawtooth Valley, the sight of cattle and sheep grazing in lush pastureland overshadowed by the peaks is pleasing to the eyes," said Dorothy Povey, Blaine County treasurer and a valley landowner.[27]

Ernie Day, vice chairman of the State Parks Board, presented Governor Smylie's statement, drafted by the Parks and Fish and Game Departments, supporting the National Recreation Area with the understanding that recreation would be the primary use and other uses would be allowed "only to the extent they do not detract from the recreational opportunities." Smylie's support for the NRA was contingent on an assumption that Congress would provide adequate funding. Smylie didn't reject a park, saying Congress had a better record of appropriating funds for parks than recreation areas. But he believed an NRA could be implemented "with a minimum of delay." In his own statement, for the Idaho Wilderness Committee, Day supported the NRA but wanted it to include immediate wilderness designation for the primitive area.[28]

Outdoor writer Ted Trueblood preferred a park that he said had been a goal of Idahoans for more than 50 years. As a Boise Capital News reporter he had covered the 1936 conference that rejected Senator Pope's park bill. It was "dominated by resource users who put their personal profits ahead of the long-term public benefit," he said. But he endorsed the recreation area because it appeared to be "the best that we can do" and a decision was needed "before it is too late to do anything." He was shocked by the unplanned development in Sawtooth Valley. "There were spots where I could barely see the mountains for the billboards." Even the state of Idaho was subdividing land on the banks of the Salmon River, denying public access, he said. Trueblood wanted better protection of fishery, wildlife and recreation values in the NRA bill with deletion of the word "substantially" from language allowing mining, grazing and timber cutting if they did not "substantially impair" those values. He favored wilderness designation for the primitive area as part of the NRA bill but accepted Church's assurance that this would be achieved pursuant to the Wilderness Act. Echoing Lincoln at Gettysburg, he said, "in a few short years nobody will remember what we say. But if the magnificent Sawtooths remain unspoiled they will stand forever as a monument to what we do."[29]

Bruce Bowler described the Sawtooths as a natural work of art, like the masterpieces hanging in the nation's galleries. He preferred a park but recognized the tide of opinion for the recreation area. He asked for stronger language in the NRA bill to protect the area's natural quality: "The Forest Service has got to make a special project here," recognizing that the area deserved park status. Church told Bowler that when the NRA was established it would be up to the Forest Service to preserve the quality. If not "it is always open for Congress to move ahead with a national park." Church's boyhood friend Stanley Burns, president of the third district of the Idaho Wildlife Federation, also saw weakness in the NRA bill, encouraging grazing, timber cutting and mining, activities that were incompatible with high-quality recreation.[30]

Ernie Day Photo

Sawtooth Lake

State Rep. Art Manley, president of the Idaho Wildlife Federation, presented the federation's statement endorsing the NRA. He said the Forest Service had managed the Sawtooth Primitive Area "wisely and well," the NRA would be managed for multiple use, and hunting would continue under management of the Idaho Fish and Game Department. He said the federation wanted immediate wilderness status for the primitive area. Manley, a realtor who had served on the Coeur d'Alene Planning and Zoning Commission, doubted that the proposed local zoning with Forest Service oversight would control the development that was "cluttering up the landscape" with an assortment of structures from A-frames to trailers.[31]

Clifford Hansen, spokesman for the Sawtooth Valley Association representing landowners, also questioned the proposed local zoning scheme. He said if the land was not to be developed, the owners preferred to be compensated, either with the purchase of scenic easements or condemnation and purchase of the land. With a scenic easement the landowner would be paid to leave the land undeveloped.[32]

A much expanded national park was proposed by Franklin Jones of the Ada Fish and Game League including, along with the Sawtooths, the White Cloud Mountains located on the east side of Sawtooth Valley, the Pioneers south of the White Clouds and the Boulders north of Sun Valley, all with wilderness status. The additional areas included 12 peaks of more than 10,000 feet, “all equal in grandeur and beauty” to the Sawtooths, said Jones. “Nestled in these high peaks are nearly 70 high mountain lakes, the East Fork of the Salmon River... fossil beds, hot springs, historic settings and all the allurements needed to make a great and wonderful park.”

The proposed Sawtooth NRA bill was not adequate to protect the Sawtooth Primitive Area in true wilderness status, said Jones, and not big enough to accommodate a growing number of tourists. The enlarged park would far exceed the proposed NRA in attracting visitors. I have been on the land over all of these areas, he said, and know they are wonderful and entitled to protection. Jones proposed park status for the mountains, with only such lowland areas as needed for administration. A hunting exclusion would not be a problem, he said, because deer and elk came down from the mountains before the fall hunting season. Both Senators Church and Jordan were taken by surprise. Church said he saw many difficulties because the wilderness system “as it is established” was confined to the existing primitive areas. Jones was alone among 78 witnesses in calling for an expanded park but it was a concept that would re-emerge.[33]

Rodger Pegues, Northwest representative for the Sierra Club, spoke against the NRA and for the park, with wilderness designation for the primitive area. The Park Service study described the Sawtooths as clearly of park quality with a combination of ice-polished canyons, alpine lakes and matterhorns forming one of the more spectacular and perhaps the peer of any such combination of such geographical features in the United States, he said. “The need here is not for an outdoor playground. The need here is to protect this area from resource exploitation, land development and excessive human use by the establishment of a national park.”[34] The Wilderness Society’s Cliff Merritt wanted Congress to proceed with designation of a Sawtooth Wilderness with additions of 13,300 acres, in advance of or concurrently with NRA legislation. If the area was to be a park, the society wanted wilderness designation included in the legislation.[35]

Following the hearing the Statesman's John Corlett wrote that the park proposal was now extinct and accurately predicted that the NRA legislation would be modified to provide for purchase of land and scenic easements rather than local zoning to maintain the scenic quality of the Sawtooth Valley. Fifty-five years after Jeanne Conly Smith proposed a Sawtooth National Park it appeared that Senators Church and Jordan had found the solution to the Sawtooth issue, a national recreation area.[36] But there would be no further movement on Sawtooth legislation until 1969, after a mining discovery in the White Cloud Mountains.

Chapter 11

A dagger in the White Clouds

"The idea that we have to carve up every nook and cranny of the quality areas of Idaho is specious reasoning." – Ernie Day

In September 1968, the war in Vietnam was raging. Polls showed Richard Nixon leading Hubert Humphrey, the Minnesota Democrat, and independent candidate George Wallace for president. In Idaho, Sen. Frank Church was being challenged by Congressman George Hansen. In Portland, the Federal Power Commission heard more testimony on the application to license a high dam on the Snake River below Hells Canyon.

Church and Sen. Len Jordan agreed to sponsor legislation for a 10-year moratorium on dams on the Middle Snake. House and Senate conferees reached agreement on a wild rivers bill that included the Middle Fork of the Salmon River and the Middle Fork of the Clearwater, plus the Lochsa and Selway.

A new Idaho dredge mining initiative fell short of the 28,000 signatures needed to put it on the ballot. The Forest Service was beginning studies on the future of the Idaho Primitive Area and the adjoining Salmon River Breaks Primitive Area. Ernie Day of the Idaho Wildlife Federation, Tom Kimball, director of the National Federation, and Dick Hronek, managing editor of The Idaho Statesman, accompanied forest administrators on a primitive area visit that included a jet boat trip on the Salmon River and a 3-day float on the middle fork.

Northeast of Sun Valley on the East Fork Salmon River drainage, the forest quiet was being broken by the sound of motors. The American Smelting and Refining Company (ASARCO), one of the largest mining companies in the world, had a crew working in the White Cloud Mountains near the base of majestic Castle Peak.

Neither the Forest Service nor ASARCO publicized the operation, and it was known to only a few people. Most Idahoans had never heard of the White Clouds. While travelers on Highway 75 could marvel at the majestic Sawtooths, the tops of the White Clouds, 20 miles to the east, were barely visible. While thousands visited the Sawtooth country, relatively few got into the White Clouds, a roadless area of eight by 10 miles. Those who did see the

White Clouds found a land of enchantment. Snowfields hung on the flanks of massive mountains. In basins carved by glaciers were many lakes, some with trout up to three pounds. Sparkling streams sent crystal clear water through meadows to the East Fork of the Salmon River, a spawning stream for salmon and steelhead, and to the main Salmon. Castle Peak at 11,820 feet was one of 13 peaks over 11,000 feet and 62 exceeded 10,000. The peaks were the summer home of bighorn sheep that wintered on the East Fork. There were also mountain goats, deer, elk and bear. Most of the lakes were yet unnamed and some not yet identified. The Forest Service had put the number at 54 but the actual total exceeded 100.

While the area was a scenic wonderland, it also had a history of mining activity. The Livingston Mine on Railroad Ridge on the northern edge of the peaks had operated sporadically from 1882 to 1958, yielding silver, lead and zinc. Near the Big Boulder Creek trailhead was an old mill, rusting machinery and tailings ponds. As of 1968, there were no significant active mines.

But in 1965, the U.S. Geological Survey published a report saying that in 1943 the Survey and the U.S. Bureau of Mines had found evidence of molybdenum near Castle Peak. Claims had been filed in 1923 but never perfected. The report drew the attention of ASARCO geologists who found that the prospector who owned the claims was still living in the area. He granted permission to check them out and then agreed to sell. Based on its 1967 findings, ASARCO planned further exploration for the following year.[1]

On May 15, 1968, a crew set up a base camp near the road along the East Fork of the Salmon River. A helicopter carried equipment and supplies to a campsite at Baker Lake at an elevation of 9,000 feet. Trees were felled to provide a clearing for a cook shack and a helicopter landing pad. Soon a drilling rig was probing deep into the ground, operating 20 hours a day with two shifts. In July, a second rig was flown in to speed up the work.[2]

The Forest Service was in no hurry to let Idahoans know what was happening. In September, newspaper editors began hearing reports from hikers about mining activity in the White Clouds. The editors asked the Forest Service what was going on. Four months after ASARCO started drilling, Clayton District Ranger Marvin Larson called Bob Johnson of Salmon, correspondent for Idaho and Utah dailies and editor of the weekly Recorder-Herald. Larson invited Johnson to join him on an 8-mile hike up Little Boulder Creek to the miner's camp. Larson and Johnson were well acquainted and Johnson was familiar with the White Clouds.

In 1963, Johnson left his job as night city editor for the Salt Lake Tribune for a more tranquil life as a free-lance writer based in Salmon, selling stories and photos to newspapers and magazines. On his way to Salmon from Salt Lake, Johnson stopped at the regional office in Ogden to ask if the Forest Service could help him get into the backcountry. The word reached Gene Powers, Salmon Forest supervisor, and when any field trip came up, "they took me along." He also worked with the Idaho Fish and Game Department and the Bureau of Land Management when they had something newsworthy.

And he traveled with local outfitters and guides. Johnson's ramblings took him into the Idaho Primitive Area, to the middle fork and the main Salmon River and into the Sawtooths and White Clouds. When he took the job editing the Salmon paper, he continued to report for regional newspapers.[3]

Larson and Johnson climbed 1,000 feet in the first mile on the Little Boulder Creek trail. At three miles, Castle Peak emerged above the trees. It took them most of the day to reach the ASARCO camp. The miners had a meal ready for them. William Salisbury, the chief geologist, told Johnson that they had found molybdenite, containing an alloy used to strengthen steel, and were using diamond tipped drills to extract core samples so ASARCO could assess the grade and tonnage of the deposit.

Helicopter pilot R.J. Nokes took Johnson on a flight over Castle Peak, tilting the craft so he could photograph some of the lakes. Since the helicopter had no doors it was an interesting ride. On September 19, Johnson's story was spread across page one of the Recorder-Herald, along with nine photos. Six days later the story appeared in the Idaho Falls Post-Register: "Mine Firm Seeks Ore in Idaho High Country." Two days later it appeared in Boise's Idaho Statesman.

Larson credited ASARCO with proceeding with care, using helicopter access rather than building a road. Salisbury said the camp demonstrated that mineral exploration could be done without destroying recreation values: "Salisbury said the firm doesn't want to construct a road into the area until it knows there is enough mineral to support a road." Larson said the company had been very cooperative in keeping a clean and respectable camp and, if it didn't find enough minerals to support a mining operation, it would be able to leave the area nearly as it was when operations began. The story indicated that the Forest Service was monitoring the work with concern for natural values. Mining company executives expected that the news of a possible new mining payroll in central Idaho would be well received.

Among Idahoans who were familiar with the White Clouds was J. Robb Brady general manager of the Post-Register. Brady's father, J. Robb Brady Sr., bought the newspaper in 1924, leaving it in the family when he died a year later. After earning a journalism degree at Notre Dame, the younger Brady served as managing editor and then general manager. Brady had hiked with his wife and sons in the White Clouds. Their ranch in the Sawtooth Valley, purchased in 1965, was "one of the few places in the valley where the White Clouds can be seen in their snow clad glory just any sunny afternoon. It is an amazing sight." Brady's reaction to the mining was anything but positive. His editorial appeared the same day as Johnson's story:[4]

Miners and Idaho's Castle Peak

"Castle Peak, at 11,820 feet, is not just one of the highest peaks in Idaho. It is one of the most majestic mountains in one of the most magnificent settings of untrammeled high country in the entire west. Because of its unique wilderness qualities, the U. S. Forest Service has kept this a roadless area, administering it much like the wilderness area it truly is. Conservation groups are advancing a wilderness concept for the White Cloud Range and its striking myriad of lakes. The country is located between the East Fork of the Salmon River on the east and the Sawtooth Valley and the upper reaches of the Salmon River on the west. But now the miners have intruded upon Castle Peak, probing its craggy base for molybdenite."

Brady acknowledged that they had taken precautions to limit the impact of their operation. "But all the precautions do not stay the pending doom of this extraordinarily beautiful area. If the mining company finds the metal in mineable quantity, one of the West's scenic citadels will be desecrated. Miners don't like that word, desecrated, but it's agonizingly appropriate if one ever backpacked, fished or hunted in that unparalleled land."

"A bulldozer will blade out a road to Castle Peak, which is in the very heart of this exalted profusion of high lakes and peaks. Mine buildings will be built. Shafts will be dug…or worse. And that great din scourging out will not just destroy the unique serenity of this setting. It will leave it forever man-scarred. Castle Peak would have to be the very last place on earth where molybdenite could be found to justify such a shocking intrusion. And obviously, the ore is not in that order of national emergency."

"Unfortunately, molybdenite comes under the 'locatable' ore laws of the nation – laws written a century ago and decidedly out of step with this time...and this place. Under the law, if the claim filer can prove a reasonably profitable operation prospect, he can mine away. The Forest Service can only exercise some control on the kind of road built into the mine. It cannot even insist on any kind of restoration. The miners can mine away, extract the mineral, dig up the mountain...and then walk away from the upheaval."

So what could people do? Brady advised them to ask members of Congress to reform the mining law, giving the land management agencies authority to reject mining "where scenic and recreation worth outweigh the ore resource worth," and to have authority, through leases, to require restoration of the land. He called for wilderness designation of the White Clouds and withdrawal of the land from mineral entry. He urged the Forest Service to contest the claim filing, a procedure that would put the issue before a panel of the Bureau of Land Management. And he issued a call to arms: "Sportsmen's organizations, the Idaho Wildlife Federation, the Idaho Alpine Club, the Idaho Chapter of the Wilderness Society, and everyone interested in preserving this area should step up and be heard." Brady also scolded the Forest Service for not letting the people of Idaho know what was happening in May: "The public is entitled to be alerted to such an unusual operation in such an unusual area."[5]

Brady's editorial was the opening salvo of one of the liveliest public policy debates in Idaho history. The White Clouds controversy would bring many more Idahoans into the conservation movement, elect a governor and contribute to a growing national interest in environmental issues. Two days after Johnson's story and Brady's editorial appeared in the Post-Register, members of the Idaho Alpine Club met in the living room of the president, Edward Anderson of Idaho Falls. The next day Anderson issued a statement expressing concern about a mine, saying the Alpine Club believed there was an urgent need to classify the White Clouds area as wilderness.

No one was more disturbed by the prospect of a mine in the White Clouds than Ernest Day of Boise, the real estate developer, photographer and Idaho Wildlife Federation leader. Day had hiked in the White Clouds with his family and recognized the quality of the area. Flying in a chartered plane, Day had captured the majesty of Castle Peak in a striking photo looking west down the spine of the mountain. It showed large snow fields hanging on the mountain's flank, a series of three smaller peaks on the left, a large lake perched part way up near the base, another peak on the right and the Sawtooth peaks in the distance.

On the day Johnson's story appeared, Day took his Castle Peak photo to Statesman editors. It appeared on an inside page the next day, accompanied by a news story with a headline: "Threat of Mine Activity Near Castle Peak Deplored by Idahoan." Day said, "Castle Peak is one of the most beautiful single mountains in Idaho. The White Cloud Mountains must be managed in such a manner as to prevent their loss to the citizens of America. A good step in this direction would be wilderness classification of the entire area. This alone would not prevent mining atrocities but could provide better security for this uniquely beautiful scenic asset." Day spoke as a regional director for the National Wildlife Federation.[6]

H. Tom Davis, a Boise engineer employed by the Idaho Water Resource Board, hiked into the White Clouds in 1968 with two friends. When they stopped at Frog Lake a Fish and Game Department conservation officer advised them that, over the ridge, a mining company was exploring.

"I was outraged," said Davis. When he returned to Boise he called Day, who he had never met, and offered to show him his White Clouds slides. Day took some to add to his collection. For Davis the discovery of the threat to the White Clouds marked the beginning of years of wild land advocacy.[7]

In November, Idaho voters gave Richard Nixon a huge margin over Hubert Humphrey. Frank Church won a third term, trouncing George Hansen 173,482 to 114,394, carrying 40 of the 44 counties. With the election behind him, Church was ready to move forward again with legislation for a Sawtooth National Recreation Area. Church had been working for protection of the Sawtooths since 1960, first in a national park and then in an NRA. The Sawtooth bill had unanimous support in the Idaho congressional delegation, which now included Second District Rep. Orval Hansen, Idaho Falls attorney, who had succeeded George Hansen.

Idahoans concerned about the White Clouds waited through the winter for news. It came on March 8, when the Challis National Forest announced that ASARCO was asking for a special use permit to build a road next to Little Boulder Creek so it could bring in heavy machinery for more extensive exploration. The Forest Service said it would probably be early summer before work on the road would begin.

The Forest Service "cannot refuse a mining operation on national forests nor can it refuse to grant permission for the construction of a road to the mine if a mining company declares that the operation is profitable," said the handout. There was no word on whether the company contemplated underground or surface mining.[8]

Ernie Day's Castle Peak photo with arrow showing location of ASARCO's claims.

Mining opponents faced big hurdles. Obviously ASARCO believed its claims had real potential. With approval of a road there would be little chance of stopping a mine. And a road could lead to additional exploration and mining. Wilderness designation would no longer be possible. Even if Congress designated the area as wilderness, existing claims that were potentially profitable could still be mined. And the Wilderness Act allowed new claims in wilderness areas until 1983.

How do you stop the Forest Service from approving a road? What kind of legislation could protect the area? The miners had the law on their side and would have powerful political support. Since most Idahoans knew nothing about the White Clouds, how many would speak up? If Senator Church should wish to sponsor effective legislation, what about Sen. Len Jordan, Rep. Orval Hansen or First District Rep. James McClure, a member of the House Interior Committee? There was also the problem of getting Idaho conservationists to agree on a solution. The first task was enlisting more public support.

On March 15, Ernie Day's Castle Peak photo showing the path of a possible road was spread across the front page of the weekly Intermountain Observer with the headline: "A Dagger in the White Clouds." While the Observer had a circulation of less than 10,000, many of its readers had an interest in public land issues.[9]

Editor Sam Day, a crusader for progressive causes, recognized the White Clouds dispute as a significant story. The Observer would give it plenty of space, keeping readers up to date and opening its columns to lengthy opinion pieces on both sides. Ernie Day also submitted a letter to the editor of the Statesman, giving the address of the president of ASARCO, suggesting that people write and make their feelings known.[10] On March 19, came news that ASARCO was speeding up its road plans. The company had hired a Boise engineering firm to design the road and surveying was to begin in May. ASARCO spokesmen had said earlier that road work might not start until middle or late summer.[11]

On March 20, the Statesman published its first editorial on the issue saying "The Beauty of the White Clouds Should Be Preserved." ASARCO should refrain from building a road before the value of the claims was determined and there should be hearings before any change in the use of public lands with recreational value, said the editors. Also the mining laws should be reformed so all values are evaluated before mining was permitted.

This prompted a rebuttal from Rollie Bruning, editor of the Wallace Miner: "Our standard of living depends on an adequate mineral base. And a higher standard of living is what caused the recreationist to proliferate and flourish." By 1980, the use of minerals in the United States would double, he wrote. "In the past 30 years the United States has consumed more minerals than the rest of the world in recorded time." He declared that all but the wealthy lack the time or money to take "guided pack train tours into wilderness areas."[12]

A group of Sun Valley area residents had been working for protection of the Sawtooths with an organization called the Sawtooth Conservation Council. In February, White Clouds mining opponents in eastern Idaho and the Sun Valley group joined forces to organize a more active and robust organization, the Greater Sawtooth Preservation Council (GSPC). Its purpose was to seek protection of the wilderness and recreation values not only of the Sawtooths and White Clouds, but also the Boulder Mountains north of Sun Valley and the Pioneers south of the White Clouds, an area of more than one million acres.

Most of the GSPC organizers were scientists and engineers employed at the National Reactor Testing Station west of Idaho Falls. Some were leaders in the recently organized Idaho Environmental Council (1968) and the Hells Canyon Preservation Council (1967).[13]

John Merriam, chairman of the economics department at Idaho State University, an avid hiker and mountain climber, was chosen as president. Merriam was born in Illinois but spent his childhood and early adulthood in southern California. He was an army veteran and had worked in Yosemite, Glacier and Yellowstone national parks during summers while earning a graduate degree in economics. It was in Yosemite that he first met his future wife, Kay. After he took a teaching job at Idaho State, Merriam and Kay explored the Idaho backcountry, including several backpack trips into the White Clouds. Merriam was thoughtful and research oriented, preferring rational argument to rhetoric. But he was also determined. In an early GSPC newsletter he was quoted as saying: "We will fight them until hell freezes over and then give them a couple of rounds on ice." Merriam would concentrate on countering the economic arguments of mine supporters.[14]

Russell Brown of Idaho Falls, a chemical engineer, and Richard Meyer, Ketchum landscape architect, were vice presidents. Other directors were Reactor Testing Station scientists Richard Miller, John McClure, Boyd Norton and Cyril Slansky of Idaho Falls, and rancher Gerald Scheid. The organization was, in Brown's words, "information rich. We were not just a bunch of environmentalists waving flags." And they were not intimidated by a historic Idaho culture that favored development over natural values.[15]

They weren't satisfied with the idea of a Sawtooth National Recreation Area administered by the Forest Service. They wanted a national park with management by the Park Service. The first newsletter reported that members were compiling recreational, geographic, mineralogical, economic and biological data to produce "an informed and workable proposal" for the greater Sawtooth area:

"The NRA, to be operated by the Forest Service, promises no effective safeguards against the neon signs, the subdivisions, the motorcycles and the high pitched noisy environment that people seek to forget on vacation. Nothing in the present NRA bill will effectively curtail real estate development, blatant concessions, logging and road building and mining." Recipients of the newsletter were asked to join at $5 per year. "Remember, this may be our last chance. The mining companies won't wait for us to philosophize about their plans. The road will go in this summer unless you commit yourselves to action." Like the Hells Canyon Preservation Council and the Idaho Environmental Council, the GSPC would be an all-volunteer organization.

Even before ASARCO submitted its road request, Gerald (Jerry) Jayne of the Idaho Environmental Council had written Senator Church urging him to substitute a national park for his Sawtooth NRA bill. The conservation movement had grown and attitudes had changed since the 1966 Sun Valley hearing, he wrote, citing the formation of the Idaho Environmental Council, Hells Canyon Preservation Council and a group now studying the Sawtooth situation (the soon to be formed GSPC). He said he was not urging a national park for the sake of having a park, but because there was no other way to protect the magnificent mountain country of the Sawtooths, White Clouds, Boulders and Pioneers.

Jayne sent copies to Senator Jordan, Congressman Hansen, Interior Secretary Walter Hickel and Parks Director George Hartzog, Jr.[16] Church replied that it had taken years to get a good proposal and even if support could be generated for a park it would take many added months or years: "I think we should concentrate our efforts on getting the National Recreation Area bill through this Congress." A Sawtooth NRA would not foreclose the option of an eventual park, wrote Church. Hansen made the same point, emphasizing the urgency of controlling development in the Sawtooth Valley. Once a recreation area bill was passed, he said, a park within and outside the NRA boundaries could be considered. Church and Jordan introduced their Sawtooth Recreation Area bill and Hansen introduced an identical bill in the House.[17]

By mid-March 1969, the regional Forest Service office in Ogden, Utah was receiving many letters for and against a White Clouds mine and requests from conservationists for public hearings on the road request. The Idaho Wildlife Federation, meeting in Burley, adopted a resolution asking for hearings. On March 26, Regional Forester Floyd Iverson announced that public informational meetings would be conducted in Boise and Idaho Falls.

"Challis National Forest management plans developed prior to the recent mining exploration in this area do not call for development of roads. Under these plans management emphasis is being given to the area's exceptionally high recreation values," Iverson said. The proposed road presented "significantly new circumstances" which required "careful consideration. We hope the public informational meetings will provide a suitable way for all who are concerned or interested to gain greater understanding of the proposed mining operation and access road--and to present their views about both the proposal and future management of the area," he said.[18] No specific law or regulation required public meetings or even consideration of public input on a request for a mining road. (The National Environmental Policy Act was not yet passed). The Forest Service decision was a victory for White Clouds defenders. It would provide a public forum, help enlist more people in the cause and generate more media coverage.

Bruce Bowler's research told him that the Forest Service had ample legal authority to deny the road request even though the 1872 mining law gave preference to mining over other uses of the public land. This meant that a decision to issue a road permit could be challenged in court. In Seattle the Sierra Club's Brock Evans was thinking along the same lines. He advised Bowler that it would be better to start with an administrative challenge, asking the Forest Service to reconsider a road permit decision before taking the issue to court.[19]

In early April, Challis Forest Supervisor Wes Carlson announced plans for a 3-year study of the White Cloud, Boulder and Pioneer mountains to identify long-range management objectives: "We will attempt to complete the study as fast as possible and will seek public opinion on the long-term status of these ranges."[20] Dates were announced for the information meetings, May 8 in Boise and May 9 in Idaho Falls. The Ada Fish and Game League sponsored a quarter-page ad in the Statesman with Ernie Day's Castle Peak photo, urging people to attend a slide presentation on the White Clouds and to speak up at the hearing: "If the beautiful, serene White Clouds country is to be saved for you and present and future generations, it must be done NOW."[21]

With the announcement of public meetings and with editorials and letters to the editor opposing a mine appearing in newspapers across the state, ASARCO executives recognized that they had a fight on their hands. They needed to do more to sell the mine. With the help of Al Minton of the State Department of Commerce and Development, they invited news organizations to send reporters for an airplane flight over the White Clouds and a briefing in Pocatello. Keith Whiting of Spokane, the company's chief geologist for the Northwest, said both he and the company were shocked by the opposition. Geologists were elated with one or two finds of commercial value in a lifetime, he said. "I thought I might be a hero, but after reading the newspapers I'm not so sure now."[22]

Whiting said the mine would be an open pit. Flotation equipment would reduce the ore at the mining site, processing up to 20,000 tons a day. Much testing remained to determine if the mine was operational, including exploration of a larger area with heavy equipment. The company had estimates of the economic benefits of a mine but was saving those for the information meetings. A crew was already at work near Castle Peak, clearing snow for a larger campsite. The mine's opponents realized that an open pit meant there would be a huge hole in the ground below Castle Peak. Reduction of ore at the site meant that a large amount of waste material, nearly all of the projected 20,000 tons a day, would be deposited in the valley of Little Boulder Creek.

The Boise hearing attracted 230 people, more than could fit into the meeting room in the YWCA building. Gov. Don Samuelson was the first speaker. In 1966, Samuelson was an upset winner in the Republican primary over 3-term Gov. Robert E. Smylie. Samuelson opposed the enactment of a state sales tax in 1965, a measure pushed by Smylie. In a 4-way general election contest, Samuelson defeated Democrat Cecil Andrus, Independent Perry Swisher and gambling candidate Phillip Jungert. Samuelson owned a sporting goods store in Sandpoint and was an outdoorsman, hunter and fisherman. He hiked in the Selkirk Mountains, often in the company of the local Fish and Game Department conservation officer, even joining on bighorn sheep counts. He had hunted bighorns in the White Clouds. Samuelson was a leader of the local gun club, a member of the Bonner County Sportsmen. He had served as vice president and as a regional director of the Idaho Wildlife

Ernie Day Photo

One of the Little Boulder lakes (named Willow Lake by Bill Platts). Pollution of this lake added to the concern of White Cloud mining opponents.

Federation. He supported wild rivers protection for the Middle Fork of the Salmon and Middle Fork of the Clearwater. He had written Frank Church in support of the Wilderness Act.[23]

Conservationists might have expected Samuelson to side with them. But Samuelson the governor had a different view of a White Clouds mine than Robb Brady, Ernie Day or Bruce Bowler. His 1966 campaign had been supported by mining executives and he had a personal fascination with mining, His administration was pushing economic development including mining. In his brief statement Samuelson endorsed both the road and an open pit mine. He also took a swipe at opponents: "I would urge that we permit no single-minded group to belittle the capability of the federal multiple use conservation program." He said his remarks were intended to be realistic, "a practical appraisal without any emotionalism. Our great agricultural, mining, timber and tourist industries are the foundations for most of the state's economy. The raw materials are here and should be exploited to the fullest possible extent."[24]

Ernie Day, waiting to speak, was visibly upset. H. Tom Davis, sitting nearby, said Day looked as if he "could hardly restrain himself." Samuelson left after he spoke and wasn't present when Day's turn came an hour later. Day declared that he would protest the governor's stand by resigning from the State Parks Board.

Appointed to the board by Smylie in 1964, Day was now the chairman. He held up a photo showing long deep scars criss crossing Railroad Ridge adjacent to the White Clouds peaks. The scars were left by recent bulldozer mining exploration, which Day had discovered in a reconnaissance flight. Challenging Samuelson's multiple use comments, Day said an open pit mine would be a true "one use, one-time use. The idea that we have to carve up every nook and cranny of the quality areas of Idaho is specious reasoning." He called for at least a 3-year delay in granting the road application pending completion of the Forest Service's study. After the meeting he told a reporter: "My resignation will be on his (Samuelson's) desk on Monday. I don't see any sense in being part of a team which doesn't have enough regard for our resources to differentiate between uses."[25]

Bruce Bowler told Forest Service representatives that they had legal authority to deny the road application: "Much law and circumstance have changed the conditions under which mining and exploration can properly be done on public lands." He cited three court decisions, including one by the U.S. Supreme Court, backing agency decisions "which implemented their trust in the actual public interest" regarding mining claimants. "The important point is for the administrative agency to have the courage, as against outmoded tradition, to do what is best for the beneficiaries of their trust, to wit, the people who really own the land."

Brock Evans, speaking for the Sierra Club and the Federation of Western Outdoor Clubs, said the Forest Service should defer action on a road until all other values had been studied. And while reasonable access must be granted, "reasonable access in this case does not mean access by road."[26]

Spokesmen for ASARCO were ready to talk about economics. Norman Visness, head of northwest mining operations, said a White Clouds mine would employ 350 directly and another 500 indirectly with $700,000 annual tax revenue to Custer County and $250,000 to the state: "Scenic grandeur and tourism alone will never sustain the state. Efforts to seal off large portions of the public domain are accelerating daily. The appeal for withdrawal of land from public use is emotional."

Keith Whiting said he believed the project was mineable. A road would let ASARCO bring in equipment for additional exploration and haul out larger ore samples for analysis. Dick Harris, assistant regional forester, said the Forest Service planned an intensive study of the White Clouds that would probably involve two field seasons "withholding any development under our control during the study period." It would be part of a 3-year study of an area also including the Boulders and Pioneers.

Dick Woodworth, director of the Idaho Fish and Game Department, was concerned about what a road would mean for fisheries: "It has been our experience that mining operations contribute directly to destruction of stream habitat, both during the operational phase and for many years after the operation has been abandoned." The general area supplies both "an average fishery by access roads throughout its perimeter and a quality fishery enhanced by wilderness surroundings in the roadless interior portion," he said, and it would be difficult to provide "even an acceptable fishery of lower quality" with the mining road.

One reason for Woodworth's concern was the Blackbird cobalt and copper mine 20 miles west of Salmon on Panther Creek, a large Salmon River tributary. Arsenic, cobalt, copper and other "heavy metals" flowing from mine tailings and waste piles had all but wiped out large runs of salmon and steelhead. Only a few seagoing fish were returning to Panther Creek. Both the Fish and Game Department and the Forest Service had been recently looking into the disaster.[27]

Bowler was keeping score. With the testimony of Doli Obee of the League of Women Voters it was 9-9. Other witnesses opposing the mine included Merrill Dubois, describing himself as "an old man" who had walked to the mine site to see it for himself, H. Tom Davis, Chet Bowers, Sandy Laidlaw, Dr. Keith Taylor and Twin Falls attorney Lloyd Webb.

With State Sen. Art Manley of Coeur d'Alene, Bowler had the score 26-10 against the mine. There is no shortage of molybdenum, said Manley, but "there is a shortage of unspoiled land." Ralph Mellon of the Boise Jaycees presented a petition asking for a 20-year mining moratorium. James Calvert of Moscow submitted petitions against a mine with 192 signatures of University of Idaho students. Speaking for the Idaho Environmental Council, Bill Meiners said mining would degrade a public resource "having far greater values to Idaho and the nation."

Al Teske of the Idaho Mining Association said the mine "would not destroy all the scenic beauty and recreational values of the area." The company only wished to exercise its legal right to construct an 8- or 9-mile road, he said. "The company has agreed to minimize the impact of their work in the event the prospect failed to prove out. The whole plan was worked out in full cooperation with the Forest Service." Max Yost of the Associated Taxpayers of Idaho, an industry lobby, said "Idaho must take advantage of every opportunity of development available." Bart Brassey of the Associated Industries complained that Idaho already had a million acres of wilderness in the Selway-Bitterroot, another 1.5 million acres being considered in the Idaho and Salmon River Breaks primitive areas, plus 200,000 acres in the Sawtooth Primitive Area. The mining industry could not grow or remain a major contributor to the economy "unless it can mine important minerals where they are found and when they are found."

Ernie Day's clash with the governor and his resignation from the Parks Board dramatized the conflict, and made news across the state. The next day in Idaho Falls the Forest Service heard 60 speakers. Fifty opposed the road, including representatives of the Greater Sawtooth Preservation Council, Idaho Alpine Club, Southeastern Rod and Gun Club of Pocatello, Bonneville County Sportsmen's Association and the Idaho Falls Chapter of the League of Women Voters. An Idaho State University student, Randy Patterson of Carey, submitted an anti-road petition with 249 signatures. From Wyoming came representatives of the Sierra Club, the Wilderness Society and the Jackson Hole Conservation Forum. Mayor S. Eddie Pedersen of Idaho Falls called for change in the mining laws to allow a choice of preserving such an area.

Miners and Challis business owners backed the mine, saying it was difficult to support the economy and provide public services in Custer County with 96 per cent of the land in public ownership. Two East Fork Salmon River ranchers spoke against the mine. The Forest Service invited people to submit letters until June 1, saying a decision on the road would be made "in the near future." Another public hearing was scheduled for Challis.[28]

On May 11, the Statesman's headline over a lengthy editorial said: "A Sacrifice Idaho Needn't Make" The editorial said that "Idaho should not lock up millions of acres from mining. But it ought to be able to protect a very few relatively small, exceptionally high quality areas (such) as the White Clouds. Mining and recreation should learn to work together and neither should attempt to lay claim to every acre of mountain terrain in the state." Molybdenum, said the Statesman, is in abundant supply and 25 per cent of U.S. production was exported while new mines were being added in Canada, the United States and South America. "Governor Samuelson said that mining and recreation use could coexist. But it seems obvious that an open pit mine from which 20,000 tons of material is taken daily and processed with over 99.5 percent of it deposited in a waste pile or settling pond, is going to have a tremendous impact. Such a waste deposit would grow at the rate of six million tons per year. A similar molybdenum mine at Climax, Colorado has seen half a mountain removed and put into a settling pond that is measured in miles. Colorado's hikers, fishermen, campers, picnickers, hunters and seekers after scenic grandeur go elsewhere." Also as population grows and industry expands "the value of unique areas like the White Clouds to the people of the state will multiply."[29]

The Twin Falls Times-News ran a front page editorial chastising the governor for backing the mine and called on the congressional delegation to get moving on the Sawtooth Recreation Area bill. The Lewiston Tribune said the tide had turned in Idaho, in favor of preserving "most of the hunting, fishing and scenic riches of the state in its present form." The Post-Register endorsed a suspension of all mining entries until the Forest Service completed its study. Robb Brady reminded readers that other Americans also had a stake in public land: "Not only people in Idaho but the unnumbered thousands outside of Idaho who were not at the information meetings in Boise or Idaho Falls will demonstrate in the future that there is an economic benefit in recreation dollars for the Challis area as well as all of Idaho."[30]

By the end of May, most of the state's dailies, plus some of the weeklies, were on record against the mine. The dailies included the Statesman, Lewiston Tribune, Pocatello's Idaho State Journal, the Blackfoot News, the Post-Register and the Times-News. Former Governor Smylie joined the debate against a mine with a column in the Intermountain Observer as did former State Senator and 1966 candidate for governor Perry Swisher: "In the 19th century, to the nation, the Far West was more to be mined than lived in. Almost everybody who came West was a miner. Some dug gold and silver and copper. Others mined timber and grass and soil and water. Or lived on those who did." wrote Swisher. "Now Samuelson has come out in favor of the rape that, if it succeeds, could set the pattern to finish the demolition for which 19th century vandals were too meagerly equipped."[31]

Mine supporters stepped up their public relations campaign. The retired manager of Food Machinery Corporation's mining department, Ot Power of Pocatello, wrote a 3-part series for the Statesman: "Has it occurred to you that certain people – federal bureaucrats, outside conservationists and others would like to see Idaho with its preponderance of federal land locked up like a great big game preserve or tourist trap? Some of these people contribute nothing to our state. Tourism could well be overdone – overemphasized. It's a 3-month deal. Many tourists come to Idaho with a dirty shirt and a $10 bill – and don't change either one of them," said Power. "Should the recreationists dictate the future course of our state's economy? Out of the 700,000 people in our state, how many back packers really see the White Clouds area? Would it be 50, 100 or 500 each year? Infinitesimal – and this number shouldn't have the power to set our rules and regulations."[32]

Woody Bean's letter to the editor reported that the Cascade Chamber of Commerce had voted unanimously in favor of the mine. Bean complained that a 2-year study wasn't needed before approval of the road: "We know first hand in Valley County what a crash followed the closing down of our mineral development in the back country."[33]

Joe Jemmett of the J. R. Simplot Company's mineral division said the land belonged to neither the mining industry nor the "recreationist cult. Do they wish to set aside this vast wonderland for the benefit of the few who possess the time and money necessary for its enjoyment or would they rather see it developed so they might enjoy its bounty?" Very few people got to the area and a road would open the way for many more, wrote Jemmett. A mine would add to the Idaho tax base, perhaps allowing better pay for teachers. "Let us get with it now before they become discouraged and abandon the whole idea in favor of a project in a less hostile climate, say in Lower Slobbovia."[34]

John Merriam attacked the economic argument, describing mining as a declining industry. Idaho mining jobs declined from 5,800 in 1940 to 3,400 in 1960: "While the value of mining production is increasing, there is every reason to believe that job opportunities in the industry will continue to decline," he wrote. Income from mining production was $68 million in 1961 but Idahoans received only $20 million with the rest going out of state, he wrote. Mining now accounted for only 1.5 percent of Idaho employment and personal income. "This industry would seem a poor candidate to hang the hopes for economic development in Idaho." Al Teske fired back, describing mining as a pillar of the Idaho economy and calling "incredible" the suggestion that it was a declining industry.[35]

Russell Brown responded to Jemmett with a point-by-point rebuttal. The issue was not unlimited mining versus abolition of the industry: "We can see the Chamber of Commerce brochures now. Come to Idaho and enjoy our scenic mine dumps. If all the revenue from such a mine went to teacher salaries, would it be as much as $2 a month? The arguments, strife and rancor are shadows beside the main issue," said Brown. "Idaho is what the rest of the world would like to be – and can't. Do we want to keep it that way or not? When this New York corporation has taken their profits and left for greener pastures, what will be left? A Castle besieged and pillaged? A vast scar on our land? Paradise lost?"[36]

Another response came from H. Tom Davis. The area was neither vast nor inaccessible and recreation use was not limited to the wealthy, he wrote. It was a crescent shaped area only four miles across and 10 miles long, accessed by six roads ending from two to six miles from the apex of the ridge touching most of the White Cloud peaks. "Last year I hiked in the peaks area for eight days for a total cost of less than $50, including food and equipment, but excluding transportation to the area. The people I saw ranged from Boy Scouts to men in their 50s, so the range of potential 'favored few' visitors is quite large."[37]

"Mining is liquidation," wrote Ted Trueblood. "You clean up and get out – and the scars last forever. A billion tourists could look at Castle Peak and still not wear it out. The history of mining in the West is an unvarying story of western wealth being taken to the East. The history of Idaho's rapidly growing tourist business is a story, equally unvarying, of eastern money coming to the West."[38]

In Washington members of the congressional delegation were hearing from Idahoans. Senator Church said it would be necessary to extend the boundaries of the proposed Sawtooth Recreation Area to include the White Clouds: "I am mindful of the need to work with Senator Jordan and Representative Hansen on this," Church said. "The important thing is to save this magnificent country." Jordan, while expressing concern over environmental damage with mining, was keeping his options open until he had more facts.

Church, Jordan and Hansen had submitted questions to the Forest Service. Chief Edward P. Cliff wrote that the agency had no authority to prohibit or restrict actual mining operations on a valid mining claim or to regulate or control the type of mining involved. No regulations had been promulgated to let the Forest Service control prospecting methods or to prohibit ingress and egress to and from a valid mining claim. But it could consider alternatives to roads.

"The Forest Service would have no authority to regulate or control the location of mill buildings or 'slag piles' as long as they are within the boundaries of valid mining claims or mill sites," Cliff said. As to withdrawals, the Forest Service had authority to withdraw small amounts of land from mineral entry for administrative purposes but counsel advised "that it would be highly questionable if we attempted to have the Forest Service land withdrawn in the White Clouds Peaks area" for such a purpose. And withdrawal could not "abrogate a valid mining claim" previously located. In other words, the Forest Service could do nothing.[39]

Washington correspondent Tom Ochiltree wrote that Church was considering the possibility of including the summit areas in a Sawtooth-White Clouds national park, leaving the valley land under management of the Forest Service as a recreation area. Ochiltree described the White Clouds fight as reminiscent of the campaign that led to designation of a North Cascades National Park in Washington State in 1968.[40]

The Greater Sawtooth Preservation Council had good and bad news for its members. The hearing testimony showed that "Idaho does not want roads and open pit mines in the heart of its mountain scenery." Church had spoken out against the mine and "is with us, the others are still on the fence." There were added threats. "J. R. Simplot Company has been exploring for molybdenum on Rock Creek, seven miles inside the Sawtooth Primitive Area near Atlanta. Williams Mining Coompany of Boise is planning to develop molybdenum deposits on Roaring River near Atlanta. Another firm is exploring deposits at the mouth of Big Pine Creek on the South Fork of the Payette River." There were rumors of a big mining operation to go into Box Canyon by Stanhope Peak in the Pioneer Mountains. "Idaho stands to lose a great deal more than the White Clouds unless people like yourself make their voices heard."[41]

Ernie Day displayed this photo of mining exploration damage on Railroad Ridge at a Forest Service hearing in 1969.

In late June came more alarming news. Ernie Day's photos taken on his latest flight over the White Clouds revealed the presence of buildings newly erected near Frog Lake. Someone else was exploring for minerals. Day's discovery led to an announcement by Vernon Taylor and Associates of Denver that it was also working in the Little Boulder Creek drainage. The company had filed 150 claims around Frog Lake and Little Boulder Lake Number One.

John Merriam sent off another letter to editors: "Although ASARCO's proposed open pit mine at Baker Lake would be tragic by itself, it is clear that a much larger area of the White Clouds is in danger of being destroyed by mining operations. Should the Forest Service grant the permit for an access road, the entire basin of Little Boulder Creek will be open for prospecting by bulldozer. Unfortunately the door is still open for other firms to join ASARCO and Taylor. The Greater Sawtooth Preservation Council urges the people of Idaho to voice their feelings on the impending destruction of this wilderness area. A wave of public protest to Idaho's congressional delegation is perhaps our last chance to prevent a disaster in the White Clouds."[42]

Meeting at Island Park, directors of the Idaho Wildlife Federation called on Congress to reform the mining law and do what the Forest Service was refusing to do, withdraw land in the White Clouds from further mineral entry: "Why should minerals be treated in any different manner than such other natural resources as oil or timber in which the government retains full control over exploitation?" asked IWF President Franklin Jones.[43]

The director of the Rocky Mountain Center on Environment, Roger Hansen of Denver, wrote Ernie Day offering to go into the area with Idaho conservationists and to act as a mediator with ASARCO. Day rejected any thought of compromise: "The issue is not *how* to develop the mine, but *whether* to develop the mine in the White Clouds." A mine was unthinkable. "If ASARCO is really desirous of 'cleaning up' their operations on an esthetic basis, they should offer their claims to the public through the federal government at a realistic figure. After the pitch by their representatives made to, and bought by our governor, the only way they can 'fence mend'' would be to withdraw from the area."

Day wrote that the issue was further complicated by the Taylor claims all around Little Boulder Lake Number One: "This, I think, makes any effort to work anything out with ASARCO even less practical. In my opinion, we must push for better mining laws and perhaps inclusion of this area in the National Parks. I have not as yet advocated this but with all of this mining activity in the White Clouds and the Sawtooths, this is beginning to look like the only real solution."

Also, Day added, there was little to gain from a trip into the area since all, or nearly all, of the conservationists were familiar with it "and the few who are not familiar with it have plans to see it in the immediate future." Hansen received a similar response from John Merriam.[44]

With the Forest Service saying it could not regulate mining in the White Clouds under existing law, Church was able to persuade Jordan and Hansen to join his effort to expand the proposed 351,000-acre Sawtooth National Recreation Area with a 157,000-acre White Clouds addition. On July 2, Church and Jordan introduced the White Clouds amendment in the Senate. It would not prevent an ASARCO mine but would give the Forest Service authority to regulate mining on any claim not yet patented, said Church. Holders of valid claims already possessed the right to mine.

Church hoped ASARCO would proceed "in such a way as to cause a minimum of adverse impact." He said he had been assured by top executives that they would make their operating plans "as compatible as possible with other resource values." Jordan said the NRA legislation made it possible to harmonize mining and recreation with "reasonable requirements" for the use and restoration of the surface and for protection of water quality.

Church reminded the Senate that the NRA legislation was the culmination of many years of work, including hearings both in Idaho and Washington and had twice been reported favorably by the Senate Interior and Insular Affairs Committee. The Senate gave the amended bill unanimous approval. The White Clouds amendment didn't satisfy Ernie Day or the leaders of the Greater Sawtooth Preservation Council because it left the door open to an ASARCO mine.[45]

As snow melted in the mountains, opening the trails, Idahoans began going into the White Clouds. Among the July visitors were Church, his 12-year-old sons Forrest and Chase and his old friend Stanley Burns. The Forest Service provided a helicopter to fly them in, passing over the ASARCO claims en route to the Little Boulder chain lakes.

"We fished in each of these sparkling alpine lakes which reach upward like liquid stones in an emerald necklace to a pinnacle elevation of over 10,600 feet. We completed our trip with a backpack hike through the verdant high mountain meadows now being staked out and claimed by mining companies," Church said. He said he "was more convinced than ever that failure to add the White Clouds to the Sawtooth NRA legislation would be a crime against nature." While he again talked about the desirability of mining with regulation, now he said it was the duty of the Forest Service to explore all other methods of access, including a railway or tramway. "A road to the heart of the White Clouds must destroy everything that is precious and unique about them. Their virginity would be lost overnight."[46]

On July 10, Church, Jordan and Hansen spoke for the Senate passed Sawtooth NRA bill, with the White Clouds amendment, before the National Parks and Recreation Subcommittee of the House Interior Committee. They hoped that Rep. James McClure, a member of the subcommittee, would join them. Instead McClure told the committee that, on the basis of present information, he could not support the White Clouds addition. [47] It might prevent Idaho from reaping the rewards of great mineral wealth, he said. "Mineral values in the White Clouds may stagger the imagination. There is a prospect that the ore body of molybdenum there may amount to at least 70 million tons, and it is reasonable to expect that it might be two or even three times that large. The worth of this ore could be somewhere between $500 million and $1,500 million." McClure questioned whether "Idaho can afford to lock up mineral lodes of such potential abundance common throughout the White Clouds."

And there had been no congressional hearings on the White Clouds amendment in Idaho or elsewhere. McClure had urged the House subcommittee to act on Orval Hansen's NRA bill but he would not support the Senate passed version with the White Clouds amendment. Mining industry lobbyists also weighed in, opposing inclusion of the White Clouds in the national recreation area. They were concerned that the regulatory authority given the Forest Service on future claims would interfere with mining.[47]

While ASARCO spokesmen had said initially that they could live with the White Clouds amendment, they later had second thoughts. Forest Service Chief Ed Cliff endorsed the legislation. Congressman Hansen spoke for the bill with the White Clouds included. "We need to act promptly to prevent unsightly development in the (Sawtooth) valley from blocking present breath-taking views." And there was no control over prospecting in the White Clouds. "Anyone who can rent a bulldozer can come in and dig into the mountainside looking for minerals. The scars left are permanent," said Hansen. Joining McClure and mining spokesmen in opposing the bill was the Greater Sawtooth Preservation Council. The council sent a telegram asking the subcommittee to reject it in favor of a combined national park-national recreation area proposal, which the council was developing.[48]

McClure's stand drew criticism from the Statesman, Post-Register and Lewiston Tribune: "Thanks largely to McClure a black cloud hangs over the White Clouds," declared the Tribune. The Twin Falls Times-News supported the White Clouds amendment but said McClure's position was understandable since he represented the Coeur d'Alene mining district. The Post-Register also chided the GSPC for opposing the "quickest and best route" to reasonable management of the Sawtooth and White Clouds areas.[49]

McClure's opposition left in doubt the prospect of any Congressional action on the White Clouds in 1969. But, responding to questions from Statesman Managing Editor Dick Hronek, he sounded as if he was softening his stand. McClure said he couldn't support the amendment without hearings on the White Clouds or passage of enough time to allow both sides to comment. He was pressing for House committee hearings. He said the mining community feared the Forest Service could use its discretion to make present valid mining claims and prospecting uneconomic, creating a de facto ban on all mining in the area. If the mineral values were as great as portrayed, he would be very reluctant to exclude their development. He was not yet ready to give a flat yes or no to the White Clouds amendment. McClure hoped the White Clouds controversy would not delay the original Sawtooth NRA proposal. And while he had given some thought to a national park "the changing climate of use in that part of Idaho means we don't have time to waste in gathering support for national park status."[50]

The summer cavalcade of White Clouds visitors included members of the Greater Sawtooth Preservation Council, the Idaho Alpine Club, high school students, reporters, photographers and others curious to learn what all the fuss was about.

The GSPC's Merriam said exploration damage was more extensive than conservationists had realized and would leave permanent scars: "A whole hillside logged off hardly seems a mere prospecting operation." There were 12 buildings plus "a good deal of industrial waste. We understand that overburden (material on top of the ore which must be removed before mining begins) is running 400 to 800 feet deep" and some of the drill rigs had not reached the end of the overburden. Merriam said conservationists were not in agreement on a solution, "going off in all directions." But the best hope might be a lawsuit to prevent the Forest Service from issuing a road-building permit on a permanent basis, on grounds that recreation values would be substantially impaired.[51]

Statesman photographer David Frazier walked in on the Little Boulder Creek trail, joining up with Idaho Alpine Club hikers from Idaho Falls. They observed survey stakes marking the possible route of the road. Frazier reported that the creek teemed with cutthroat and eastern brook trout. They camped near the trail and Frazier reported on their campfire conversation.

"As an ex-mining engineer, I can see no other place except this creek and meadow for a settling pond," said Bill Richardson. "When you let someone put in a mine, there is nothing but a hole in the ground and a dirty stream when you finish," said Joe Gasidlo, a Detroit native who said he had fallen in love with the Idaho wilderness. The next day Frazier visited the ASARCO camp. Asked about relations with the hikers, geologist Greg Prescott said: "We haven't had any helicopters shot down yet." After visiting a drill site, Frazier was given a ride on the helicopter back to the east fork.[52]

The Statesman's Walter Johnson and wife, Clara, hiked in to Frog Lake in August with four companions for a week of camping and exploring. The party included Jim Humbird of the Fish and Game Department and his daughter, Michelle. They met James Hoxie of Boise who said he had camped in the White Clouds for 13 years. Hoxie believed the daily helicopter traffic near Castle Peak had chased most of the bighorn sheep and mountain goats to new habitat. Johnson said that "Hoxie reminisced over fabulous deer hunting after storms when 800 deer bunched on Railroad Ridge, the 8-pound trout that he had landed in Frog Lake, the trophy bighorn rams that he had stalked in the peaks."

With Forest Service permission the ASARCO crew had managed to "walk" a bulldozer in to its camp, an operation that took two days. "A bulldozed road carves through the trees from the mining camp straight up the mountain," Johnson said. A sign welcomed visitors. "Little Boulder Camp, Unincorporated, Recreation Unlimited." There was information: $2 million to be spent on exploration, a $70 million investment required before a pound of molybdenum is delivered; only one in 10,000 investigations of mineral properties prove profitable; three drills are operating to obtain samples; the plywood shanty camp sits in the center of the molybdenum deposits.

Johnson found the mine crew courteous and helpful. The helicopter pilot gave them a ride back to their camp, two at a time, and a key to allow them to use his boat at Frog Lake. Willis Titmus of Homedale, one of their party, used the boat to hook 100 fish in two days, releasing all but a 15-incher that went into the frying pan. Johnson reported that the trip had cost an average of only $6.75 per day per person, including the $28 per person cost of hiring a packer who carried their gear eight miles up the trail to Frog Lake. This was a rebuttal to mining advocates who said that only the wealthy could get into the White Clouds.[53]

Later in the month Jim and Michelle Humbird returned with Statesman editorial page editor Ken Robison. On the Big Boulder Creek trail they met a horse rider, Charles McAbery, Forest Service patrolman for the White Clouds. McAbery accompanied them to Walker Lake, where they camped for the night. The next day they explored the picturesque Big Boulder Lakes and hiked over two ridges to the Tin Cup Lakes.[54]

One of the people working in the White Clouds was Bill Platts, regional fishery biologist for the Forest Service. He was inventorying, studying and naming lakes. In early August, Platts found that the Vernon Taylor crew had a drill rig operating at a lake he had named Willow, the lowest of 12 lakes in the Little Boulder chain, and was pumping "drilling mud," a mixture of bentonite and drill tailings, into the lake. About one-fourth of the lake had turned chalky white. The crew proceeded even after being warned by Fish and Game Biologist Mel Reingold of Salmon that its drilling operation would almost certainly pollute the lake and Little Boulder Creek. Even though he didn't know if he had legal authority to do it, Platts ordered Wallace Fulghum, engineer in charge, to shut down the operation. When Fulghum objected, he said: "You have your choice. You can shut down or continue and see if I have the authority."[55]

Bill Platts

The drilling continued. After receiving a report from Fulghum, Taylor spokesmen complained to members of Congress who complained to the chief of the Forest Service. A few days later when Platts returned to his Boise home, his wife advised him that the deputy regional forester had left a message directing him to report to Ogden immediately.

"We have a problem in the White Clouds," the message said. It sounded as if he was about to be fired. Platts called some environmental friends to let them know what was happening, then drove through the night to reach Ogden. When he reported, he learned that phone calls had been received on his behalf and he still had a job. Platts believed one of the callers was Bill Meiners of Boise. He had met Meiners and his wife, Lynne, in the White Clouds earlier in the summer. While Platts still had a job, the Taylor crew was still pumping bentonite and tailings into the lake at the rate of a ton a day and the Forest Service was doing nothing about it.

The state of Idaho had legal authority to act. Putting a pollutant into a lake or stream was a violation of state law. The Department of Health and Welfare sent Gordon Hopson of Pocatello to confront the Taylor crew. On August 8, accompanied by Platts and Fish and Game conservation officer James Gannaway, Hopson told Fulghum to stop polluting the lake. Fulghum replied that the bentonite was harmless, "you can drink it, and you can eat it." Yes, said Gannaway, but it would seal the bottom of the lake, leaving it barren of aquatic life. Fulghum said that the discussion was meaningless. If molybdenum was discovered the lake wouldn't be there. It would be drained and replaced by an open pit.[56]

Hopson gave Fulghum a week to stop polluting the lake and asked the Forest Service to report to him on compliance with the order. After a week, Dan Pence, district Forest Service ranger at Clayton, found that nothing had changed: "Mr. Fulghum told me that as far as he was concerned there was nothing harmful in the material discharging into the lake and he did not believe any damage was being done."

Three days later the Forest Service's White Clouds ranger, Charles McAbery, radioed a report to Pence that the bentonite was still going into the lake. It was now one-half to three-fourths milky white. Hopson contacted the Custer County prosecutor, Willis Benjamin, asking him to seek a court injunction. Benjamin did nothing. "I understand the situation isn't that serious. Too many people are screaming bloody murder," he said. Media reports finally made a difference. On August 20, 12 days after Hopson's order, McAbery radioed Pence that the Taylor crew was now recycling the bentonite and very little was going into the lake. It was only one-third milky white and was clearing.[57]

While the Taylor crew was polluting Willow Lake, the Idaho Mining Association was meeting in Pocatello. Conferees heard a blistering attack on White Clouds defenders from William R. Green, mining engineer for the Idaho Bureau of Mines and Geology. Green described the ASARCO find as one of the most significant in the state in many years and complained that the requested road had been contested by "hysterical preservationists. During the next few months this group, assisted by people from outside the state, began a scare campaign in the state press aimed at prohibiting all mining in the area. Blatantly prejudiced individuals were interviewed, crews of cameramen were sent into the area to try to catch exploration teams doing something that could be considered as wrong."

The publicity succeeded, said Green, because three of the four members of the Idaho congressional delegation now supported adding the White Clouds to the proposed Sawtooth Recreation Area.[58]

As the summer progressed, more Idahoans were discovering the White Clouds. Ranger McAbery estimated that there had been 800 visitors from June 30 to late August, nearly all Idahoans. About 40 percent were back packers, 30 percent rode horses and 30 percent rode scooters or trail bikes. Much of the area was inaccessible to the motorbikes but they could get to the popular Frog Lake.

Governor Samuelson stepped up his campaign for the mine. At a national governor's conference in Seattle he chastised the Forest Service for publicizing the road request and for conducting hearings. Speaking directly to Ed Cliff, chief of the Forest Service, he said, "If the agency had issued a permit for the road and not held hearings, there would be no controversy and people would not be stirred up all over the nation." Samuelson described the area below Castle Peak as having "nothing but sagebrush on one side and scraggly trees on the other."[59]

His comments generated a flurry of critical calls and letters to the governor's office. The governor was flailed in a Statesman editorial accompanied by a photo of the canyon and the mountain: "If the canyon is as scraggly and ugly as the governor says it is, maybe it won't make a difference if it becomes the site for a massive tailing pond spreading out across the valley floor along with a mill and an open pit." And, "It's too bad the governor has to be the chief executive of a state in which people cling to the idea that questions affecting them ought to be known and discussed." Russell Brown of the GSPC described the governor's comments as an assault on American democracy. Speaking for the Hells Canyon Preservation Council, Jerry Jayne said the governor would deny the public the right to be heard on keeping a few wild areas wild.[60]

Samuelson followed up with a press conference saying he had been "misquoted and half quoted" in Seattle and his remarks had been taken out of context. But he continued his assault on the Forest Service saying the agency misled the people of Idaho by suggesting it had authority to deny the road application. The meetings "actually and lawfully were meaningless," and a "hoax" was perpetrated on the people of Idaho. Asked about Senator Church's suggestion of a railway or tramway for access, Samuelson said Church "suggests a lot of things. He doesn't give a darn about the economy of Idaho."[61]

By this time the Greater Sawtooth Preservation Council had put together and sent to the congressional delegation its concept of a 1.3 million-acre combined national park and national recreation area including the Sawtooth, White Cloud, Boulder and Pioneer mountains. The pastoral valley lands would have recreation area status while the peaks would be under Park Service jurisdiction with wilderness status. "The broad protective powers of the NRA will preserve the ranching, farming, hunting and fishing of the Sawtooth and Pioneer valleys. These prime use areas, which include some of the finest hunting territory in the state, have been included in the NRA. The high mountain country, faced with imminent and irreversible mining destruction, can only be saved by park status." There was also an economic argument. A park would bring more visitors and more tourist dollars to Idaho. "Last year more than 2.5 million people visited both Yellowstone and Grand Teton National park." Over $57 million was poured into the economies of the communities surrounding Yellowstone in 1968 and annual tourist income in Teton County Wyoming was $18 million, said the GSPC.[62]

Senator Church met with GSPC directors in late July and tried to persuade them that language in the NRA bill emphasizing scenic, recreational and water quality values gave the Forest Service authority to regulate mining of existing claims. They disagreed. And they disputed the claim by mining advocates that the Park Service could do no more than the Forest Service to stop a mine. Russ Brown sent Church, Jordan and Hansen a detailed analysis, pointing out that all parks and monuments were withdrawn from further mineral entry when established except as expressly provided otherwise by legislation or executive order. Withdrawal would not eliminate existing mining claims but would bar new claims and could make it more difficult to develop existing claims, he wrote. It could prevent acquisition of a mill site. That would mean the miners would have to incur the cost of removing all excavated material. There was no right in common law or statute for access to a pre-existing mineral claim across a national park or monument, Brown wrote, but with the NRA bill mineral rights could be expanded indefinitely. The White Clouds "could be mined out of existence." Its passage would "only put an official stamp of approval on the wreckage." Brown saw no merit in a strategy of passing the NRA bill with the possibility of park legislation to follow. Having approved an NRA, Congress was unlikely to approve a park.[63]

The GSPC's position was supported by analysis done by a Park Service attorney and provided by Paul Fritz, superintendent of the Craters of the Moon National Monument. A native of Yonkers, N.Y., Fritz studied at Utah State University and the University of Arizona. After Air Force service in 1958, he joined the Forest Service as a landscape architect in the Salmon Forest. There he was credited with stopping a road-building program in the approaches to the Big Horn Crags. Hired by the Park Service in 1961 as a landscape architect at the Flaming Gorge National Recreation Area in Colorado, he also worked at Canyonlands and Arches national parks and Natural Bridges National Monument before coming to Idaho.[64]

Fritz sent a copy of the legal analysis to Bruce Bowler with a note: "Here are some sneaky questions showing how the N.R.A. bill is weak. If questioned in the courts, the results could actually aid the opposition."[65]

John Merriam also sent a copy to Bowler describing it as the basis "of our contention that a park will save the White Clouds and vicinity. This was done by a NPS lawyer but we obviously can't publicize that aspect." The Park Service analysis said the Forest Service already had legal authority to regulate mining. The NRA bill would weaken that authority, allowing regulation only with claims filed after it was established. Rather than withdrawing the NRA from further mineral entry, it allowed unlimited additional claims. The NRA bill would reduce, not enhance, protection of the White Clouds and Sawtooths.[66]

Responding to opposition, ASARCO's chief geologist announced that the company was prepared to put up a bond or create a sinking fund to assure rehabilitation of the area disturbed by a mine. John Collins said the company was "anxious and willing" to maintain lines of communication with conservationists in Idaho. "We are willing to sit down and talk about our project and what we can do within reason to accommodate the desires of conservationists in planning the mine." Collins said that ASARCO had not supplied the $1 billion figure being used by Samuelson as the potential output of a mine. Until the mineralized zone was fully defined, he said $100 million might be an appropriate figure. And he rejected the suggestions of a railway to remove the ore or a tramway to provide access.[67]

Ernie Day responded: "The real question is not how to mine the scenic White Clouds country around Castle Peak, but whether to mine at all." As to a bond or sinking fund for restoration, "no amount of money can replace the beauty of the high cirques and alpine lakes in anything like their natural condition. You just can't sweep 20,000 tons of tailings a day under the rug." And, even if the $100 million figure were correct, "Idaho would net only a fraction of that. Projected over a long period, the scenic grandeur of the area is worth more in dollars and cents than a one-time one-use destruction."[68]

McClure defended his opposition to the White Clouds amendment in his summer newsletter. After repeating his estimate of possible economic impact of an ASARCO mine he added: "But if the claims are untrue, it would be equally wrong to disturb the area. For these reasons I am trying to find all the facts and give all parties a chance to be heard. I am also trying to develop legislative language to solve the problem." McClure said he had asked the committee to act without delay on the House Sawtooth NRA bill. "I am also doing everything possible to have the Committee give full consideration to the White Clouds proposal so that a decision can be made there, too."[69]

The mining industry showed its gratitude to Samuelson with a party in his honor at the home of Henry Day on Lake Coeur d'Alene. John Corlett, the Statesman's political editor, wrote that one possible purpose was to suggest to potential rivals that Samuelson would be well financed and difficult to beat in a 1970 primary election: "The word has gone around that the mining industry will make certain that Samuelson need not worry about campaign funds in his bid for re-election next year."[70]

In September, House Interior Committee Chairman Wayne Aspinall said he was suspending consideration of all bills to designate park or recreation areas because of concern about the cost of land acquisition. There would be no Sawtooth legislation in 1969. The Statesman said Aspinall's decision made no sense for the Sawtooth-White Clouds because land acquisition costs would be minimal, with purchase of scenic easements on 23,000 acres and acquisition of only 700 acres. [71] Aspinall's position was in line with that of Robert Mayo, President Nixon's budget director, who advised him that there was little prospect of increased funding from the Land and Water Conservation Fund for three or four years. Funding had been cut from $200 million to $124 million for fiscal 1970, with acquiescence of House and Senate appropriations committees, even though 1968 legislation provided for annual funding of $200 million through 1973 with added Outer Continental Mineral Leasing receipts to be used to make up any difference between normal income to the fund and $200 million.[72]

Samuelson continued his criticism of the Forest Service. Speaking in Idaho Falls, he said "the administration of the Forest Service in this district stinks to high heaven." He accused the agency of trying to block the ASARCO mine. At a recent meeting of governors in Colorado Springs, the governor said he had corrected a statement by Chief Forester Ed Cliff that the mine would be in the center of the White Clouds. Cliff had apologized, he said. "Mr. Cliff is an honorable man."[73] While Samuelson was speaking in Idaho Falls, Ernie Day was addressing the Boise Rotary Club, saying mining in the White Clouds would be "a crime against nature." Day said the man in the most strategic position was Rep. James McClure. "McClure, if he would get back of the amendment, weak as it is, could help some."[74]

The governor took his crusade for the mine to Washington, meeting with Agriculture Secretary Clifford Hardin to urge approval of the road. Five days later, he told county officials in Burley that a road permit would be issued "as soon as the engineering is completed." Also he said he was assured that "there will not again be misrepresentation." The Forest Service had deceived the people of Idaho by saying the proposed mine was in the center of the White Clouds area.[75]

Alex Smith, assistant regional forester for information and education in Ogden, denied that a road decision had been made, saying Governor Samuelson had been informed that a decision would be made in the fall. The question was still under study. "Regardless of what the decision is, when a decision is made we will announce it." Smith also responded to the governor's repeated complaints of Forest Service deception. "It has never been clear what the governor has inferred to be misrepresentation," said Smith. "We have made every effort from the beginning of the announcement of the public information meetings to correctly and factually present the true situation. At this point we are not aware of any misrepresentation knowingly or unknowingly done."[76]

Four days later the Forest Service issued a 9-page report, saying a road route had been located by the engineering firm employed by ASARCO but had not been presented to the agency. Permission to locate a possible route "does not imply that the need for road access has been recognized. When presented, the design will be evaluated. Both the location and design are subject to modification as needed to meet Forest Service requirements to protect other resource uses and values if a road is approved." As to requests that the Forest Service withdraw the area from mineral entry, the General Counsel advised "that it would be highly questionable that the large acreage of the White Clouds could be withdrawn. It could not, in any event, abrogate a valid mining claim previously located within the area." Valid unpatented claims could be eliminated only by voluntary relinquishment or by federal acquisition. Meanwhile the Forest Service "is working – with varying degrees of success – to encourage prospectors and miners to provide maximum feasible protection to other resource values."[77]

Three days later, Floyd Iverson reported that Forest Service mining engineers had found that a significant number of ASARCO's claims were definitely valid. "The full extent of the ore body has not been determined but more than 140 claims have been staked." Data and exploration work indicated that a "very sizable" additional quantity of ore was likely involved. As exploration continued, further examinations would be necessary to determine the validity of other claims, said Iverson. It was anticipated that a decision on an access road would be made before the end of the year, following receipt of a report on the feasibility of using a tramway as an alternative.[78]

On the same day Samuelson again called on the Forest Service to "obey the laws" and issue a road permit. Samuelson said ASARCO had proved its claims and informed him the value would run over a billion dollars. "The more they drill the better it looks." The governor released a letter to Thomas Cowden, assistant secretary of agriculture, calling for an investigation to reverse Forest Service policies that were "detrimental to the economic, social and environmental conditions of the people of Idaho." Rather than following the law, the Forest Service had responded "to pressures against mineral development."[79]

No road permit was forthcoming. In late October, ASARCO issued a statement saying the company would delay filing final plans for an access road until completion of further studies: "For the immediate future we propose to conduct a number of ecological studies of the area involving ecologists, an agronomist and hydrologist, fishery and wildlife experts and a landscape architect. We have received a preliminary report with recommendations from Dr. Beatrice Willard of the Thorne Ecological Foundation of Boulder, Colo. In addition – at our request –a team of specialists from the Forest Service's Intermountain Forest and Range Experiment Station have studied the area and have made recommendations and have provided guidelines on revegetation. This program was initiated in September. Under the circumstances, we have notified the Forest Service that final engineering plans for the proposed access road to the claims will not be filed until some later date. The final design will take account of the special conditions of the area."

Future planning would include "choice of a plant site and mining and waste disposal methods designed to assure the least practical impact of the mine development on the natural characteristics and ecology of the area."[80]

Speaking to mining students in Moscow in December, Keith Whiting acknowledged growing concern for the environment. He estimated a 20-year life for the mine with $50 million in value produced – far less than the $1 billion figure used repeatedly by Gov. Samuelson.[81]

Another threat to the White Clouds was revealed in November, a second request for a mining road. In August, five Pocatello employees of the J.R. Simplot Company filed 12 claims on about 240 acres in the Quicksand Meadows area in the Big Boulder Creek drainage, two miles from Island Lake and about four miles from the Livingston Mill. The Forest Service received the road request shortly after the claims were recorded in September. A spokesman, Edward Hansen, said the group had formed a limited partnership, the Meadow Valley Mining Group. He said the Simplot Company had no financial interest in the claims. No explanation was given for the Forest Service's delay in revealing the road request. This new threat generated more press coverage and more editorials calling for Congressional action.[82]

As the year ended the defenders could claim credit for temporarily saving the White Clouds. A barrage of news releases, letters and testimony had generated media coverage and won public support. Many more Idahoans had joined the movement to protect the state's best natural areas. Frank Church was on record against a White Clouds mine and Senator Jordan and Orval Hansen were supporting the recreation area legislation with the White Clouds included. State Rep. Vernon Ravenscroft, D-Tuttle, had proposed state legislation to require reclamation when a mining operation ended. Governor Samuelson's campaign for the mine, with his sledge hammer rhetoric and attacks on the Forest Service had so far failed. Some White Cloud defenders believed the governor had helped them. His assertion that there should have been no hearings had created a backlash and his exaggeration of the mine's potential economic benefits had been exposed. At the beginning of the year ASARCO executives were confident of success. They were now on the defensive, proclaiming their intention to prepare a less damaging mining plan.

Ernie Day, with his photos, his dramatic clash with the governor and his consistent stand against any mine, had done more than anyone else to make the White Clouds a defining public policy issue. Thousands of Idahoans had seen his images of the peaks and lakes. He and Samuelson had spent the year marching across the Idaho stage, describing their contrasting visions of the state's future. The Greater Sawtooth Preservation Council had mobilized opposition and was helping make the White Clouds a national issue. GSPC directors summarized the year's developments in their October newsletter: On the bright side, no road had been started. "Last March the company had applied for their road permit with the bulldozers scheduled to roll by May. Stop a billion-dollar mining company in a period of eight weeks? They said it couldn't be done." GSPC members had taken a writer and photographer for Life magazine into the White Clouds in early September. "These people are sympathetic to conservation problems and their article will bring the issue to millions of readers."

Vice President Russ Brown flew to San Francisco for a presentation to directors of the Sierra Club. Brown would have an article in the November Sierra Club Bulletin. GSPC director Boyd Norton was now a full time employee of the Wilderness Society in Denver and the society would be a valuable source of support. The National Wildlife Federation was preparing to go to court if the road permit was granted. "There is optimism that such a suit can win; this would be a landmark decision establishing that mining companies must respect the public interest."[83]

On the not so bright side, members of the Idaho congressional delegation seemed to feel that the NRA bill was the best that could be achieved. "The bill clearly is not enough. Existing mining claims (and there are thousands of these) are subject to no controls. The lands are left open to future prospecting and new mining. The NRA bill would allow the Sawtooths and White Clouds to be "quite literally torn to pieces." With the NRA bill stalled "the door is open for a bill strong enough to do the job." The most depressing news was the amount of new claim staking. "Virtually all of the White Clouds are now staked. The activity has spread to the Pioneers and the Sawtooths as well; even the area near Little Redfish Lake is claimed. If this region is going to be kept intact, action must come very soon; in two or three years there won't be much scenery to preserve."

The Intermountain-Observer named Castle Peak its "man of the year" and the White Clouds battle the number one Idaho news story of the year: "Of all the Idahoans who made news in 1969 – and many did – none made as much as the silent, majestic mountain range itself, symbolized by 11,820-foot Castle Peak, which presides over the scene of battle. If Idaho had a 'man of the year' for 1969, it was not a man at all, but a mountain," wrote Alice Dieter.[84]

The Statesman suggested that the "man of the year" was all of those Idahoans who had discovered the natural value of the White Clouds and had stalled plans for the ASARCO mine. The Lewiston Tribune's Bill Hall had written in July that Idaho had turned a corner in favor of conservation, of living quality over wealth.[85]

Despite the campaign of White Cloud defenders, opinion in Idaho was mixed. In a year-end report released in early January the Forest Service said it had received 800 statements and letters at and after the May hearings: "Nearly equal numbers express support and opposition for the proposed road and mineral development and for keeping the area essentially undeveloped."

Regional Forester Iverson said slightly over half favored maintaining the area in a roadless condition with 25 per cent favoring management of the peaks as a wilderness area. Principal reasons for opposing mining were damage to esthetic values, damage to anadromous and other fish and wildlife values, the need for more roadless areas, damage to water quality and the surplus of molybdenum elsewhere in the nation. Nearly half supported a road permit and strongly favored mineral development. Main reasons were to boost the economy of Custer County and the state, a need for increased industrial development and job opportunities in Idaho, present 'wild' acreages in excess of public needs and access that a road would provide for visitors to the area.

"The number of statements received is impressive but it cannot be considered as an opinion poll on which a decision can be based. Each statement has been and is being thoughtfully reviewed as it may relate to the management objectives and responsibilities of the Forest Service." Iverson said earlier in the year "we anticipated and indicated that a Forest Service decision on the road permit application would need to be reached by Forest Supervisor G.W. Carlson by the end of 1969 to avoid needless delays in the company's mining activities. ASARCO's announcement in October of plans to defer its presentation of proposed road plans to the Forest Service has changed this timetable. ASARCO officials have announced plans to further evaluate the mineralization and ecology of the White Clouds Peaks country. Their studies will continue in 1970. Our action on the road application must be deferred until plans for the proposed road are submitted by ASARCO."[86]

Donald Jackson's story in Life magazine was published January 9, 1970. Life's editors saw the battle as symbolic, reflecting growing national support for environmental protection: "This complex, bitterly fought battle between use and waste, progress and preservation, has been going on for years. It is going on today in the White Cloud Mountains."

Whiting told Jackson there would be an open pit and a tailing pond for the waste. "We'll probably elevate the level of the valley a bit. Perhaps we should say we'll rehabilitate, not restore." A Forest Service spokesman in Washington, who declined to be quoted by name, told Jackson the mining law's preference for mining made multiple use management impossible. Senator Church pointed out that any change in the mining law would probably be blocked by Wayne Aspinall, chairman of the House Interior Committee. Jackson described an imaginary boxing ring with conservationists in one corner, miners in the other and the Forest Service, which should be refereeing, hiding under the ring. "The Forest Service says it can't refuse the road," wrote Jackson. "Goodbye wilderness."[87]

Russ Brown followed up with a letter to the editor saying: "Every major conservation effort of the last decade was a lost cause at its inception." Mildred Campbell of Challis wrote that she "would welcome with open arms the mining companies or any industry which would widen our tax base." Pat Bartholomew of Ketchum felt an "unbearable ache" for the fragile land of the White Clouds but "I know, in all truth, as the law now stands, we cannot protect them from 'progress'."[88]

Chapter 12

Stopping the ASARCO mine

"It has been maintained that people have a right to harness the rivers' power, a right to harvest the timber, a right to mine the minerals. I maintain that man also has the right to enjoy the unparalleled beauty of mountains unscarred, virgin forest uncut, swift flowing streams unchecked and unpolluted and wildlife in its natural habitat." – Mrs. Karl Holte.

As 1970 began it was apparent that White Clouds mining would be a factor in the election of a governor. Three Democrats were preparing to run, 1966 nominee Cecil Andrus, Twin Falls attorney Lloyd Walker and Rep. Vernon Ravenscroft of Tuttle, author of a 1969 mine reclamation bill rejected by the legislature. Don Samuelson might also be challenged in the Republican primary.

The Greater Sawtooth Preservation Council (GSPC) would push its park plan as a substitute for a national recreation area. The National Wildlife Federation would step up efforts to convince the Forest Service that it had authority to reject a road while also making it clear that a road permit would be challenged in court. More national attention would come with stories in the New York Times and Christian Science Monitor. John Merriam's account appeared in The Living Wilderness and Merriam collaborated with Max Dahlstrom of Pocatello on a piece for the Environmental Journal. The mining threat was also described in the Sierra Club Bulletin and the National Wildlife Federation and National Parks magazines.[1]

Responding to the renewed threat of a Sawtooth Park, the Forest Service brought in Tom Kovalicky to serve as Stanley District ranger. "My job was to get this community cohesive to support the Forest Service."[2] Kovalicky had helped the Forest Service win a contest over management of the Flaming Gorge Reservoir area in northeast Utah and southwest Wyoming. He would be countering the efforts of Craters of the Moon Manager Paul Fritz.

The Forest Service printed a brochure citing the benefits of Sawtooth National Recreation Area with Forest Service management. Emphasis would be on recreation, wildlife, fisheries and scenery with continued livestock grazing, timber cutting and mining. Recreation use of the Sawtooth area had quadrupled from 1958 to 1967.[3]

H. Tom Davis organized a Boise chapter of the Greater Sawtooth Preservation Council to bolster the cause in Southwest Idaho. The GSPC Boise would be loosely affiliated with the GSPC based in Idaho Falls. Twenty-five people, including high school students, attended the February organizing meeting. Wildlife Federation veterans Ernie Day, Bruce Bowler and Stanley Burns were named to an advisory panel that included Statesman Managing Editor Dick Hronek and Doli Obee of the League of Women Voters.[4]

In November 1969, Director Tom Kimball of the National Wildlife Federation had asked Agriculture Secretary Clifford Hardin to direct the Forest Service to prepare regulations for ingress and egress to mining claims before any action was taken on the ASARCO road request. Disappointed by the response, he renewed the request, pointing out that the Boundary Waters canoe area in Minnesota was now threatened with mining exploration with heavy equipment. He also hinted at a possible lawsuit if ASARCO received a road permit.[5]

A copy of the letter went to Edward Weinberg of Los Angeles, the federation's attorney. Weinberg met with Forest Service attorneys, asking them to consider whether the test of economic feasibility could be based on individual claims rather than a grouping of claims and whether a road permit could be refused because of potential harm to salmon in the Salmon River, now being studied for wild and scenic designation. He followed up with a letter calling attention to the National Environmental Policy Act recently signed by President Nixon with its mandate to federal agencies to avoid "needless impairment and degradation of the environment." Weinberg advised Kimball that his meeting with the attorneys told him that "at least at the level of the Forest Service, ASARCO has little, if any, support."[6]

Weinberg also asked regional directors of the Bureau of Sports Fisheries and Wildlife and the Bureau of Commercial Fisheries what a White Clouds mine might mean for salmon. Kimball wrote Interior Secretary Walter Hickel a second time proposing to allow concerned citizens to challenge the validity of mining claims. Kimball said the case for change in Interior's regulations had been strengthened by the National Environmental Policy Act.[7]

In the Idaho Legislature, Senators Cecil Andrus and Diane Bilyeu proposed state regulation of open pit and strip mining. Miners would be required to provide plans to control pollution, restore disturbed areas, restore streams and avoid damage to fish, wildlife and humans, with regulation by the State Land Department. Milder legislation was proposed by Rep. Vernon Ravenscroft, requiring prior state review of mining plans and regulations for open pit mines impacting a lake or flowing stream. Even the Ravenscroft bill was too much for ASARCO and the mining industry whose spokesmen ripped into it at a committee hearing.

S. Norman Kesten of ASARCO said legislation should be framed "to minimize all damage to the surface of Idaho" rather than penalize one industry. George Atwood of Soda Springs, superintendent for Monsanto, said regulation would mean substantial cost increases and an end to phosphate mining and prospecting in Idaho. Raymond Miles of Wallace, superintendent of Day Mines, said: "if it is wrong to pollute a stream, then it is wrong whether the polluting is done by a miner, a minister or a farmer." The mining spokesmen endorsed the proposal of Governor Samuelson, a study of environmental problems related to mining. Ernie Day also spoke against the Ravenscroft bill: "This is so nebulous; it doesn't mean a thing" relating only to how mining should take place, "not whether it should take place."[8]

Day showed members of the Senate Resources Committee White Clouds slides and endorsed the Andrus-Bilyeu bill. Supporting it also were the greater Sawtooth Preservation Council, the League of Women Voters and former State Forester Roger Guernsey, who had been fired by Samuelson.

Mining spokesmen were even more adamant in opposition and were joined by Idaho Power Company and construction contractors. For 80 years mining companies dumped mine waste into the South Fork of the Coeur d'Alene River and "nobody cared very much" said ASARCO's Kesten. The practice was halted in 1968 but communities continued to dump sewage into the river. "Certain publications and individuals" had misrepresented the proposed mine, said Kesten, and the company's rehabilitation plans would make the area "at least as useful to the people of Idaho as it is today."[9]

Mining won. No legislation was passed. Instead there would be a study by a legislative committee. This approach was approved after the Senate rejected, 16-17, Ravenscroft's proposal, backed by Andrus, for a study by a special committee including legislators, representatives of the Forest Service and Bureau of Land Management, the Greater Sawtooth Preservation Council, general contractors and the mining industry. Three Republicans and 13 Democrats voted yes while 16 Republicans and one Democrat voted no. "It would appear that the Senate Republicans opposed the House passed measure because it provided for a conservation member on the study committee," wrote John Corlett.[10]

In March, Travis Roberts, acting regional director of the U.S. Fish and Wildlife Service in Portland, responded to Weinberg's questions. Chemical drainage from a White Clouds mine "could and probably would" eliminate both salmon and resident fish downstream from the mine in the East Fork of the Salmon River, he wrote. Fishery damage could extend for many miles down the main Salmon River. Also "any change in siltation, turbidity or water quality could eliminate all forms of aquatic life in the East Fork and tributaries within the area of influence of mining activity." Roberts cited research by Bill Platts showing the loss of salmon and trout to heavy metals draining from the Blackbird mine on Panther Creek. Roberts also advised that mining activity would adversely affect bighorn sheep and mountain goats.[11]

Roberts' comments were included in a Fish and Wildlife Service memorandum, an "Environmental Early Warning" that found its way to the news media. There was more. "Because of intervention by the governor's office in Idaho, agencies responsible for maintaining a good environment are unable to act."

Samuelson struck back saying it was "wild-eyed misinformation" and "a deliberate lie. We have done nothing but push for clean water and clean air." State agencies had been charged "to do it, but do it realistically." Samuelson said mining would have "absolutely no effect" on East Fork salmon. "We can stop it (pollution) before it gets there. We know we can. This is someone flying on emotions."[12]

Bruce Bowler wrote John Findley, Fish and Wildlife Service regional director, commending his office for the Roberts report and urging him not to back down. Bowler added that Samuelson's advocacy for the mine "militates against any Idaho state employee doing anything contrary to his wishes." Dr. Walt Blackadar of Salmon also wrote Findley saying state agencies had failed to protect Panther Creek: "I salute you and the federal agencies that are trying hard to protect our environment and wish you to stand firm against any amount of Samuelson's pressure."[13]

Directors of the Greater Sawtooth Preservation Council announced that they would push for introduction of their plan for a 1.3 million-acre park-national recreation area. They said the congressional delegation's NRA bill, S853, was too weak, a "sweetheart deal" accepted by ASARCO and the American Mining Congress. They believed ASARCO had deferred further exploration in the White Clouds because of financial commitments to projects in South America and lawsuits against the company involving air pollution in Tacoma, Wash., Maricopa County Arizona and El Paso, Texas. The directors approved the formation of GSPC chapters in Moscow, Ketchum and Boise.[14]

Three hundred people turned out for a White Clouds symposium and slide show sponsored by GSPC Boise. Yellowstone Park contributes $60 million a year to surrounding areas, said John Merriam, the kind of income Idaho could have on a continuing basis with a park. The potential benefit "makes a $2 million mining payroll look a little anemic." Dr. Donald Obee, chairman of the Division of Science and Health at Boise State University, said a report from Bill Platts projected the loss of East Fork salmon and resident fish with a mine. Brock Evans said there were six billion tons of known molybdenum reserves in the U.S. without ASARCO's mine and it would only add to the 28 million tons being exported annually. Bruce Bowler said the Forest Service and Interior Department had authority to deny a road permit and reject a mine but public pressure was needed to persuade them to act. H. Tom Davis asked for letters to Congress supporting park legislation.[15]

Idaho Department of Commerce Director Al Minton told a Boise audience that opposition to a mine was marked by "bitterness and emotion" and factual analysis was needed. With 80 percent of its land off the tax rolls, Idaho needed a broader tax base to avoid higher taxes, he said. In Custer County only four percent of the land was taxable. "We can have progress without pollution." The issue should not be projected into politics.

The Statesman's Ken Robison responded with "A Non-emotional Case Against Mine." Federally managed public land plus state land was about 70 percent of Idaho's total land area, not 80 percent. Idaho had more privately owned land in relation to its population than most states. Private forest and rangeland similar to the public land was assessed for tax purposes at an average $3 per acre. All of it on the tax rolls with similar assessed value would add no more than 10 percent to total Idaho property taxes. Idaho had an abundance of low cost land that could accommodate industries and business "without marring an exceptional area like the White Clouds." A White Clouds mine would not reduce taxes a dime for most Idahoans, Robison wrote. With added costs for roads, schools and services a mine would probably not even reduce taxes in Custer County.[16]

In late March, ASARCO announced that it would defer development work in the White Clouds pending completion of the Forest Service study, projected for July 1971. The company's work in the coming season would be limited to getting its environmental studies underway, tidying up the site, removal of equipment no longer required and minor additional work to assist in long-term planning. While there was no mention of any political consideration, it seemed obvious that both the company and Governor Samuelson would be better off if the controversy subsided.[17]

The Forest Service declined a request from the National Wildlife Federation to withdraw the White Clouds from further mineral entry. For Idaho Wildlife Federation leaders this was further evidence that the Forest Service would not protect the area. At its annual convention in early April, the federation endorsed the concept of a combined national park and national recreation area with park status for the Sawtooth, White Cloud, Boulder, Pioneer and Smoky Mountains. It was even more ambitious than the current plan of the Greater Sawtooth Preservation Council. It reflected the thinking of the federation president, Franklin Jones, who had advocated a similar combined park and NRA at the 1966 Sawtooth hearing.

National parks prohibited hunting but Jones said that during hunting season the game was usually found at lower elevations that would have NRA management. The federation planned to present the proposal to the Idaho congressional delegation. It had become evident, said Jones, that the Forest Service was unwilling to exercise its authority provided by a 1955 law allowing regulation to protect surface resources on public lands.[18] The Statesman said the "larger and more influential" federation's endorsement of a park reflected growing public concern for the White Clouds.[19]

Franklin Jones again asked the Forest Service to recognize that it could regulate mining under existing law, enclosing a copy of the federation's resolution. This time the response was different. Acting Chief E.M. Bacon replied that, with the National Environmental Policy Act, "we are now in the process of making a thorough study of our present statutory authorities, administrative regulations and current policies and procedures to determine whether action is needed to bring them into line with the purposes of the Act."[20]

Park legislation was endorsed by the Idaho Innkeepers Association. H. Tom Davis reported that Wes Carlson had revealed at a Forest Service meeting that ASARCO now believed it would need not one but four dams to contain waste material, stair stepping down to within two miles of the East Fork of the Salmon. Davis credited Idaho conservationists with winning the attention of the state and nation "to a degree heretofore thought impossible" with the help of growing environmental concern and "the inadvertent help" of Samuelson, Al Minton, ASARCO and Al Teske, but more commitment was needed, more time and more money. GSPC Boise membership had reached 70.[21]

White Clouds mining was enthusiastically endorsed by the state's most prominent business leader, Jack Simplot. Speaking before the Idaho Press Club, he said: "There will be a big hole there one day but it will be a great one. It is just a speck on that wall but it could support a great industry and I am all for it. I don't think we can lock up our resources." Simplot said the open pit copper mine near Salt Lake City attracted more tourists than the Mormon Temple. He said his company was spending several million dollars a year to control pollution and would comply with all regulations. "You play by the rules," he said, adding that "we won't spend millions unless we have to." John Corlett followed up, reporting that the Utah open pit was indeed a tourist attraction with 300,000 visitors in the past year but not more than the Temple's 2.4 million.[22]

In a move to counter support for the GSPC's proposed park-NRA, the Forest Service released a report on current activity in the 1.3 million-acre area that it encompassed. Two mines operated year-round with 10 employees and 30 intermittent mining and exploring operations employed 135. More than 165 ranch families depended on summer grazing for 12,500 cattle and 109,000 sheep. Annual timber sales totaled 27 million board feet, employing more than 160. In 1969 there were 98,000 visitor days of hunting and 145,000 for fishing with a game harvest of 4,487 deer, 636 elk, 38 mountain goat, 93 antelope and 93 bear. Three new skiing area proposals were nearing the final approval stage.[23]

In July the Forest Service discovered that it did indeed have legal authority to regulate mining exploration. The White Clouds area would be closed to the use of heavy equipment except on valid mining claims served by existing roads. This came more than a year after Ernie Day displayed his photos of bulldozer damage on Railroad Ridge. Challis and Sawtooth forest supervisors Wes Carlson and Ed Fournier said that pursuant to the National Environmental Policy Act and President Nixon's executive order 11514, the agency was obligated "to use all practicable means, consistent with other essential considerations of national policy, to prevent, eliminate or minimize damage to the natural environment on the national forest lands."[24]

Ed Weinberg, attorney for the National Wildlife Federation and Sierra Club attorney Don Harris of San Francisco flew to Idaho for a hike into the White Clouds with conservationists and a conference on legal strategy. They met in Hailey with Bruce Bowler, Brock Evans and John Chapman of Boise, attorney for the Greater Sawtooth Preservation Council. The media was advised, giving the Forest Service another reminder that a road permit would bring a court challenge. Ernie Day advised Tom Kimball that the attorneys would now be working together and acting "only after the exchange of information and ideas and mutual decision." Day had feared that the Sierra Club might take some action that would hurt the cause: "It seems we have won a small part of our battle with the Forest Service's issuance of new rules on heavy equipment use. Perhaps this means they will invoke the National Environmental Policy Act in the future against ASARCO and we will not have to go to court at all."[25]

Members of the legislature's Land Committee visited the White Clouds. In groups of four they flew for 50 minutes over central Idaho viewing "a panorama of hundreds of jagged peaks." They also flew by helicopter to the exploration area near Castle Peak. At a briefing in Challis, Keith Whiting told them ASARCO would "re-establish the ecological system in the area to as high a value as it is now. We're sure we can do that. The landscape won't look the same as it does now. Maybe it might be even a little better."

Tailings in the valley of Little Boulder Creek would extend over an area two and a half miles long by a half mile wide and "would have the effect of leveling off the steep gulley," he said. Another possibility would be to build a new lake to cover the tailings. Norman Kesten said there was "no likelihood of any silt getting into the East Fork of the Salmon River."[26]

BSU Albertson's Library Archives Photo

Cecil Andrus ran for governor on an environmental platform, an Idaho first.

Sen. John Peavey endorsed the road and the mine. He said he had hiked into nine lakes "but there aren't many people who do." He caught only skinny, malformed trout (Some of the lakes were overpopulated with brook trout.) Peavey was a rancher who ran sheep on public lands, the son of Mary Brooks, widow of former U.S. Senator James Brooks. Rep. George Brocke, D-Kendrick, also favored a mine: "It looks to me as if there's mountains enough for everyone." Peavey and Brocke said that with controls to prevent stream pollution and guaranteed restoration of the land, there was no reason mining shouldn't proceed.[27] Conservationists and legislators from Pocatello hiked in. Sen. Diane Bilyeu, representing Cecil Andrus, said the area was as beautiful as the Tetons and should be left as it was: "If we could walk in with six men, four women and two children, they don't need a road."[28]

Candidates for governor had staked out their positions. Cecil Andrus and Lloyd Walker opposed White Clouds mining. Vernon Ravenscroft favored an ASARCO mine with reclamation. The Republican challenger, State Sen. Dick Smith of Rexburg, favored a mining moratorium. Smith had the support of Sportsmen and Outdoorsmen for Dick Smith, headed by Ernie Day and Coeur d'Alene attorney Scott Reed. In the August primary election Idahoans had their first opportunity to speak on the White Clouds issue. Andrus won the Democratic nomination for governor with 29,036 votes, a margin of 5,667 over Ravenscroft. Lloyd Walker was third with 10,664. Governor Samuelson received 46,719 votes, Smith 33,338. Candidates who opposed a White Clouds mine had 73,038 votes, Samuelson and Ravenscroft a combined 70,088. The results could be considered a victory for White Clouds defenders. Still the margin was thin and other issues were in play including the question of support or lack of support for Idaho schools and universities.

Neither Congressmen James McClure nor Orval Hansen had primary opposition but both would be challenged in November, McClure by William Brauner of Caldwell who opposed a mine. Hansen would face Democrat J. Marsden Williams of Roberts, an ardent mine advocate. Both parties were divided on White Clouds mining.

Having heard from many White Clouds defenders, Jim McClure had changed his position. After months of discussion, Church, Jordan, Hansen and McClure had agreed to legislation. McClure would now support the Senate passed National Recreation Area bill including the White Clouds and Boulders. The four were also proposing two other bills, one declaring a 5-year moratorium on new mining claims and the second making the peaks a national park. Identical park and moratorium bills were introduced by Church and Jordan in the Senate and by McClure and Hansen in the House. The park legislation would not extinguish existing mining claims but would allow regulation by the Park Service.

The Park Service would have authority to purchase "lands, waters and interests" with appropriated funds. With the moratorium, patents that might be issued for mining claims existing at the time of enactment of the legislation would convey title to the minerals but not the land. And the Forest Service would be given authority to regulate land disturbances by motorized equipment. The park legislation would direct the Secretary of Interior to review the areas within two years for suitability for designation as wilderness. The congressional delegation wanted the National Recreation Area and moratorium legislation passed first, hopefully in the current year, with consideration of the park legislation to follow. Prompt action on the NRA would protect the Sawtooth Valley from unsightly development. The moratorium would prevent the filing of additional mining claims, allowing time for future action on the park bill. The Statesman said the legislative combination "means a rejection of the concept that Idaho must make any sacrifice, no matter how great, for the sake of a mining payroll" and must always "accept the leftovers of commercial use."[29]

Idahoans would soon have an opportunity to comment on the legislation because Rep. Roy Taylor's House Subcommittee on Parks and Land had scheduled a field trip to Idaho and an August 26 hearing in Sun Valley.[30]

What about Governor Samuelson? Would he go along with fellow Republicans Jordan, Hansen and McClure? The question was soon answered. The governor called a press conference and declared that he wanted "no part of a national park." The economic damage to Idaho would be too great. "There would be no hunting, no grazing…no management." The Park Service would "lock up a piece of ground and let it sit there and die and this is not good management." An economic study should be conducted before a park was proposed. He could accept a Sawtooth Recreation Area but only the earlier version that excluded the White Clouds.[31]

John Corlett chided Samuelson for undermining the congressional delegation's proposal. Samuelson had been thoroughly briefed "and was well aware of the priority of the park legislation to be considered last." The governor might have said he agreed in part with the delegation. "Instead he preferred to take up the cudgel of an antagonist." Corlett's column reflected his own changing views on public land issues.[32] In his weekly column former Governor Smylie was not so gentle: "Samuelson is apparently determined to mine that mountain if it is the last thing he does. It may well be just that." Smylie feared that Samuelson's stand could rob the state "of a last clear chance to save the Sawtooth Valley," preventing enactment of either the NRA or the park bill.[33]

Introduction of the park bill changed the debate. The primary question had been mine or no mine. Now it was National Recreation Area versus park. All of the historic anti-park arguments were revived. Mine supporters found more allies, including some who opposed White Clouds mining but also opposed a park. Vernon Taylor, speaking for the recently organized Central Idaho Mining Association, issued a statement saying that with a park, the sheep, cattle and mining industries would cease to exist in central Idaho. It had been Taylor's exploration that made headlines with pollution of Willow Lake. Taylor said his firm was not working claims this summer because 1969 drilling didn't show enough mineralization to justify the cost of a helicopter operation.[34] He was waiting for a decision "one way or another." As part of the Forest Service's anti-park campaign Tom Kovalicky hosted a rally of motorcyclists who camped on the grounds of the Stanley Ranger Station.

Both sides recognized that the Sun Valley hearing would be a critical showdown in the White Clouds battle and both went to work to line up speakers. Witnesses were to sign up in advance and would be limited to five minutes. By the time the committee arrived in Idaho, 356 people had signed up to speak. GSPC Boise chartered a bus for pro-park witnesses.

On the morning of August 25, committee members flew by helicopter to Frog Lake for a look at the area and a briefing. Regional Forester Vern Hamre told them the 1872 mining law should be changed to let the Forest Service regulate exploration and mining. In the entire White Clouds area only a few tons of ore had been hauled out since 1950 and yet there had been "a lot of surface disturbing activity," he said, adding that a miner had built a road to Crater Lake that was likely to wash out into the Salmon River drainage. Hamre suggested that no matter what legislation was passed, the ASARCO claims would remain because the government was unlikely to buy them out. Rep. McClure agreed and said members of the congressional delegation were in accord that the claims should remain. Committee members flew on to Toxaway Lake in the Sawtooths where they spent the night.[34]

Capacity of the Sun Valley Opera House was 300 but 500 people were on hand, far more than Chairman Taylor had expected. The committee was scheduled to conduct another hearing in Oregon the next day. With so many wishing to speak Taylor announced that witnesses would be limited to three minutes and were to stop with a warning bell. They could submit longer written statements. Al Minton, director of the Idaho Department of Commerce, spoke for the governor. Reading from Samuelson's 13-page statement, Minton plodded on and on. He continued even after Taylor brought down his gavel, speaking for 15 minutes and through four warning bells. After answering questions from Rep. Morris Udall, Minton demanded more time. Taylor cut him off, calling for the next witness, a member of Minton's staff. "If we can't have cooperation we can't proceed."

An indignant Minton walked out of the room, got in his car and drove away after telling a reporter "the governor was not given an opportunity to present his views." Samuelson was asking that all legislation be held in abeyance pending an economic impact study.[35] After Minton, the hearing settled down. At noon it was divided into two parts, with Rep. Morris Udall taking testimony in the Challenger Inn and the time limit was reduced to one minute.

Cecil Andrus endorsed a park, large enough to protect the mountain high country "but small enough to allow hunting, fishing and grazing in the lower elevation areas." He said park status would assure that mining would be regulated "with the utmost in protection should mining occur."[36] The Idaho Fish and Game Commission was not going along with the governor. Chairman Roy Holmes of Twin Falls spoke for the national park concept to "preserve mountain habitat and scenic values" but with continued state fish and wildlife management in both the park and NRA areas.[36]

Most of the testimony was either pro-park or pro-NRA. Many speakers called for enactment of the GSPC park plan, including the Pioneer Mountains, with immediate wilderness designation for the Sawtooths, rather than the congressional delegation's park bill. John Merriam and Pete Henault of the Greater Sawtooth Preservation Council objected to language in that bill authorizing special use permits to exercise "valid existing rights." They feared this would make mining more likely, even with Park Service administration. The same issue was raised by Jerry Jayne, Franklin Jones, Brock Evans, Pat Bartholomew and Nelle Tobias. Jones presented petitions opposing White Clouds mining with more than 8,000 signatures. Many of the pro-park witnesses were speaking in a public forum for the first time, including Caldwell High School student Greg Clopton, 13-year-old Peter Huebner of Idaho Falls and 12-year-old Terry Long, niece of John and Pat Bartholomew. She had hiked in the Sawtooths, White Clouds, Pioneers and Boulders.

Spokesmen for the Idaho State Chamber of Commerce, Idaho Cattlemen's Association, Idaho Woolgrowers, Idaho Farm Bureau, Stanley Basin homeowners and the 7-county North Side Communities spoke for an NRA and against a park.

Also favoring the NRA and opposing a park were the Twin Falls, Salmon and Burley chambers of commerce. Custer County Commissioner John Rovetto, objected to any "lockup of our resources from whatever agency" adding that this could be "Custer's last stand." Miners and mining industry spokesmen opposed both the park and moratorium and some wanted no NRA. Not all Idaho Wildlife Federation members agreed with the federation's position. Bud Esterholdt, president of the 13-county Fourth District spoke for the NRA and against a park. He doubted that most federation members wanted a park.

Senator Peavey and Democratic Sen. Don Frederickson of Gooding favored the NRA and opposed a park. Fredericksen, speaking for the Wood River Resource Area, supported mining with rehabilitation. Peavey used the occasion to blast The Idaho Statesman. He said it had fostered misunderstanding and reflected the views of its Michigan owners, not Idahoans.[36] Republican State Rep. Bill Onweiler of Boise and Sen. Diane Bilyeu endorsed the GSPC park plan. Onweiler challenged the claim that Custer County suffered because of a high proportion of public land and a limited tax base. Its property tax levies were well below the state average, its per capita assessed value was 40 per cent above the state average and it was 24th of 44 counties in per capita income, he said.

To save time many witnesses spoke for others with similar views, as requested by Chairman Taylor. A total of 213 had been heard when the committee adjourned at 5:45 p.m. Leaders of the GSPC counted a large majority for a park or combined park-NRA and considered the hearing a victory. The Associated Press reported that more supported an NRA than a park. It was clear that opinion was divided and there was still substantial opposition to a park, particularly in central Idaho.

Concern that a park would bring too many visitors was a frequent theme. J. Robb Brady, the first to sound the alarm about a possible White Clouds mine, wrote an editorial endorsing a park as offering the best protection but added that the time was past when a park was needed to attract tourists.[37]

Hopes for congressional action in 1970 quickly vanished. Chairman Wayne Aspinall announced in early September that the House Interior Committee would shut down for the session. In his October newsletter Frank Church advised constituents that nothing would be done until 1971, while citing the merits of a park: It would "never be another congested Yellowstone or Yosemite, nor should we want that many people crowding into the Sawtooth Basin." It would compare to such parks as Teton and the North Cascades "which offer a setting of mountain splendor." As for open pit mining in the White Clouds, even a national park could not extinguish vested rights stemming from a prior mining claim, he wrote. But regulation by the Park Service would assure "the largest feasible measure of protection for the soil, water and scenic values." And no new mining claims could be located within a park.[38]

The next showdown would come with the November election. Samuelson adjusted his message, emphasizing opposition to a park rather than support for a mine. Cecil Andrus at times found himself on the defensive because of the exclusion of hunting in parks. Fellow Democrat J. Marsden Williams denounced the park proposal at every opportunity as he campaigned across the Second District.

Timber industry representatives and livestock grazers joined with ASARCO, the Simplot Company and the Idaho Farm Bureau to organize the Idaho Multiple Use Resources Council. It would lobby to prevent "preservation or non use of resources." Simplot's Bill Maxwell said the commercial users of the public land had not been telling their story. "We have never stood together in a unified voice," he said, "and therefore we are not winning." One of the organizers was Vernon Ravenscroft, the defeated Democratic candidate for governor.[39] The Statesman printed H. Tom Davis's detailed analysis of the water pollution threat. Spokesmen for ASARCO had said no sediment would enter the streams. Davis said the primary issue was not sediment but the leaching of metallic ions from a massive amount of mine tailings that would be carried into ground and surface water. Leaching from much smaller mine waste dumps had wiped out seagoing fish in Panther Creek.[40]

Ernie Day, who had supported Dick Smith in the primary campaign, asked fellow Republicans to join The Committee of 10,000 for Andrus. When

State Rep. Arvil Millar questioned his endorsement of a Democrat, Day responded: "Today there are many honestly concerned, perhaps even frightened people, who worry more about our environmental chances of survival than they do about the fading traditional party lines of the past. Anyone in public office who is willing to trade this gem of the Gem State for surplus metal, the profits of which go out of state, is not living up to the tradition of the party of Theodore Roosevelt and Gifford Pinchot."[40]

The Eastern Idaho Chamber of Commerce, representing 15 local chambers in 22 counties, invited Al Teske to speak for White Clouds mining at its annual meeting. A newsletter distributed by park opponents warned of "endless streams of bumper to bumper traffic and acres of campers and tents so thick that you can't see the shorelines of a lake or the trees behind them."

It raised the specter of eventual designation of the valley floors as well as the peaks as a national park with loss of all hunting and grazing rights and the confiscation of deeded land.[41] Speaking in Idaho Falls, Governor Samuelson attempted to move the proposed mine out of the White Clouds, drawing a rebuke from Pete Henault. Samuelson pursued the theme in other appearances, saying that "all the back country is on the other side of the peak (Castle Peak)."[42] Beginning a campaign swing through the Magic Valley, Cecil Andrus told a Gooding audience that he had come to explain and clarify his position. He cited his Sun Valley testimony for a park only large enough to protect the alpine beauty from surface mining "but small enough to allow hunting, fishing and grazing in the lower elevation areas."[43]

Speaking in Gooding the next day, J. Marsden Williams said a park would lock hunters out of large areas, eliminate sheep grazing and result in summer homes being boarded up or burned to the ground.[44] In a Pocatello news conference, Andrus said the hunter lockout charge was an attempt to avoid the real issue, "whether we are going to allow mining interests to destroy this area for everyone."[45]

While the Idaho Wildlife Federation had traditionally stayed out of election politics, the Idaho Environmental Council (IEC) plunged in. Pete Henault organized an IEC sponsored Pocatello fund raising dinner for Andrus. The organization endorsed Andrus, Orval Hansen and James McClure's challenger, William Brauner. While McClure was now a co-sponsor of Sawtooth park legislation, the IEC said his foot dragging delayed introduction of the bill until it was too late to be considered in the 1970 session.

Also, McClure had refused to support the Jordan-Church moratorium legislation on dams in Hells Canyon. Why was the IEC so much involved in the political campaign? "Conservationists have traditionally fought the battles with the written or spoken word," said Henault. "We're winning a few battles but we're losing the war." Bob Leeright of the Associated Press described the IEC's political efforts, noting that environmental concerns, including the White Clouds, Hells Canyon and water pollution were of major significance in the upcoming election.[46]

A magazine endorsement created a stir in late October. Field and Stream, edited by Idaho native Clare Conley, endorsed Cecil Andrus. Conley said the magazine had become more vocal in expressing its views on governors and members of Congress since he became editor. The endorsement was announced at a Boise press conference sponsored by Republicans for Andrus. Standing beside Conley was Jack Hemingway of Sun Valley, son of Ernest Hemingway. He said he had been a Republican but "the issues are so vital here they absolutely transcend partisan politics."

When Samuelson criticized the magazine and questioned the sincerity of its editors the Idaho Environmental Council's Jerry Jayne responded: "George Bird Grinnell, founder of Forest and Stream magazine, the predecessor of Field and Stream, ranks with John Muir and Teddy Roosevelt as one of the great conservationists. Grinnell founded the Boone and Crockett Club, the first Audubon Club, fought against poaching in Yellowstone Park and was responsible for creating Glacier National Park." Added Jayne: "This is one of the greatest endorsements that any candidate could receive and we regret that the governor has tried to discredit it."[47] GSPC Boise sponsored a $700 full-page ad in the Statesman before the election endorsing Andrus.[48]

Two weeks before the election three Idaho political writers predicted Andrus would win. Four picked Samuelson. On election night votes in counties south of the Salmon River gave Samuelson an early lead. His margin dwindled as results were reported from northern Idaho where voting ended an hour later. Andrus moved ahead to win by 10,896 votes. He carried nine of the 10 counties north of the Salmon River including a narrow margin in Samuelson's home county, Bonner. Strong showings in the Lewiston area, in his home county, Clearwater, in Latah County, home of the University of Idaho and in Shoshone County, the Coeur d'Alene mining district, provided most of his 15,480-vote margin in the north.

Though Samuelson carried 27 of 34 counties south of the Salmon his margin was only 4,584 votes, much less than in 1966. Andrus carried Ada County by 249 votes, lost by only 1,434 in Canyon and by 1,787 in Bonneville, the Idaho Falls area. In the Pocatello area, he won by more than two to one, 11,625 to 5,690. Custer County wanted a mine, voting nearly ten to one for Samuelson, 1,164 to 135. Republican and independent voters who wanted the White Clouds protected helped Andrus offset the usual Republican advantage in the south. In his autobiography, he would write that the White Clouds issue helped him become the first western governor elected on an environmental platform. He was Idaho's first Democratic governor in 24 years.[49]

Idaho would now have a governor who opposed mining in the White Clouds and more dams on the Snake River below Hells Canyon, a governor who would more aggressively pursue control of water pollution. People concerned about the environment would now qualify for appointment to state boards and commissions. Andrus would make environmental concern a theme of his administration, saying Idaho could have both "living quality" and a strong economy. During the campaign Samuelson traveled around the state in the private plane of Jack Simplot. Early in his administration Andrus would meet with Simplot and get his commitment to control the waste flowing from his potato processing plants into the Snake River.[50]

W. Anthony (Tony) Park, a Boise attorney whose environmental positions mirrored those of Andrus, defeated Atty. Gen. Robert Robson. Orval Hansen won by 34,000 votes over mining advocate J. Marsden Williams while McClure won by 21,000 in the First District.

White Clouds defenders hoped that their impressive showing at Sun Valley and the Andrus victory, reflecting a new level of environmental concern in Idaho, meant there would be no mine. The 1970 legislation expired with the previous Congress. In February 1971 the GSPC, Idaho Wildlife Federation and Idaho Environmental Council submitted their revised park-NRA plan to the congressional delegation. Boundaries had been revised after consultation with the Fish and Game Department to reduce the size of the park areas and limit the impact on hunting. The park would include the Sawtooth, White Cloud, Boulder and Pioneer mountains. Both the park and national recreation area would be administered by the Park Service. There would be three recreation areas: a Salmon River NRA in the Stanley Basin; Boise-Payette NRA on the west side of the Sawtooths; and a Lost River NRA east of the Boulders and Pioneers.[51]

Word came back from Washington that the congressional delegation was developing a proposal, not for immediate park legislation, but for a national recreation area with a 5-year moratorium on new mining claims. H. Tom Davis wrote Senator Church saying GSPC Boise did not want to see another national recreation area bill: "It would give the impression both to Congress and the public that the problem has been solved, while in reality it would only be complicated."

The moratorium could be interpreted as recognizing existing claims, he warned, while verifying the Forest Service position that it was powerless to regulate mining of existing claims.[52] There was more bad news in late March. A divided Idaho Wildlife Federation, meeting in Coeur d'Alene, adopted the Fourth District's resolution opposing a park.[53]

On March 29, the congressional delegation introduced bills in the House and Senate establishing a Sawtooth National Recreation Area with a 5-year moratorium on new mining claims and instructing the Interior Department to submit a park proposal within two years. The NRA included the Sawtooth, White Cloud and Boulder mountains with wilderness designation for the Sawtooth Primitive Area and wilderness study for the White Clouds and Boulders. It did not include the Pioneers. While the Forest Service was theoretically given added regulatory authority, the bill included language the GSPC and its legal advisers believed not only suggested that mining would proceed, but seemed to guarantee it, authorizing special use permits for existing claims.[54]

BSU Albertson's Library and Archives photo

Idaho's Congressional delegation joined in sponsoring Sawtooth National Recreation Area legislation in 1971. From left: Sen. Len Jordan, Sen. Frank Church, Rep. James McClure and Rep. Orval Hansen.

White Clouds defenders were stunned. After two years of rallying public support, the Sun Valley hearing and the Andrus victory, they had expected a Sawtooth park bill. Instead they were confronted with legislation not much better than the Senate-passed bill of 1969. John Merriam advised Church,

Jordan and Hansen that "the language of the bill seems designed to insure that nothing shall prevent open pit mining in the White Clouds. We are well aware of who is blocking truly effective legislation." He was referring to Congressman McClure. "We want the best for Idaho, not the poor compromise of commercial exploitation with a recreation area label."

Merriam promised that the council would continue to fight for better protection and would be "out in great numbers" in 1972 to support candidates based on their environmental records.[55] The GSPC leaders resolved to oppose the NRA bill, advising members that its passage would eliminate any chance of park status for the mountains and would assure mining destruction of the White Clouds. "We must turn the situation around in the next three months." Members were asked to speak out publicly and in letters to the editor and to pepper members of Congress with letters.

Responding to frustrated park supporters, Church conceded that the bill "doesn't accomplish everything you and I would like to see accomplished" but was "the best to which I could get agreement from all members of the delegation." Without such unanimity previous bills had died in the House. "After ten years of trying, I am convinced that enactment of protective legislation must not be delayed further." He hoped the bill would be the first step toward eventual creation of a national park. Church was making the Sawtooth legislation his first legislative priority while resisting conservationist requests to abandon the proposed Snake River dam moratorium in favor of permanent protection. Church needed the continuing cooperation of Senator Jordan, the moratorium co-sponsor, on the Sawtooth legislation.[56]

Rep. Taylor's subcommittee conducted a 2-day Washington hearing on the NRA bill in June 1971. Rep. McClure said while the 1960s park proposal was overwhelmingly rejected, "I still believe that a properly formulated park and recreation bill could gain acceptance" and would be a "superior proposal." He said he was giving the NRA bill his full support because "it is absolutely imperative to move now – and this bill is not surrounded by the controversy which will delay its acceptance." While HR 6957 called for a park study to be completed within two years, the intent was for the Park Service to bring forward a park proposal, he said.

The Sawtooths had already been studied and study was underway on the White Clouds. John McGuire, deputy chief of the Forest Service, said the NRA bill would allow the agency to regulate mining of existing claims "to minimize adverse environmental impacts." ASARCO's Keith Whiting endorsed the bill but objected to language saying patents could no longer be issued on "claims previously made." Company attorneys believed this would be an unconstitutional taking of private property, he said.[57]

Russ Brown presented the case for park designation: "The new NRA bill represents a step backward from the less than ideal park and NRA bills of the last session." He said the 5-year moratorium would not affect the old claims including "300 or more that blanket the Little Boulder Creek area." A park study had been requested by Governor Andrus and could be requested by any member of the congressional delegation without legislation. The special use permit language in the NRA bill "would provide a legislative guarantee to the miners" to build roads and to claim and use additional land and waterways for ore processing, waste disposal dumps and tailings ponds, he said. "Any pretense of protection of the White Clouds disappears when the special use permits are considered."

Brown contended that park designation could protect the area with permanent mineral entry withdrawal as in the bill establishing the North Cascades National Park and NRA. The White Clouds claims had not gone through the final validation process. "Where lands are withdrawn from mineral entry, an entry man could have a mill site only if he made a valid mill site entry before the area is withdrawn. The economic burden of transporting low grade ore (99.8 percent waste) would make the proposed White Clouds operation uneconomical."

Brown provided the text of the GSPC bill for a 1.4 million-acre national park and NRA to be managed by the Park Service. McClure challenged Brown, saying he was proposing to extinguish valid mining claims and this would be a taking of private property.

"While they have a right to the mineral, it is not actually their property, not in the sense that you and I own property," said Brown. Pat Bartholomew of the GSPC, H. Tom Davis, speaking for the Idaho Environmental Council, and Pete Henault of the Hells Canyon Preservation Council, also called for a park.

Jack Hemingway, now a member of the Idaho Fish and Game Commission, presented the statement of Governor Andrus calling for a combined park-NRA with permanent withdrawal of the high country from further mineral claims. Andrus asked that Congress proceed immediately with NRA legislation for the valley areas only, following up as quickly as possible with park designation for the Sawtooths, White Clouds, Boulders and Pioneers. The proposed NRA legislation would create an image of protection while allowing "exploitive uses to continue."

"By comparison to many areas of the nation, Idaho is a portrait of unspoiled America with some of the finest mountain scenery in the world. Idaho's beauty will increase in value in years to come because of its growing rarity," said the Andrus statement. In response to questions Hemingway confessed that his personal view differed from the governor because of the hunting exclusion in national parks. He favored a Forest Service national recreation area.

The Idaho Wildlife Federation was no longer supporting a park and neither was the national federation. National Director Tom Kimball testified for the Idaho Federation, endorsing the NRA bill but calling for a phase out of mining, with wilderness designation for the White Clouds and Boulders as well as the Sawtooths. Ernie Day still wanted a park and his statement was added to the hearing record. Only park status "will have the required muscle to protect the base of Castle Peak and the upper Little Boulder Creek drainage from a vast open pit mining operation for a metal in surplus supply," said Day.

Don Zuck of Twin Falls testified for the Southern Idaho Wildlife Federation, with 700 members, backing the NRA bill but with wilderness designation for the White Clouds, Boulders and Pioneers as well as the Sawtooths. Zuck said a leasing system should be adopted for mining. Meanwhile the Park Service had no more authority to extinguish existing mining claims than the Forest Service. Zuck said the federation agreed with the legislature's NRA endorsement and disagreed with Andrus. A statement submitted by Steven Mealy of the Idaho Outfitters and Guides Association said the association opposed park management and specifically the GSPC proposal.

On November 10, the House Interior Committee approved a revised bill by voice vote. Rep. McClure objected to two changes, giving the Forest Service rather than the state jurisdiction over fish and game management and separating the Sawtooth Wilderness from the national recreation area.[58]

The House vote in early February 1972 was 369-9. The only opposition speaker was Rep. John Saylor who described the bill as a sham, providing "the form of protection but not the substance." It was a poor "second best proposition with loophole provisions that would bring mining and other incompatible uses into the very heart of the area." Saylor inserted in the record a copy of the GSPC analysis.

Meanwhile, White Clouds defenders had convinced Senator Church that the bill was inadequate. While they were in Washington for the House hearing Russ Brown, Pat Bartholomew and H. Tom Davis met with Church in his office, asking for amendments. In February 1972, Church advised the news media that the House bill had serious weaknesses and that he would attempt to amend it in the Senate to delete the special use permit language and to make the 5-year mineral withdrawal permanent. The GSPC strategy was to support the Church amendments while continuing to speak for a park. Members were asked to contribute to help send as many witnesses as possible to Washington for the Senate subcommittee hearing. It cost about $400 for each witnesses.

Previously Idaho witnesses had paid their own way, hoping for compensation later. "That expedient is no longer practical."[59]

A week before the Senate hearing a task force representing eight federal agencies, with a representative of Governor Andrus, released a preliminary report saying there should be no molybdenum mining in the White Clouds, at least until a national need was demonstrated. The task force said there was no evidence that mining could be done "without seriously impairing the high

Photo Courtesy of H. Tom Davis

Greater Sawtooth Preservation Council representatives told Frank Church the National Recreation Area bill would leave the door open to an ASARCO mine. Church won approval of their proposed amendments in the Senate-House conference committee. From left: Russell Brown, Church, Pat Bartholomew and H. Tom Davis

quality environment" with severe damage to water quality, fisheries, wildlife and recreation. It said the nation had a molybdenum surplus with a current stockpile of 48 million pounds. The report said mining operations in Idaho and other states "have been disastrous to fish populations in many instances" including virtual elimination of fish in Panther Creek with toxic mine waste. It said an open pit mine in the White Clouds would destroy some lakes and streams. Heavy sedimentation of the East Fork of the Salmon River and some of its tributaries from mining, ore processing and roads could be expected.

The report continued: "These operations could be disastrous to production of anadromous fish and resident fish by destroying spawning and rearing habitat, reducing fish food organisms and adversely affecting water quality." Wildlife populations would be affected by air pollution, noise pollution, roads and mining activity, said the report. Landscape alteration would destroy the area's wilderness character, even with conscientious rehabilitation efforts. With the tailing ponds "it is difficult to conceive that the beauty of the area will ever approach an unaltered state." Agencies represented were the Bureau of Mines, U.S. Geological Survey, Bureau of Land Management, Bureau of Outdoor Recreation, Bureau of Sports Fisheries and Wildlife, Environmental Protection Agency, National Marine Fisheries Service and the Park Service. The Forest Service and Idaho Fish and Game Commission acted as consultants. The governor's representative was Pete Henault.[60]

Governor Andrus was in Japan with the National Governor's Association executive committee. He issued a statement describing the report as "a victory for Idaho's people who have overwhelmingly supported preservation of the high-altitude, pristine White Cloud Mountains." He said it supported his stand in favor of a national park and could be the most significant development in many years for the protection of Idaho's salmon and steelhead fisheries. "Millions spent downstream on fish passage improvement would be wasted if a molybdenum mine in the White Clouds poisoned the headwaters of the Salmon River," said the governor. Rep. McClure saw it differently. He disputed the report's conclusions and said there was "no evidence that area can't be mined without harming the environment."[61]

The Interior Department's Northwest representative, Emmett Willard, attempted to discredit the report, saying the conclusions should be considered tentative and held in abeyance for reconsideration in light of additional information to be gathered.[62] Andrus complained that photos included in a draft version had been left out of the final report. The Statesman reported that the photos had been removed "by order of a high Interior Department official." The source of this information was Pete Henault. Willard said the photos were omitted to save printing costs. Henault said they were taken out because of pressure from the Bureau of Mines. One was a photo of Castle Peak and another showed mining exploration scars.[63] Willard's statement and the photo omissions aroused suspicion that the Nixon administration was being influenced by the mining lobby. J. Robb Brady saw it as evidence of a possible behind the scenes deal.[64]

Church and McClure clashed on Church's proposed amendment to the House bill to make the mining claim withdrawal permanent. Speaking before the Senate subcommittee, McClure again said there was no evidence the area could not be mined without damage to the environment, disagreeing with results of the multi-agency study. "I want to ask the gentleman if he's ever seen an open pit that's a thing of beauty," said Church. "I've never seen a forest operation that did, either, but we do it because we have to," McClure answered. He said the Senate should go along with the 5-year moratorium until completion of a U.S. Bureau of Mines mineral study begun in 1971 at the request of the Idaho Mining Association. Senator Jordan questioned the idea of a permanent withdrawal: "I don't think we can continually keep booting this 5-year period ahead." Church responded, saying "we risk the possibility of legislation not coming along to protect it after the 5-year period has passed."

Associate Forest Service Chief John McGuire agreed a permanent ban could be enacted and reopened later by Congress if necessary. The mining study would still continue. Governor Andrus, in a statement presented by Franklin Jones, supported a permanent ban and again endorsed a combination park-NRA. Also speaking for the permanent ban was Glen Wegner of Kendrick who, like McClure, former Gov. Smylie and former congressman George Hansen, was seeking the Republican nomination to succeed Jordan.

ASARCO's Keith Whiting said the company was willing to return mined-over areas to the Forest Service after mining. Church likened the offer to "returning a wife to a husband after she's been raped." Jordan said he was concerned about Whiting's statement that the company would have to be paid should the United States take over its unpatented claims. "If that's so," said Jordan, "we've got a lot of problems out West." He said he didn't believe that the mere location of a claim vested a right to patent it under the law. Whiting said ASARCO had reduced its claims from 150 a year ago to 56 now.[65]

Jordan joined Church in sponsoring amendments; a permanent withdrawal from further mineral entry of all 750,000 acres in the NRA, Forest Service authority to purchase valid mineral interests, elimination of the special use permit language, inclusion of the Pioneer Mountains in the park study, inclusion of the Sawtooth Wilderness within the NRA and continued state control of hunting and fishing. The amended bill won unanimous approval in the Senate by voice vote, sending it to a Senate-House conference committee to resolve differences. The committee, which included Church, Jordan and McClure, adopted all of the key Senate amendments including the permanent mineral withdrawal and elimination of language authorizing special use permits.[66] With the amendments the Forest Service was given ample authority to prevent mining of existing claims. White Clouds defenders and Frank

Church had transformed a weak bill backed by the mining industry into a strong instrument for protection of the White Clouds, Boulders and Sawtooths.

Church, Jordan, Hansen and McClure joined in a chorus of praise for the revised bill. Church said it was the culmination of the effort he began "more than a decade ago to bring protection to this area. This is a strong bill and will safeguard this part of Idaho from serious injury." Jordan called it the culmination of a delegation effort begun in 1970. Hansen said it "insures for our own and future generations the protection and utilization of one of the most scenic places in the nation."[67]

On September 1, 1972, ten days after President Richard Nixon signed the bill, 375 people gathered for a dedication ceremony at Redfish Lake. Church, Jordan, Hansen, McClure and Andrus were on hand as speakers along with Forest Service Chief John McGuire. McClure said he believed there would ultimately be a park-NRA but it was up to the people of Idaho. Andrus advised the Park Service people present to keep their (Forest Service) feet to the fire. McGuire said the Forest Service would concentrate on determining the validity of mining claims, challenging those found to be invalid, and on preparing guidelines for land use in the Sawtooth Valley.[68]

Three weeks earlier McClure had won the Republican U.S. Senate nomination by 11,100 votes over George Hansen in a 4-way race. While he tried to keep the door open to White Clouds mining, McClure ultimately accepted the Church amendments. The final bill included his Sawtooth Wilderness prescription with all of the acreage the Forest Service had proposed to exclude and all that conservationists wanted to add for a total of 216,000 acres. All members of the congressional delegation contributed to the creation of the national recreation area, but Church was the primary author and advocate beginning with his Sawtooth wilderness park bill of 1960. His cordial relationship with Senator Jordan helped win Jordan's support for the White Clouds addition and the mining amendments. Orval Hansen was an early convert to White Clouds protection. Governor Andrus played a key role with his 1970 election victory and continuing advocacy for a park. But there would have been no legislation to protect the White Clouds without Ernie Day and the campaign waged by the Greater Sawtooth Preservation Council.

Day's Castle Peak photo, his clash with Samuelson and his dogged insistence that there could be no mine fueled the successful citizen's movement. The GSPC leaders refused to settle for a weak national recreation area bill and persuaded Church to sponsor the strengthening amendments. Credit should also go to Jeanne Conly Smith and the Idaho Federation of Women's Clubs for their Sawtooth Park campaign begun in 1911. Idahoans had been seeking recognition and protection of the Sawtooth country for 61 years.

Ernie Day Photo

Amendments strengthened the Sawtooth NRA bill, reducing the threat of mining in the White Clouds.

Even with the amendments, White Cloud defenders weren't sure they had stopped ASARCO's mine. Would the Forest Service have enough backbone to use the legal tools it had been given? Would a future presidential administration cave to the mining industry? Would future Idaho Congressional representatives and governors attempt to reopen the mining question? In 1975, the Forest Service issued a progress report. In three years $19 million had been spent to acquire land and scenic easements from 193 Sawtooth Valley landowners. Private land use regulations were in place and condemnation was in progress on three subdivisions. It was apparent that the original $19 million authorization for acquisition of land and scenic easements was inadequate. In 1978 Church and McClure were able to increase the authorization from the Land and Water Conservation Fund to $42 million. The total would ultimately exceed $60 million.

As of 1975, the Forest Service had identified 7,000 unpatented mining claims in the national recreation area. The owners had relinquished 620 claims, 273 were being contested and 250 were being processed for possible challenge. Seventy-five claims appeared to be valid. The Forest Service was studying the White Cloud, Boulder and Smoky mountains and the Hanson Lakes area for possible wilderness designation. Trailing of cattle through important bighorn sheep habitat in the White Clouds would be discontinued. Recreation use of the area had reached one million visitor days.[69]

The Park Service proceeded with its study and produced a report recommending a combined national park and national recreation area including the Pioneer Mountains and Copper Basin. The area was described as eminently worthy of park status. The plan called for management of the peaks as wilderness with closure of some roads and trails. Livestock grazing would continue in the lowland areas but would be phased out in the mountains after 25 years. Mining would be extinguished in the park but allowed in the recreation area. Hunting would be allowed in the NRA portion but not in the park, except for mountain goats and to control game populations.[70]

The study was completed and forwarded to Washington by the regional director in March 1975 but languished there without a recommendation by the Interior Secretary. Cecil Andrus didn't recommend it either, after he became Interior Secretary in 1977. With the strengthened NRA bill, with the Forest Service demonstrating a commitment to protect natural values, with visitor numbers growing rapidly and with no revival of ASARCO's attempt to mine, there was little interest in pursuing park legislation even among Idaho conservationists.

Responding to an editorial in the South Idaho Press in September 1974 Church's press secretary, Cleve Corlett, advised editor Bill MacKnight that Church was not supporting a national park. The Park Service study was only "informational," he wrote. It had been added to the National Recreation Area legislation in response to sentiment for such an option at that time. Senator Church believed the NRA would prove to be the best management plan for the area.[71]

Custer County got its mining payroll without a White Clouds mine. A molybdenum discovery a few miles north of the Salmon River in 1967 led to development of the Thompson Creek Mine on a mountain ridge 21 air miles southwest of Challis. This was not an area of spectacular beauty with snow-capped peaks and, after the bruising White Clouds battle, the Andrus and John Evans administrations were willing to work with miners so long as the mining plan approved by the Forest Service and Bureau of Land Management provided safeguards to protect the water quality of the Salmon River. Conservationists were concerned about the threat to Salmon River water quality but did not oppose the mine. Interior Secretary Andrus approved the mining plan with its water quality provisions. By 1983, earth-moving machines were scooping up thousands of tons of rock a day, carving away the side of a mountain at 8,000 feet elevation. Giant trucks carried the ore to an on-site mill for processing. Waste material was deposited behind a 730-foot high earth fill dam.

In November 1973, the Idaho conservation community lost John Merriam, leader of the Greater Sawtooth Preservation Council's campaign for the White Clouds and chairman of the economics department at Idaho State University. He died in a boating accident on Palisades Reservoir while deer hunting. Frank Church and Cecil Andrus called his widow, Kay, asking that she select a mountain to bear his name. She chose the unnamed peak that flanks Castle Peak on the north and it became Merriam Peak. Kay and friends scattered John's ashes near a White Cloud lake.[72]

In July 1981, ASARCO showed renewed interest in its White Cloud claims. Richard Brown director of exploration, planned to meet with Forest Service officials to talk about possible permits to allow added exploration. He said the ultimate goal was an open pit mine. The added exploration would help determine whether a mine could be profitable, he said. This news generated a barrage of editorial comment and a statement by Governor John Evans opposing a mine. Evans said the issue was settled by Idaho voters in 1970. Sawtooth Forest Supervisor Paul Barker said it was unlikely that the Forest Service would approve an open pit mine.

John Corlett suggested that ASARCO's move was prompted by the anti-environmental tilt of the Reagan administration. He wrote that the company had learned that "the feeling for protection of the White Clouds is as deep and lasting as it was a decade ago"[73]

Chapter 13

Saving Hells Canyon

"View the scenic alpine meadows and lakes of the Seven Devils Mountains of Idaho. Descend from the shade of these sentinels down wooded slopes into Hells Canyon, the deepest and narrowest gorge on our continent. See and hear the mighty river flowing swift and clear between the wild rapids. Now then, consider linkage of the awesome escarpments with the living, surging river." – T. Russell Mager.

Talmon Russell Mager fell under the spell of the deep canyon and the mighty river in the 1960s, descending trails thousands of feet to fish for white sturgeon. With his family in 1957, 1958 and 1959, Mager made weekend horseback treks to the Seven Devils Mountains on the Idaho side of the canyon. Using flies, they pulled 2- to 4-pound cutthroat trout from Echo, Baldy and Bernard lakes. From Bernard, they could hike up to Dry Diggins lookout and see a "little ribbon of water" far below, the Snake River.

In June 1961, Mager and his 15-year-old son, Ron, made their first descent into the canyon. It was a 5-hour drive from Lewiston with their horse trailer to Cold Springs camp near the trailhead. To the west they could see snow-capped mountains in Oregon. The descent took them four hours by way of a branch of Sheep Creek. They reached the river at Johnson's Bar and then rode south to the mouth of Bernard Creek in the deepest part of the canyon, camping on land that had been a homestead. Rising at dawn, they saw the sun illuminate the tops of the mountains to the west and then watched the sunlight slowly move down the canyon wall to the river. Mager thought it was a marvelous spectacle.[1]

Then it was time to fish. Using sucker meat as bait, they cast their lines weighted with railroad spikes and waited. A sturgeon didn't grab the bait. "They'd nibble. You'd let them chew on it, then jerk back," Mager explained.

Then the fight was on. It could take more than an hour to land a 100-pound sturgeon. "Most of the time we'd lose them. They'd just keep going downstream," breaking off the 30-pound leader. Only fish between three and six feet could be kept. "We always brought one back."

In February 1964, Mager learned that the Federal Power Commission had issued a license to Pacific Northwest Power Company to build the 670-foot Mountain Sheep dam. The dam would silence the mighty river and flood the canyon. On the trail that summer he met an old sheepherder and told him about the dam. He agreed that it would be a calamity but said: "You can't fight those guys." Well, perhaps someone could fight them.

Russell Mager

Mager was born in Buffalo, New York in 1917. His mother was a minister and her influence contributed to his decision to study social work. Because of its low tuition, he enrolled at the University of Alabama in Tuscaloosa, where he got acquainted with some U.S. Air Force trainees. He wanted to learn to fly. He enlisted in 1940, completed advanced flight school in May 1941, and was assigned as a cadet instructor. His students included members of the Royal Air Force who would soon be in combat with the Luftwaffe.

In the fall of 1944, he was assigned to command a B29 bomber on Guam in the Marianas Islands. He brought plane and crew back from 26 combat missions.

"The closest we came to curtains was being barely missed by a Japanese suicide pilot over Tokyo," he recalled. After the war, with the help of the GI bill, Mager earned a masters degree in social work at the University of Buffalo and went to work for the Veterans Administration. He also continued as an officer in the active Air Force Reserve.

Looking for a new challenge and attracted by the idea of living in the West with its rivers and mountains, Mager accepted a job with the state of Washington. Next came a project at Idaho's State Hospital North in Orofino, moving patients into foster homes with support services. In Orofino the Mager family lived on the former hospital farm, allowing them to pasture horses. They rode into the Selway-Bitterroot Primitive Area and the Seven Devils. In 1960, they moved to Lewiston where Mager headed a new community health center. He joined the Sierra Club and was among those meeting occasionally in the back room of a café to talk about land and water issues. His wife, Marian, typed his letters to members of Congress opposing Bruces Eddy dam and the Forest Service decision to exclude 400,000 acres of the Selway-Bitterroot Primitive Area from wilderness.[2]

White Sturgeon from the free-flowing Snake River in Hells Canyon

In September 1965, Mager read an article in the Idaho Fish and Game Department's magazine, Idaho Wildlife Review. Fisheries Biologist Bill Platts described the destruction of Snake River white sturgeon habitat by dams and warned that one of the last sturgeon strongholds would be lost with High Mountain Sheep dam. With Idaho Power Company's dams, with Mountain Sheep and its re-regulating dam, China Gardens, plus the proposed federal Asotin dam near Lewiston, 165 miles of flowing river would become flat water. The Snake would be a continuous pond from its mouth all the way to Weiser. Sturgeon needed shallow riffle areas and fast moving water, preferably rapids, plus relatively silt free river bottoms. With still water behind dams only a small remnant population would survive.[3]

Mager wrote the Federal Power Commission (FPC) protesting its licensing decision, saying Mountain Sheep would destroy the sturgeon. An FPC attorney replied that the commission had conducted extensive hearings with participation by fish and game agencies and the Interior Department. Mager sent another protest letter.[4] With the commission's decision now before the U.S. Supreme Court in November 1966, Mager wrote Justice William O. Douglas urging denial of the license. He enclosed a photo of a sturgeon caught by his son and cited the Platts article. "Considering the resulting loss of fish life, is this dam really necessary in view of the early possibility of a nuclear source?" In February he wrote again.[5]

Mager left Lewiston and moved to eastern Idaho to teach at Idaho State University in Pocatello. In December, he testified at a Boise hearing conducted by the Selke Committee as part of its review of Forest Service plans for the Magruder Corridor.

Floyd Harvey

There he met four members of the Idaho Alpine Club from Idaho Falls: Boyd Norton, Jerry Jayne, Al McGlinsky and Dick Wilde. They all worked at the National Reactor Testing Station (NRTS), the federal nuclear research and development complex located on 890 square miles in the Lost River desert west of Idaho Falls. NRTS physicists, engineers and technicians conducted research and testing to advance the use of nuclear power and develop power plants for Navy submarines and carriers. Most of the Alpine Club members were new to the west. They enjoyed the freedom to explore millions of acres of public land, scaling mountains, hiking wilderness trails, fishing rivers and high lakes. With the wild country available to them, "we were rich beyond belief," said Jayne. Mager told them about Hells Canyon and they invited him to show his slides at a future Alpine Club meeting. They were impressed when they saw the slides in March 1967.[6]

In April, Mager wrote Sanford Stepfer, chairman of the Sierra Club's Pacific Northwest chapter, asking that the club oppose the dam. Stepfer said it could not be considered unless local people made the case. Mager agreed with Stepfer's suggestion for an in-depth study by Idaho dam opponents. But he noted that the Wildlife Federation's Ernie Day and others felt strongly that it would be hazardous to re-open the issue because of the danger of rekindling interest in the Nez Perce dam site.[7]

Meanwhile, in Lewiston the canyon and river had another defender. Floyd Harvey had built up a river excursion business, carrying passengers from Lewiston to the deepest part of the canyon. They stayed overnight at his camp on a bar at Willow Creek after a 6-hour, 93-mile trip. A Lewiston native and son of a service station owner, Harvey was selling insurance in the 1950s. He loaned money and co-signed a note for a friend who wanted to buy a boat and carry passengers up the river into Hells Canyon. The business faltered and Harvey became the owner of the boat and a lease from the Forest Service on land at Willow Creek.[8]

Relatively few people had ever seen Hells Canyon. Development of "jet boats" with no protruding propeller and power enough to push across the larger rapids allowed easier access to big water rivers. While thousands of people were floating the Salmon River and its middle fork in rubber rafts in the

1960s, commercial outfitters were just getting started running raft trips on the Snake below Idaho Power's Hells Canyon dam.

Harvey promoted his business with magazine ads and invitations to newspaper and magazine travel writers for free excursions. He sent invitations to prominent people including California Gov. Ronald Reagan and Idaho's Robert Smylie. Smylie accepted and Reagan sent an aide. Curt Gowdy came to film a program for the American Sportsman television series.

Harvey recognized that High Mountain Sheep dam would destroy his business. But there might be a way to offset the loss. He met with Pacific Northwest Power (PNP) executives in Spokane and asked for a contract to carry workers and supplies to the dam site. With a contract he could borrow money to build the bigger boat he would need. Upon returning to Lewiston he learned that PNP had contracted with and was building a boat for his rival, Rivers Navigation Company.

Dick Rivers ran a weekly mail boat that served ranchers in the canyon. He also ran daily excursions from Lewiston and trips to his camp 58 miles upriver. Harvey was incensed. He wrote Pacific Northwest Power executives telling them he would now do everything he could to stop the dam: "I told them you will never build Mountain Sheep dam." It seemed like an idle threat.[9]

Harvey went to the Lewiston Chamber of Commerce, the Fish and Game Department and the Wildlife Federation looking for allies. No one would help. They were all supporting High Mountain Sheep dam. "I was an outcast," Harvey said. "No one would talk to me." He began looking elsewhere.

In the spring of 1967, he contacted Brock Evans, the young attorney recently hired as the Sierra Club's Northwest representative based in Seattle. Evans invited him to make his case to the club's Northwest Executive Committee meeting at a private home on Puget Sound. Committee members were impressed with his photos and his description of the virtues of the river and canyon. They directed Evans to see what he could do. But what would that be? "The license had been granted and the only issue before the Supreme Court was who would build the dam."[10]

On June 5, 1967, came a surprising development. The U.S. Supreme Court, in a 6-2 decision, set aside the license for High Mountain Sheep dam and directed the Federal Power Commission to reopen the case and consider whether any dam should be built. Justice William O. Douglas wrote the majority opinion: "The test is whether the project is in the public interest. And that determination can only be made after exploration of all issues relative to the 'public interest' including future power demand and supply, alternate sources of power, the public interest in preserving reaches of wild rivers and wilderness areas, the preservation of anadromous fish for commercial and recreational purposes and the protection of wildlife."[11]

Douglas cited the Anadromous Fish Act of 1965, expressing the concern of Congress about declining salmon and steelhead: "The importance of salmon and steelhead in our outdoor life as well as commerce is so great that there certainly comes a time when their destruction might necessitate a halt to so-called 'improvement' or 'development' of waterways. The destruction of anadromous fish in our western waterways is so notorious that we cannot believe that Congress, through the present Act (Federal Power Act of 1920), authorized their demise."

Douglas cited the November 1960 letter to the FPC from Assistant Interior Secretary Elmer Bennett saying proposed Mountain Sheep fish passage facilities were "unproved" and that losses of habitat for mule deer and other wildlife could not be mitigated. He quoted the commission itself in its licensing decision: "…we understandably must assume that the best efforts will be only partly successful and that real damage may and probably will be done to such fish runs." He cited the Fish and Wildlife Coordination Act that called for equal consideration for wildlife in water development programs. And Douglas cited Senate approval of the Wild Rivers Act in 1966 and its reintroduction in the current Congress as evidence of a renewed interest by Congress in "preserving our nation's rivers in their wild, unexploited state."

He noted that Interior Secretary Stewart Udall had advised the FPC in 1962 that immediate construction of High Mountain Sheep was not required for Northwest power needs. Douglas cited the 1962 authorization by Congress of Bruces Eddy and Asotin dams, an appropriation for Little Goose dam (downstream from Lewiston on the Snake) and approval of the Hanford Thermal Project. A pending treaty with Canada might add 1,399 megawatts of generating capacity and open the door to construction of Libby dam with 397.

While making the case for a no-dam decision, Douglas also directed the FPC to consider a federal dam, saying the Federal Power Act required the commission to evaluate the merits of federal development of any hydroelectric project and submit its findings and recommendations to Congress. The commission hadn't allowed Interior to present evidence in support of a federal dam. "If another dam is built the question of whether it should be under federal auspices looms large in view of federal projects on the Snake-Columbia waterway and the effect of operation of a new dam on the vast river complex."

Five justices concurred in the opinion. Justices John Harlan and Potter Stewart dissented. Harlan wrote that the majority: "in its haste to give force to its own findings of fact on the breeding requirements of anadromous fish and the likelihood that solar and nuclear power will shortly be alternate sources of power supply, substituted its own preferences for the discretion given by Congress to the Federal Power Commission. In particular it must be emphasized that the Court, alone among the Secretary of Interior, the commission, Pacific Northwest Power, the Washington Public Power Supply System and the various other interveners apparently supposes that no dam at all may now be needed at High Mountain Sheep."

Harlan added that nothing "in the terms or legislative history of the Anadromous Fish Act of 1965 suggest in any way that it was expected to provide the Secretary or this court with any retroactive mandate to overturn the commission's judgment."

Harlan was right. None of the interveners, including the Idaho, Oregon and Washington wildlife federations and fish and game agencies had spoken up for flowing rivers, for salmon above High Mountain Sheep or for wildlife habitat to be flooded by the dam. The majority opinion reflected the personal views of Justice Douglas, a native of Yakima, Wash. Douglas was a nature lover and friend of wilderness and rivers. His book, "My Wilderness" published in 1960 celebrated wild places he had explored in the Northwest, including the Middle Fork of the Salmon River.

Not everyone recognized the court decision's significance. Among those who did were Russ Mager and Brock Evans. Hells Canyon and the river were not saved but had won a stay of execution and a new trial. Mager wrote Douglas applauding the wisdom of the court: "Those of us who favor preserving this grand gorge and river now have the opportunity to throw some light on the questions raised by the Supreme Court around power, recreation, wildlife and wild rivers."

Mager believed the opponents now needed to prepare an in-depth study. He recognized that the canyon was relatively "undiscovered and unknown," particularly the "approximately 20 miles of magnificent gorge and river between Johnson Bar and Granite Creek rapids."[12]

In their forays into the canyon Mager and his son had seen only two other people, both sheepherders. Few people had experienced the power of the river's many roaring rapids as it passed between sheer rock walls below Idaho Power's dams. Not many knew that it was deeper than the Colorado's Grand Canyon with a greater variety of wildlife and fish or that its history included 7,000 years of human occupation. Relatively few knew about the 19th century attempts to pass steam powered paddle wheel boats through the rapids, the brutal 1887 massacre of 32 Chinese miners, or the difficult high water crossing of the river by Joseph's Wallowa band of Nez Perce in the spring of 1877 after they were ordered onto the reservation. Not many knew that the canyon's geology included rock spewed from ocean volcanoes.

Some of the local people, residents of Weiser, Grangeville and Lewiston, had recognized it as exceptional. They had called attention to the jagged peaks and glacial lakes of the Seven Devils and the deep canyon as a potential tourist attraction in the 1930s and again in 1950, proposing it as a national park.[13] The

National Park Service took a look but the resulting reports were negative. The author of the 1930s report concluded that the canyon was "an unimpressive, drab, rocky, snake-infested area totally unsuitable for a national park."

The Forest Service designated a Seven Devils-Hells Canyon Scenic Area in 1962. But since 1947, the canyon had been recognized primarily for its power potential. In considering the Wild Rivers Act the Senate Interior Committee recognized the Middle Snake as a river of great beauty but did not recommend it as a wild river because of the pending dam license applications.

Brock Evans had learned of Mager's interest and wrote asking about local sentiment: "I believe if enough local sportsmen and others express their concerns in an organized way about this project, there may be a chance to do something about it."[14] Evans wrote the Supreme Court asking if new parties could now intervene, becoming participants in the Federal Power Commission proceedings. The answer was yes. Gathering all the information he could find on Hells Canyon, he began drafting a petition for intervention by the Sierra Club and the Federation of Western Outdoor Clubs, a coalition organized in 1932 that now included 41 Northwest mountaineering, outdoor and conservation organizations.

To add credibility Evans also wanted a local organization: "Given the overwhelming pro-dam climate of the times, we were certain to be attacked by politicians and media." The Idaho Alpine Club signed on. Members had seen Russ Mager's slides, knew about the court decision and needed no persuasion. Evans got the required 30 copies of the petition to intervene in the mail just before the midnight deadline on August 31, 1967.[15]

By that time Mager and Alpine Club members had formed a new organization to campaign for protection of the river and the canyon. On July 19, Mager hosted the organizing meeting of the Hells Canyon Preservation Council at his home. Also present were Boyd Norton, Jerry Jayne, Paul Fritz, Al McGlinsky, Cyril Slansky and James Campbell.[16] All but Mager and Fritz worked at the National Reactor Testing Station. Slansky was the respected elder statesman among NRTS scientists. He had led a team in pioneering research on the recovery of enriched uranium from the spent fuel of nuclear reactors. Norton was a talented writer and photographer with a growing passion for wilderness protection. Fritz was supervisor of the Craters of the Moon National Monument. Jerry Jayne grew up on a Pennsylvania apple farm, came west with wife, Joyce, to study at the University of Idaho and left an Idaho Falls teaching job to become a computer programmer at the testing station.[17]

In the Idaho Alpine Club, Mager, Evans and Harvey had found a talented and spirited band of conservation advocates. With Mager as president, Jayne

Gerald (Jerry) Jayne

as vice president and James Campbell as secretary, the Hells Canyon Preservation Council (HCPC) would take the lead in working for protection of the river and the canyon. It would gather information, recruit supporters, court possible allies, seek political support, and carry the message to local and national media. The organization had no staff, no office and no money and would depend entirely on the work of volunteers.[18]

A September visit to Hells Canyon was scheduled so HCPC members and Evans could see what they were trying to save. Jayne, Campbell and Tom Davis, the Wilderness Society's Cliff Merritt and Evans made the trip up the river to Willow Creek camp with Floyd Harvey. The next day he took them another 12 miles to Granite Creek. They marveled at the majesty of the canyon, absorbed the sights and sounds of the river, explored and fished.

They caught smallmouth bass, trout, catfish and sturgeon including one six feet long and another eight, estimated to weigh 250 pounds. Campbell described his impressions: "This stretch of the river gorge (above Willow Creek) is tremendous with one rapid after another and walls on both sides of the river towering over a mile above you. We all felt after this trip that this unique piece of America should be protected against another needless dam."[19] Evans and Merritt talked strategy.

It was not enough to oppose Mountain Sheep dam before the Federal Power Commission. They needed a plan for permanent protection that people could rally around, that could gain national attention and support. They settled on the idea of Congressional legislation for a Hells Canyon-Snake National River, protecting the river from Hells Canyon Dam to Lewiston, barring not only Mountain Sheep but also all other possible dams. They talked about including a corridor of land along either side if the river.[20]

Filled with enthusiasm after the sojourn in the canyon, HCPC members assembled their first newsletter in Jayne's living room, sending it to Northwest Sierra Club members, members of the Federation of Western Outdoor Clubs and to Floyd Harvey's past river excursion patrons. People were asked to join with annual dues of $2, support the Hells Canyon-National River and help

Ernie Day photo

Snake River in Hells Canyon

save the continent's deepest gorge, last stronghold of the white sturgeon, some of Idaho and Oregon's best game habitat and "a unique archeological and ecological" area.

The national river was still a concept without defined boundaries. In late September, the Federal Power Commission accepted the anti-dam interveners as full participants. Pacific Northwest Power had argued that they should be allowed only limited participation and should not be admitted as "parties" with legal standing to appeal the FPC's decision. Other new interveners were the National Wildlife Federation and the Idaho Water Resource Board.[21]

Evans and the council leaders were hoping the Idaho Wildlife Federation would join the campaign. He talked by phone with Bruce Bowler, who advised him that he was still considering what the federation should do in view of the Supreme Court decision. Bowler felt obligated to Pacific Northwest Power for filing on the Mountain Sheep site rather than Nez Perce, for showing concern for Salmon River salmon and for working with the fish advocates against Nez Perce. He was impressed with the research PNP was conducting on its plan to pass Imnaha River fish past Mountain Sheep dam through a 19-mile canal.[22]

In the second newsletter in February 1968, the council reported gaining more allies, the North Idaho Wilderness Committee headed by Morton Brigham and the Oregon Fish and Game Council of Richland, Ore., a small community near Brownlee reservoir. The 400-member Idaho Outfitters and Guides Association was opposing any dam.

Despite the reticence of Bruce Bowler the Idaho Wildlife Federation, by vote of its directors, was now opposing Mountain Sheep. But it was not opposing a dam above the mouth of the Imnaha at the Appaloosa or Pleasant Valley sites. The other news was that, in the wake of the Supreme Court decision, Northwest Power Company and Washington Water Power had ended their long feud and joined forces. They were now joint applicants for a license. They wanted to build High Mountain Sheep but would settle for Appaloosa, eight miles above the Salmon, or Pleasant Valley, 24 miles above. Private and public power interests would now be working together.

Appaloosa and Pleasant Valley would be less damaging to seagoing fish since they would not obstruct the Imnaha and would not require a low re-regulating dam at China Gardens, 15 miles below the Salmon. With the failure of Idaho Power's skimmer at Brownlee, fishery agencies had agreed that there would be no more experiments with fish passage at high dams. No attempt would be made to pass seagoing fish in the Snake River beyond any of the possible dams, Mountain Sheep, Appaloosa or Pleasant Valley. Adults would be trapped below the dam and their progeny would be reared in a hatchery. But the Mountain Sheep plan still included a canal to pass Imnaha fish. Appaloosa was the site favored by Interior Secretary Stewart Udall for a federal dam built by the Bureau of Reclamation. And Udall was trying to partner with PNP and Washington Public Power Supply System (WPPSS) to build it.[23]

Cyril Slansky prepared a detailed paper describing the case against Mountain Sheep or another high dam and presented it, with Hells Canyon slides and a film of HCPC members landing sturgeon, at a meeting of the Bonneville Sportsmen's Association. Don Thomas of Lewiston persuaded the Lewiston Chamber of Commerce to withdraw its support for Mountain Sheep. Boyd Norton spoke for the river and canyon at the Northwest Wilderness Conference in Seattle.[24]

Russ Mager was invited to speak as part of a panel discussion on Snake dams at the annual meeting of the Idaho Wildlife Federation in late March. He hoped to persuade the federation, with its many affiliates and 20,000 members, to join the no-dam campaign. But federation members adopted the earlier position of the directors, opposing only dams below the Imnaha. While the decision disappointed river defenders, it ended the federation's 8-year alliance with Pacific Northwest Power in support of High Mountain Sheep.

Hugh Smith, the PNP attorney, tried to keep the federation on board, claiming that Mountain Sheep would not harm salmon or steelhead while conceding that it would eliminate sturgeon. The resolution passed unanimously by voice vote. The only one who spoke against it was Bruce Bowler who said he didn't yet feel qualified to make a judgment.

Morton Brigham responded: "I've had 15 years to make up my mind and the biggest mistake I ever made was once, years ago, believing dams could be of benefit." Brigham had lobbied for the resolution, warning federation members of the scheme to divert Salmon River water through a tunnel to the reservoir behind Mountain Sheep. Speaking on the panel, Bowler had said he believed Mountain Sheep would be the last big dam built in the Northwest with the emergence of nuclear power. He applauded the Supreme Court decision that echoed his years of pleading for the public interest value of fish, wildlife, wilderness and rivers: "It was probably the greatest conservation law of all times."[25]

Slansky presented his paper to the Pacific Northwest Conservation Council in Missoula. With Mountain Sheep dam, he said, there would be "no more falls and wild cascades, no life along the flooded sand bars and beaches" and no wild river boating. The four commercial boat operators reported that visitation was up 300 per cent since 1962, to 4,000 visitor days a year. The white sturgeon would be lost and 17,200 acres of big game habitat would be inundated with potential loss of half the estimated 28,600 deer and 5,400 elk in a severe winter. Salmon runs would be reduced and a re-regulating dam at China Gardens would back water into the mouth of the Salmon, said Slansky.

Archeological and other historic sites would be flooded along with 80 per cent of the camping and recreation land along the river and important trails. More reservoir recreation was not needed, he said. Idaho Power's three dam complex had 19,000 acres of reservoirs. Slansky said nuclear plants contracted in 1966 would have capacity equaling the country's 20 largest hydroelectric installations.[26]

In hearings, articles, interviews and pleadings before the Federal Power Commission defenders would try to make a basic point: Hells Canyon, the surging river, the plants, wildlife, fish, geology and historical sites plus the adjoining streams and canyons were, in combination, a rare treasure, unique on the continent. The issue was much more than river versus reservoir recreation, far more than fish versus dams or the cost of hydroelectric power versus nuclear power, far more than scenic quality or current or future numbers of visitors. This was a test of the ability of 20th century humanity to recognize and retain a masterpiece, the product of millions of years of nature's handiwork.

In April, New York Times Reporter William Blair, responding to a council invitation, accompanied a group that included Jayne, Norton, Campbell and his wife, Ruth, on a 4-day excursion in the canyon with Floyd Harvey. Blair described how Harvey took two passengers at a time through the biggest rapids. One of them, Sluice Creek, shattered the boat's windshield. Blair described some of the canyon's history and the wildlife. Part of the party climbed 3,000 feet toward Hat Point on the Oregon side, sighting a dozen elk and enjoying a spectacular view of the canyon. The Times followed up with an editorial calling for protection of the river and canyon with no more dams. This was a coup in the continuing effort by the council to win national media attention and support.[27]

In mid-May, Stewart Udall announced that a federal interagency study showed that Appaloosa was the most desirable site for a dam on the Middle Snake. Interior fish experts believed Mountain Sheep would reduce both Imnaha and Salmon River salmon. Oxygen-short water releases flowing past the mouth of the Salmon would kill some upstream migrants and the fluctuating river flows would disorient others. Udall claimed that Appaloosa would actually help upstream migrants by releasing cold water, reducing Snake River summer temperatures all the way to the Columbia. The experts projected a million-pound increase in commercial salmon harvest and 250,000 pounds of steelhead with a million more angler days of sports fishing.[28]

The Preservation Council's August newsletter focused on the upcoming hearings scheduled by the Federal Power Commission in Lewiston and Portland, asking people to testify or write letters for the record. Departing from its usual procedure, the FPC was inviting public testimony, not limiting

H. Tom Davis Photo

Sheep Creek Rapids in Hells Canyon.

participation to interveners. This would be the first opportunity for Hells Canyon defenders to speak in a forum with extensive media coverage. Jim Campbell got off a letter to Gov. Don Samuelson asking him to oppose any dams, with copies to members of the Idaho congressional delegation, media, chambers of commerce, Idaho Wildlife Federation and the Idaho Water Resource Board.[29]

A few days before the Lewiston hearing, Idaho Senators Frank Church and Len Jordan announced that they would co-sponsor legislation for a 10-year moratorium on licensing further dams in the Middle Snake, allowing time for further study. Jordan favored eventual construction of a dam at the Nez Perce site, impounding Salmon River as well as Snake River water. From a Nez Perce reservoir, water might be pumped back over the Idaho Power dams upstream, allowing the irrigation of more desert land in Idaho and eastern Oregon. Jordan believed as many as seven million additional acres could be irrigated rather than the two million projected without Salmon River water. He opposed the FPC licensing of a dam at Mountain Sheep, Appaloosa or Pleasant Valley because it would mean there could be no dam at the Nez Perce site. He also feared that the amount of water needed to turn turbines in a dam licensed by the FPC might limit future upstream development. Hugh Smith tried to persuade him that Mountain Sheep or Appaloosa could also store Salmon River water by diverting part of the Salmon's flow through a tunnel. But Jordan wouldn't bite.[30]

Jordan was considered an authority on water and its use in the West. In a University of Oregon thesis written in the 1920s, he advocated construction of a series of dams on the Columbia and Snake to permit slack water navigation below Lewiston. After ending his term as Idaho governor, he was appointed by President Eisenhower to serve on the International Joint Commission that was working on the U.S.-Canada Columbia River water treaty. He helped define water resource policy for the Eisenhower administration. Jordan considered himself a friend of conservation and wildlife. But he had no reservations about submerging land bordering the river under a reservoir, including the Kirkwood Bar sheep ranch where his family lived for eight years during the depression, if the result was more irrigated land. A moratorium would give the Idaho Water Resource Board time to prepare a state water plan including the use of Salmon River water.[31]

Frank Church preferred preservation of the river and canyon. A moratorium would delay a licensing decision by the FPC and give Hells Canyon advocates more time: "In the next decade, technological advances in electrical power generation may make the need for high, single purpose hydroelectric dams obsolete – and it may turn out that this magnificent gorge can be preserved in all its wonderful recreational aspects," said Church.

The 10-year moratorium would coincide with the 10-year moratorium that Church, Jordan and other Northwest senators had won on federal study of the diversion of Northwest water to the Southwest. They had been able to attach that provision to the $779 million Central Arizona Project. The Snake River legislation reflected the close working relationship of the Idaho senators on resource issues, based on personal respect. Church had accepted a compromise with Jordan on the Wild and Scenic Rivers bill, giving up protection of the Salmon River in exchange for protection of the Clearwater. The senators were also working together for a Sawtooth National Recreation Area.

More than 100 witnesses signed up in advance of the Lewiston hearing. Floyd Harvey opened his home to HCPC members from Pocatello and Idaho Falls. Dam advocates outnumbered anti-dam witnesses but the count was close. The Lewiston Morning Tribune reported that 54 witnesses favored a Pacific Northwest Power-Washington Public Power Supply System dam, 12 favored a federal dam, 49 wanted no dam and 10 supported the 10-year moratorium. This represented a huge shift in sentiment since the Supreme

Court decision. River protection advocates also submitted petitions with 6,000 names.[32]

Russ Mager said the emergence of nuclear power made a dam unnecessary. "Must we build every dam, destroy every river?" asked Art Manley, the past year's president of the Idaho Wildlife Federation. He endorsed the moratorium. "When will we stop paving, damming and fencing?" asked HCPC member Dick Wild. The Washington Environmental Council's George Hudson said the river belonged to the people of the United States, not the local communities backing a dam. Allen Slickpoo said the Nez Perce tribe opposed any additional dams on the Snake, Salmon or Clearwater. George Reed of the Oregon Wildlife Federation said the organization's previous support for High Mountain Sheep was a mistake: "No amount of fish passage facilities" would preserve the Imnaha runs.

Carmelita Holland of Richland, Ore. said the Idaho Power dams destroyed the seagoing fish and the economic benefit to nearby communities was short-lived. She mocked a PNP display showing a completed dam with a blue water reservoir: "Your little exhibit out there made me feel at home – clear water with no fish." Morton Brigham disputed assertions that few people used the canyon, citing an annual deer harvest of 400. Floyd Harvey said his excursion business had increased six times in six years but would be destroyed by a dam. The Idaho Fish and Game Department was now opposing any dam on the Middle Snake. Director Dick Woodworth said construction of Mountain Sheep or Appaloosa "would seriously damage and could even eliminate the Salmon and Imnaha runs of anadromous fish" while inundating big game winter range. The department wasn't buying the theory that Idaho salmon would benefit from cold-water releases from an Appaloosa reservoir. Rancher Jack McClaran of Enterprise, Ore. said any dam would inundate the headquarters of most of the sheep and cattle ranches along the river.

Dam supporters included spokesmen for Northwest unions, the North Idaho Chamber of Commerce and the Washington State Grange. Ken Billings of the Washington Public Utility Commission said: "it would be a sacrilege to waste the water without developing the Middle Snake." Hugh Smith said Pacific Northwest Power favored the High Mountain Sheep site but only if it could build the China Gardens re-regulating dam downstream. Its second choice was Pleasant Valley, the site of its original filing in 1954. Gov. Don Samuelson presented what he described as the official Idaho position, opposing any development unless the state received a sizable share of the monetary benefits. This was also the position of the Idaho Water Resource Board. The board wanted revenue to help pay for irrigation development. A few days later in Portland, dam opponents outnumbered supporters 30-9.

With the strong showing of anti-dam sentiment in the Lewiston and Portland hearings, Pacific Northwest Power and WPPSS were persuaded to accept Stewart Udall's proposed joint venture for a federal Appaloosa Dam. As a sweetener, to help win Congressional approval, the power combine would pay construction costs in exchange for 50 years of cheap power. This approach would bypass the Federal Power Commission and avoid the risk of Supreme Court rejection of a license for a dam. The applicants asked for a 6-month delay in the FPC proceedings while they sought congressional approval. The HCPC urged its members to write members of Congress opposing the Udall plan.[33]

Brock Evans completed his draft of the Hells Canyon-National River bill and it was unveiled at a Seattle press conference on Nov. 10, 1968. It would protect 100 miles of river from Hells Canyon dam to Asotin, Wash., just upstream from Lewiston. It would also ban dams on 85 miles of the lower Salmon River and on the Imnaha. It included 256,000 acres in a Seven Devils unit in Idaho and 335,000 acres in the Oregon Imnaha unit to be managed by the Forest Service primarily for scenic, wilderness and recreation values. Livestock grazing would continue but logging and mining would be banned. Included were areas to remain roadless with consideration for wilderness designation – 115,000 acres in Idaho and 250,000 in Oregon.

From the northern boundaries of the designated areas to Lewiston a quarter-mile strip would be included on both sides of the Snake with a similar strip on the lower Salmon. The Secretary of Agriculture would protect public use by purchasing easements on privately owned land. He could also acquire private land for access and for administration. Motorized boat traffic would continue. With the river corridors, total acreage was 721,000. With this bill, the Middle Snake River, the lower Salmon and the Imnaha would have protection similar to that given to wild rivers, under the Wild Rivers Act passed by Congress in September.[34]

"This is one conservation issue on which all the various groups – sportsmen, conservationists and foresters agree," said Russ Mager. "All the national conservation organizations from the Sierra Club, the National Wildlife Federation and the American Forestry Association down to local sportsmen and rod and gun clubs are unanimously opposed to the dams."

It wasn't entirely unanimous, since the Idaho Wildlife Federation was not yet opposing all dams and the national federation was three months away from a no-dam position. But the anti-dam coalition was growing. The upstart Hells Canyon Preservation Council, with the legal work of Brock Evans and considerable help from Floyd Harvey, had made remarkable progress in 17 months. Far more people, in and out of the Northwest, knew about Hells

Canyon and agreed that it was a national treasure deserving permanent protection.

The HCPC assembled a packet of information, including the proposed national river bill, a sampling of letters from across the country that had been sent to the FPC and a history of the controversy, and sent it off to members of Congress. The cover letter praised the 90th Congress for its conservation record including protection of California Redwoods and the North Cascades in Washington State and approval of the Wild and Scenic Rivers Act. However, the election of Richard Nixon as President in November 1968 meant that Stewart Udall would be leaving office. Would Nixon's Interior Secretary support federal construction of Appaloosa Dam?[35]

In January public power representatives invited Brock Evans to lunch and offered a deal. They wanted river defenders to support a federal dam authorized by Congress. They told Evans that, based on the history of the case, the Federal Power Commission was sure to issue a license for a private dam. It would be better to have a dam in public hands. Evans advised Russ Mager: "They suggest that the project might be more palatable to us if it included a proposal to make the areas flooded by the dam and also the areas downstream a 'water quality laboratory' to test the affect on fish, etc." Evans agreed that the FPC would grant a license to private power: "But I do not believe a court will do the same thing. And that is what we have thought all along and that has been our strategy. I don't see how we can do anything but fight this project to the end. I believe we can win." Evans wrote that the concept of a water quality laboratory "shows how little they understand what we are thinking about."[36]

Mager sent a letter to Oregon and Washington HCPC members urging them to write their congressional representatives opposing any Middle Snake dam. Letters had already gone to the Idaho delegation. Federal dam supporters would need to find a senator or congressman from the Northwest to sponsor their bill. Brock Evans went to Washington to lobby Nixon administration officials. Nixon aide John Ehrlichman arranged for him to meet with Interior Undersecretary Russell Train who was receptive to river protection.[37]

In their January 1969 newsletter, HCPC leaders described the Church-Jordan moratorium as the second best bill expected to be introduced in the 91st Congress. The best was the Hells Canyon-Snake National River. A moratorium could be lifted long before the end of 10 years and there was no need for further study. But finding sponsors for the national river bill turned out to be more difficult than had been expected.

Senator Church, a sponsor of the Wild and Scenic Rivers Act and champion of the Wilderness Act, was the preferred candidate but he refused. Church was committed to the moratorium and would not go back on his agreement with Senator Jordan. Church also needed Jordan's cooperation on the Sawtooth Recreation Area legislation. He not only declined to sponsor the national river bill but also opposed its introduction, recognizing that it would make it more difficult to pass the moratorium: "As long as I am committed to the moratorium, I will oppose any attempt to authorize any dams on the Middle Snake. Similarly, I would also oppose any effort to dedicate the river to single use recreation, since either action would defeat the very purpose of the moratorium," he wrote Mager. "Should you wish to have someone introduce such a bill, Russ, that is your prerogative. But I hope you will understand that I will have to oppose its introduction at this time."[38]

In July, Church accepted an invitation to meet with Preservation Council directors in Idaho Falls. He softened his position, saying he would not oppose introduction of their bill. In the August HCPC newsletter, members were told Church refused to support the national river bill because of his agreement with Senator Jordan and because he "seemed to underestimate the tremendous national support" for the measure. "Rather, he has been very much impressed by the apparent strength of those few (and we might add local) interests lobbying for a dam. Getting congressional approval for our bill, already a tough job, will be made even tougher by the conspicuous front line absence of Senator Church, one of the Senate's most respected conservationists."[39]

The Idaho Wildlife Federation was still withholding its support for the National River bill, proceeding on the assumption that a dam was inevitable. Some of its members, notably Ted Trueblood, were swayed by the Interior Department's assertion that cold-water releases from an Appaloosa or Pleasant Valley reservoir would help adult salmon bound for the Salmon River. Trueblood wrote some Northwest conservationists urging support for a federal dam, describing the Snake River canyon as a "hot hole in the summer and a cold one in winter." Brock Evans advised one of the letter's recipients, Lew Bell of Everett, Wash., that two days of FPC hearings on the subject, including cross-examination of Interior's witnesses, had convinced him that a dam's alleged benefit to salmon was only theory and speculation.[40]

While the Idaho Wildlife Federation continued to withhold support for the national river bill, one of its foremost leaders, Ernie Day, signed on as an HCPC director along with long-time IWF member Al Klotz of Boise. And the federation's First District adopted a no-dam resolution. (The federation didn't declare its opposition to all dams until 1970, when Bruce Bowler submitted a brief to the Federal Power Commission saying that "the whole voluminous record of these proceedings add up to the fact that the undammed portion of the Middle Snake River in Hells Canyon is a most unique resource that belongs to all the people of this nation.")[41]

In the Federal Power Commission proceeding, Brock Evans found well-qualified witnesses to speak for the unique value of the river and canyon.

They included river runner Martin Litton, plant ecologist Frank Craighead, archeologist Earl Swanson of Idaho State University and geologist Tracy Vallier. In a brief filed in October 1970, Evans also cited the testimony of Fishery Supervisor Monte Richards of the Idaho Fish and Game Department, Stuart Murrell of Idaho Fish and Game, the Idaho Wildlife Federation's witness, and Wade Hall of the Wallowa-Whitman National Forest.[42]

In 1969 Idaho conservationists rallied to fight the proposed open pit mine near picturesque Castle Peak in the White Cloud mountains northeast of Sun Valley. The threat to the White Clouds energized conservation leaders and, like the Hells Canyon issue, brought a new generation into the activist ranks. The White Clouds fight generated far more Idaho media attention and citizen interest than Hells Canyon but the surge in environmental sentiment helped win more defenders for the river and canyon. The White Clouds found determined advocates among leaders of the Hells Canyon Preservation Council. With allies in Pocatello, Ketchum, Moscow and Boise they organized the Greater Sawtooth Preservation Council, modeled on the Hells Canyon Council.

Some of them also helped form a third organization, the Idaho Environmental Council (IEC), to work on multiple issues. Like the Oregon and Washington environmental councils, Brock Evans had suggested it. Bruce Bowler drew up articles of incorporation in April 1969, and the IEC was organized with University of Idaho faculty members James Calvert and Fred Rabe of Moscow, Art Manley, Russ Mager and Paul Fritz as directors. Soon added were Jerry Jayne, plus Lyle Stanford and Donna Parsons, both of the College of Idaho, Max Walker and Salmon physician Walt Blackadar.

The goals included increased public awareness of man's impact on the environment, protecting scenic, historic and open space resources, wilderness and wildlife. The directors dived into an imposing list of issues and goals including the White Clouds, Hells Canyon, upper Selway River wilderness, Lower Granite dam on the Snake below Lewiston, state prohibition of dredge mining on wild and scenic rivers and creation of a state department of ecology. In December, Jayne was named the first president.[43]

Hells Canyon was gaining more national attention with a photo and article in Life magazine and prominent mention in the Readers Digest. Idaho Outdoor Writer Ferris Weddle's plea for the river and canyon had appeared in the Defenders of Wildlife Magazine in October 1968. In July 1969, Field and Stream magazine published Michael Frome's article "Must This Be Lost to the Sight of Man?" The National Parks Association and Wilderness Society magazines published articles by Cyril Slansky and Russ Mager.

But the most significant development was the emergence of a prominent ally, radio and television personality Arthur Godfrey. Godfrey wrote the

Russell Mager Photo

Arthur Godfrey landing a trout in Hells Canyon. Floyd Harvey in background.

Federal Power Commission in 1968 opposing the licensing of a dam. Boyd Norton wrote thanking him and invited him to join HCPC members on a Hells Canyon trip with Floyd Harvey. Godfrey replied that he would like nothing better, but it would depend on his professional schedule.

A few months later Godfrey called Harvey and scheduled a trip for the July 4, 1969 weekend, flying to Lewiston on a friend's Learjet. Harvey and the mayor of Lewiston hosted the entertainer at a private dinner with a few conservationists. It was late afternoon the next day when Godfrey and Harvey reached Willow Creek "having battered our way through 30 thrilling rapids. The walls of the canyon grow steep and towering, rising to 6,000 feet. Here, one reflects, are God's cathedrals," Godfrey would write.

Godfrey and Harvey slept under the stars on the beach. Next day they fished for sturgeon and Godfrey landed a 7-footer. Further upstream at the mouth of Sheep Creek that flowed from Sheep Lake, high in the Seven Devils, he caught six rainbow trout in an hour. In a helicopter flight arranged by Harvey he flew over the reservoir behind Hells Canyon dam before returning to Lewiston.[44]

Russ Mager was also in the canyon that weekend with a National Broadcasting Company crew that was filming a segment on Hells Canyon for the Huntley-Brinkley news program. They interviewed Mager at the mouth of the Salmon River and filmed a fisherman landing a sturgeon. Mager then rode with Harvey upriver to Sheep Creek where he got a photo of Godfrey hooking a trout. Godfrey rhapsodized at length about the river and canyon on his national radio program. He also wrote Interior Secretary Walter Hickel describing his experience, releasing his letter to the news media: "Mr.

Secretary, you must not allow anyone to build a dam on that river." Godfrey offered to arrange a trip for Hickel. "I beg you to see it personally." Hickel at that time was considering whether to pursue authorization of a federal dam as proposed by his predecessor.[45]

The HCPC, Floyd Harvey and Brock Evans had succeeded in making Hells Canyon a national issue. In August, Hickel announced that the Nixon administration would not pursue construction of a federal dam. And he called for a 3- to 5-year moratorium on a Federal Power Commission license decision to allow further study. But the commission was renewing its deliberations, accepting more testimony from applicants and interveners.

With Senator Church's assurance that he would not oppose introduction of the Hells Canyon-National River bill, HCPC directors expected to soon find a sponsor. But three months passed without success. In early November 1969, Boyd Norton was in New York and stopped in the offices of Audubon Magazine, which was preparing his Hells Canyon article and photo essay for publication. The editor had just received page proofs and gave him several sets.

Brock Evans had suggested that the freshman senator from Oregon, Robert Packwood, seemed to be conservation-oriented and should be approached. Norton caught a flight to Washington and made an appointment with Packwood. After studying the proofs, looking carefully at each photo, Packwood agreed to sponsor the bill. Norton also met with a potential House sponsor, veteran Pennsylvania Republican John Saylor. Saylor had played a key role in keeping a bill for a high federal Hells Canyon dam in committee and had also helped delay construction of Bruces Eddy on the North Fork of the Clearwater. In a visit to Washington, Russ Mager talked with Saylor who told him he had decided to introduce the bill after meeting with Norton earlier in the week. Mager also visited with an aide to Sen. George McGovern and the conversation gave him hope that McGovern would co-sponsor a bill with Packwood. Mager called Church's assistant, Porter Ward, who reaffirmed Church's pledge not to oppose the bill's introduction.[46]

With modest changes by congressional staff, Brock Evans' draft of the national river bill was introduced in the House by Saylor on Jan. 8 and in the Senate by Packwood four days later. Getting the bills introduced was one thing, getting them considered in committee was another. Neither Senator Church nor Jordan had any desire to have the Packwood bill considered. They were pushing for action on their moratorium bill that would have a hearing on Feb. 16 before the Senate Interior Committee's Subcommittee on Water and Power Resources. HCPC members were urged to write members of the Senate Interior Committee urging support for the Packwood bill rather than the moratorium. The canyon deserved permanent protection, they were told, and the moratorium was a poor second choice: "For us to be immobilized for 10 years would mean fighting the whole battle over again then." By that time the power and reclamation interests might have a new set of arguments. While many organizations were helping, council members were advised that "the bulk of the work must be done by you." A "multitude of letters" was needed. The council's membership list now included 900 in 42 states.[47]

Hells Canyon advocates hoped to avoid offending Senator Church while advocating passage of their bill rather than the moratorium. The day before the hearing Church called Evans, Harvey and other river defenders into his office and asked them to support the moratorium. They met later in the day and changed their testimony, in support of the moratorium as a first step toward protection of the river and canyon with the Packwood bill.[48]

Church opened the hearing by telling the committee there was a growing movement to protect the river and acknowledging introduction of the Packwood bill. He described the natural, fish and wildlife values of Hells Canyon in generous terms and spoke of gains in nuclear technology. Senator Jordan predicted that further study by state and federal water planners would confirm the need for irrigation water for a tremendous area in southern Idaho and Eastern Oregon. He described the possible benefits of a dam at the Nez Perce site, impounding Salmon River water and suggested that a decade's delay might resolve the salmon issue with destruction of the fish by downstream dams either built, under construction or authorized. Senator Packwood credited Church and Jordan with foresight in proposing the moratorium but said the preservation of river and canyon could best be achieved with his bill. He asked for inclusion of Norton's Audubon article in the hearing record and provided a Hells Canyon film for the committee's viewing.

River defenders, including Jerry Jayne, Norton (who was now western representative for the Wilderness Society), Floyd Harvey, Carmelita Holland, Annette Tussing of Clarkston, Wash. and the Sierra Club's Lloyd Tupling, used the hearing to plead for the Packwood bill while endorsing the moratorium as a first step. The moratorium was also endorsed by the National Wildlife Federation, Lewiston Tribune Editorial Page Editor Bill Hall and by the Interior and Agriculture departments. Deputy Forest Service Chief M.M. Nelson called the Middle Snake "a magnificent, irreplaceable natural feature" that should be left as it was. The Forest Service had advised the FPC in November 1968 that no dam should be licensed. A surprise witness, former Interior Secretary Stewart Udall, endorsed the moratorium and described the canyon as an awe-inspiring place deserving national park status. He was apologetic about his previous advocacy for a federal dam that he said was based on the assumption that the alternative was a dam licensed by the Federal

Power Commission. He said the whole history of the commission indicated that if there was an application a dam would be licensed.[49]

Church clashed with Idaho Water Resource Board Director Robert R. Lee, who did not endorse the moratorium but spoke in favor of a dam licensed by the FPC, Pleasant Valley or Appaloosa. The board was pursuing an agreement with the applicants to participate in the project so it could receive $1.5 to $3 million a year in power revenue to use for irrigation development, said Lee. Ten percent of the dam's power output was to be reserved for Idaho and marketed by the Idaho Power Company.

Church told Lee that support for a dam was at odds with the purpose of the moratorium, to allow more time to determine the best course. He said his meetings with the board had led him to believe it would support the moratorium. Church challenged Lee's comments dismissing the recreation benefits of a free flowing river. He said Lee's testimony on the board's position was a surprise and came "at the eleventh hour."

Pacific Northwest Power's Hugh Smith said the power combine had been pursuing a license for 14 years. Congressional approval of the moratorium would mean river protection advocates had won because "we will not return to this struggle 10 years from now." Also speaking against the moratorium were spokesmen for Washington Water Power, the American Public Power Association, the Washington Grange, the Oregon Water Resources Board and Idaho Power Company.

To help counter the rising tide of public support for a free flowing river, Pacific Northwest Power hired former Park Service director Conrad Wirth to put a more attractive face on a dam and reservoir. It would be part of a concept called "the great mountain country of the West." PNP would pay for a study of possible road and other development in the region to foster tourism but didn't offer to pay for roads. Preservation council leaders denounced the plan as a public relations gimmick. Replacing one of the wildest and most beautiful stretches of river with a huge reservoir with a 150-foot drawdown was "a bad joke," they said.[50] When FPC hearings resumed in March 1970, the dam applicants also attempted to bolster their position by announcing the completion of agreements for participation by the Idaho Water Resource Board and Idaho Power Company.

In May the Senate approved the moratorium bill on a voice vote. River defenders continued to ask for a hearing for the Packwood bill. And Arthur Godfrey came back to Hells Canyon, this time with Interior Secretary Walter Hickel and entertainer Burl Ives. They would be accompanied by a platoon of lesser-known dignitaries invited by Floyd Harvey. National media came, including the major news services, CBS, and Look magazine.[51] Godfrey, Hickel and Ives were guests at a Lewiston dinner before starting up the river.

Stacy Gebhards of the Idaho Fish and Game Department and two Idaho folk singers put on a program with songs about wild rivers, salmon and water pollution. Governor Samuelson had traveled to Lewiston to greet Hickel and Godfrey at the airport and sat next to Hickel at the dinner. The governor had been defending his record on pollution control, White Clouds mining and Hells Canyon in his re-election campaign and was offended by the pollution slides. After returning to Boise he called the chairman of the Fish and Game Commission with threats to remove the commissioners and Director Dick Woodworth. In view of the governor's wrath, Woodworth advised Gebhards to participate in no more programs.[52]

On the river excursion two press boats took turns passing the celebrity boats, taking photos. Ives emerged from a trip through Rush Creek rapids "with his huge frame dripping wet." In the evening Ives and Godfrey led a sing along around the campfire. Like Godfrey, Ives wanted the canyon left as is. Hickel described it as a great natural area, but did not call for permanent protection, endorsing the moratorium and saying, "time will show the highest use." Godfrey, Hickel and Ives also spent a day on horses high above the canyon on the Oregon side.[53]

The widely publicized Godfrey-Ives-Hickel trip was a public relations triumph for Hells Canyon defenders. But while they were winning with public opinion, House and Senate leaders were not allowing the national river bills to have a hearing.

In an attempt to counter the publicity generated by the Godfrey, Hickel, Ives trip, Pacific Northwest Power brought in another entertainer, Art Linkletter, to speak for dams and progress. He did not get into Hells Canyon on his brief visit but traveled with Dick Rivers only to the mouth of the Salmon with Governor Samuelson and a few Idaho business leaders including industrialist Jack Simplot. The Linkletter visit generated little media coverage and none of the excitement that surrounded the 3-day Godfrey, Hickel, Ives excursion.[54]

November's Idaho election was largely a referendum on White Clouds mining. Conservationists actively supported Cecil Andrus and were delighted with his victory. The Hells Canyon Preservation Council did not endorse candidates but the Idaho Environmental Council did. Hells Canyon was a factor in the IEC's endorsement of Andrus, of Second District Rep. Orval Hansen, who supported the moratorium, and the non-endorsement of Rep. McClure who easily won re-election. When the new Congress convened in 1971, Senators Church and Jordan reintroduced the moratorium bill, dashing the hopes of Hells Canyon defenders that Church would now embrace their bill. Orval Hansen introduced an identical moratorium bill in the House.

Senator Packwood introduced a slightly modified version of the Hells Canyon-National River bill.

In February 1971, Examiner William Levy recommended that the Federal Power Commission grant a license for Pleasant Valley dam with a re-regulating dam, Low Mountain Sheep, at a site just upstream from the Imnaha. Pleasant Valley was to be 550 feet high, backing water for 30 miles, almost to Hells Canyon dam. Low Mountain Sheep would be 175 feet high with a pool extending for 20 miles to Pleasant Valley.

Levy had not been convinced by the extensive testimony of river defenders. Nor was he swayed by the case against a dam presented by the commission staff. He wrote that the Pleasant Valley site, 24 miles above the mouth of the Salmon, would be less environmentally damaging than Appaloosa or High Mountain Sheep. Levy questioned whether future Northwest energy needs would be met with nuclear and coal-fired plants. While a coal-fired plant at Centralia, Wash. was on schedule, the first two proposed nuclear plants, Trojan and Eugene, had been delayed by environmental opposition. Not a single nuclear plant was yet under construction or authorized. Projected hydropower additions at existing dams were also uncertain, he wrote. There was no assurance that more reliable or less environmentally damaging alternative power sources could be provided by 1980. Moreover, "denial now" as a practical matter, would "eliminate the Middle Snake as a regional power resource."

Levy astounded river defenders with a declaration that echoed the position of the power combine: "Pleasant Valley can be constructed without substantial adverse impact on the existing fishery, the natural beauty of the canyon or its scenic values." The reservoirs would make "available a vast area of incomparable beauty to more people rather than to have it remain inaccessible, except to a rugged few." Levy reached this conclusion despite an Idaho Fish and Game Department survey showing far more recreation use of the river below Idaho Power Company's Hells Canyon dam than on the reservoir above. Levy accepted the proposed seagoing fish plan. Adults were to be trapped below the low Mountain Sheep dam and transported by truck to a hatchery. Fifty miles of river habitat would be lost to seagoing fish and sturgeon, including gravel beds where fall chinook spawned.[55]

Levy's recommendation didn't surprise Brock Evans and other river defenders who all along feared the commission would give more weight to its Federal Power Act mandate to promote "comprehensive development" than to Justice Douglas's plea for wild rivers and fish. The only way to protect the river and adjoining wild country was with congressional legislation. There would be more time because Levy recommended delaying an FPC decision until Sept. 11, 1975, allowing Congress to consider the pending studies by the

Agriculture and Interior departments on designation of the Middle Snake from Hells Canyon dam to Lewiston as a wild and scenic river.

River protection received a boost in June, when Gov. Cecil Andrus persuaded Oregon Gov. Tom McCall and Washington's Dan Evans to join him in a letter to the power commission saying another dam in Hells Canyon would not serve the interests of the people of the Northwest or the nation. With this statement Andrus and McCall rejected the positions of their state water resource boards and Evans rejected the previous position of the Washington Public Utilities Commission. Andrus, however, was supporting the Jordan-Church moratorium, not wanting to undercut Church. He refused to endorse the Packwood bill despite continuing pleas from the HCPC.[56]

Packwood took his campaign for the national river bill to Idaho, conducting a press conference in Boise before joining river defenders on a Memorial Day weekend Hells Canyon float trip, accompanied by a CBS film crew. He described the moratorium as, at best, a fallback position.

"He says he wants to build a fire under Church and other Northwest senators on the Senate Interior Committee who have declined to support the Hells Canyon bill," wrote Sam Day of the Intermountain Observer. Packwood's Boise appearance and comments were a direct challenge to Church who responded at his own press conference later in the day: "I welcome him to Idaho. Going down the river will bring additional publicity to the canyon and that's all to the good."

Church said he agreed with the goal of saving the Middle Snake but the moratorium had a better chance of passing. The Intermountain Observer's Day wrote that some of the leaders of Idaho's "more militant" conservation groups no longer regarded Church as their hero. Church refused to support the national river bill and his Sawtooth National Recreation Area bill was considered a "sell out" and was opposed by the Greater Sawtooth Preservation Council.[57]

Packwood was still being denied a hearing on the national river bill. So he adopted a strategy of finding additional co-sponsors, courting senators in one on one conversations. His 25 co-sponsors included some of the most prominent names in the Senate: Edward Kennedy, George McGovern, Edward Brooke, Barry Goldwater, Robert Taft, Jacob Javits, Ernest Hollings, Gaylord Nelson and William Proxmire. Still, the bill was getting no hearing so Packwood adopted a desperate plan, advising Church and Jordan that, when their moratorium bill came up for a Senate vote, he would move to substitute the national river bill.[58]

Church, Jordan and Oregon Sen. Mark Hatfield, a moratorium co-sponsor, sent a letter to all members of the Senate asking them to oppose the Packwood substitute. Church urged Packwood to avoid a floor fight, telling him he would lose. Packwood agreed, after receiving assurance from Nevada Sen. Alan Bible, chairman of the Parks and Recreation Subcommittee of the Interior Committee, that his bill would get a hearing. The HCPC credited Packwood with a great victory as a result of his courageous action.

The directors no longer saw the moratorium bill as a positive step but as an obstacle to passing the national river bill. They advised council members that the situation had changed since the moratorium was introduced in 1968. There was now more public and political support for environmental protection. The moratorium would not curb the latest threat to the canyon, a proliferation of subdividing of private ranch land along the river with the threatened loss of public access. Because of publicity generated by Hells Canyon defenders, the land was now worth more for recreation lots than it had ever been for ranching. The moratorium would put off dam construction only a little longer than the delay the FPC was imposing on itself. Preservation Council leaders had hoped it would go away: "It has not and now its proponents are actively working against us. We feel we no longer have any choice but to oppose it."[59]

On June 28, the Senate passed the moratorium bill for the second time. It was now a 7-year moratorium because three years had passed since the earlier bill's introduction. Russ Mager sent Church a copy of his letter to George McGovern thanking him for signing on as a national river co-sponsor. Church responded, reporting Senate approval of the moratorium: "As I have indicated in my statement to you, if the House does not act this year I plan to reconsider my position on the legislation needed to conserve the Middle Snake." A month earlier Church had asked the Department of Agriculture to begin its proposed wild rivers study. Packwood had made the same request in April.[60]

In an effort to generate more support for the national river bill, Lewis Bell, Everett, Wash. attorney and leader of a coalition of Northwest fly fishing clubs, spearheaded the formation of a new organization, the Coalition to Save the Snake. It included conservation groups, northwest commercial fishing interests and Indian tribes, a total of 40 organizations. The chairman was Jack Hemingway, son of the author, recently appointed to the Idaho Fish and Game Commission by Andrus.

The Hells Canyon Preservation Council had a new president. Russ Mager had stepped aside and the current president was 33-year-old Pete Henault, an energetic nuclear scientist. Henault was a director of the Idaho Environmental Council, had been active in the White Clouds campaign and had worked for the election of Cecil Andrus, organizing an IEC-sponsored fund raising dinner. He also helped organize the Save the Snake Coalition.[61]

Three weeks before the scheduled September hearing, Senator Jordan attacked the Packwood bill in a Boise press conference, calling it the "Idaho water export act of 1971." In an appearance in Lewiston Packwood had said his bill would limit future upstream irrigation development on the Snake River. This was a call to arms for Jordan and southern Idaho irrigation promoters and was recognized by Senator Church as political poison. River defenders looked forward to the opportunity to speak for the national river bill and explain why the moratorium was no longer relevant.

But Packwood's attempt to bypass the Interior Committee had ruffled feathers. His Lewiston comment had been a strategic mistake and Church had been wounded by harsh criticism by Preservation Council leaders. The Hells Canyon advocates were in for some tough questioning.[62]

Before allowing Packwood to explain his bill, Senator Bible gave Jordan 10 minutes to assail it as a threat to all future southern Idaho irrigation development. Questioned by Church, Packwood attempted to clarify his Lewiston statement, saying that upstream irrigation development would be limited only if it depended on construction of a Middle Snake dam. The answer didn't satisfy Church or Jordan and it suggested that Packwood didn't fully understand the issue. Church tried to get him to agree to amend his bill with specific language saying river protection could not limit upstream development. But he refused, saying the volume of water needed for recreation in the river below Hells Canyon dam was a question to be determined in the future.[63]

River defenders, including Pete Henault, Arthur Godfrey, Boyd Norton, Jerry Jayne, Brock Evans, Michael Frome, James Campbell and Hells Canyon float trip guide John Barker, called for enactment of the national river bill rather than the moratorium. Evans said the purpose of the moratorium was to allow reopening of the dam question at a later date. There was already a de facto moratorium and an FPC license decision would be appealed in the courts, insuring a further 3- to 4-year delay. The moratorium bill would do nothing to prevent sale of bench land needed for public access. It wouldn't protect adjacent lands, including the Seven Devils and the canyons of the Snake, Salmon and the Imnaha. Church responded, saying there was no assurance an appeal would succeed. He believed that with a 7-year delay, "no single purpose dam will be built on that river."

When Boyd Norton testified for Friends of the Earth, Church challenged him for writing that "Conservationists now consider the moratorium a sellout to the reclamation dam builders." Church said he supported the moratorium in the honest belief that it had the best chance of becoming law, stopping the FPC from licensing a dam. He said his interest in the river was "every bit as keen and went back every bit as long" as Norton's.

Church had also been incensed by an article in the last HCPC newsletter under the headline "Frank Church, White Hat or Black?" questioning his commitment to conservation and accusing him of doing nothing about the heavy loss of downstream migrating salmon to excess nitrogen saturation below lower Snake and Columbia River dams. Church had the article inserted in the hearing record along with his letters to the Corps of Engineers calling for action on the nitrogen problem and supporting the Corps request for $12 million for dam modification.

When Henault testified, Church pounced on him, citing the record of his efforts for salmon. Henault promised to consider a retraction and an apology in the next newsletter. In his testimony Henault focused on the threatened loss of public access to land along the river. Lots were being offered for sale at Wild Goose rapids with a sign painted on the canyon wall. Above Asotin, cattle feedlots extending to the river's edge were polluting the river. Timber was being cut in the Rapid River drainage above the fish hatchery developed as part of the mitigation for salmon and steelhead runs lost to the Idaho Power dams. "Mr. Chairman, we are losing Hells Canyon today," said Henault. "Time is running out and soon we will not have the opportunity to save the unique treasure we have the opportunity to save today."

Arthur Godfrey shocked committee members by calling for removal of Idaho Power's dams and all other western dams. He stood his ground despite grilling by Senators Hatfield and Clinton Anderson. A platoon of witnesses attacked the national river bill, including Director Robert Lee of the Idaho Water Resource Board, spokesmen for the Southwest Idaho Water Development Association, the timber industry and the license applicants. Conrad Wirth, greeted by Bible as an old friend of the committee, spoke for reservoir recreation. Only in response to Packwood's questions did he reveal that he was working for the license applicants.

Floyd Dominy, former director of the Bureau of Reclamation and ardent dam promoter, said it would be a disaster to forego the multiple benefits of a dam. Church challenged him and they debated at length the merits of dams versus flowing rivers. Church said he believed the public had a gut feeling about this river in the deepest gorge on the continent: "It is the only part that has not been dammed and it ought to be left alone." The Interior and Agriculture departments and the Idaho Fish and Game Commission supported the moratorium, not the river bill.

The hearing disappointed river defenders. Most of their witnesses were limited to five minutes while Lee was given more than hour to speak and answer questions. Church had made it clear that the Packwood bill was unacceptable without clear language to protect southern Idaho water rights and future development. Timber industry spokesmen said the ban on timber cutting would eliminate jobs in Idaho and Oregon. Henault described the hearing as a setback: "It became apparent that this was a hearing, not on the national river bill, but on reclamation in Idaho," he wrote in the Intermountain Observer. "Much of what conservationists and hydroelectric interests came to say was lost in the uproar of how Idaho needed to make the desert bloom." It had been "the Len Jordan show and testimony to the power that this man wields in Washington." Packwood conceded that there was no hope for his bill in the current session of Congress, predicting that river protection could take three to five years.[64]

While the Hells Canyon-National River bill was dead, so was the moratorium. Rep. Orval Hansen tried to move his bill through the House Interstate and Foreign Commerce Committee without success. While the National Wildlife Federation supported both the Packwood bill and the moratorium, the Sierra Club, Wilderness Society, Audubon Society and other Preservation Council allies were generating letters only for the Packwood bill. Church, Jordan and Hansen appealed to eastern seaboard conservation organizations for help with some success but the moratorium bills remained in committee.[65]

Hells Canyon defenders considered the failure of the moratorium a plus. Otherwise, 1971 had been a year of disappointment. Packwood had stirred up the easily frightened southern Idaho irrigation establishment. The "for sale" signs continued to sprout along the Middle Snake and 19 lots had been sold at Wild Goose rapids. The FPC examiner had recommended the licensing of Pleasant Valley dam and the clock was moving on his moratorium.

The next year would be better as canyon defenders began to realize the benefits of four years of advocacy. Concern about the impending loss of public access to riverside land brought Packwood and Church together to work on a solution. Governors Andrus and McCall, and a representative of Dan Evans joined the two senators in a White House meeting and in testimony before Senator Bible's appropriations subcommittee and a House committee.

The White House provided no help but Congress authorized $4 million in Land and Water Conservation Fund money for land acquisition. The Forest Service had been talking with landowners and they were willing to sell. Now the agency had the money to acquire the 10,600 acres that were at risk. The next step was having the land appraised. Unfortunately the appraisals didn't satisfy the landowners and some prepared to sell to private buyers. The Forest Service then turned to condemnation. There were howls of protest but the condemnation process stopped any private sales. Eventually the landowners were handsomely paid as courts awarded prices more than double the government appraisals. Lem Wilson received $2.1 million for 4,000 acres on the Oregon side of the river. The California and Texas residents who had purchased the historic Circle C ranch from James Campbell of New Meadows received $2,014,000 for their land at Pittsburg Landing.[66]

After denouncing the Packwood bill at his August 1971 press conference, Senator Jordan had announced that he would not seek re-election in 1972. With Jordan's retirement Church would no longer be bound by their moratorium agreement. In mid-summer 1972, Church advised HCPC leaders that he was ready to work with them on Hells Canyon legislation modeled on the just passed Sawtooth National Recreation Area bill. Church met with Idaho and Oregon environmentalists in Washington, agreeing that the area would include designated wilderness. Timber cutting would not be barred on non-wilderness land as it had been in the national rivers bill. Church would provide the critical water language.

"We think we have found a workable formula which offers permanent protection for Hells Canyon, which will have the strong backing of Senator Church, Packwood and ourselves, and which we hope will have the support of Senators Hatfield and McClure and Congressmen Ullman and Symms," HCPC members were advised in the November newsletter. Henault went to work drafting a bill based on the terms agreed upon with Church, seeking input from boaters, landowners, the Forest Service and fish and game departments as well as environmentalists. HCPC directors accepted the recreation area name but didn't like it: "It's like calling the Notre Dame Cathedral the Notre Dame recreation hall." They recognized the water provision was necessary if the bill was to become law but complained that it favored reclamation over "an adequate water flow in Hells Canyon."[67]

James McClure was elected to succeed Jordan in the Senate. As the First District representative McClure had opposed both the national river bill and the moratorium. His position was that a moratorium on dams licensed by the FPC should be accompanied by a moratorium on legislation protecting the river. Conservationists believed he was siding with the dam advocates. The HCPC leaders considered him an adversary and favored Democrat Bud Davis in the Senate race.

But McClure had been rethinking his position, recognizing the surge in Idaho environmental sentiment. His First District constituent poll in 1971 showed 71.8 percent opposed any Middle Snake dam, 67 percent favored wild river designation and 55 percent favored preservation of the river even if it limited upstream irrigation development. A statewide poll for the Idaho Water Resource Board in 1972 found 71 percent favoring a flowing river over a reservoir. McClure had hiked in the Seven Devils and recognized the natural quality of the canyon. He supported the $4 million appropriation to acquire ranch land for public use. When HCPC vice president Dick Farman visited him in Washington after the election, McClure told him his position had been misrepresented; he wanted to see Hells Canyon protected: "I want you to go back to Idaho and kick that Pete Henault in the kneecap." The HCPC directors advised members that they hadn't kicked Henault but admitted, "we may have been unfair." They would work with McClure, doing everything "in our power to create a friendly and respectful relationship."[68]

River protection also gained a key convert on the Oregon side of the river where polls also showed strong no-dam sentiment. Rep. Al Ullman of Baker announced in December that he would introduce a Hells Canyon National Parklands bill barring further dams. Ullman had first been elected as a champion of the federal high Hells Canyon dam and had long been allied with public power interests favoring a Middle Snake dam. In 1971, he had introduced a bill for a Hells Canyon Recreation Area with no prohibition on dams. His conversion and his seniority on the House Interior Committee greatly improved prospects for protection of the river and canyon.

Ullman and Oregon Reps. Green and Wyatt introduced the 723,000-acre Hells Canyon National Parklands bill on Jan. 22, 1973. It would ban further dams on the Middle Snake and direct the Forest Service to emphasize recreation with conservation of fish, wildlife, scenic and historical values. Some of the area was to be kept roadless and studied for wilderness designation. No provision was to conflict with present and future upstream use of the water of the Snake and its tributaries. Oregon Sen. Mark Hatfield introduced the Ullman bill in the Senate but said he would also co-sponsor the bill being prepared by Church and McClure.[69]

Henault submitted his draft bill to Church and Packwood on Dec. 5, 1972, along with a detailed explanation. His effort had included 120 working hours in the Hells Canyon area and 5,000 miles of travel. Many more hours had been contributed by 10 other conservationists in three states. His draft had been added to by Jerry Jayne and polished by Preservation Council attorney Schuyler Bradley. What he proposed was a much more acreage than in the discarded national river bill: 1.5 million total acres with 590,000 acres of designated wilderness, 170,000 acres in Idaho and 420,000 in Oregon. The Oregon wilderness would be designated the Tu-ek-kas Wilderness, honoring Old Joseph, chief of the Wallowa Nez Perce and father of the well-known Chief Joseph. The acreage proposed by Henault would have made the bill difficult or impossible to pass and the senators would pare it down.

But it was a solid achievement of citizen effort in drafting major legislation. Henault's job at the National Reactor Testing Station would be eliminated in the spring of 1973, and he would leave Idaho for a job with Seattle City Light. But he would continue to work for protection of Hells Canyon.[70]

McClure and Church began work on the National Recreation Area bill when the new congress convened. The senators and the two staffs, working with Henault's draft, massaged management language and looked for common

Ernie Day Photo

Jet boating on the Snake River in Hells Canyon.

ground on boundaries. Church assistant Mike Wetherell traveled into the area by boat, by air and on horseback to gather information. Church and McClure stepped in when the staffs disagreed.

"The efforts made between the staffs and the two senators involving long hours, innumerable sets of maps and at least a hundred revisions in language resulted in an extremely well thought out bill with respect to the Idaho side," Wetherell advised writer Bill Ashworth in 1976. After the Idaho compromises were worked out Church and McClure asked Senators Packwood and Hatfield for their input on the Oregon boundaries.[71]

It was a slow process and the bill was not ready for introduction until July 23, 1973. The four senators issued a joint statement describing it as a consensus plan. It would protect 82 miles of river from Hells Canyon dam to Asotin in the wild and scenic river system with the 32 miles above Pittsburg Landing to be managed as a wild river. The Asotin dam, authorized through

Church's efforts in 1962, would be de-authorized. A Hells Canyon wilderness would include the Seven Devils Mountains, the canyon face in Idaho north to Pittsburg Landing, and the canyon face on the Oregon side from above Hells Canyon dam to the Grand Ronde in Washington. The Rapid River drainage in Idaho would receive wilderness study. Existing and future upstream water use would be protected.

The total area in the NRA was 860,000 acres, far less than Henault had proposed but more than in the national river bill. Language taken from the Sawtooth National Recreation Area bill said the Forest Service would be denied authority to use condemnation to acquire more than 5 percent of the total land area. Scenic easements were to be used as an alternative to purchase by condemnation. "I feel we have written a good bill," said Church. "Our next step is to take it to the people of Idaho and Oregon for their recommendations."[72]

Supporters outnumbered opponents at the first hearing on what the media labeled the "four senators bill" at LaGrande, Ore. in December 1973, chaired by Senator Packwood. It was the same in two days of hearings in Lewiston a week later chaired by Church and McClure. Governor Andrus endorsed protection of the river and canyon as "a unique and magnificent national treasure." But he wanted boundary changes to reduce the acreage outside the canyon that might be made off limits to timber cutting. Bob Lee was no longer with the Idaho Water Resource Board but spoke for the influential Committee of Nine of Water District 1 representing irrigators of 1,250,000 acres from Ashton to Twin Falls. Despite the language saying the NRA could not limit future upstream water use, the Committee of Nine wasn't satisfied. Lee said river recreation users would inevitably resist efforts to add irrigated acreage upstream and "in a showdown between the federal government and Idaho water users, the water users would lose." Church replied that the bill protected upstream rights "the best that can be done by statute."[73]

Ernie Day, speaking for the National Wildlife Federation, asked for a minimum river flow greater than the 5,000 cubic feet per second in Idaho Power's license. McClure told him this would mean no bill at all. John Barker, current chairman of the Coalition to Save the Snake, said de-authorization of Asotin dam would protect a key river recreation use area for Lewiston and Clarkston. Paul Keeton, Lewiston attorney and chairman of the Idaho Fish and Game Commission said future generations would consider this a "great law." When J.J. Stein, managing director of Washington Water Power pointed out that WWP had been pursuing a dam license for 18 years, Church told him: "If you have been trying to build a dam for 18 years you must recognize that there is some resistance."

While prospects for Hells Canyon legislation improved in 1973, the river claimed the life of former State Rep. Eddie Williams of Lewiston and his cousin, Jack Bowman. Williams was a close friend and adviser to Cecil Andrus. He helped persuade Andrus to run for governor in 1970 and served as his first administrative assistant. Williams ran for Congress in 1972, losing to Steve Symms by 10,000 votes. Four members of the Andrus staff and administration and their spouses had enjoyed an April hike from Hells Canyon dam to Pittsburg Landing. Bowman and Williams picked them up in Bowman's 18-foot boat and headed downriver. Four hours later, about 52 miles from Lewiston, the boat was hit by a powerful wave that ripped off the windshield. Realizing that the swamped boat would sink, Williams advised everyone to get out. The eight hikers survived, some after being in the water for hours. Williams and Bowman, without life preservers, were lost.[74]

Hells Canyon defenders expected victory in 1974. Most members of the Idaho and Oregon congressional delegations favored a bill. Opinion surveys were favorable and all three Northwest governors backed the legislation. Al Ullman was preparing to move ahead with his House bill, revised to include wilderness designation for the face of the canyon on both sides of the river.

But the dam license applicants had not given up. And they had an Idaho ally, First District Rep. Steve Symms. When he ran to succeed McClure in 1972, Symms said he favored protection of the river. But now he was trying to head off the Ullman bill, introducing legislation for a 4-year study. He had the backing of former Senator Jordan.[75]

McClure, in a joint press release with Church, answered Jordan and other critics who were assailing the Senate bill as a threat to Idaho water: "There is no existing law that curbs the present authority of the federal government to impose minimum stream flows or the federal government's ability to use the waters of the Snake River in defiance of water rights given under state law. This bill, for the first time, extends some protection against the establishment of minimum stream flows and for the first time in any statute would guarantee the future of upstream water rights."[76]

A scheduled April hearing on the Senate bill in Washington was postponed because the Bureau of Outdoor Recreation asked for more time to evaluate an alternative plan proposed by the Forest Service. The Forest Service wanted to cut the National Recreation Area's acreage from 860,000 to 540,000, with no designated wilderness, no immediate wild and scenic river designation and no de-authorization of Asotin dam. When the Senate hearing was conducted in July, the Forest Service had a new position, supporting wild rivers protection for the Snake but opposing the inclusion of any acreage in a National Recreation Area. Governor Andrus supported the bill but wanted to reduce the acreage to protect the timber industry in Idaho and Adams counties. Senator McClure said the bill would be modified to reflect his concern.[77]

The Senate approved the modified four senators bill in the fall of 1974. In the House, Hells Canyon supporters were in the majority at a July hearing on the 726,000-acre Forest Parkland bill sponsored by Ullman. Richard Farman, who had succeeded Pete Henault as HCPC president, said a dam would provide only nine months of projected growth in Northwest energy demand. Ullman denounced the alternate plan of the Nixon administration, backed by the Forest Service and Department of Interior, to protect none of the adjoining canyon land. Idaho Atty. Gen. Anthony Park, speaking for himself and Governor Andrus, endorsed the Ullman bill "in principal" while Lt. Gov. Jack Murphy, the Republican nominee for governor, opposed it, backing Symms' 4-year study.[78]

Ullman's bill didn't come up for a subcommittee vote until November 21, late in the session. California Republican Craig Hosmer was determined to stop it. He demanded a quorum requiring the presence of 13 of the 25 committee members. Ullman, Doug Scott and Brock Evans of the Sierra Club called enough missing members to get the count to 14 but then two walked out. Eventually, the Interior Committee would vote to bring the bill from the subcommittee but it had to wait for the new Organic Act for the Bureau of Land Management. Time ran out leaving the power combine still in the game.[79]

Floyd Harvey was looking forward to his 1974 camp opening trip. He had again invited Godfrey, along with Russell Train, head of the Environmental Protection Agency, and former Atty. Gen. Elliot Richardson. It would be another high profile event helping the cause. But on the night of January 31, 1973, a boat went up the river. Two buildings at Willow Creek Camp were burned to the ground, acid was poured over equipment and $500 worth of fishing tackle was stolen. The May trip was cancelled. Harvey was out of business. Boats, equipment and the remains of the Willow Creek Camp were sold at auction in June to satisfy a Small Business Administration loan. Idaho County officials investigated but said they found too little evidence to file criminal charges.

In 1977, a frustrated Harvey filed a civil suit asking $3 million from three people. After a long civil trial, Harvey won a large settlement. The arson at Willow Creek not only destroyed Hells Canyon Excursions but left Harvey destitute for years until he received the lawsuit settlement. Harvey believed his Hells Canyon advocacy was a factor in the arson and vandalism.[80]

Frank Church won re-election in 1974 despite attacks by the John Birch Society questioning his patriotism and the campaign of Republican Bob Smith, an ally of Steve Symms and his former administrative assistant. Church received 55 percent of the vote, carrying 34 of the 44 counties. Cecil Andrus easily won a second term with 70 percent. Conservationists lost a friend in the House as George Hansen defeated Orval Hansen in the Republican primary. George Hansen would be joining Symms as a foe of Hells Canyon protection.[81]

In 1975, Ullman introduced a Hells Canyon National Recreation Area bill that was nearly identical to the bill passed by the Senate the previous year. Hells Canyon backers got a majority of House subcommittee members to sign on as co-sponsors. The power interests countered, seeking to muddy the water by having Wyoming Rep. Teno Roncalio propose an amendment, allowing construction of Pleasant Valley and low Mountain Sheep dams, barring further dams only below the Imnaha.

At an April hearing before Rep. Roy Taylor's subcommittee the power spokesmen raised the specter of an energy shortage. They said they had invested $9 million in pursuit of a dam and it would be wrong for Congress to intervene. Pacific Northwest Power's Wendell Sartre said the "dangerous waters" in the 50 miles of river below Hells Canyon dam had limited recreation potential. Reps. Symms and George Hansen spoke for their substitute, a 3-year moratorium on action by Congress and study of a recreation area. Gov. Cecil Andrus endorsed the Ullman bill. Speaking also for Oregon Gov. Robert Straub and Washington's Dan Evans, he said the people of the Northwest had made their choice. Idaho Fish and Game Director Joe Greenley said the NRA bill would preserve the last remaining Snake River habitat for salmon and steelhead.[82]

In Idaho an industry coalition that included the J.R. Simplot Company, Morrison Knudsen Corporation, the Boise based construction company, and Idaho Power Company launched an advertising campaign opposing the Hells Canyon bills with Jordan as the primary spokesman. Full-page newspaper ads carried the text of his "open letter" to the people of Idaho.

The coalition included the Southwest Idaho Development Association, Idaho Water Users, Idaho Farm Bureau, Idaho Mining Association, Food Producers of Idaho and the Idaho Association of Commerce and Industry. Idahoans were told that all available Snake River water would be needed for future development, protective language in the Hells Canyon National Recreation Area bill was not enough and only a few hardy souls who back pack or run rivers could enjoy Hells Canyon. The coalition called for hearings in southern Idaho. The Idaho Statesman denounced the move as a stall, designed to allow the FPC to issue a license. While not wanting Congress to act, the industry coalition was willing to let an unelected federal commission wipe out 50 miles of river, said the Statesman.[83]

Idaho's Department of Health and Welfare stepped into the controversy, denying certification of the proposed dams on water quality grounds. The agency said the dams would eliminate salmon and sturgeon habitat, foster algae growth, reduce dissolved oxygen and raise the water temperature. The agency also proposed to intervene with the FPC. The State of Oregon also refused to certify the dams. Pacific Northwest Power prepared to challenge the decisions in court.[84]

The Senate passed the Church, McClure, Packwood, Hatfield bill in June but the House Interior Committee was again slow to act, finally clearing the Ullman bill for a House vote on Oct. 30. When the bill came up in the order of business permitting amendments, few members were present to vote. Symms failed to win approval of his substitute by only five votes, 20-15. A few minutes later the power combine amendment, sponsored by Oregon Rep. Robert Duncan and Teno Roncalio failed 43-27. The final vote was 342-53 reflecting the strong bipartisan support generated by the 8-year campaign of Hells Canyon defenders. Symms and Hansen voted no. Symms declared that economic growth would be stifled so much that "people will be in bread lines."[85]

President Gerald Ford signed the Hells Canyon National Recreation Area bill on New Year's Eve, Dec. 31, 1975. The final version, agreed to by House and Senate conferees, encompassed 652,488 acres. It protected 66.9 miles of the Snake with 32.5 miles as wild from Hells Canyon dam to Pittsburg Landing and 34.4 miles as scenic. Wild river protection was also given 26.8 miles of the Rapid River. Asotin dam was de-authorized. The Idaho NRA acreage was 141,073 with 84,100 as wilderness including the Seven Devils and the canyon face. The Oregon acreage was 511,415 with 193,840 acres of wilderness. Powerboat use would continue on the Snake. Grazing, timber cutting and mining of existing claims were not barred in the NRA but the Forest Service was directed to protect natural values. The final boundaries excluded areas that the Forest Service believed had the greatest mineral potential. By the time the bill was signed the most critical bench lands along the river had been purchased by the Forest Service.

The campaign begun by a former bomber pilot, an inexperienced young attorney, a river captain and a few novice environmental crusaders had blossomed into an irresistible national movement. A cause that was lost had been won; a condemned river had been saved. One of nature's masterpieces was rescued.

In their final newsletter Hells Canyon Preservation Council directors gave primary credit to Senators Packwood, Church, McClure and Hatfield, Ullman and Rep. Lloyd Meeds of Washington and to Governors Andrus, Straub and Evans. They thanked members for writing countless letters and sustaining the council's effort. And they noted that Justice Douglas, the man who made it possible to save Hells Canyon was retiring. Many others could have been mentioned, including Russ Mager, Floyd Harvey, Brock Evans, Pete Henault, Jerry Jayne, Boyd Norton and Arthur Godfrey. Credit could also have been given to Bruce Bowler, the Idaho Wildlife Federation and other interveners whose 1960s defense of Salmon River seagoing fish stopped Nez Perce dam and delayed an FPC decision.[86]

On June 8, 1976, the Federal Power Commission dismissed all license applications as requested by the Sierra Club, Federation of Western Outdoor Clubs and the Idaho Alpine Club. It had been 22 years since Pacific Northwest Power asked for a license to build Pleasant Valley dam.[87]

On June 20, 500 people gathered to celebrate at Lewiston's Hellsgate Marina. Frank Church, who was now running for President, gave credit to the citizen advocates who changed public opinion: "I think that as we look ahead in this age when we display so much pride in man's work it is a welcome thing, once in a while to celebrate God's work." Forest Service Chief John McGuire displayed a plaque to be placed at Heaven's Gate lookout above the canyon paying tribute to "those who had the perception and the foresight and willingly made sacrifices to preserve forever the untamed reaches of Hells Canyon of the Snake River." Senator McClure called attention to the significance of the canyon as a former home of the Nez Perce. The Lewiston Tribune credited McClure for working "long and hard" on the legislation while Church was busy with his investigation of the Central Intelligence Agency and preparation for a presidential run.

On July 31, the victory was celebrated on the Oregon side of the canyon at Hat Point 7,700 feet above the river, with Al Ullman, Bob Packwood and Governor Straub among the speakers. Wade Hall, the retired Forest Service staffer, was recognized for his role as a long-time river and canyon defender.

Chapter 14

Saving the River of No Return Wilderness

"These remarkable wild lands support one of the most significant wildlife communities found anywhere in the coterminous United States. The perpetuation of significant numbers of many of the species depends on the wilderness classification of these lands. This could be the most far reaching decision to ever effect wildlife in Idaho" – Martel Morache

"Like bare bones tossed back to a dog, the skeleton of a wilderness would be stripped of its flesh and blood by the deletion of Chamberlain Basin and the headwaters of Big Creek." – Nelle Tobias to President Gerald Ford, Dec. 11, 1974.

The Idaho Primitive Area (IPA) was established in 1931 with unanimous approval by Gov. Clarence Baldridge's committee representing sportsmen, timber, mining and grazing interests. Harry Shellworth described the decision as "entirely satisfactory to Idaho."

In 1968, as the Forest Service prepared to review the IPA and the adjoining Salmon River Breaks Primitive Area for possible wilderness designation under the Wilderness Act, the political climate was much different. The nation's appetite for wood had increased tremendously and the timber industry was pushing for increased volumes from the national forests.

Industry groups in Idaho had conducted a furious campaign against the Wilderness Act and helped win an amendment requiring Congress to approve any wilderness designation for primitive areas. Idaho wilderness supporters could count on fierce opposition from timber and mining interests and their political allies. The primitive areas had a substantial volume of potential timber, particularly in the Chamberlain Basin, a high plateau area with rolling hills and many meadows, prime summer habitat for the largest elk herd south of the Salmon River. Boise Cascade Corporation, successor to the

Boise-Payette Company that employed Harry Shellworth, had its eyes on Chamberlain Basin.

In October 1968, at the urging of Brock Evans of the Sierra Club, Idaho conservation leaders gathered in Coeur d'Alene to consider forming a new organization, the Idaho Environmental Council (IEC).[1] The purpose was to bring activists from all parts of the state together in a coalition that would have more political influence. It would be an organization "where everybody gets behind each issue whether it be in the north or the south." A steering committee was formed early in 1969, and Bruce Bowler filed articles of incorporation. Fourteen directors were chosen to lead the organization.[2]

The IEC leadership included veterans of the Idaho Wildlife Federation and a younger generation from northern, southern, central and eastern Idaho. The IEC immediately joined the campaigns to stop a proposed open pit mine in the White Cloud Mountains and to keep more dams out of Hells Canyon. Its leaders also began thinking about the Idaho and Salmon River Breaks primitive areas.

Don Calvert of Moscow, an IEC director, and Doris Milner of Hamilton, Mont., a leader in the Magruder Corridor campaign, organized a strategy meeting at the Milner home in September 1969 and a follow-up meeting in November to consider what boundaries the conservationists should propose to the Forest Service and what adjoining areas should be included. The two primitive areas totaled 1,441,059 acres but there was another two million acres of adjoining or nearby wild country with few or no roads.

The Idaho and Montana conservationists agreed that they should ultimately work for a single wilderness encompassing the two primitive areas, plus some adjoining areas, to be called the River of No Return Wilderness.[3] The Salmon River had been known as the "River of No Return" since early in the century because boats couldn't travel upstream through the turbulent rapids. That had changed with the advent of powerful jet boats but the name was known nationwide and had obvious appeal.

The conservationists also agreed with Ernie Day, who cautioned against calling for a single large wilderness at that time and against asking the Forest Service to consider both primitive areas in a single study. Separate studies were being done by the Forest Service's Region One north of the Salmon River and by Region Four south of the Salmon. The areas were quite large "and it cannot help our case to have the total areas emphasized." They agreed to endorse continued jet boat use on the Salmon River, recognizing that they needed the support of the Idaho outfitters and guides. While studying the primitive areas, the Forest Service would also be studying the Salmon River for wild and scenic river status, pursuant to the Wild Rivers Act.[4]

There was agreement on expanding the proposed wilderness beyond the primitive areas, adding the Horse Creek area east of the Salmon River Breaks Primitive Area and north of the Salmon River, the Bighorn Crags-Clear Creek area south of the Salmon and the Camas Creek area adjoining the Middle Fork of the Salmon.[5] The conservationists had learned that the timber industry was preparing to fight wilderness status for the primitive areas. The Southern Idaho Forestry Association had hired resource consultant Joel Fryckman of Ogden, Utah to conduct an 18-month study. And Gov. Don Samuelson had made it clear he would side with the industry, telling the association: "They (the Forest Service) had no business in completely tieing up all that good sound timber."

Directors of the IEC approved proposed additions to the primitive areas at a December meeting in Caldwell and Calvert submitted the IEC proposal for the Salmon River Breaks area at a meeting with Forest Service representatives in Moscow. Along with the entire primitive area, the IEC wanted to include the Magruder Corridor area south of the Magruder Road, the upper Bargamin Creek drainage and the Horse Creek area. Calvert said the proposal also generally reflected the wishes of the Montana Wilderness Association, North Idaho Wilderness Committee, Idaho Alpine Club, Idaho Outfitters and Guides, the Sierra Club and the Wilderness Society.

In November 1970, Cecil Andrus defeated Gov. Don Samuelson. Andrus was not on record on the primitive areas but he was elected with the help of his opposition to a mine in the White Clouds and to further dams in Hells Canyon. The IEC had publicly supported him and Idaho environmentalists had worked for his election. They were hopeful that he would help on the primitive areas.

In March 1971, the IEC urged its members to turn out and speak up at seven April information meetings scheduled by the Forest Service to receive input on its study plan for the Idaho Primitive Area: "The Idaho Primitive Area is the largest national forest primitive area in the United States with about 1.25 million acres. It is a vast, beautiful mountainous area drained by the Middle Fork of the Salmon and the Salmon itself, the famous 'River of No Return.' It is one of the last strongholds of the cougar and excellent habitat for many other species of wildlife. It furnishes some of the finest primitive type recreation in the country – fishing, hunting, wilderness travel and survival, nature study, mountain climbing, floating, etc."[5]

Carl Hocevar of Idaho Falls, Calvert's successor as wilderness chairman, presented the IEC proposal at the Idaho Falls meeting, wilderness for the entire IPA plus four adjoining areas totaling185,000 acres – Horse Creek, Clear Creek, Camas Creek and Jacobs Ladder Creek.[6]

The IEC proposal continued to expand as people nominated more adjoining areas. The Forest Service scheduled a series of "information meetings" in March 1973, inviting public input on possible alternatives ranging from no wilderness to wilderness for nearly all of the primitive areas plus some contiguous areas. But this alternative excluded 100,000 acres of the Idaho Primitive Area on upper Big Creek and its largest tributary, Monumental Creek, because of past and present mining activity and mining roads. It included a prohibition of powerboats on the Salmon River and the elimination of airplane access to the wilderness landing fields. Wilderness supporters favored continued powerboat use and air access, both clearly allowed by the Wilderness Act. They believed the Forest Service was deliberately trying to turn the outfitters and guides and the public against wilderness by espousing an unwarranted "purity" standard.[7]

Dr. Walt Blackadar invited Idaho and Montana conservationists to Salmon in February 1973 to make a final decision on a wilderness proposal for the primitive areas in advance of the Forest Service meetings.[8] Twenty-five people gathered at the Blackadar home, located on a hill overlooking the Salmon River. Pete Henault's account appeared a week later in the Intermountain Observer. He reported that Doris Milner had suggested a cautious approach, going along with the least unsatisfactory Forest Service proposal and fighting for the rest later. But Don Aldrich, veteran Montana conservationist and consultant for the Wilderness Society, disagreed: "This may be the last chance we get. If we don't stand up for exactly what we think is right now, it's going to be a lot harder later to convince people that what we really wanted was something else." Aldrich said they should forget the theory that "we must cooperate with the Forest Service to get a good wilderness. It's Congress that's going to decide this issue, not the Forest Service."[9]

Aldrich's view prevailed. The participants hung a large map of the primitive areas on the wall and identified adjacent areas they wanted to include, marking the boundaries with a felt marker. They wanted to include as much of the Middle Fork of the Salmon River drainage as possible to protect its water quality and habitat for salmon, steelhead and cutthroat trout. They included areas important to bighorn sheep and mountain goats and areas with clusters of high lakes. They agreed unanimously to reject all of the Forest Service alternatives and to support a single River of No Return Wilderness of 2.3 million acres including 13 roadless areas adjacent to the primitive areas. They endorsed continued airplane use of backcountry airstrips and supported wild river status for the Salmon from its north fork to its junction with the Snake, with continued use of powerboats.

The finished map excluded most roads that reached the primitive areas so the boundaries of most of the adjacent areas appeared as bulges on the map. It looked like "a many-lobed and highly asymmetrical amoeba."[10] If Congress agreed, it would be the largest designated wilderness in the continental United States.

Both conservationists and the timber industry mobilized supporters to turn out for the 10 workshops, seven in Idaho and one each in Hamilton, Mont., Spokane, Wash. and Salt Lake City. The workshops attracted 3,000 participants including nearly 1,000 in Boise. The Forest Service received over 6,800 "inputs" including response forms, letters and petitions representing 8,775 people. Most came from Idahoans, 82 percent, with 15 percent from other western states and less than 2 percent from other parts of the country.[11] Among the wilderness supporters at the Pocatello workshop was Ron Watters who, with three companions, had made a 150-mile winter trek across the Idaho Primitive Area on skis and on foot.

The Forest Service provided only a vague summary of the results, saying there was "public support for the current management of the areas" including continued use of aircraft and powerboats on the Salmon. Most wanted no dams on the Salmon River. Opinion was sharply divided on wilderness with "very little support for middle ground alternatives."[11]

Wilderness advocates knew the real test would come with public hearings to be conducted in the fall of 1973. There was no imminent threat to the primitive areas as there had been with the White Clouds and still was with Hells Canyon. And while thousands of Idahoans had hunted and hiked in the Idaho Primitive Area and thousands more had floated the Middle Fork and the Salmon, most people knew little about the areas. The Idaho conservationists would also work with the National Wildlife Federation, Wilderness Society and Sierra Club to make the River of No Return Wilderness a national issue.

For months a group of conservationists had been meeting weekly for lunch at a motel near the Boise State College campus, sharing information on issues and developments. This "environmental lunch bunch" had been convened by H. Tom Davis, an engineer formerly with the Idaho Water Resource Board and with Boise Cascade. He was now employed by a Boise engineering firm. Among the participants were Wildlife Federation stalwarts Ernie Day, Bruce Bowler, Bill Meiners and Franklin Jones, Ken Cameron of Trout Unlimited, Duane Marler of the Federation of Fly Fishermen, Doli Obee of the League of Women Voters, Ken Robison, Idaho Statesman editorial page editor, and Janet Ward of the American Association of University Women.

Mary Lou Reed of Coeur d'Alene, wife of attorney Scott Reed, was interested in promoting the creation of a new conservation organization. She sent two organizers from Montana to meet with Boise area conservationists. That meeting led to the establishment of the Idaho Conservation League. Unlike the Idaho Wildlife Federation and the Idaho Environmental Council, the league was to have an office and a paid director. It would lobby the legislature on environmental issues and form local chapters to help mobilize conservation efforts statewide. One of the organizers, Boise dentist Ken Cameron, was chosen as president and Marcia Pursley was hired as director.

Meanwhile, H. Tom Davis had talked with Day and Bowler about forming an organization to work exclusively for the River of No Return Wilderness, believing that a single purpose organization would be more effective than the multi-purpose Idaho Environmental Council. It was going to take a robust campaign for public support to overcome the opposition. They agreed to organize the River of No Return Wilderness Council and Bowler drafted articles of incorporation. The first directors of the council were Davis, Day, Bowler, Jerry Jayne, Mary Lou Reed and outdoor writer Ted Trueblood. More would soon be added. River of No Return Council volunteers went to work in a basement room of the Boise YWCA building shared with the Idaho Conservation League. They mailed fliers and brochures to thousands of Idahoans, urging them to speak up at the upcoming Forest Service hearings and to write letters supporting a 2.3 million-acre River of No Return Wilderness.

Ted Trueblood's article, "The Battle of the Salmon River," appeared in the October issue of Field and Stream magazine. Trueblood, an Idaho native who grew up on an irrigated farm near Wilder, was one of the nation's best-known and most respected outdoor writers. Hundreds of his hunting and fishing stories had appeared in Field and Stream, True and other magazines. After a few years with Field and Stream in New York, he had convinced the editors to let him return to Idaho while continuing to serve as associate editor.

For Trueblood the Middle Fork Salmon River country was sacred ground and he had seen "nearly all of it, on foot, on horseback and by boat." Ted and wife Ellen had honeymooned in 1939 on Sulphur Creek, a middle fork tributary just outside the Idaho Primitive Area. For years he and Ellen had flown into Chamberlain Basin for fall elk hunts. His Field and Stream article described the boyhood adventures of Ted and brother Burtt during two months of hiking, camping, fishing and exploring on the middle fork in the early 1930s. The middle fork's water, he wrote, "is so clear you can count the spots on a trout 20 feet beneath the surface."

He described the South Fork Salmon River debacle. Salmon spawning beds had been covered with silt because of erosion from logging roads and logging "on the fragile decomposed granite slopes. The pools and the food producing and spawning riffles are full of sand." (The south fork disaster would be cited repeatedly by wilderness supporters. Rain on snow storms in the winter of 1964-65 sent 1.5 million cubic yards of soil into the river, covering spawning gravels. The south fork was the most important summer

Spawning salmon in a Middle Fork Salmon River tributary.

chinook stream in the Columbia Basin with runs of 10,000 in the 1950s. Only 250 returned in 1979. The same highly erodible soils extended over much of central Idaho.) Ted urged readers to write letters to the RNR Council supporting wilderness protection for the primitive areas and wild river status for the Salmon.

Before the Forest Service hearings Boise Cascade ran full-page newspaper ads across the state describing its proposal, based on the Fryckman review. Boise Cascade wanted no wilderness while suggesting that 579,000 acres of the canyon country along the middle fork and the Salmon should be managed as a "roadless recreation area." President John Fery described it as a "middle road" plan that would allow removal of 40 million board feet of timber a year. Boise Cascade's ads also said the primitive areas were highly mineralized with 5,400 mining claims and historic production of $95 million. Boise Cascade also wanted no wild river protection for the Salmon River.[12] The Forest Service had unveiled its proposal, a Salmon River Wilderness north of the Salmon and an Idaho Wilderness south of the Salmon with a total 1,532,000 acres. Included were 1,347,000 acres of the existing primitive

Martel Morache

Nelle Tobias

areas (deleting 94,000 acres) and 185,000 acres of contiguous areas. The primary deletions were 30,000 acres each on upper Big Creek and its tributary, Monumental Creek, left out because of mining roads, historic mining activity and potential for more mining. Along the Salmon would be a 16,000-acre wild river corridor. The river would be protected from the north fork to its juncture with the Snake, 237 miles.[13]

Martel Morache of the Idaho Fish and Game Department had spent eight years gathering information on the primitive areas and adjoining country. He was the department's point man on the primitive areas and an articulate advocate for wilderness status based on habitat for fish and wildlife. Morache wanted to protect the integrity of the middle fork, including as many of its tributaries as possible. "If we can preserve an entire river system intact, from now to perpetuity, we will have done one of the finest things that could be done," he told audiences at his slide show presentations.

Morache pointed out that the area's range of elevation, from 10,000 feet to 2,200 feet, provided habitat for more than 190 species of wildlife. The largest bighorn sheep population in Idaho resided in the canyon complex of the lower middle fork and the main Salmon River, while mountain goats occupied most of the crest areas. Elk wintered in the canyons of the Salmon River, middle fork and south fork, migrating to Chamberlain Basin in the spring where calves were born. The elk spent the summer in Chamberlain, feeding on the abundant forage.

Morache was instrumental in shaping the wilderness proposal of Gov. Cecil Andrus, a single wilderness area of 1.8 million acres. In his testimony at the Forest Service hearing in Boise, Andrus answered the industry advocates who were describing wilderness as a lockup, single use, a playground for easterners, anti-economy and anti-development: "Wilderness is hunting and fishing, clean air and clean water. Wilderness is big game habitat, salmon and steelhead spawning in the waters of untouched streams and creeks. Wilderness is Idaho the way it was, or more clearly, a small portion of Idaho that should remain the way it was for future generations."

Wilderness was compatible with the intent of the multiple use acts of 1961 and 1964 that guided the Forest Service, said Andrus. "Multiple use does not mean that every acre should be logged, every acre mined, every acre grazed nor every acre withheld for recreation… For example, surface mining is the reverse of multiple use. The Boise Basin is a perfect illustration. After 100 years much of it still provides virtually no grazing, no timber, no watershed, no hunting, no fishing – nothing in fact but piles and piles of cobblestones."

The Andrus proposal included the areas on Big Creek and Monumental Creek that the Forest Service proposed to exclude. Also included were 80,000 acres of the Clear Creek drainage on the east side of the Idaho Primitive Area and the Soldier Lakes area on the south. It excluded 10 areas adjoining the primitive areas that were included in the RNR Council's 2.3 million acres. It was regarded favorably by most conservationists, much less than they wanted but better than the Forest Service proposal and a good answer to Boise Cascade. Andrus would receive many letters of support from Idahoans for his wilderness position.

Ernie Day spoke for the RNR Council's plan. Ted and Ellen Trueblood presented 63 pro-wilderness letters received in response to Ted's Field and Stream article. Some of speakers said the issue was not more Idaho wilderness, but how much less. Actual wilderness acreage was shrinking every year, as more roadless areas were roaded and logged.[14] More than 70 percent of the people who spoke at the three hearings in Lewiston, Boise and Pocatello favored wilderness and most of those endorsed the council's 2.3 million acres. After the hearings the RNR Council forwarded to the Forest Service more than 1,000 individual letters of support along with petitions with thousands of signatures.[15]

With their impressive showing in the hearings, wilderness supporters hoped that the Gerald Ford administration would submit an improved recommendation for the primitive areas. But in February 1974, an anti-wilderness delegation from Idaho went to Washington to meet with Agriculture Secretary Earl Butz and his assistant, Robert Long. It included Glen Youngblood of Boise Cascade, Al Teske of the Idaho Mining Association, plus representatives of the Idaho Farm Bureau, Idaho Cattlemen's Association, Idaho Woolgrowers and State Representatives

Vernon Ravenscroft and Herb Fitz. Ravenscroft had switched to the Republican Party after losing to Andrus in the 1970 Democratic primary election. The Republican controlled Idaho Legislature also got into the fray, sending Butz and the Congress an anti-wilderness memorial.

In June, Governor Andrus asked Regional Forester Vern Hamre to release for public view the recommendation for the primitive areas that he had sent to Washington.[16] Andrus feared that the industry coalition might persuade Butz to recommend less wilderness. Assistant Agriculture Secretary Robert Long wrote Andrus, acknowledging the request, indicating that Hamre's report would not be released but would "weigh heavily" in the final decision. A decision had not been made. "We need to take into account the national perspective and needs as factors in the study," Long said.[17] Long followed up, meeting with Andrus on a visit to Idaho. Andrus didn't find the meeting encouraging. He sought a court order for release of Hamre's recommendation but U.S. District Judge Fred M. Taylor sided with the Forest Service, ruling that the regional forester's recommendation could not be released until President Gerald Ford sent his proposal to Congress.

Cecil Andrus was elected to a second term in November with a huge margin over Republican nominee Jack Murphy, 182,182 to 68,731. Sen. Frank Church won a fourth term with 145,140 votes to 109,702 for Robert Smith, former aide to First District Rep. Steve Symms. Smith, like Symms, was a foe of wilderness.

A month after the election the worst fears of wilderness supporters were realized. President Ford proposed that Congress designate two Idaho wilderness areas totaling 1,143,000 acres, excluding the 386,000-acre Chamberlain Basin.

Andrus responded immediately, calling a press conference to denounce the administration for proposing, "to totally destroy the heartland of Idaho," bowing to mining and timber "power brokers" and acting "without regard for the people or the professional foresters." The regional forester's recommendation had now been released and Andrus held up a booklet describing it – 1,541,000 acres with Chamberlain Basin included: "If you give up the Chamberlain Basin, the headwaters of Big Creek and Monumental Creek, you've destroyed the water quality of the entire wilderness area." Andrus said the primitive areas were part of the heritage of Idaho "and I'm not about to see it destroyed." He said he would go to Washington to speak for a larger wilderness.[18]

There was more reaction the following day. Ernie Day denounced the Ford proposal as "an extension of Watergate politics," adding that the potential timber cut from Chamberlain would probably equal less than one percent of the Northwest's annual log exports to Japan. Ted Trueblood described the Chamberlain Basin as the finest elk habitat in America and cited the destruction of salmon habitat with roads and logging on the South Fork of the Salmon. Senator Church issued a statement saying he had "no intention of presiding over the destruction of the Idaho and Salmon River Breaks primitive areas," adding that Congress, not the Forest Service or the administration would determine the boundaries. Church said he would insist on hearings in Idaho so "the views of Idahoans can be fully heard."[19]

The Idaho Statesman's editorial denouncing the proposal said it made a mockery of the process of analysis and public hearings by the Forest Service. The Forest Service reported that 9,000 inputs had been received and the responses showed "strong support for wilderness classification," said the Statesman. The Idaho Falls Post-Register called it a "tragic decision" and urged readers to work for congressional approval of nothing less than the 1.8 million acre wilderness advocated by Andrus: "The hearings held in Idaho and Wyoming registered overwhelmingly for expanding the Salmon River wilderness. Nobody bothered to check the decision with the people."[20]

The Ford proposal generated a flurry of letters to Andrus and Church applauding their stand as well as letters to the White House. Gerald Jayne advised the President that his proposal was atrocious: "It not only proposes the destruction of existing wilderness but makes a mockery of public involvement in government."[21] After reading an article by Trueblood in the Lewiston Tribune, Duke Parkening of Kooskia wrote Secretary Butz asking how he could overrule the wishes of the majority, Andrus, Church and the Forest Service?[22] But the Grangeville Chamber of Commerce praised Ford. And 41 Idaho legislators, 38 Republicans and three Democrats, signed a letter supporting exclusion of the Chamberlain Basin, sending it to Ford and members of Congress.[23]

Directors of the River of No Return Wilderness Council feared that the Forest Service would proceed with timber sales in some of the contiguous areas included in their 2.3 million acres, making those areas ineligible for wilderness status. H. Tom Davis wanted wilderness advocates to seek a court order barring any roads or sales in all contiguous areas until Congress acted. [24] In February 1970, a federal judge in Colorado had ruled that, pursuant to the Wilderness Act, the Forest Service must consider the wilderness suitability of all contiguous areas in its review of primitive areas.

The Forest Service was maintaining that the decision applied only to the Tenth Judicial District, which did not include Idaho. Following the advice of Senator Church, RNR Council directors voted not to go to court.[25] Church discussed the matter with Davis, Trueblood and Bruce Bowler in a mid-March meeting in Boise and followed up with a letter to Forest Service Chief John

McGuire asking for a moratorium on planning or conducting timber sales in the contiguous areas until Congress acted.

The furor over the Ford proposal helped wilderness advocates win more public and media support. Now there was a real threat, a potential loss of wilderness, salmon, elk and other wildlife as the result of political influence, overriding the will of the majority. The River of No Return Council was able to promote more media coverage of the issue in April 1975, chartering planes to fly Boise area newspaper and television reporters and photographers over the primitive area and into Mackay Bar on the Salmon River, taking them upriver by boat for photos of bighorn sheep along the shore. Ted Trueblood advised Frank Church that both television and newspaper coverage were excellent, enclosing full-page photo spreads from the Statesman and Idaho Free Press.[26] The Council also sent newspapers across the country copies of Trueblood's latest River of No Return article, warning of the potential loss of Chamberlain Basin.

Bruce Bowler sent Church a draft of a 2.3 million-acre River of No Return Wilderness bill in March 1975. In early June, the Sierra Club's regional representative, Doug Scott, asked Church to introduce the bill. He believed its introduction would help wilderness advocates rally support in Idaho and nationally, call attention to the inadequacy of the administration's 1.1 million-acre proposal and might persuade the Forest Service to delay logging in the contiguous areas.[27] Church was not ready to introduce the RNR bill. His assistant, Ben Yamagata, advised him that conservationists had already made the future of the Idaho primitive areas a national issue, "based on the inquiries I've received from various congressional offices." But he saw potential pitfalls with the request. Church might become identified with the proposal and Sen. James McClure was unlikely to join him as a co-sponsor. (As he had on the Hells Canyon National Recreation Area.)[28]

The problem of potential timber sales in the contiguous areas was put to rest in late June in a meeting of wilderness supporters with Forest Service officials in Salt Lake City, arranged by Doug Scott of the Sierra Club and Region Four Supervisor Vern Hamre. Scott advised River of No Return campaign leaders that a review of 5-year action plans in the Payette, Boise and Challis national forests showed that "perhaps as much to their surprise as ours" no timber sales or other adverse actions were planned in any of the contiguous areas in the 2.3 million-acre proposal in the next five years. The Forest Service could add sales or road projects in the future "but we can stay on top of such additions and the burden would be on them to pick the fight which I don't think they would do lightly."[29] So no lawsuit was needed. Instead, Scott advised wilderness supporters to concentrate on winning more support, particularly in Idaho, and in laying a foundation for a favorable vote in

Congress. Congress was not likely to proceed this year or next, he believed. He was right.

In 1975 Senators Church and McClure were focusing on their Hells Canyon National Recreation Area bill and Church was busy chairing an investigation of the Central Intelligence Agency. The Hells Canyon legislation was signed by President Ford on Dec. 31, 1975. In 1976 Church was running for President. He got a late start on his underfinanced campaign and despite primary victories in Oregon, Nebraska, Idaho and Montana, was compelled to drop out after finishing a distant third in Ohio. Church had indicated that he would introduce the River of No Return bill when the time was right but the time was not right in 1975 or 1976.

Two months before the 1976 election, Cecil Andrus persuaded the Ford administration to revise its proposal for the primitive areas to include the Chamberlain Basin. In a campaign speech in Montana, President Ford had vowed to expand public recreational lands. Andrus wrote Ford's assistant for domestic affairs, James Cannon, suggesting that the President could take a significant step toward that goal by reversing the Chamberlain proposal.[30] He followed up with a trip to Washington and a meeting with White House officials.[31]

The election of Jimmy Carter as president in November 1976 meant that there would be a new primitive area proposal from the new administration. And wilderness advocates would have a friend in a key position because Carter chose Cecil Andrus to serve as his Secretary of Interior. Most Idaho conservationists were delighted with the news that Andrus was being considered for Interior. They had enthusiastically supported his candidacy in 1970 and 1974. They appreciated his leadership as governor in stopping an open pit mine in the White Clouds and in keeping further dams out of Hells Canyon.

Andrus had persuaded the legislature to pass a Stream Protection Act that required a review of plans for stream alterations. He had also gained approval of a local Land Use Planning Act that gave cities and counties authority to consider wildlife habitat in land use decision-making. He had sought legislation to allow state designation of protected rivers and sponsored an "Idaho's Tomorrow" program that invited citizens to express their desires in local forums. Andrus was also supporting a proposal to reserve public land along the Snake River south of Boise as hunting habitat for an exceptional population of hawks, eagles and falcons.

While Andrus consistently spoke up for living quality, he tempered his environmental advocacy with concern for jobs, including jobs in timber, mining and agriculture. On Hells Canyon he had opposed wilderness designation for the Rapid River drainage in deference to concern about the timber supply in Adams and Idaho counties. On the primitive areas he had not embraced the 2.3 million acre proposal of Idaho conservationists but continued to speak for 1.8 million acres. And he had not backed the conservationist effort to block construction of the Teton Dam in eastern Idaho.

The Andrus environmental record wasn't good enough for some Idaho activists. They put together a critical memo that the Sierra Club circulated to other conservation groups in Washington. As a result 12 conservation and wildlife organizations left Andrus off their list of acceptable candidates for the Interior position.[32] News of the memo and the omission came as a shock to the governor's environmental friends in Idaho. They drafted a letter urging Carter to appoint Andrus, saying that the unsigned memo did not represent the thinking or wishes of the large majority of conservationists and environmentalists in Idaho:

"Gov. Andrus has, on balance, an outstanding record on conservation and resource protection. We and the vast majority of the Idaho conservation community were neither contacted nor consulted relative to this anonymous and scurrilous attack on Gov. Andrus." Organizations endorsing the letter included the Idaho Wildlife Federation, River of No Return Wilderness Council, Idaho Conservation League and the Ada County Fish and Game League. It was signed by 33 Idaho conservationists.[33] Ted Trueblood issued a separate statement for the River of No Return Wilderness Council denouncing the letter: "I believe that nine out of 10 Idaho sportsmen would support him for the job."[34] Andrus sent Trueblood a note, thanking him for "setting the record straight."[35] One of the critical memo's authors was H. Tom Davis, chairman of the RNR council. He resigned the chairmanship, under pressure from the council directors, primarily Bruce Bowler, but continued to serve as a director. Davis maintained that the memo was factually correct and even offered to debate it with Andrus and his staff.[36]

Andrus was a personal as well as a political friend of Trueblood and RNR Council directors Day and Bruce Bowler. He had known Day since 1965. They met on a State Land Board tour that included a raft ride on the North Fork of the Clearwater River. Day was thrown overboard after playfully attempting to push another rafter. Recognizing that he was in trouble, Andrus went to his rescue, helping him to shore. Their friendship continued before and after Andrus became governor. Andrus sometimes joined Trueblood, Day, Bowler and other wildlife federation stalwarts on their annual crappie fishing excursions to Owyhee Reservoir. In May 1977, Field and Stream carried Trueblood's article praising the new Interior Secretary and describing his environmental leadership. He wrote that the Andrus record had been "consistently on the side of the environment. He has repeatedly said that protecting it is not inconsistent with orderly growth, that you can provide jobs and still preserve air and water quality, wild areas, fish and game."[37]

Idaho wilderness advocates recognized that Andrus would probably determine the Carter administration's primitive area recommendation. They were hoping that he would embrace their 2.3 million acres. Church met with RNR directors in December and promised to introduce their bill and to call for public hearings in Idaho and Washington. He followed up by writing to Trueblood asking for "the RNRWC proposal in its most current form" with up to date supporting materials. Church had not endorsed the bill but the directors got the impression that he favored it. He was also optimistic about moving ahead on the issue with Andrus as Interior Secretary and Morris Udall as chairman of the House Interior Committee.[40] Udall had floated the middle fork in 1974 and had written Andrus pledging his support of a central Idaho wilderness.[38]

In 1977, wilderness was becoming a much bigger political issue in Idaho, making the task of the RNR advocates more difficult. The Forest Service began a review in 1972 of roadless areas in all of the national forests to identify those it considered suitable for wilderness designation by Congress. This was part of a planning process pursuant to the Multiple Use and Sustained Yield Act of 1960 and the National Environmental Policy Act. When President Ford proposed to delete the Chamberlain Basin from the central Idaho wilderness in December 1974, he also asked Congress to designate 36 wilderness areas in other states totaling eight million acres.

This proposal was criticized by wilderness supporters as inadequate, omitting many high quality areas. In 1977, with Jimmy Carter in the White House, the Forest Service undertook a second review (Roadless Area Review and Evaluation, RARE II). The review had two purposes, to identify areas that Congress might want to add to the wilderness system and to allow roading, logging and other development to proceed in areas that were not recommended for wilderness or for further study. Nothing would happen before the review was completed. This meant that many proposed timber sales would be delayed.

Idaho had more publicly owned unroaded land than any state other than Alaska, 11 million acres in the national forests and five million acres under jurisdiction of the Interior Department's Bureau of Land Management.

The unroaded national forest areas included 2.4 million acres in the existing wilderness and primitive areas. Much of the forest land was rugged mountain and canyon country and the Forest Service rated 44 percent as unsuitable for timber harvest. Still, much of it was coveted by the timber industry. The Forest Service identified 115 roadless areas for review, a total of seven million acres, nearly a third of Idaho's national forest acreage.

Wilderness advocates expected most of that acreage to be left open to roads and logging. But they identified areas in all parts of the state that they wanted protected as wilderness. These included the Mallard-Larkin and Great Burn areas in the north, the Magruder Corridor and Meadow Creek areas on the Selway, the Palisades area in eastern Idaho and the Pioneer and White Cloud Mountains in central Idaho.

The roadless area review process set off alarm bells in mill towns across the state. Loggers and mill workers were told that they could lose their jobs. Industry ads in newspapers and on television warned that 51 percent of Idaho's national forest land would be off limits to timber harvest if all of the roadless areas were designated for wilderness management. Wives of loggers and mill workers organized to fight wilderness. Church and other members of the Idaho congressional delegation received hundreds of anti-wilderness letters. Ethel Kimball of Salmon recalled that in 1965 she had supported the campaign to save the upper Selway, arranging a meeting in Salmon attended by Church, Doris Milner and Guy Brandborg. She had wished then to preserve "one particular area." Now she believed the pendulum had swung too far. The country had been taken over by "ecoholics," who didn't care about the economies of timber communities: "Idaho has had enough, Senator Church, and as our senior and most powerful man in Congress, surely you can use your strength to help your state during this critical time."[39]

Nowhere was the conflict more intense than in Idaho County. Morton Brigham of Lewiston and Dennis Baird of Moscow were leading a movement to gain wilderness designation for a portion of the 330,000-acre Gospel Hump roadless area. Located to the west of the Salmon River Breaks Primitive Area, it included Gospel Peak and Buffalo Hump mountains north of the Salmon River, had many high lakes and was home to elk, moose, deer and mountain goats.

The Forest Service had recommended none of the area for wilderness study in the first roadless area review. In April 1976, the Nez Perce Forest adopted land use plans allocating parts of the area to timber harvest. Idaho environmentalists appealed to Forest Service Chief John McGuire. McGuire agreed that the Forest Service, in dividing the area into eight separate planning units, hadn't fairly considered its wilderness potential. He directed his agency to evaluate the entire roadless area including a portion south of the Salmon River.[40]

This meant delay in proceeding with planned timber sales, reducing the amount of timber available to area mills. The timber industry and the Grangeville Chamber of Commerce were also concerned about potential Forest Service wilderness recommendations for the 160,000-acre Meadow Creek area in the Selway River drainage and the Jersey Jack roadless area north of the Salmon River. The Grangeville Chamber of Commerce asked Church for help to resolve the situation. Church was sympathetic, advising chamber and timber industry spokesmen that he shared their concern that the roadless area review process and the threat of appeals and lawsuits by conservationists could reduce the supply of logs to Idaho mills and eliminate jobs.

Church asked conservationists and representatives of the Grangeville Chamber to sit down together to see if they could reach a compromise. With an agreement, he could propose a Gospel Hump amendment to a bill that he was sponsoring, the Endangered American Wilderness Act. This bill would designate 18 wilderness areas in seven western states, areas prized by wilderness supporters but not recommended in the first Forest Service review.[41]

Church attended the first meeting of the conferees in Grangeville on April 28. The four environmentalists, Brigham, Baird, Doug Scott of the Sierra Club and Dan Lechefsky of the Wilderness Society, insisted on wilderness designation for part of the area but said they would agree to release 80,000 acres for logging. The five Grangeville Chamber representatives were not ready to accept any wilderness, only further study for part of the area. But after more meetings an agreement was reached on July 13. It called for 220,000 acres of wilderness in the high peaks area and the breaks of the Salmon River. Another 45,000 acres, heavily timbered and accessible, would be made instantly available for logging. Another 78,000 acres would become available for development pursuant to a comprehensive resource plan yet to be developed. The potential timber would be included in the Nez Perce Forest's determination of its "allowable cut."

Church praised the conferees for reaching an agreement that could protect timber jobs, avoiding "years of uncertainty and delay," saying that he believed the negotiation process could serve as a model to resolve other wilderness disputes. Negotiators credited Church for his leadership. Baird thanked the senator for his courage "and for having retained the trust of all sides in the matter. Your past work in the area of wilderness preservation has earned you a vast amount of goodwill and respect from conservationists, and your help in settling the fate of Gospel Hump has only increased our respect for you (and your staff)."[42]

Church introduced the compromise plan in the Senate and scheduled a hearing in Grangeville before the Senate Energy and Natural Resources Committee's Parks and Recreation Subcommittee. He spent two days exploring the Gospel Hump country by air and on horseback in advance of the hearing. Most of the 70 speakers, including the Idaho County Commissioners and a spokesman for First District Rep. Steve Symms, opposed any wilderness and rejected the compromise.

Gov. John Evans and Idaho County legislators supported it, as did the Grangeville and Cottonwood chambers of commerce. The opposition testimony, some of it highly critical of Church for his role in passing the Wilderness Act, reflected intense anti-wilderness sentiment generated by the roadless area review and environmental appeals of proposed timber sales. Some complained of "economic blackmail" by environmentalists.[43]

C. H. Ketcham of the Prairie Land and Timber Company said the compromise was made "with a loaded gun pointed directly at the heart of the timber industry and the economy of Idaho County."[44] Two months earlier Church and Sen. James McClure had heard 47 anti-wilderness witnesses at a hearing in McCall. Only two spoke for wilderness.[45] In his opening statement in Grangeville, Church cited a 1972 court ruling pursuant to the National Environmental Policy Act that required the Forest Service to prepare an environmental impact statement before taking any action that would alter the wilderness character of any inventoried roadless area: "Because of new appeals and the likelihood of future court battles, the harvesting of timber from the heavily forested portions of roadless areas in Idaho's national forests still remains under a pall of uncertainty."[46]

In early October, Church was able to win Senate Energy and Natural Resources Committee approval of the Gospel Hump compromise as part of his Endangered American Wilderness Act. To help gain the support of Senator McClure, he agreed to two changes, allowing snowmobile use on a trail across the wilderness and extending the deadline for new mining claims from 1983 to 1988. Church and McClure said they would seek further Idaho wilderness compromises to free up timber supplies. And Church was quoted as saying that the Gospel Hump negotiation process might be used next for the Idaho primitive areas.[47]

This suggestion generated shock and disbelief among River of No Return advocates. They believed the 1974 Forest Service hearings had demonstrated strong public support in Idaho for their 2.3 million acres. Their hopes had soared with the Andrus Interior appointment and with Church's promise to introduce their bill. They were encouraged further when President Carter mentioned the central Idaho wilderness in his environmental message. But in July 1977, Interior Secretary Andrus told a Lewiston Tribune reporter that the Carter administration's proposal would be his 1.8 million acres. And in an August meeting Church told RNR directors he would support no more than the 1.8 million. He had also suggested linking the River of No Return issue to the roadless area review, asking the RNR directors if they would compromise by accepting non-wilderness status for other areas. It was apparent that Church had been swayed by the timber industry's anti-wilderness offensive and the fear of timber job losses.

Ted Trueblood advised River of No Return directors: "The elation we all felt when President Carter mentioned the RNR Wilderness in his environmental message, even though the acreage was vague, has now faded. The prospects of getting the 2.3 million acre wilderness we want, and should have, are very poor." They might not even get 1.8 million acres. "Industry, with the help of its mouthpiece, Steve Symms, and others like him, has launched an intensive, clever and effective anti-wilderness campaign. There are people who believe Idaho will be half wilderness unless the designation of new areas is stopped now." The timing of the Buffalo Hump compromise was unfortunate, Trueblood wrote. "We may gain 220,000 acres of wilderness there, but we could lose five times as much because the opposition is waving it as the red flag of danger to future economic development."[48]

Trueblood got off a letter to Church: "We were dismayed by the news release in the Statesman on October 7 quoting you and Senator McClure. Two amendments adopted by the Senate Energy and Natural Resources Committee are in clear contradiction to the intent of the Wilderness Act – which we might not have had but for you – and further set a dangerous precedent that could jeopardize the entire wilderness system."

Of even greater concern, wrote Trueblood, was the suggestion of a negotiated settlement for the primitive areas: "This is simply unthinkable. In the first place, the two cases are not parallel. Gospel Hump was a study area. The Idaho and Salmon River Breaks primitive areas were established, at the request of the people of Idaho, long before the passage of the Wilderness Act. Secondly, only in Congressional hearings – which you have promised – can the people express their wishes on the River of No Return Wilderness. No committee, no matter how good its intentions, can speak for all Idahoans who have a right to express their opinions on the River of No Return Wilderness. In addition, since the land is nearly all national forest and belongs equally to all Americans, their desires must also be considered."[49]

River of No Return Council directors Nelle Tobias of McCall and Ernie Day sent Church similar letters, as did other River of No Return supporters.[50] Church did not reply, preferring to wait until Congress completed action on the Endangered American Wilderness Act and Gospel Hump. After nearly two months with no response, Trueblood wrote Church again. He began by quoting the hero of the Hemingway novel "For Whom the Bell Tolls": "This government has much money, much gold. They will give nothing to their friends. You are a friend. All right. You will do it for nothing and should not be rewarded. But to people representing an important firm or country

Ted Trueblood Photo

Elk in Chamberlain Basin

which is not friendly but must be influenced – to such people they give much."[51]

"We are your friends," wrote Trueblood. "We have overlooked much since the day you lost your courage at Dworshak Dam but we have remained your friends. We have been patient for five years waiting for you to recover your courage and help us obtain the River of No Return Wilderness. Last August 18, it was obvious that your courage was completely gone. You asked me *twice* if there was any way we could make a trade-off with the 2.3 million acres we must have in the River of No Return Wilderness. I said, 'no way.' Now there is a way. There is a way in which you can redeem yourself with your friends and still go all out for the tradeoff you want." Trueblood noted that the Forest Industry Council's newspaper and television ads warned of possible wilderness designation of 11 million acres. The RNR supporters were willing to compromise based on that figure, he advised Church. "Then, early in the next session of this Congress, we want you to introduce a bill for a 2.3 million acre RNR Wilderness. You can make it clear that you are doing it by request, which will take the heat off you. And you can make trade-offs and compromises all over the place, using the 11 million acre figure."

Trueblood's relationship with Church had always been friendly. Now, he was questioning the senator's courage. It was a severe rebuke as well as a reminder that Idaho conservation leaders had supported Church in every election campaign.

In December, Church won a unanimous Senate vote to include Gospel Hump in the Endangered American Wilderness Act. After the House passed Rep. Morris Udall's version of the act, Senate and House conferees agreed to include Gospel Hump in the final bill. With final passage assured, Church called Trueblood and followed up with a letter. The McClure snowmobile amendment had been stricken out by the conferees, he reported. By agreeing to the amendment in the Senate, Church said he had been able to secure a unanimous vote to add Gospel Hump to the bill. The strong Senate vote had given him leverage to persuade House conferees to include Gospel Hump in the final bill, despite the determined opposition of Rep. Steve Symms. "Even though Symms himself was a conferee, in the end he was voted down by his own colleagues."

Church said he was "well satisfied with the final product" which differed only slightly from the compromise agreement, creating a 206,000 acre "pristine wilderness in the summits of the Gospel Hump area. I am proud of that accomplishment and think you would be too." As to the primitive areas, he had never intended use of the Gospel Hump approach. "Any newspaper account suggesting that I favored a different course is mistaken." Church expected the Carter administration would soon submit its proposal. "In January, I will be willing to introduce, by request, the 2.3 million-acre proposal advocated by the River of No Return Wilderness Council. Other proposals may also be introduced."[52]

H. Tom Davis photo

Welcome Lake in the River of no Return Wilderness

Then there would be public hearings in Idaho and Washington. Trueblood was delighted. He sent Church a warm note addressed "Dear Frank," thanking the senator for his "wonderful encouraging letter," and "wishing you and yours a Very Merry Christmas and a great 1978. Your friend, Ted."[53] A copy of Church's letter went to RNR Council directors. After a long period when things looked pretty bleak, Trueblood wrote: "I am heartened. Senator Church will introduce the bill we want and there will be public hearings. If we can demonstrate overwhelming public support, we have a chance."

As he had promised, Church introduced the 2.3 million-acre River of No Return Wilderness Bill Feb. 6, 1978, making clear that it was not his bill but was introduced "by request." Now the River of No Return backers had a bill they could rally around, S2494. Trueblood's memo to council members asked them to write letters of support to Church, McClure, Andrus and Gov. John Evans and renew their memberships. Money was needed to help demonstrate overwhelming public support at public hearings. "The end is now in sight and, hopefully, a bill will be passed later this year."[54]

But in late May, RNR Council members were advised that there would be no congressional action on the River of No Return in 1978. The Senate Energy and Natural Resources Committee was busy with other issues including the roadless area review, the Alaska lands bill and the Carter energy plan. The Carter administration still had not submitted its primitive area proposal. And, as yet, there was no recommendation from Gov. John Evans. Trueblood suggested that the council close its office, suspend activity and hang on to its money, $2,000, until a bill was introduced in the next Congress.[55] Directors Morton Brigham and Jerry Jayne both advised that the council should continue operations, working for the 2.3 million acres. "It has been my experience that a start-stop approach to such an issue doesn't go anywhere," wrote Brigham. "It takes steady support, year after year, for such a far-reaching measure. Even a trickle of letters over a long period can work wonders."[56]

Frank Church planned to move ahead on the central Idaho wilderness early in 1979 and hoped to see legislation passed before the end of the year. Church was looking ahead to the election year, 1980. He expected that he would be challenged by First District Rep. Steve Symms and that Symms would use the wilderness issue against him. It would be better to resolve the issue in 1979 than in the election year. Church also recognized that he might not be re-elected, that the next two years might offer the last chance for a large Salmon River wilderness.

Cecil Andrus arranged for Jimmy Carter to float the Middle Fork of the Salmon in the summer of 1978 with Salmon outfitter Norm Guth, letting the President see some of the Idaho Primitive Area. The Carter administration announced its River of No Return proposal in December, a wilderness of 1,889,000 acres. It was similar to the 1.8 million acres that Andrus had supported as governor but also included 72,000 acres in the Selway River drainage north of the Salmon River and the Magruder Corridor south of the Magruder road.

In January, Frank Church introduced "by request" three bills, the 2.3 million-acre River of No Return Wilderness, the Carter administration's 1,889,000 acres and an Idaho Forest Industry Council bill for a wilderness of 1.3 million acres. The industry bill also proposed to authorize logging in other nearby roadless areas. It authorized implementation of the current Forest Service land use plan for the Warren Planning Unit in the South Fork Salmon River drainage and provided for $2 million a year for five years for logging roads. It would ban further wilderness consideration for all roadless areas in the Nez Perce Forest.

The timber industry proposal would deny wilderness protection to a million acres in the River of No Return Council's plan and would also open to development several hundred thousand acres of additional roadless land that was outside the proposed boundaries of the River of No Return Wilderness.[57]

River of No Return leaders knew that they needed to demonstrate strong public support in Idaho to persuade Senator Church to support their 2.3 million acres. The council and its allies prepared an extensive public outreach campaign that included slide show presentations, letters to the editor and distribution of thousands of copies of an illustrated tabloid newspaper. They organized committees in the larger cities to prepare for the hearings. And they formed a new organization, Friends of the River of No Return Wilderness, inviting other organizations to endorse the 2.3 million-acre bill and to ask their members to turn out for the hearings and write letters to Church and McClure. Simultaneous press conferences were conducted in Boise, Lewiston and Idaho Falls to announce that 24 Idaho organizations had joined the friend's coalition. (The number would eventually reach 39.)

Five days later, Senators Church and McClure conducted the first public hearing in Lewiston. Most of the 140 witnesses supported the 2.3 million-acre River of No Return Wilderness. The anti-wilderness witnesses supported the timber industry bill as the least objectionable alternative. Many came from Elk City, a village of 400 and home to the Bennett Lumber Company sawmill. They had been told the sawmill would shut down if large roadless areas in the Selway River drainage became wilderness.[58]

Two weeks after the Lewiston hearing the Carter administration sent Congress its Roadless Area Review recommendations, proposing wilderness designation for 9.9 million acres of undeveloped national forest land in 15 states. In Idaho, the President recommended areas totaling 1.5 million acres for wilderness and 1.4 million acres for further study. The remaining 4.6 million acres was proposed for development, including timber removal.

The recommendation was well received by the timber industry because Carter had reduced the Forest Service's proposed further study areas by 357,373 acres. It was also applauded by Gov. John Evans who had proposed less wildernesses. Senator McClure described it as a good starting point for further discussion. Jerry Jayne of the Idaho Environmental Council and Pat Ford, director of the Idaho Conservation League, expressed disappointment. Ford said more than half of Idahoans responding to a Forest Service request for input had favored wilderness for areas recommended for development by Carter. On the plus side, Carter's proposed wilderness included 200,000 acres of primitive area contiguous areas that had been omitted from his River of No Return proposal. In effect, he was now proposing a central Idaho wilderness of 2.1 million acres.[59] It was apparent that both Carter and Evans were proposing a tradeoff, a large wilderness in central Idaho but roads and logging in most of the roadless area review areas.

Anti-wilderness feeling was strong in Salmon, site of the second Senate committee hearing. Champion International had recently gone from two shifts to one at its mills in Salmon and North Fork, laying off 36 workers. Champion's problem was not wilderness, but a Forest Service regulation giving a preference to small business on 40 percent of the timber sale volume. A small mill in Darby, Mont. was buying some of the timber Champion had expected to purchase.[60]

Senator McClure was unable to attend and Senator Church conducted the hearing alone. Champion gave mill workers the day off so they could go to the hearing and parked a logging truck outside the building with a large sign: "Save our jobs." Pickups in the parking lot displayed anti-wilderness signs such as "Don't Californicate Idaho, environmentalists go home" and "Charles Manson was an environmentalist." Crushed beer cans were dumped on a table with a River of No Return display and bumper stickers were torn up.

A crowd of 400 filled the Elks Lodge and others stood outside by the windows to hear the speakers. River of No Return supporters came from Idaho Falls, Pocatello, the Wood River area and western Montana. The crowd cheered anti-wilderness speakers and booed River of No Return supporters, causing Church to intervene to maintain order. The senator listened to speakers for eight and a half hours with no break for lunch.[61] Although 158 testified another 100 had signed up to speak. Church extended the hearing to a second day.

Among the first day's speakers was Rep. Steve Symms, who called for an acreage limit on Idaho wilderness. He said that Congress should resolve the entire Idaho wilderness issue including the primitive areas, the roadless area review areas and wilderness on land administered by the Bureau of Land Management.

While anti-wilderness speakers said timber and mining jobs would be lost with a large central Idaho wilderness, River of No Return advocates cited the millions contributed to the Idaho economy by backcountry recreation. Salmon Dentist Richard Smith said the volume of timber sold on the Salmon National Forest had increased from 10 million board feet in 1955 to 36 million in 1979, evidence that the industry was not suffering because of wilderness.[62] Both the Boise and Idaho Falls papers reported that advocates for the 2.3 million-acre River of No Return wilderness outnumbered those favoring the timber industry bill by a ratio of two to one. There was no support for the 1.9 million-acre Carter proposal.[66] Church told a reporter that he hoped to see a solution that considered both the needs "of the local economy" and wilderness values.

The day before the Boise hearing, Ted Trueblood called attention to the large volume of logs being shipped out of the state to an Oregon mill. While the timber industry was telling Idahoans that jobs would be lost with a central Idaho wilderness, he said, it had chosen not to buy 20 million board feet of timber from the Boise National Forest. A Boise Cascade spokesman said the company had tried to buy the timber but was outbid because the Oregon Company was willing to pay astronomical prices.[63]

Most of the 373 people who had signed up to testify in Boise were River of No Return supporters. Also signed up were 37 residents of Elk City who chartered a bus for the hearing. Tim Mueller of Bennett Lumber Company said the Elk City mill would close without timber from 255,000 acres of roadless lands in the Nez Perce Forest adjoining the primitive areas. This land was outside the proposed River of No Return boundaries.

Senator Church was sensitive to Elk City's concern and had already advised the residents that the mill's timber supply would be protected. More than 300 testified in Boise, pushing the total for the three hearings past 600. River of No Return supporters outnumbered the opposition by a large margin in all three hearings but there was tremendous concern about timber supply, related to roadless area review lands, particularly in Elk City and other Idaho County communities. After the Boise hearing, Senator Church said it was apparent "that no one of these bills commands the support of the Idaho people in sufficient number" and that an ultimate bill must bring the various interests "into fair balance." Senator McClure said it was likely that a compromise bill would be approved by Congress.[64]

What did Church mean by a "fair balance" in the ultimate bill? In late August, Church and his north Idaho field director, Larry LaRocco, met with wilderness advocates Dennis Baird, Scott and Mary Lou Reed, Art Manley and Fred Paige in Coeur d'Alene. River of No Return leaders were advised that "The general impression received is that Church is personally familiar with the issues involved, is personally overseeing the putting together of a compromise bill, is sympathetic to our goals and is very sensitive to the political implications of the issue."

Church planned to resolve the issue of roadless lands in the Nez Perce Forest as part of the bill. He preferred not to address the issue of the Warren land use plan but feared McClure might demand its inclusion as a price for supporting the bill. Church reported that the Noranda Mining Co. proposed to reopen the Blackbird cobalt mine on Panther Creek and had been pressuring him to reduce the potential wilderness area. The RNR Council had recently moved its proposed boundary to exclude about 5,000 acres of mining claims adjacent to the existing mine but Noranda wanted to exclude far more.[65]

In early November, the Senate Energy and Natural Resources Committee approved, on a 17-0 vote, a bill drafted primarily by Church. It included most of the River of No Return Council's acreage and added 65,000 acres of the Magruder Corridor south of the Magruder Road. It also added 105,000 acres north of the road to the Selway-Bitterroot Wilderness, leaving a 300-foot non-wilderness buffer on either side of the road. Idaho and Montana conservations had been working to restore the Magruder Corridor to wilderness status ever since the Forest Service excluded it in the reclassification of the Selway-Bitterroot Primitive Area in 1963.

But Church excluded from wilderness the 24,000 acre Big Mallard Creek and Jersey Jack roadless areas on the Northwest side of the Salmon River Breaks Primitive Area. His bill also omitted the 97,000-acre Meadow Creek East roadless area that the Forest Service and Carter administration had proposed for wilderness. Meadow Creek was the largest tributary of the Selway River and Meadow Creek East included large meadows used by elk. By excluding Big Mallard, Jersey Jack and Meadow Creek, Church hoped to gain the support of Wickes Forest Industries of Grangeville and the Bennett Lumber Company.

While McClure had agreed with Church on most of the wilderness acreage and voted for the bill in committee, he was not satisfied. He sought two amendments that the committee rejected. One would have mandated non-wilderness status for a total of 900,000 acres of roadless areas in central Idaho outside the proposed River of No Return boundaries.

Without the amendment he said at least two sawmills would probably close. Church said the Forest Service had already promised to treat those areas in McClure's 900,000 acres as non-wilderness and that such statutory language would "scuttle the bill" because it would not be accepted by the House Interior Committee. Church had language included in the Senate

Ernie Day photo

Ship Island Lake in the Idaho Primitive Area, later included in the River of No Return Wilderness.

Interior Committee report that he said would achieve the same result, assuring that the 900,000 acres would be managed to allow timber removal.

The other McClure amendment would have reduced the acreage sought by the RNR Council in the Clear Creek roadless area to leave it available for possible cobalt mining. Church said most of the potential deposits of cobalt were outside the proposed wilderness boundary. Wilderness advocates had emphasized the importance of the area as habitat for bighorn sheep. Boise Cascade didn't get the language it wanted to assure logging in the Warren and Landmark planning areas. But Church included a provision saying court appeals of those plans must be completed by the fall of 1980. McClure vowed to offer his amendments again when the Senate considered the bill.[66]

While Idaho conservationists were generally pleased with the River of No Return acreage and with restored wilderness protection for the Magruder Corridor, they were disappointed with the exclusion of the Jersey Jack, Big Mallard and East Meadow Creek areas north of the Salmon. Some felt that Church had gone too far to accommodate the timber industry.

They were further disappointed that 112 miles of the lower Salmon River were not given wild and scenic river status.[67] The Forest Service, Carter administration and Gov. John Evans had recommended protection for the entire river from the north fork downstream. McClure insisted on the exclusion and Church reluctantly went along. Most of the testimony at Forest Service hearings had favored inclusion of all 237 miles but there was spirited opposition from landowners along the river. Without wild river protection, the river would remain at risk for the licensing of a salmon-killing dam by the Federal Power Commission.[68]

When the bill came up for consideration in the Senate on November 20, McClure again offered his amendments. Most of the 5-hour debate was taken up by a sometimes-heated clash between the Idaho senators. At one point McClure described Church's comments as "baloney, sheer unadulterated baloney." The Senate rejected 67-21 McClure's amendment to mandate non-wilderness management for 900,000 acres of central Idaho roadless area review land.

Church again maintained that language in the committee report would achieve the same result and that a statutory mandate would not be accepted by the House Interior Committee. He introduced letters from Wickes Forest Industries of Grangeville and Bennett Lumber Company of Elk City opposing McClure's statutory release language. At one point, while Church was off the floor, McClure questioned his actions in gaining the support of the lumber companies. When Church returned and challenged his comments, McClure clarified his remarks. But he later told a reporter that he believed Church had "manipulated" the support of Wickes and Bennett.

McClure withdrew his amendment to exclude 45,000 acres in the Clear Creek area from wilderness after Church won approval of a substitute amendment allowing underground mining, but not surface mining, if cobalt was found within the wilderness boundary. McClure argued that cobalt was a strategic metal and that national security was more important than bighorn sheep habitat. The final Senate vote was 69-18 with McClure voting no.[69]

Church said the bill struck a balance between competing uses demonstrating that "by careful draftsmanship of substantive legislation, we can wisely provide for a thriving forest products industry, continued mining and a magnificent wilderness that will be one of the jewels of the national wilderness system."[70] Ted Trueblood said "the people of Idaho are deeply indebted to Frank Church for his years of dedication to establishing an adequate wilderness in the Salmon River country."[71]

It was now no secret that Rep. Steve Symms would try to oust Church from the Senate in 1980 and that the Central Idaho Wilderness Act would be an issue. After the Senate vote, Symms issued a press release saying the bill would mean job losses and that Idahoans were being asked to contribute more than their share to the national wilderness system.[72] Both Symms and Second District Rep. George Hansen opposed the Senate bill.

Symms was a member of the House Interior Committee and was prepared to offer as a substitute a bill mandating non-wilderness management for 5.9 million acres included in the roadless area review with 375,000 acres designated for further study, limiting the River of No Return Wilderness to 1.4 million acres and excluding the entire Salmon River from wild and scenic river protection. Church and wilderness advocates would have to depend on other members of the House committee including the chairman, Rep. Morris Udall. Udall had offered his help to Andrus for a central Idaho wilderness after floating the middle fork in 1972. Another key House supporter would be Rep. John Seiberling, D-Ohio, and chairman of the Interior Committee's Public Lands Subcommittee.

Testifying in support of his bill before Seiberling's subcommittee in early December, Church said the Symms substitute would produce "an emasculated Salmon River wilderness" excluding parts of the drainages of Camas Creek, Loon Creek and Sulphur Creek. These were all major tributaries of the middle fork and important salmon and steelhead streams. Church said the Symms bill also made a mockery of the deliberative and studied process the Forest Service and Congress had followed in determining the best uses of national forests. Other roadless area review areas deserved individual consideration, he said, adding that he expected the River of No Return Wilderness to be the last large addition to the wilderness system in Idaho.[73]

Martel Morache of the Idaho Fish and Game Department spoke for the Church bill, emphasizing the importance of protecting the integrity of the middle fork tributaries and habitat for wildlife, including bighorn sheep in the Clear Creek area. The boundaries were not the result of capricious or arbitrary decisions but of "15 years of critical, searching review," he said. Gov. John Evans supported the Church bill's wilderness boundaries and urged an amendment to include the lower 112 miles of the Salmon in the wild and scenic river system and protect it from dams.

Coeur d'Alene attorney Scott Reed, speaking for the National Audubon Society, asked for an amendment to bar dredge mining on the Salmon River and all of its tributaries. At that time there was a renewed threat of dredge mining of Bear Valley Creek, a middle fork tributary. Salmon outfitter

Norman Guth, president of the Idaho Outfitters and Guides and a director of the River of No Return Wilderness Council, cited the economic value of backcountry recreation, an estimated $23 million a year.[74] Ralph Maughan of Pocatello, an RNR Council director, asked for boundary changes to improve the Senate bill including the addition of the Elk Creek roadless area. He noted that Elk Creek was one of the most productive salmon spawning streams in the Middle Fork drainage.[75] Both Symms and Hansen spoke against the Church bill and for the Symms substitute. Hansen said Idaho already had more wild and scenic river mileage than any other state.

Seiberling's committee endorsed a bill modeled on the Church bill with some changes. It added the lower 53 miles of the Salmon to the wild and scenic system but, because of the opposition of Symms, left out a 59-mile section, 33 miles below Riggins and 26 miles above. It also adopted a prohibition on dredge mining on the Middle Fork of the Salmon and all of its tributaries both inside and outside the wilderness. But the Interior Committee accepted an amendment by Rep. James Santini, D-Nevada, to exclude from wilderness 50,000 acres of the Clear Creek roadless area because of its potential for cobalt.

Seiberling acted as floor sponsor of the House bill on April 16, 1980, saying it would give wilderness protection to the largest forest roadless area in the lower 48 states. Quoting the testimony of Martel Morache, he said the Salmon drainage provided spawning and rearing habitat for more spring and summer migrating chinook salmon than any other drainage of the Columbia River Basin. It also accounted for 98 percent of Idaho sport fishing for salmon and produced half of all Columbia River steelhead. "The survival of salmon is inexorably tied to the Salmon River remaining a free flowing stream." The middle fork and the main Salmon were among the most popular whitewater rivers in the nation, said Seiberling. He credited Church with crafting a bill that would also protect the timber industry: "There will be no jobs lost but rather jobs continued."[76]

Symms said three-fourths of the Idaho delegation opposed the bill. He offered his substitute, a Central Idaho wilderness of 1.4 million acres and further study of 375,000 acres of roadless area review land. All other Idaho forest roadless areas would be open to development by statute. Symms said the committee bill reflected the wishes of the "environmental sector" while his was a balanced approach. Rep. George Hansen backed Symms, saying wilderness served only the hiking and picture taking privileges of "rich and dedicated outdoor sportsmen."

Symms said it was a myth that the Church bill had broad support, citing opposition by the Idaho AFL-CIO, the state Chamber of Commerce, Cattlemen's Association, Farm Bureau and the Idaho legislature. With his bill, said Symms, the central Idaho wilderness would still be the largest wilderness in the lower 48 states. Oregon Democrat James Weaver said the 3.7 billion board feet of timber a year being exported from the Northwest exceeded by many times the potential cut in the proposed wilderness.

The tendency of House members to support their colleagues on issues in their districts helped Symms get 179 votes for his substitute. It was rejected 179-214. The modified Church bill passed 301-93. Rep. Peter Kostmeyer of Pennsylvania failed in his attempt to protect the omitted 53 miles of the Salmon River. Church persuaded the House-Senate conference committee to omit the Santini amendment. The final bill protected 125 miles of the Salmon River with wild and scenic river status, excluding 112 miles. But the lower 53 miles was protected from dams and placer mining. The size of the River of No Return Wilderness was believed to be 2.2 million acres when the legislation was passed but later land surveys showed that it was 2,373,331 acres.

Jimmy Carter signed the Central Idaho Wilderness Act on July 23, 1980. River of No Return council directors Ernie Day and Norman Guth were present, having accompanied Interior Secretary Cecil Andrus to the White House. They gave Carter a smoked Idaho steelhead.

The River of No Return Wilderness would be recognized as one of Church's finest achievements. He had given wilderness advocates what they wanted, a large wilderness embracing most of the Middle Fork Salmon River drainage. He had restored wilderness status to the Magruder Corridor. And he had protected the timber industry, particularly the mills in Idaho County. The River of No Return Council and its allies made it possible for Church to prevail by winning public support in Idaho with an aggressive information campaign that included numerous slide show presentations, newspaper ads and Ted Trueblood's writing. They never wavered on their 2.3 million acres, even when Church asked them to accept less.

Many people contributed to the victory. Among them was a young artist, Ron Walker of Boise, who, at the request of H. Tom Davis, produced a remarkable poster with line drawings of wilderness scenes based on photos by Ernie Day, Trueblood and Davis. The poster was given to all members of Congress. Martel Morache played a key role in shaping the proposals of governors Andrus and Evans. He made numerous slide show presentations in Idaho and neighboring states, briefed officials of the Ford and Carter administrations and worked with Church's staff in drawing boundaries for Church's bill. National conservation organizations, the Wilderness Society, Sierra Club, and the National Wildlife Federation all contributed, calling on their members for support and lobbying members of Congress.

By the time President Carter signed the Central Idaho Wilderness Act, Frank Church was engaged in a difficult campaign for re-election. He had been under attack since 1977 by conservative political action committees accusing him of weakening the Central Intelligence Agency with his investigation of the agency and questioning his loyalty for supporting the treaties that would return the Panama Canal to Panama in 1999.

The barrage of radio and television messages had convinced many Idaho voters that Steve Symms was a better choice for the Senate. Symms was supporting the "sagebrush rebellion," a movement to transfer the national forests and the public land managed by the Bureau of Land management to the states. Sen. Orrin Hatch of Utah, a rebellion supporter, said the ultimate purpose was sale of the land to private owners.

Ted Trueblood, Ernie Day and Bruce Bowler formed an organization, Save Our Public Lands, to fight the rebellion and help Frank Church. Trueblood had written an article for Field and Stream magazine describing the rebellion as a movement to sell the land. He pointed out that the public land in the west provided most of the habitat for game animals, most of the hunting for big game and most of the access to lakes and streams. If the land was sold, no trespassing signs would go up and the public would lose.

The article, "They're Fixin' to Steal Your Land," was reprinted in a 4-page tabloid by Save Our Public Lands (SOPL) and thousands were distributed door to door. SOPL criticized Symms for supporting the land transfer and Church made it a campaign issue. It probably helped but Symms won the election by 4,262 votes.

When Church was stricken with cancer and near death in 1984, Sen. James McClure pushed through legislation to rename the River of No Return Wilderness the Frank Church River of No Return Wilderness.[77]

Notes

Chapter 1

Happy hunting ground notes

1. Marshall Edson, *A Century of Idaho Wildlife, The Early Years*, Idaho Wildlife Review, September-October 1967, Pages 3-4. Edson, *The Winds of Change*, Idaho Wildlife November-December 1988, Page 4.
2. Idaho Session Laws 1873, Pages 10-12.
3. Idaho Session Laws 1875, Pages 46, 671-672.
4. Idaho Session Laws 1883, Pages 55-57.
5. Idaho Session Laws 1885, Pages 120-122.
6. Idaho Session Laws 1887.
7. Idaho Session Laws 1893, Pages 157-162.
8. *The Game and Fish Law*, Kendrick Gazette, reprinted in Idaho Statesman, April 23, 1893, Page 4. *Protect the Game*, Idaho Statesman, June 13, 1893.
9. Idaho Session Laws 1895, Page 156.
10. Idaho Session Laws 1897, Pages 130-134.
11. Idaho Session Laws 1899, Pages 427-430.
12. Charles H. Arbuckle, *First Biennial Report of the State Fish and Game Warden of the State of Idaho 1900,* Pages 1-15. *Idaho's First Fish and Game Warden*, Idaho Wildlife Review, January-February 1976, Pages 18-19. Marshall Edson, *Winds of Change*, Idaho Wildlife Review, November-December 1988, Page 4.
13. *Killing the Game*, Idaho Statesman, November 26, 1900.
14. *State Recognizes Treaty Rights of Nez Perce Tribe*, Idaho Statesman, April 26, 1922, Page 5. Arbuckle would later serve as a U.S. Marshall and as Boise City chief of police.
15. *T.W. Bartley Appointed Game Warden*, Idaho Statesman, January 20, 1901, Page 4.
16. *The Game Law*, Idaho Statesman, August 24, 1901. *Protect the Game*, Idaho Statesman, July 1, 1902, Page 4.
17. *Report of the State Game Warden*, Idaho Statesman, January 6, 1903, Page 6.
18. *For Protection of the Game*, Idaho Statesman, January 30, 1903, Page 4.
19. *Wants Changes in Game Law*, Idaho Statesman, January 21, 1903, Page 5.
20. Idaho Session Laws 1903, Pages 188-201.
21. *How Game Law Will Operate*, Idaho Statesman, April 9, 1903, Page 3. *Workings of the Game Law*, Idaho Statesman, June 24, 1903, Page 4.
22. *Strong Delegation*, Idaho Statesman, March 5, 1905.
23. William Stephens, *Second Biennial Report of the Fish and Game Warden of the State of Idaho 1905-1906.*
24. *Wanton Slaughter of Elk, Idaho Game Wardens Testify In Case in Los Angeles*, Idaho Statesman, December 15, 1906, Page 1.
25. William Stephens, *Biennial Report of the Fish and Game Warden of Idaho 1909-1910. Otto M. Jones, Annual Report of the Fish and Game Department of Idaho 1922.*
26. *Reply of Game Warden to Arraignment of His Policy by State Sportsmen's Association,* Idaho Statesman, May 14, 1907, Page 10. *Stephens Reply Answered*, Idaho Statesman, May 15, 1907, Page 2.
27. *Attack Made on Game Warden*, Idaho Statesman, February 24, 1909, Page 3.

28. *Asks Game Reserve in Boise National Forest*, Idaho Statesman, February 7, 1909.
29. Gordon S. Bowen, *Grandjean Man of the Forests*, Idaho State Historical Society 1987, Pages 33-37.
30. Idaho Session Laws 1909, Pages 152-153.
31. *New Law Suits Sportsmen*, Idaho Statesman, March 14, 1909, Page 2. *Forest Officers Busy*, Idaho Statesman, March 19, 1909, Page 7.
32. *Much Criticism of Warden Stephens – Forest Supervisor Says Fish and Game Department Has Been Negligent,* Idaho Statesman, June 19, 1909, Page 6. Bowen, Pages 33-37.
33. *Governor Goes to Aid of Warden*, Idaho Statesman, June 20, 1909, Page 5.
34. Bowen, Pages 40-41.
35. *Lawbreakers in Jeopardy,* Idaho Statesman, August 3, 1909, Page 4. *Brief Local News*, Idaho Statesman, August 4, 1909, Page 5.
36. *State Made a Mistake*, Idaho Statesman, September 12, 1909, Page 6. *Famous Game Preserve Is Possible*, Idaho Statesman, May 13, 1910, Page 12.
37. J.B. Gowen, *Report of the Fish and Game Warden of Idaho, 1914-1915,* Page 42.
38. *Editor Barber Given Reward for Service,* Idaho Statesman, December 29, 1912. *Governor-Elect Announces His Appointments,* Idaho Statesman, December 9, 1912, Page 8.
39. *Frank M. Kendall Report of the Fish and Game Warden of Idaho 1911-1912*, Pages 14-19.
40. *Governor Replies to Sportsmen's Complaints*, Idaho Statesman, February 3, 1913, Page 5. *Sportsmen To Go On With Fight for Recognition,* Idaho Statesman, March 14, 1913, Page 6.
41. *Asks Sportsmen for Real Help for State*, Idaho Statesman, March 26, 1913, Page 6. *Sportsmen and the Department in Full Harmony*, Idaho Statesman, June 19, 1914, Page 3. *Interesting Letter from E.F. Walton, president State Sportsmen's Association,* Idaho Fish and Game, July 1914, Pages 14-15.
42. *The Minimum Fine*, Idaho Fish and Game, July 14, Page 7.
43. *Barber Ousted to Make Room for Gowen*, Idaho Statesman, July 4, 1914, Page 1.
44. *Barber Surprised by Ouster by Governor*, Idaho Statesman, July 11, 1914, Page 5.
45. *Barber Denies Graft Charges in Rumors*, Idaho Statesman, July 13, 1914, Page 4.
46. *Revokes Orders of Predecessors on Fish Screens*, Idaho Statesman, July 7, 1914, Page 2. *Robert C. Sims and Hope P. Benedict, Idaho's Governors*, Boise State University 1992, Page 80.
47. *J.B. Gowen Fifth Biennial Report of the Fish and Game Warden of Idaho, 1913-1914*, Pages 2-16. Idaho Session Laws 1915 (The Black Lake Preserve was abolished by the legislature in 1935.)
48. *Fish and Game Bill Passes in House*, Idaho Statesman, February 25, 1915, Page 6. *Senate Passes Kiger-Koelsch Fish and Game Bill*, Idaho Statesman, March 2, 1915, Page 6.
49. *Governor Kills Eight More Measures by Veto*, Idaho Statesman, March 11, 1915, Page 1.
50. *A Political Adjunct*, Idaho Statesman, March 12, 1915, Page 4. *Same Old Motive*, Pocatello Tribune editorial reprinted in Idaho Statesman March 26, 1915, Page 4.
51. Idaho Session Laws 1915, Page 183 and 221. Idaho Session Laws 1917, Pages 25-26 and 70-72. Idaho Session Laws 1919, Pages 92-93, 186.
52. Jim Humbird, *Modern Day Elk More Plentiful*, Idaho Wildlife Review January-February 1975, Pages 16-17.
53. Idaho Session Laws 1915, Pages 184-186. Idaho Session Laws 1919, Page 241.
54. *W. H. Thorp Seventh Biennial Report of the Fish and Game Warden of Idaho 1917-1918*, Page 15.
55. Thorp, pages 21-22.
56. *Otto M. Jones to be Game Warden*, Idaho Statesman, January 5, 1919, Page 7. James H. Hawley, *History of Idaho Volume 2*, S.J. Clarke Publishing Co. 1920, Page 486.

57. *Idaho Sportsmen May Reorganize*, Idaho Statesman, May 29, 1920, Page 6.
58. *Game Warden Distributes Frogs*, Idaho Statesman, July 22, 1919, Page 8. *Deputies Will Assume Duties Unknown Before*, Idaho Statesman, February 15, 1920, Page 6.
59. Idaho Session Laws 1921, Pages 261-285. *Otto M. Jones Ninth Biennial Report of the Game Warden of Idaho 1921-1922.*
60. *Otto M. Jones Eighth Biennial Report of the Game Warden of Idaho 1919-1920*, Pages 25-26.
61. *Gov. Davis Saves Otto Jones Life*, Idaho Statesman, July 26, 1921, Page 1.
62. *Otto M. Jones Ninth Biennial Report of the Fish and Game Warden of Idaho 1921-1922*, Pages 1-35.
63. *Reply Made to Woolgrowers Request to Abolish State Game Department*, Idaho Statesman, February 3, 1922, Page 2.
64. *Sportsmen to Unite to Save Game of Idaho*, Idaho Statesman, February 12, 1922, Page 4.
65. *Will Ask Sheep to Quit Reserves*, Idaho Statesman, February 16, 1922, Page 6. *Woolgrowers Bout Goes Merrily On*, Idaho Statesman, February 18, 1922, Page 3.
66. *Otto M. Jones Ninth Biennial Report*, Pages 24-27.
67. *Outdoor League Stages Banquet*, Idaho Statesman, February 17, 1923, Page 6. *Fish and Game Bodies Organize*, Idaho Statesman, February 18, 1923, Page 2. *Mr. Sportsman and Citizens*, Idaho Statesman, March 18, 1923, Page 14.
68. *Deputy Warden Will Succeed Otto M. Jones*, Idaho Statesman, March 25, 1923, Page 4. Idaho Session Laws 1923, Pages 182-183.
69. Kliess Brown, *A Century of Idaho Wildlife*, Idaho Wildlife Review January-February 1968, Page 3. *R.E. Thomas Tenth Biennial Report of the Fish and Game Warden of Idaho 1923-1924,* Page 43.
70. Idaho Session Laws 1923, Pages 45, 84. Idaho Session Laws 1925, Pages 42, 71, 135, 255. Idaho Session Laws 1927, Pages 150, 217.
71. *R.E. Thomas Thirteenth Biennial Report of the Fish and Game Warden of Idaho 1929-1930*, Pages 13-18.
72. Lorayne O. Smith, *Southern Idaho Game Association History*, College of Southern Idaho 2007.
73. *Nearly Fifty Years of Service*, Idaho Wildlife Review, March-April 1974, Page 14.
74. *Gooding Host to Sportsmen of Southwest Idaho,* Idaho Statesman, December 15, 1930, Page 1. *Sport Group Urges Changes*, Idaho Statesman, December 16, 1930, Page 1.
75. *Sportsmen See Victory Ahead Says Spokesman*, Idaho Statesman, December 1, 1932, Page 9.
76. *Sportsmen Fail to Admit Game Change Is Lost*, Idaho Statesman, January 13, 1933, Page 7. *Senate Starts Week By Swinging Ax on Five Bills, Game Commission Killed*, Idaho Statesman, February 21, 1933, Page 8.
77. *Fish and Game Commission Measure to Come Before Legislature*, Idaho Statesman, February 3, 1935, Page 12.
78. *Sportsmen Get Together Here*, Idaho Statesman, February 11, 1935, Page 1.
79. *Sportsmen Lose Their Fight for Commission Bill*, Idaho Statesman, February 27, 1935, Page 6. *Cato the Censor*, Idaho Statesman, February 27, 1935, Page 6.
80. David L. Lendt, *Ding, the Life of Jay Norwood Darling*, Iowa State University Press, Ames, Iowa 1979. Pages 66-67, 85, and 97-101.
81. *Idaho Sportsmen to Hold Special Meeting in Boise*, Idaho Statesman, January 23, 1936, Page 3. *Game Meeting Convenes Today*, Idaho Statesman, January 26, 1936, Page 6. *Group seeks Conservation*, Idaho Statesman, January 27, 1936, Page 1.
82. Frank Lundburg, *The Idaho Wildlife Federation Then, Now and Tomorrow, 60 Years of Conservation Leadership*, Idaho Wildlife Federation 1995. Pages 5-10. *All States to Be*

Represented at Conference, Boise Capital News, January 28, 1936, Page 8. *Articles of Incorporation Idaho Wildlife Federation*, Bruce Bowler papers.
83. *Ickes Urges Conservation on Big Scale*, Boise Capital News, February 6, 1936, Page 1.
84. *Darling Urges Use of Votes to Save Game,* Idaho Statesman, February 5, 1936, Page 1. *Cartoonist Named Leader of Drive to Save Wildlife,* Idaho Statesman, February 6, 1936, Page 1.
85. *Game Meeting Opens in Boise,* Idaho Statesman, April 6, 1936. *Idaho Sportsmen End Organizational Parley,* Boise Capital News, April 7, 1936, Page 1.
86. Lundburg, Pages 7-8. *Chart Wildlife Program*, Boise Capital News, April 6, 1936, Page 1.
87. Byron Johnson, *What It Means To Be A Poacher*, unpublished manuscript 2011, Page 3.
88. Idaho Fish and Game Act, Session Laws 1939, Pages 1-14. Marshall Edson and Diane Ronayne, *The Winds of Change*, Idaho Wildlife November-December 1988, Page 6.
89. *Fish and Game Session Opens in Idaho Capital City*, Idaho Statesman, January 12, 1937, Page 1. *Game Leaders Re-elect Cole As President,* Idaho Statesman, January 13, 1937, Page 1.
90. *Support Grows for Bi-Partisan Bureau Control*, Idaho Statesman, January 7, 1937, Page 6.
91. *Proposal Puts Bureau Control Under Five Men*, Idaho Statesman, January 19, 1937. *Game Measure Passes House*, Idaho Statesman February 9, 1937, Page 1.
92. *Game Commission Meets Opposition Among Legislators*, Idaho Statesman, January 23, 1937, Page 2. *Game Measure Meets Defeat*, Idaho Statesman February 14, 1937, Page 1.
93. *Sportsmen Flay Senate's Action*, Idaho Statesman, February 14, 1937, Page 5.
94. *Game League Files Papers*, Idaho Statesman, July 8, 1938, Page 1.
95. *Game Program Meetings Slated*, Idaho Statesman, November 2, 1938.
96. *Idaho Fish and Game Commission Minutes*, December 13, 1938, April 29, 1939, May 6 1939.
97. *Idaho Fish and Game Commission Minutes*, July 8, 1939.
98. *Idaho Fish and Game Commission Minutes*, July 21, 1939.
99. *Owen Morris Eighteenth Biennial Report of the Fish and Game Department of Idaho 1939-1940*, Pages 1-41.
100. *Idaho Wildlife Federation Bulletin,* February 4, 1949, Bowler papers.
101. *Here We Have Idaho*, Statewide, May 15, 1952, Page 5. Ted Trueblood, *Sportsmen Should Get Together and Prepare a Program for the Legislature*, Statewide June 12, 1952, Page 15. *Sports Group Urges Firing of Director,* Idaho Statesman, January 26, 1953.
102. Gov. Len B. Jordan message to legislature, Idaho Statesman, January 7, 1953, Page 14.
103. John Corlett, *Politically Speaking,* Idaho Statesman, January 7, 1953, Page 6. *Fish and Game Matters Said 'Hot Issues',* Idaho Statesman, January 10, 1953, Page 6.
104. *Senate Receives Bill to Create New Fish and Game Commission*, Idaho Statesman, March 1, 1953, Page 6. *House Passes Bill to Abolish Fish and Game Commission*, Idaho Statesman, March 4, 1953, Page 2. Bowler papers, Box 6, Folder 25.
105. *Idaho Wildlife Federation Bulletin*, April 12, 1955, Bowler papers

Chapter 2

Taking on the Dredge Miners

1. *Era Stirred By Dredgers*, Arthur Hart, Idaho Statesman, Aug. 21, 1972, Page 12. *Pioneer Days in Idaho County,* Volume 2, Sister M. Elfreda Elsensohn, The Caxton Printers 1951, Pages 26-30.

2. *Gold Dredge on the Yankee Fork,* Howard A. Packer, Jr., Yankee Fork Publishing Co. 1983. *Guidebook to the Geology of Central and Southern Idaho,* edited by Paul K. Link and William R. Hackett, Idaho Geological Survey, 1988, Page 226.
3. *Violently Opposed to Dredging,* Walter Johnson editorial, Statewide, July 20, 1950, Bowler papers, Box 4, Folder 4. *State Rejects Request to Dredge Salmon River,* Idaho Statesman, Aug. 25, 1950, Page 24. *Dredging Permit Denied,* Twin Falls Times-News, Aug. 27, 1950, Page 4.
4. *Land Board Hears Anti-Dredge Views,* Idaho County Free Press, Sept. 14, 1950, Page 1. *Ten Groups Protest Clearwater Dredging,* Lewiston Tribune, Sept. 12, 1950, Page 8.
5. *Plant in Boise to Mill Monazite Sand,* Idaho Statesman, Nov. 26, 1950, Page 8.
6. Martin brief, Bowler papers, Box 4, Folder 5.
7. *View on Dredges*, David Brazil letter, Idaho Statesman, Dec. 30, 1951, Page 4. Ted Wegener memo to Idaho Wildlife Federation members, Dec 7, 1950, Bowler papers, Box 4, Folder 5. Bruce Bowler to Randall Wallis, Senate attorney, Feb. 7, 1951, Bowler papers, Box 32, Folder 5.
8. *Senate Blocks Bill to Set Dredging Rule,* Idaho Statesman, March 8, 1951, Page 5.
9. *Dredging on Idaho Rivers,* editorial, Idaho Statesman, Aug. 23, 1951, Page 3, Bowler papers, Box 32, Folder 5.
10. *Dredge Work on Salmon River Flayed,* Idaho Statesman, Aug. 4, 1951, Page 2. *Not Indifferent to Dredging,* Statewide, Aug. 9, 1951, Page 4, Bowler papers, Box 32, Folder 5. *Lease Request Turned Down by Land Board,* Idaho Statesman, Aug. 18, 1951, Bowler papers, Box 32, Folder 5. *Report of the State Land Department*, Edward Woozley, 1946-48, Page 23.
11. *Battle Seen Over Dredging Lease Request,* Idaho Statesman, Aug. 5, 1951, Bowler papers, Box 4, Folder 5. *Payette Valley Joins Dredging Outcry,* Statewide, Sept. 4, 1951, Page 4. Bowler papers, Box 4, Folder 5. *Dredge Firm's Lease Request Is Withdrawn,* Idaho Statesman, Sept. 11, 1951, Page 16.
12. *Senators Told Rare Minerals Found in Idaho,* Idaho Statesman, Nov. 14, 1953. *Fifty-seventh Report of the Mining Industry in Idaho,* Idaho Inspector of Mines, 1955.
13. Ada Fish and Game League resolution, Bowler papers, Box 29, Folder 9.
14. *Dredge Owners In Bear Valley Given Warning,* Idaho Statesman, July 13, 1951. Idaho Fish and Game Department resolution, July 1951, Bowler papers, Box 32, Folder 5.
15. Johnson to Budge, July 13, 1954, Bowler papers, Box 29, Folder 9. Bowler to Budge, July 13, 1954, Bowler papers, Box 29, Folder 9.
16. D.B. Patterson, John Eaton, Art Smith letter to sportsmen, March 12, 1951, Bowler papers, Box 32, Folder 5.
17. Bowler to Wegener, Sept. 1, 1951, Bowler papers, Box 32, Folder 5.
18. Frank Cullen to Bowler, Dec. 15, 1952, Bowler papers, Box 32, Folder 6. Pierre Pulling to Bowler, Dec. 30, 1952, Bowler papers, Box 32, Folder 2.
19. *Burstedt Says Dredging Bill Right Step,* Idaho Statesman, Feb. 11, 1953, Page 6.
20. Bowler letter to Idaho Wildlife Federation Members, Feb. 17, 1953, Bowler papers, Box 32, Folder 7.
21. *Burstedt to Back New Dredge Bill,* Idaho Falls Post-Register, Feb. 25, 1953, Page 2.
22. *Dredging Control Proposal Blasted,* Idaho Statesman, Feb. 27, 1953, Page 11, Bowler papers, Box 32, Folder 7.
23. *Senate Passes Dredge Mining Control Bill,* Idaho Statesman, March 4, 1953, Page 5. *Idaho House Passes Two Conflicting Bills to Regulate Dredge Mining,* Idaho Statesman, March 5, 1953, Page 2. Bruce Bowler argument for dredge mining initiative, Idaho Granger, August 1954.
24. *Dredge Operators Fight Move of Sportsmen to Tighten Idaho Laws,* Coeur d'Alene Press, May 13, 1954. *McDowell says Idahoans Comply With Dredge Law,* Idaho Statesman, July 14,

1954, Bowler papers, Box 32, Folder 7. *State Auditor Sees Mining Initiative 'Useless' Effort,* Idaho Statesman, July 31, 1954, Bowler papers, Box 32, Folder 7. *Gordon Lucky letter,* Idaho Statesman, Aug. 1, 1954, Page 4, Bowler papers, Box 32, Folder 8.

25. *R.G. Cole letter*, July 12, 1954, Bowler papers, Box 32, Folder 8. Idaho Statesman, July 2, 1954, Page 6.

26. *Public Action Needed to Save Fish,* Emmett Messenger-Index editorial, Feb. 17, 1955, Page 16.

27. *Bear Valley Dredgers Suspend Operations Pending Provision for Clarification,* Emmett Messenger-Index. Feb. 17. 1955. Page 1. *Overruling the Jury*, editorial, Emmett Messenger-Index, May 5, 1955, Page 4.

28. *Dredge Men Set Meet for Monday,* Idaho Statesman, March 9, 1955.

29. *Be It Enacted, Republic or Dredge Rule?,* editorial, Emmett Messenger-Index, April 7, 1955, Page 4.

30. *State Engineer Tells Wildlife Club Dredges Can't Be Closed Arbitrarily,* Lewiston Tribune, Sept 22, 1955, Page 8. *Report of the Mining Industry of Idaho for 1956*, Page 143. Roberts letter to Wilson, July 30, 1955, Bowler papers, Box 39, Folder 2.

31. Morton Brigham to Glen Wegener, April 25, 1955, Bowler papers, Box 4, Folder 6. Charles Scribner to Bruce Bowler, May 2, 1955. Brigham to District Two sportsmen's clubs, April 28, 1955. Brigham to Scribner, June 6, 1955, Bowler papers, Box 39, Folder 2.

32. *Governor to Investigate Dredging Law Accusation,* Idaho Statesman, May 27, 1956, Page 6.

33. Idaho Session Laws 1969, Page 845-854. Idaho Session Laws 1970, Page 659.

34. *Salmon Land Withdrawal Is Debated,* Idaho Statesman, Sept. 20, 1957, Page 1. *Closure Hearing Ended After Two Days*, Idaho Statesman, Sept. 21, 1957, Page 1.

35. *Dredging Proposed for Bear Valley,* Idaho Citizen, June 1979, Page 1. *Some Salmon River Riddles: Why Was Door to Dams Left Open?,* Scott Reed, Idaho Citizen, August 1980, Page 3. *Boise South Fork Mining Sought,* Idaho Statesman, May 13, 1980, Page 1A.

36. *Boise South Fork Miners Protest New State Rules on Dredging,* Idaho Statesman, June 26, 1980, Page 1B.

Chapter 3

Salmon and steelhead lose habitat to dams

1. Anthony Netboy, *The Columbia River Salmon and Steelhead Trout – Their Fight for Survival*, University of Washington Press, Seattle 1980, page 53.

2. Jim Lichatowich, *Salmon Without Rivers,* Island Press 1999, Page 13.

3. Barton W. Evermann, *Salmon Investigations in Idaho,* Bulletin of the United States Fish Commission 1894.

4. David W. Ortmann, *Idaho Salmon Versus Dams,* Idaho Wildlife Review, March-April, 1970, Page 60.

5. Netboy, Pages 21-22.

6. Idaho Legislature Session Laws 1875, Page 871. Session Laws 1899, Pages 430-431.

7. Susan Stacy, *A Legacy of Light – A History of Idaho Power Company,* Idaho Power Co. 1999, Page 206.

8. *When Salmon Ran The Payette,* Idaho Wildlife Review, July-August 1975, Page 14.

9. Marshall Edson, *Idaho Wildlife in the Early Days,* Idaho Wildlife Review, September-October 1963, Page 8.

10. *Boise River Salmon,* Idaho Wildlife Review, January-February 1966, Page 15.

11. Victoria Mitchell, *History of the Sunbeam Dam,* Custer County Idaho, Idaho Geological Survey, 1997.
12. Bert Bowler, *Removing and Breaching Dams in Idaho* 1934-1993, April 2010.
13. Frank Kendall, *Biennial Report of the State Game Warden 1911-1912*, Page 41.
14. J.B. Gowen, *Biennial Report of the State Game Warden 1915-1916*, Page 27.
15. Assistant Reclamation Commissioner to Ben Anderson, Jan. 7, 1930, Bowler papers, Box 27, File 34.
16. Commissioner of Reclamation to C. Ben Ross, March 6, 1934 , Bowler papers, Box 27, File 34.
17. *Sunbeam Dam Notes 100-Year History,* Upper Salmon River Watershed News, Summer 2009, Page 3.
18. *Fish Can Pass Sunbeam Dam,* Idaho Recorder, July 11, 1934, Bowler papers, Box 4, File 5.
19. Forrest Hauck, *Return of the Big Redfish,* Idaho Wildlife Review, May-June 1955, Page 4.
20. Victoria Mitchell, *History of the Dewey Mine,* Idaho Geological Survey, February 2007. *To Blow Out $12,000 Dam – Dewey Company's Structure to be Destroyed by Game Warden,* Spokane Spokesman-Review, Sept. 14, 1905 page 4.
21. Otto M. Jones, *Eighth Biennial Report of the Game Warden of the State of Idaho 1919-1920,* Pages 48-49. Bert Bowler, page 2.
22. Brooks, Karl, *Public Power, Private Dams,* University of Washington Press, Seattle 2008, Pages 48-49.
23. Brooks, Page 185.
24 Brooks, Pages 211-212.
25. Bob Lorimer, *Salmon Saving Program Begun in 1964 by Power Firm Shows First Results,* Idaho Statesman, June 20, 1986, Page 1C.

Chapter 4

Fighting for the Clearwater

1. Department of Interior Fish and Wildlife Service, *A Report on the Fish and Wildlife Resources Affected by the Bruces Eddy Dam and Reservoir*, June 1960.
2. Darcy Williamson, *River Tales of Idaho*, Page 308.
3. Charles McCollister and Sandra McCollister, *The Clearwater River Log Drives*, Forest History Today, Fall 2000, Pages 20-26.
4. David W. Ortmann, *Salmon vs. Dams, Idaho Environmental Issues*, Idaho Wildlife Federation 1976, Page 60. Ralph B. Pirtle, *Fish Counts at the Lewiston Dam*, Idaho Wildlife Review, July-August 1956, Page 6.
5. Ross Leonard to Frank Church, April 26, 1957, Church papers, Series 1.1, Box 119, Folder 2.
6. *Chamber Gives Qualified Support to Clearwater Storage Projects*, Lewiston Tribune, Nov. 14, 1953, Page 2.
7. Ross Leonard, *Effects of Proposed Dams Upon the Anadromous and Resident Fishery of the Clearwater River*, November 1953, Frank Church papers, Series 1.1, Box 119, Folder 2. *Effects of Proposed Dams on the Clearwater River Upon Game Populations*, Idaho Fish and Game Department 1953, Church papers, Series 1.1, Box 119, Folder 2.
8. *Are Wildlife Objections Overstated?,* Lewiston Tribune Editorial, Nov. 14, 1953, Page 4.
9. John Corlett, *Writer Prognosticates on Orofino Hearing*, Lewiston Tribune, Nov. 15, 1953, Page 4.

10. *Army Engineers Two Dam Plan Meets Wide Approval,* Lewiston Tribune, Nov. 11, 1953, Page 12.
11. *Wildlife Group Opposes Clearwater, Snake Dams*, Idaho Daily Statesman, Jan. 11, 1954, Bowler papers, Box 29, Folder 33.
12. *O'Connor Defends Wildlifer's Fight Against Bruces Eddy Dam*, Lewiston Tribune, Feb. 26, 1957, Church papers, Series 1.1, Box 119, Folder 1.
13. John Corlett, *Idaho Wildlife Federation Like Spoiled Child,* Lewiston Tribune, Jan. 18, 1954, Page 4. John Corlett, *Politically Speaking*, Idaho Statesman, Jan. 12, 1954, Bowler papers, Box 29, Folder 33.
14. *Morton Brigham, diligent worker for wildlife and wilderness*, Idaho Citizen, December 1977-January 1978, Page 6.
15. Stuart Murrell, *Conservationist Morton R. Brigham,* Idaho Wildlife Review. *Laurel Darrow, Conservation is a Tradition, Too*, Lewiston Tribune, Sept. 30, 1990. Morton Brigham, (obituary) Lewiston Tribune, Dec. 19 2001.
16. *WWP President Lambasts Lack of Unity in Region Over Power Development*, Lewiston Tribune, Jan. 22, 1954, Page 16.
17. Bruce Bowler, Idaho Wildlife Federation to the Federal Power Commission, March 2, 1954, Bowler papers, Box 29, Folder 33.William Ashworth, *Hells Canyon, the Deepest Gorge on Earth*, Hawthorn Books 1977, Pages 91-92.
18. *Clearwater Battle Is Not Won, Dr. Wygant Tells Sportsmen*, Lewiston Tribune, Nov. 29, 1954, Page 8.
19. *A Shift Toward a Positive View*, Lewiston Tribune, Nov. 30, 1954, Page 4.
20. *Don't Dam the Clearwater*, brochure published by the Committee for the Preservation of the Clearwater, Bowler papers, Box 29, Folder 33.
21. Morton Brigham to Bruce Bowler, Nov. 18, 1956, Bowler papers, Box 29, Folder 33.
22. *The Current Status of Proposals for the Bruces Eddy and Penny Cliffs Dams on the Clearwater River*, memo from Stewart Brandborg, National Wildlife Federation, May 24, 1956, Church papers, Series 1.1, Box 119, Folder 2.
23. *Senate Votes to Authorize Bruces Eddy*; *No Funds Seen,* Lewiston Tribune, July 27, 1956, Page 12, Church papers, Series 1.1, Box 119, Folder 2.
24. *Bruces Eddy – A Conservation Test in River Basin Planning,* Congressional Record, July 26, 1956, Pages 1-13.
25. Stanley Burns interview, August 7, 2008.
26. Instructions for Bruce Bowler, Bowler papers, Box 29, Folder 9.
27. Ed Zern and Tom Linaweaver, *Senator Welker Will Oppose Dams on Clearwater River*, Outdoor Week, Sports Illustrated, May 21, 1956, Church papers, Series 1.1, Box 119, Folder 2.
28. Morton Brigham to Frank Church, Sept. 17, 1956. Bowler papers, Box 27, Folder 8.
29. Frank Church to Morton Brigham, Oct. 16,1956, Bowler papers, Box 27, Folder 5.
30. Carl Burke to Bruce Bowler, Sept. 21, 1956, Bowler papers, Box 27, Folder 8. Church letter to Idaho Outdoorsmen, October 1956, Bowler papers, Box 27, Folder 8. Stanley Burns interview, August 7, 2008.
31. Brigham to Bowler, Dec. 18, 1956, Bowler papers, Box 29, Folder 33.
32. A.B. Curtis to Church, Jan. 22, 1957, Church papers, Series 1.1, Box 119, Folder 1.
33. Brigham to Church, Jan. 27, 1957 Church papers series 1.1 box 119 Folder 1.
34. Church to Ross Hall Feb. 6 1957, Church papers, Box 119, Folder 1.
35. Warren Magnuson to Church, Feb. 8, 1957, Church papers, Series 1.1, Box 119, Folder 1.
36. Brigham to Church, Feb. 10, 1957, Church papers, Series 1.1, Box 119, Folder 1. Church statement to Subcommittee on Rivers and Harbors of the Senate Committee on Public Works, Feb. 5, 1957, Church papers, Series 1.1, Box 119, Folder 2.

37. E.M. Wygant to Church, April 2, 1957, Bowler papers, Box 27, Folder 19.
38. Church to E.M. Wygant, April 17, 1957, Bowler papers, Box 27, Folder 10.
39. Bowler to Church, May 1, 1957, Bowler papers, Box 27, Folder 10.
40. Brigham to Church, March 3, 1957, Church papers, Series 1.1, Box 119, Folder 6.
41. Church to Eli Rapaich, April 9, 1957, Church papers, Series 1.1, Box 119, Folder 6.
42. *Church and Dworshak on Bruces Eddy*, Lewiston Tribune Editorial, Feb. 8, 1957, Page 4.
43. John Corlett, *Two Projects Dear to Orofino's Heart*, Lewiston Tribune, Church papers, Series 1.1, Box 119, Folder 1.
44. Shearl Lomax to Church, Feb. 9, 1957, Church papers, Series 1.1, Box 119 Folder 1.
45. *Wildlife Studies Show Whitetails Would Suffer Most in Pool Area*, Lewiston Tribune, Feb. 13, 1957, Church papers, Series 1.1, Box 119, Folder 2.
46. *Some Sweeping Conclusions Demolished*, Lewiston Tribune Editorial, Feb. 15, 1957, Page 4.
47. Ross Leonard to Frank Church, April 26, 1957, Church papers, Series 1.1, Box 119, Folder 6. Church statement in Congressional Record, May 3, 1957, Church papers, Series 1.1, Box 119, Folder 1.
48. Bruce Bowler to Rep. Charles Buckley, Aug. 7, 1957, Church papers, Series 1.1, Box 119, Folder 1.
49. *Committee Okehs Bruces Eddy*, Lewiston Tribune, Aug. 10, 1957, Page 12.
50. *Bruces Eddy Funds Cut As Works Bill Passes*, Lewiston Tribune, Aug. 14, 1957, Page 1.
51. *Ike Vetoes Water Projects, May OK Road Measure*, Lewiston Tribune, April 16, 1958, Page 1.
52. *Ike Signs Bill Providing Cash for Bruces Eddy*, Lewiston Tribune, Sept. 3, 1958, Page 1.
53. *Exact Bruces Eddy Site, Best Materials Will Be Known*, Lewiston Tribune, March 10, 1959, Page 5.
54. William Ashworth, *Hells Canyon, Deepest Gorge on Earth,* Pages 107-120.
55. *A Report on Fish Passage Problems at Oxbow and Brownlee Dams, Snake River,* U.S. Fish and Wildlife Service, December 1958, Church papers, Series 1.1, Box 155, Folder 18. Assistant Interior Secretary Ross Leffler to Frank Church, Oct. 27, 1959, Church papers, Series 1.1, Box 155, Folder 19.
56. *Oregon Governor Declares Fish Loss 'Catastrophic' at Oxbow*, Lewiston Tribune, Oct. 8, 1958, Page 14.
57. *Power Company Disputes Fish Loss Claim, Says Politics Behind It*, Lewiston Tribune, Oct. 9, 1958, Page 14. *Oxbow Fish Loss A Disaster, Oregon Game Director Asserts*, Lewiston Tribune, Oct. 10, 1958, Page 12.
58. Karl Brooks, *Public Power, Private Dams, the Hells Canyon High Dam Controversy*, University of Washington Press 2006, Page 218.
59. District Two resolution, March 7, 1957, Church papers, Series 1.1, Box 119, Folder 1.
60. Wendell Smith, *Progress of Fish Handling at High Dams*, April 15, 1960, Bowler papers, Box 1, Folder 7.
61. Joseph T. Mijich, Statement before Sen. Frank Church, Seattle, Wash., Nov. 16, 1961, Church papers, Series 1.1, Box 119, Folder 4.
62. Eli Rapaich to Church, May 18, 1959 and Rapaich statement to Senate Public Works Appropriations Subcommittee, Church papers, Series 1.1, Box 119, Folder 6.
63. Brigham to Bowler, June 5, 1959, Bowler papers, Box 29, Folder 33.
64. *A Report on Fish and Wildlife Resources Affected By the Bruces Eddy Dam and Reservoir*, U.S. Fish and Wildlife Service, Department of Interior, June 1960. Church papers, Series 1.1, Box 118, Folder 7.

65. *Bruces Eddy Would Harm Wildlife, Department Says*, Lewiston Tribune, July 7, 1960, Page 12. *Dam's Effects Out of Reason, Curtis Says*, Lewiston Tribune, July 7, 1960, Page 12. *Wildlifers Use Bruces Eddy As Vehicle to Plug for New Millions in Federal Funds*, Clearwater Tribune (Orofino), July 21, 1960, Page 1.
66. Frank Church to Tom Boise, Aug. 13, 1960, Church papers, Series 1.1, Box 119, Folder 4.
67. *Kennedy Says Water Assets Being Wasted*, Lewiston Tribune, March 1960, Page 1.
68. Church news release, March 5, 1961. Church papers, Series 7.4, Box 1, Folder 8.
69. Manley to Church, March 17, 1961. Harland to Church, March 7, 1961. Church to Manley, March 24, 1961, Church papers, Series 1.1, Box 119, Folder 5.
70. Tom Kimball to Bowler, Aug. 30, 1962, Bowler papers, Box 29, Folder 39. Bowler to Kimball, Sept. 7, 1962, Bowler papers, Box 29. Folder 38.
71. Bowler to Kerr, Sept. 10, 1962. Brigham to Kerr, Sept. 10, 1962. Day to Kerr, Sept. 10, 1962, Church papers, Series 1.1, Box 119, Folder 4.
72. Brigham to Church, March 29, 1962. Church to Brigham, April 9, 1962, Church papers, Series 1.1, Box 119, Folder 4.
73. Bowler to Glenn Brewer, Oct. 2, 1962, Bowler papers, Box 27, Folder 14.
74. Church press releases, Sept. 27 and 28, Oct. 10 and Nov. 11, 1962, Church papers, Series 1.1, Box 119. Folder 4.
75. *Sen. Church Says He'll Filibuster for Bruces Eddy*, Idaho Statesman, Oct. 12, 1962, Page 1.
76. *House Votes to Authorize Bruces Eddy*, Lewiston Tribune, Oct. 13, 1961, Page 1.
77. *Bethine Church, A Lifelong Affair*, The Frances Press, Washington 2003, Pages 146-147.
78. *Backer Hails Bruces Eddy Realization,* Lewiston Tribune, Oct. 13, 1962, Page 12.
79. Tom Boise to Church, Oct. 13, 1962, Church papers, Series 1.1, Box 119, Folder 4.
80. Church to Wynne Blake, March 7, 1963, Church papers, Series 1.1, Box 119. Folder 7.
81. Jay F. Kalez, *How Will Fish Get Over Bruces Eddy Dam?* Seattle Sunday Times, Nov. 17, 1963, Church papers, Series 1.1, Box 120, Folder 16.
82. *Bruces Eddy Dam Will Jeopardize PFE Operations at Lewiston – Cancell*, Lewiston Tribune, Aug. 17, 1963, Bowler papers, Box 29, Folder 33.
83. Conservation News, Idaho Wildlife Federation, Oct. 1, 1963, Church papers, Series 1.1, Box 119, Folder 7.
51. Church press release, May 9, 1967, Church papers, Series 7.4, Box 3, Folder 2.
84. *Engineers Plan Studies of a Re-regulating Dam on the Clearwater River Near Lenore*, Lewiston Tribune, June 6, 1967, Bowler papers, Box 32, Folder 16.
85. *Strong Opposition Voiced to Any Additional Dams on Clearwater River*, Lewiston Tribune, Nov. 20, 1970, Page 16, Bowler papers, Box 32, Folder 16.
86. *Governor Asked to Halt Filling of Dworshak Dam Reservoir*, Idaho Statesman, Sept. 14, 1971, Page 6, Bowler papers, Box 32, Folder 16.
87. Liven Peterson, *Idaho's Great Pyramid*, Idaho Environmental Issues, Idaho Wildlife Federation, 1976, Pages 61-66.
88. *Dworshak Called Last of Its Kind*, Lewiston Tribune, June 16, 1973, Page 12.
89. Bert Bowler, *Removing and Breaching Dams in Idaho (1934-1973)*, Pages 2 and 3.
90. *Dam Removal Success Stories, Removal of Grangeville and Lewiston dams in Idaho*, American Rivers.

Chapter 5

Creation of the Idaho and
Selway-Bitterroot primitive areas

1. Johnny Carrey and Cort Conley, *The Middle Fork, A Guide,* Back Eddy Books, Cambridge, Idaho 1992, Pages 301-348. Carrey and Conley provide a detailed account of the Sheepeater campaign.
2. Carrey and Conley, Pages 287-300.
3. Ralph W. Hidy, *Harry Shellworth interview 1955*, Oral History Research Office's Weyerhauser project, Idaho State Historical Society Library and Archives, Pages 1-6.
4. Pat Cary Peek, *Cougar Dave, Mountain Man of Idaho,* Ninebark Publications, 2004, Pages 137-138.
5. Idaho Session Laws 1917, Pages 125-126.
6. W.H. Thorp, *Seventh Biennial Report of the Fish and Game Warden of Idaho 1919*, Page 15.
7. Idaho Session Laws 1925, Page 255.
8. Robert G. Bailey, *River of No Return (The Great Salmon River of Idaho),* R.G. Bailey, Lewiston 1935, Pages 640-643.
9. S.B. Locke, *report reprinted in Tenth Biennial Report of the Idaho Fish and Game Warden 1925*, Pages 34-41.
10. Bud Moore, *The Lochsa Story, Land Ethics in the Bitterroot Mountains,* Mountain Press Publishing Co., Missoula, Mont. 1996, Page 262.
11. Dennis and Lynn Baird, *A Campfire Vision, Establishing the Idaho Primitive Area,* Journal of the West, July 1975, Pages 52-53.
12. Baird, p 53.
13. Minutes of the Dec. 20, 1930 meeting of the Governor's Committee on the Proposed Primitive Area, Harry Shellworth papers, Idaho State Historical Society Library and Archives.
14. Pat Cary Peek, Pages 137-154.
15. Baird, Page 52.
16. Baird, Page 54.
17. *Idaho to Have Million-Acre Primitive Area*, Idaho Statesman, Nov. 15,1930, Page 1. *Area Will Be Monument to Mother Nature,* Boise Capital News, Nov. 17, 1930, Page 9.
18. The resolution was included in the minutes of the governor's committee meeting.
19. Watson Humphrey, *They Would Keep the State's Wildest Area Unspoiled*, Idaho Statesman, Dec. 28, 1930, Page 1, section 2.
20. *The Forest Primeval*, Idaho Capital News, Dec. 21, 1930, Page 4.
21. *Mining Chief Opposes Area*, Idaho Statesman, Nov. 30, 1930, Page 1.
22. *Woodsman Raps Primitive Area*, Idaho Statesman, Jan. 4, 1931, Page 2 section 2.
23. Judith Austin, *The CCC in Idaho,* Idaho Yesterdays, Fall 1983, Page 13.
24. Peek, Pages 218-220.
25. Primitive Areas, U.S. Forest Service History, Forest History Society.
26. Bernard Devoto, *Journals of Lewis and Clark,* Houghton Mifflin Co., Boston 1953, Page 239.
27. Selway-Bitterroot Primitive Area, U. S. Forest Service, report from Region One and order by Earle Clapp July 3, 1936, reproduced at the National Archives and Records Administration, Pacific Alaska region, Seattle.
28. James M. Glover, *A Wilderness Original, the Life of Bob Marshall*, The Mountaineers, Seattle, Wash. 1986, Page 145.

29. Lynn and Dennis Baird, *In Nez Perce Country, Accounts of the Bitterroots and the Clearwater After Lewis and Clark*, University of Idaho Library, Moscow 2003, Page 223.
30. Bud Moore, Page 217.
31. Moore, Page 218.
32. James M. Glover, *A Wilderness Original, the Life of Bob Marshall*, The Mountaineers, Seattle, Wash. 1986, Page 145.
33. Glover, Page 191.
34. Selway-Bitterroot Primitive Area Report.
35. Notes from Moose Creek Ranger District Historical Files, Clearwater National Forest, compiled by forester Edward Slusher Nov. 25, 1958, University of Idaho Library.
36. Slusher, Moose Creek Historical File.
37. Slusher, Moose Creek Historical File.
38. Mark Harvey, *Wilderness Forever, Howard Zahniser and the Wilderness Act,* University of Washington Press, Seattle 2005, Pages 161-162.
39. Proposed Selway-Bitterroot Wilderness, U.S. Forest Service, November 1960, Frank Church papers, Series 1.1, Box 119, Folder 5
40. Zahniser to Wilderness Society members, Feb. 15, 1961, Church papers, Series 1.1, Box 119, Folder 5.
41. E.C. Rettig to Potlatch employees, Feb. 23, 1961, Church papers Series 1.1, Box 152, Folder 7.
42. *First Hearing on Wilderness Plan Conducted*, Lewiston Tribune, March 8, 1961, Page 14.
43. Frederick H. Swanson, *The Bitterroot and Mr. Brandborg*, University of Utah Press, Salt Lake City 2011, Page 128.
44. *Four Wilderness Views Expounded,* Lewiston Tribune, March 10, 1961, Page 14.
45. Bruce Bowler testimony, March 9, 1961, Church papers, Series 1.1, Box 152, File 4.
46. *Final Hearing on Wilderness Is Concluded*, Lewiston Tribune, March 15, 1961, Page 14.
47. Decision of the Secretary of Agriculture Establishing the Selway-Bitterroot Wilderness Area, Lolo, Bitterroot, Clearwater and Nez Perce National Forests, Montana and Idaho, U.S. Forest Service, January 11, 1963.
48. Swanson, Page 131.
49. Swanson, Page 132.
50. Bruce Bowler to Orville Freeman, March 16, 1965, Bowler papers, Box 40, File 20.
51. Vern Haslett to Frank Church, March 23, 1965, Church papers, Series 1.1, Box 156, Folder 8.
52. Harold Anderson to Morton Brigham, Jan. 5, 1965, University of Idaho Library, Selway-Bitterroot History papers.
53. Morton Brigham to Doris Milner, Jan. 8, 1965, University of Idaho Library, Selway-Bitterroot History papers.
54. Swanson, Page 135.
55. William P. Cunningham and Douglas W. Scott, *The Magruder Corridor Controversy,* The Living Wilderness, Autumn 1969, Page 37, University of Idaho Library, Selway-Bitterroot History.
56. Cunningham and Scott, Page 38.
57. Cunningham and Scott, Page 39.

Chapter 6

Club women campaign for Sawtooth National Park

1. Idaho Statesman, Nov. 14, 1915, Page 3.
2. Douglas W. Dodd, *A National Park for the Gem State*, Idaho Yesterdays, Spring 2009, Page 17.
3. Minutes of the Second District Meeting of the Idaho Federation of Club Women, 1911, MS 628, Idaho State Historical Society Library.
4. Jeanne Conly Smith, *Would Preserve Marvels and Beauties of the Sawtooth, Clubwomen Want National Park Set Aside*, Idaho Statesman, Oct. 22, 1911, Page 1, second section.
5. *The Proposed Sawtooth National Park*, Press Comments Pamphlet, 1916, Jeanne Conly Smith file, Idaho Historical Library.
6. *Women Tackle Many Serious Problems*, Idaho Statesman, June 21, 1912, Page 4. Josephine Conly Smith Vaughan to Frank Church, June 5, 1966, Church papers, Series 1.1, Box 93, Folder 2.
7. *Women Should Aid in Building Good Roads in State*, Idaho Statesman, June 19, 1912, Page 3. *"See Idaho First" Organization – Public Spirited Women Determine to Bring Natural Beauty of State Within Reach*, Idaho Statesman, June 13, 1912, Page 3. Idaho Club Woman, October 1912.
8. Jeanne Conly Smith, *On the Trail in Sawtooth National Park*, Idaho Club Woman, October 1912, Pages 2-7. *Explore Sawtooth Country for Many Miles*, Idaho Statesman, Aug. 26, 1912, Page 3.
9. Emil Grandjean, *Report for Forest Atlas*, Boise National Forest, Jan. 15, 1909, Boise National Forest Archives. Dodd, Idaho Yesterdays, Page 19.
10. *Park in Sawtooth Reserve Reduced in Area*, Idaho Statesman, March 23, 1913, Page 2.
11. *Grandest Natural Scenery in the World at Boise's Door*, Wood River Times, April 23, 1913, Page 1. Reprinted from the Sunday Boise Capital News, April 20, 1913.
12. Dodd, Page 20.
13. Jeanne Conly Smith, *Entrancing Beauties, Delightful Recreation in the Proposed Sawtooth National Park*, Idaho Statesman, Jan. 2, 1916, Page 1, second section. *Sees Money in Tourist Crop for Idaho*, Idaho Statesman, Nov. 14, 1914, Page 2
14. Senate Joint Memorial Number 8, Petitioning the Congress of the United States to Create the Sawtooth National Park, Idaho Session Laws 1915, Pages 411-414.
15. Report of the Committee on Public Lands on HR 6799, a bill to establish the Sawtooth National Park, Jan. 25, 1917, Church papers, Series 1.1, Box 93, Folder 1.
16. D.F. Houston to Scott Ferris, chairman of the House Committee on Public Lands, March 14, 1916, Committee report.
17. *Sawtooth National Park Objected to by Woolgrowers – Its Creation Would Shut Out Large Areas of Valuable Grazing Land*, Idaho Statesman, Jan. 1, 1916, Page 10. *Sawtooth Park No Detriment to Woolgrowers*, Idaho Statesman, Jan. 15, 1916, Page 4. *Sawtooth Park Appears to be Dead for Time*, Idaho Statesman, March 21, 1916, Page 7.
18. Irvin Rockwell, *Sheep, Scenery, Public Park or Pasture*, Idaho Statesman, March 31, 1916, Page 6.
19. *Unduly Scared*, Idaho Statesman editorial, April 1, 1916, Page 6. *Want the Part Suitable Only for Grazing*, Idaho Statesman, April 2, 1916, Page 2.
20. Enos Mills, *For Sawtooth Park*, Idaho Statesman, May 3, 1916, Page 4.
21. *Boundaries of Sawtooth Park,* Idaho Statesman, Feb. 1, 1917.
22. *Sawtooth Park Bill Favorably Reported by House Committee*, Idaho Statesman, Jan. 26, 1917, Page 1.

23. Idaho State Planning Board, *Brief Report of the First Statewide Recreation Conference*, Hailey, Idaho, 1936, Page 39.
24. Idaho Statesman, April 8, 1917, Page 14.
25. Dodd, Pages 24-27.
26. Robert Limbert, *A Trip to the Moon Right Here in Idaho*, Idaho Statesman, April 21, 1921, Pages 7-9, second section. *Idaho Lands Are Considered As Parks*, Idaho Statesman, June 28, 1921, Page 5.
27. *New Expedition Ready to Explore the Moon Valley*, Idaho Statesman, June 15, 1921, Page 11. *Moon Valley Trampers Back Friday Morning*, Idaho Statesman, June 25 1921, Page 7.
28. David Louter, *Administrative History, Craters of the Moon National Monument*, National Park Service, 1922, Pages 7-16.
29. Douglas W. Dodd, *Preserving Multiple Use Management*, PhD Thesis, University of California, 2000, Pages 71-73. *Sawtooth National Park Is Given a Great Boost*, Hailey Times, July 30, 1936, Page 1.
30. *State Planning Board Will Sponsor Hailey Conference*, Hailey Times, August 27, 1936, Page 1. *Idaho's Winter Sports Mecca*, Idaho Statesman, Aug. 30, 1936, Page 1, second section.
31. Dick d'Easum, *Idaho Wants A National Park*, Idaho Statesman, July 24, 1936, Page 1, second section.
32. *Sawtooth National Park Is Given A Great Boost*, Hailey Times, July 30, 1936, Page 1. *All Idaho Is Stirred Over New Park*, Hailey Times, Aug. 6, 1936, Page 1.
33. *Sawtooth National Park Discussion Opens Today at Conclave in Hailey*, Idaho Statesman, Aug. 30, 1936. *Sawtooth Park Battle Opens at Hailey Meet*, Boise Capital News, Aug. 31, 1936, Page 1.
34. C.J. Olson, *Primitive Areas, Briefed Report, First Statewide Conference on Recreation*, Idaho Planning Board, Hailey, Idaho, Aug. 30-31, 1936. *Regional Forester's Report on the Sawtooth Primitive Area,* Jan. 20, 1936, Harry Shellworth papers, MS 269, Idaho State Historical Library.
35. R.G. Cole, Discussion, Briefed Report, Pages 37-39.
36. John B. Williams, *National Parks and Monuments*, Briefed Report, pages 35-36.
37. Richard Rutledge, *Management of Idaho Wild Lands*, Briefed Report, Pages 49-60.
38. E.C. Schmidt, *Advertising a State's Recreational Resource*, Briefed Report. H.J. Plumhoff, Briefed Report, Page 42.
39. *Gray Inspects Stanley Basin*, Idaho Statesman, July 11, 1936, Page 1. R.E. Shepherd to Harry Shellworth, June 24, 1936. Shepherd to H.J. Plumhoff, July 3, 1936, Harry Shellworth papers, MS 269, Idaho State Historical Library.
40. *Wonders of Interior Idaho Have Their Praises Sung By All Who Appreciate Them*, Hailey Times, Sept. 3, 1936, Page 1. Briefed Report, page 62.
41. *National Park Opinions Vary at Conference*, Idaho Statesman, Sept. 1, 1936, Page 1. *Development of Sawtooth Area Pushed by Forest Service*, Idaho Statesman, Sept. 2, 1936, Page 6. *Park Issue Fades*, Twin Falls Evening Times, Sept. 2, 1936, Page 4. Dodd thesis, Page 110.
42.Richard Rutledge, *A Program for the Sawtooth-Salmon River Country*, Idaho Frontier Club, Shoshone Idaho, May 24, 1937. *Forester Envisions Great Sawtooth Development,* Lincoln County Journal, May 28, 1937, Page 1. Hailey Times, July 16, 1937, Page 7.
43. *Idaho to Have Primitive Area in Sawtooths*, Idaho Statesman, Sept. 10, 1937, Page 1. *Board Favors Rugged Area,* Idaho Statesman, Sept. 11, 1937, Page 1.
44. *Second Primitive Area Designated*, Lincoln County Journal, Nov. 12, 1937.
45. *Famous Sawtooth Range in Idaho to Be Kept As Primitive Area*, Department of Agriculture press release, Nov. 5, 1937. Dodd thesis, Page 112.

46. Dodd, thesis, Pages 116-121. Hugh Lovin, *A Century of Efforts Trying to Reclaim the Mountain Home Plateau*, Idaho Yesterdays, Spring 1966, Page 10.
47. *Boise Writer Attacks Grazing, Asks Sawtooth Park*, Boise Capital News, Nov. 26, 1937, Page 12.

Chapter 7

Frank Church and the Wilderness Act

1. Mark Harvey, *Wilderness Forever, Howard Zahniser and the Path to the Wilderness Act*. University of Washington Press, 2005, Pages 186-188.
2. Harvey, Page 189.
3. *Senator Agrees to Sponsor National Wilderness Preservation Act*, Feb. 11, 1957, Church papers, Series 1.1, Box 151, Folder 9. Morton Brigham to Frank Church, Jan. 7, 1958. Church papers, Series 1.1, Box 151, Folder 8. ("I have read your letter of Dec. 11 and am somewhat disappointed that you will not join others who are sponsoring the bill.")
4. Dennis Donahue to Frank Church, Nov. 26, 1958, Church papers, Series 1.1, Box 151, Folder 8.
5. Mr. and Mrs. Calvin Hazelbaker to Frank Church, Aug. 17, 1958. Nancy Mae Larson to Henry Dworshak, Oct. 14, 1958. Gertrude Maxwell to Church, June 16, 1958. Elaine Kilgore to Church, June 12, 1958, Church papers, Series 1.1, Box 151, File 12.
6. John Saylor to Bruce Bowler, June 7, 1957. Hubert Humphrey to Bruce Bowler, May 20, 1959, Bowler papers, Box 40, Folder 29. Bowler to Church, July 30, 1959, Church papers, Series 1.1, Box 152, Folder 4.
7. Lyle Stanford to Church, Oct. 2, 1958, Church papers, Series 1.1, Box 151, Folder 12. George Saviers to Church, May 13, 1958, Church papers, Series 1.1, Box 152, Folder 4. Frank Church to Don Samuelson, Feb. 1, 1960, Church papers, Series 1.1, Box 92, Folder 20. Russell Mager to Frank Church, June 5, 1961. Andy Anderson to Church, June 2, 1961, Church papers, Series 1.1, Box 152, Folder 4.
8. Harvey, Page 210.
9. Idaho Wildlife Federation resolution, November 1958, Church papers, Series 1.1, Box 151, Folder 11.
10. Art Manley to John F. Kennedy, March 28, 1961, Church papers, Series 1.1, Box 152, Folder 6.
11. Church press release, March 28, 1961, Church papers, Series 56, Box 1, Folder 9. *Proposed Amendments to the Wilderness Bill*, Congressional Record, March 28, 1961, Church papers, Series 1.1, Box 151, Folder 17.
12. Bruce Bowler to Church, May 29, 1961, Morton Brigham to Church, Church papers, Series 1.1, Box 152, Folder 6. Ernest Day to Church, April 17, 1961, Church papers, Series 1.1, Box 152, Folder 5. Ted Trueblood to Church, May 18, 1961, Church papers, Series 1.1, Box 152, Folder 4.
13. L.G. Randall, Hecla Mining Co. to Church, April 6, 1961. North Idaho Forestry Association to Church, April 10, 1961, Church papers, Series 1.1, Box 152, Folder 2. Mel Claar, Idaho Woolgrowers Association to Church, April 5, 1961, Church papers, Series 1.1, Box 152, Folder 7.
14. Clinton Anderson to Frank Church, July 14, 1961, Church papers, Series 1.1, Box 152, Folder 7.
15. Frank Church to Howard Zahniser, Aug. 2, 1961, Church papers, Series 1.1, Box 152, Folder 7.
16. *Excerpts from the Wilderness Act Debate*, Congressional Record, Sept. 5-6, 1961, Church papers, Series 7.7, Box 1, Folder 8.

17. Ernest Day to Frank Church, Sept. 5, 1961. Morton Brigham to Church, Sept. 5 1961. Ted Trueblood to Church, Sept. 13, 1961. John Carver to Church, Nov. 7, 1961. *Wilderness Bill's Defender Speaks*, Idaho Statesman, Sept. 3, 1961, Page 4. Zahniser to Church, Sept. 23, 1961, Church papers, Series 1.1, Box 152, Folder 5. Bruce Bowler to Church, Aug. 9, 1961, Church papers, Series 1.1, Box 152, Folder 4.
18. Church newsletter 87-12-5 7.7 56, Box 1 folder 18.
19. Church news release, Oct. 17, 1961, Church papers, Series 7.7, Box 1, Folder 8.
20. Naomi Steffens to Church, Sept. 25, 1961, Church papers, Series 1.1, Box 152, Folder 5. Ray McNichols to Church, Nov. 7, 1961, Church papers, Series 1.1, Box 152, Folder 6.
21. John Corlett, *Politically Speaking*, Idaho Statesman, Oct. 29, 1961, Page 9.
22. *House Group Hears Foes, Backers Battle Over Wilderness Bill*, Idaho Statesman, Oct. 31, 1961, Page 1.
23. Bruce Bowler testimony, Oct. 31, 1961, Bowler papers, Box 40, Folder 16.
24. *House Committee Member Says Result of Wilderness Bill Not to Stop Contest*, Idaho Statesman, Nov. 1, 1961, Page 10.
25. Bowler to Church, Nov. 3, 1961, Church papers, Series 1.1, Box 152, Folder 6. Wilderness Users Committee of Idaho, *A Memo for Idaho Citizens,* Dec. 1, 1961, Church papers, Series 1.1, Box 152, Folder 10.
26. Harvey, Page 231.
27. House Subcommittee on Public Lands press release, August 1962.
28. Art Manley to Gracie Pfost, Sept. 14, 1962, Church papers, Series 1.1, Box 152, Folder 11.
29. John Corlett, *Politically Speaking,* Oct. 29, 1962, Page 6.
30. Morton Brigham to Church, July 1, 1964, Church papers, Series 1.1, Box 152, Folder 15.
31. Church to Art Manley, Aug. 18, 1964, Church papers, Series 1.1, Box 152, Fold

Chapter 8

Must the Salmon River Die?

1. William Ashworth, *Hells Canyon, the Deepest Gorge on Earth,* Hawthorn Books, New York, 1977, Page 104.
2. Bowler to Church, May 4, 1959. Franklin Jones to Church, July 27, 1959, Church papers, Series 1.1, Box 155, Folder 19.
3. *Fish, Wildlife, Private Dam Interests Oppose Dam Moratorium*, Lewiston Tribune, Nov. 13, 1959, Page 12.
4. *Conservation of Anadromous Fish Spawning Areas in Salmon River, Idaho – Amendment*, Congressional Record, Jan. 19, 1960, Church papers, Series 1.1, Box 155, Folder 21.
5. Jerome Kuykendall memo for Federal Power Commission to members of Congress, Feb. 26, 1961, Church papers, Series 1.1, Box 155, Folder 22
6. Ashworth, Page 121.
7. Bruce Bowler to Rollin Bowles, March 21, 1960, Church papers, Series 1.1, Box 155, Folder 21.
8. Minutes of the Board of Directors of the Idaho Wildlife Federation, March 2, 1960, Church papers, Series 1.1, Box 155, Folder 22.
9. Bruce Bowler to Thomas Kimball, Feb. 24, 1961, Church papers, Series 1.1, Box 156, Folder 1.
10.Ted Trueblood, *Must the Salmon River Die?,* Field and Stream Magazine, October 1960, Pages 11-13.
11. Kenneth Reynolds to local sportsmen's clubs, October 1960, Bowler papers, Box 32, Folder 5.

12. Brief of Idaho Wildlife Federation with Federal Power Commission concerning project 2273, Oct. 4, 1960, Bowler papers, Box 4, Folder 19.
13. Statement by T.J. Jones, Federal Power Commission pre-hearing conference, Portland, Ore., June 15, 1960, Bowler papers, Box 4, Folder 19.
14. Bruce Bowler response to motions to strike, Oct. 23, 1960. Hearing transcript, Pages 9,433-9,437, Bowler papers, Box 6, Folder 2.
15. *The Preservation of Salmon Is One Important Issue, Using the Plea in Behalf of Public Power Is Another*, Idaho Statesman, Oct. 23, 1960, Page 4.
16. *Sportsmen Stand on Dams Defined*, Ted Trueblood letter, Idaho Statesman, Oct. 30, 1960, Page 5, Bowler papers, Box 32, Folder 5.
17. Elmer Bennett to Jerome Kuykendall, Nov. 21, 1960, Bowler papers, Box 4, Folder 19.
18. Owen Hurd to Ted Trueblood, Oct. 4, 1960. Trueblood to Bowler, Oct. 10, 1960, Bowler papers, Box 6, Folder 1.
19. Bowler to Hugh Smith, March 8, 1961. Smith to Bowler, April 17, 1961, Bowler papers, Box 6, Folder 1.
20. *Hearing Airs Questions of Damage to Salmon,* Portland Oregonian, March 18, 1961, Bowler papers, Box 6, Folder 1.
21. *WPPS Announces Plans to File on Mountain Sheep Dam Site*, Idaho Statesman, April 16, 1961, Page 12, Bowler papers, Box 6, Folder 1.
22. *Brownlee Fish Facility Said Failure*, Idaho Statesman, March 17, 1961, Page 20. Stewart Udall to Jerome Kuykendall, March 15, 1961.
23. Bruce Bowler to Stewart Udall, March 8, 1961, Bowler papers, Box 6, Folder 1.
24. *Hearing Examiner's Recommendation for License for High Mountain Sheep Dam*, Federal Power Commission, Oct. 8, 1962, Stewart Udall comments, Page 59.
25. *Rejection Asked By Udall*, Idaho Statesman, Dec. 4, 1962, Page 3.
26. Federal Power Commission News Release, Feb. 5, 1964, Church papers, Series 1.1, Box 156, Folder 4.
27. Tim Vaughan to Bruce Bowler, Feb. 11, 1964, Bowler papers, Box 6, Folder 12. *Smylie Hails FPC Ruling on Project as Fishing Victory*, Idaho Statesman, Feb. 6, 1964, Page 1.
28. Bowler to Frank Reifsnyder, Oct. 12, 1966, Bowler papers, Box 7, Folder 1.
29. Brief of Respondent Intervener, Idaho Wildlife Federation, U.S. Supreme Court, March 20, 1967.

Chapter 9

Rivers Wild and Free

1. Stewart Udall to Frank Church, June 6, 1962, Church papers, Series 3.3, Box 119, Folder 4. *Secretary Udall Sends Draft Bill to Congress to Establish National Wild Rivers System*, Department of Interior news release, March 5, 1965, Church papers, Series 1.1, Box 156, Folder 6.
2. Congressional Record, March 8, 1965, Pages 4178-4180.
3. Art Manley to Church, April 4, 1965, Bowler papers, Box 40, Folder 16.
4. Bruce Bowler to S. Eddie Pedersen, March 29, 1965, Bowler papers, Box 40, Folder 15.
5. Ted Trueblood testimony, Senate Interior Committee, April 25, 1965, Bowler papers, Box 40, Folder 16.
6. Cullen, Burke and Jones statements, Senate Interior Committee, April 25, 1965, Bowler papers, Box 40, Folder 16.

7. Record of Boise hearing, May 18, 1965, Public Lands Subcommittee, Church papers, Series 1.1, Box 156, Folder 7.
8. *Congress to Soften Wild Rivers Law, Boise Meeting Told*, Idaho Statesman, May 19,1965, Page 1.
9. *Good Sendoff for the Wild Rivers Bill*, Lewiston Tribune, Sept. 16, 1965, Page 4. *Legislation for 'Wild Rivers' Must Be Promoted in Order to Preserve Idaho's Salmon, Clearwater*, Idaho Statesman, Sept. 5, 1965, Page 4A. *No Lockup*, Idaho State Journal, May 14, 1962. *Wild Rivers Basically Sound*, Idaho Falls Post-Register, Page 4 (no date), Bowler papers, Box 40, Folder 18.
10. *Water Board Favors Delay on Rivers Bill,* Idaho Statesman, Aug. 27, 1965, Page 11, Bowler papers, Box 40, Folder 18.
11. Church press release, Sept. 14, 1965, Church papers, Series 1.1, Box 156, Folder 6.
12. *Wild Rivers Bill Obstruction Labeled Unnecessary By Church to Insure Columbia River Account; Lewiston Hearing Awaits Jordan Testimony Today*, Idaho Statesman, Oct. 26, 1965, Page 10. Roger Guernsey statement, Bowler papers, Box 40, Folder 19. Church statement to Idaho Water Resource Board, Oct. 25, 1966, Church papers, Series 1.1, Box 156, Folder 12.
13. Roger Guernsey statement, Bowler papers, Box 40, Folder 19.
14. Frank McElwee statement, Bowler papers, Box 40, Folder 19. *Board Urged to Take Note of Multiple Use Potential*, Lewiston Tribune, Oct. 26, 1965, Page 24.
15. *Tourism Is Using the Rivers Too*, Lewiston Tribune, Oct. 28, 1965, Page 4.
16. *Wild River Views Mesh in Change*, Idaho Statesman, Jan. 16, 1966, Page 9A. *71-1 Vote Passes Bill for Rivers*, Idaho Statesman, Jan. 19, 1966, Page 1. *Water Resource Board Decides to Postpone Decision on Rivers Bill*, Idaho Statesman, Jan. 19, 1966, Page 12A.
17. Jordan to Church, Jan. 13, 1967, Jordan papers, Box 32 Folder 24. *Wild Rivers Need Study, Board Says*, Idaho Statesman, April 15, 1967, Page 1. *Water Hassle on Wild Rivers Affects Salmon Clearwater,* Idaho Statesman, April 16, 1967, Page 11. Art Manley to Idaho Wildlife Federation affiliates, May 12, 1967, Bowler papers, Box 40, Folder 22. *Wild Rivers in Trouble*, Ferris Weddle, Intermountain Observer, June 3, 1967, Bowler papers, Box 40, Folder 22.
18. *Church, Jordan Achieve Wild Rivers Compromise*, Idaho Statesman, July 27, 1967, Page 1. *Gem Solons Cooperate,* Cleve Corlett, Idaho Statesman, July 31, 1967, Page 4. *Why Was the Salmon River Compromised?* Idaho Wildlife Federation newsletter, September 1967. Bowler to Church, Jan. 15, 1966, Bowler papers.
19. *Wild Rivers Turndown Irks Church*, Idaho Statesman, July 17, 1968, Page 2. House *Vote Passes Bill to Preserve Wild Rivers*, Idaho Statesman, Sept. 13, 1968, Page 1. Bowler papers, Box 40, Folder 23. *Wild Rivers Bill of Senate Favored,* John Corlett, Idaho Statesman, Sept. 11, 1968, Page 11. *Idaho Solon Lauds Vote On Rivers*, Idaho Statesman, Sept. 28, 1968, Page 9A.
20. *Middle Fork Salmon River Wild and Scenic River Plan, U.S. Forest Service 1969*, Bowler papers, Box 40, Folder 25.
21. Clarence F. Pautzke, U.S. Fish and Wildlife Service, to Frank Church, Aug. 20, 1965. Jordan papers, Box 32, Folder 24.
22. *Rivers Act Contested by Robson*, Idaho Statesman, Dec. 24, 1969, Page 1, Bowler papers, Box 40, Folder 23. *House Republicans Clout Andrus Veto*, Idaho Statesman, March 23, 1974, Page 8. *Senators Fail to Override Veto of Plea for Rivers Compensation*, Idaho Statesman, March 26, 1974, Page 8, Bowler papers, Box 40, Folder 27.

Chapter 10

Church proposes Sawtooth Park

1. Church statement, Jan. 18, 1960. *Washington on the Line*, Church newsletter, January 1960, Church papers, Series 1.1, Box 92, Folder 19.
2. *Definition of Issues Over Proposed Park Plan Urged by Forest Official*, Challis Messenger, Jan. 28, 1960. *C of C Rips Sawtooth Park Plan*, Salt Lake Tribune, Page 1, second section, Feb. 8, 1960, Church papers, Series 1.1, Box 93, Folder 2.
3. *Stanley Basin Group Attacks Park Proposal*, Idaho Statesman, Jan. 16, 1960, Page 8. Fred M. Cooper, Idaho Reclamation Association to Frank Church, Jan. 25, 1960, Church papers, Series 1.1, Box 92, Folder 20. Sandy Brooks to Frank Church, April 25, 1960, Church papers, Series 1.1, Box 92, Folder 25.
4. *A Sawtooth National Park*, Idaho State Journal, Feb. 9, 1960. *Big Business in the National Parks*, Lewiston Tribune, Feb. 11, 1960. Don Frederickson to Frank Church, Jan. 21, 1960, Church papers, Series 1.1, Box 92, Folder 19. Ben Plastino to Frank Church, Feb. 10, 1960, Church papers, Series 1.1, Box 12, Folder 20.
5. Bruce Bowler to Frank Church, Jan. 19, 1960. Church to Bowler, Jan. 27, 1960, Church papers, Series 1.1, Box 92, Folder 19.
6. Ernest Day to Frank Church, Jan. 28, 1960, Church papers, Series 1.1, Box 12, Folder 20.
7. Church to Glenn Brewer, Jan. 28, 1960, Church papers, Series 1.1, Box 92, Folder 19.
8. Church news release, April 7, 1960, Church papers, Series 1.1, Box 93, Folder 1.
9. Bruce Bowler, *Why a Sawtooth National Park?*, March 11, 1960. Floyd Iverson, *The Sawtooth Mountain Region and the Program for the National Forests*, March 11, 1960, Church papers, Series 1.1, Box 93, Folder 3. Bowler to Church. March 3. 1960, Church papers, Series 1.1, Box 92, Folder 24.
10. Parley Rigby to Church, April 6, 1960, Church papers, Series 1.1, Box 92, Folder 25. Michael Throckmorton to Church, Feb. 10, 1960, Church papers, Series 1.1, Box 92, Folder 22. C.W. Mulhall to Church, Feb. 12, 1960, Church papers, Series 1.1, Box 92, Folder 21. Businessmen and women to Church, Feb. 8, 1960, Church papers, Series 1.1, Box 12, Folder 20. Harry Caldwell to Church, Jan. 27, 1960, Church papers, Series 1.1, Box 92, Folder 19. Resolution No. 21, Idaho Intertribal Council, Feb. 17, 1960, Church papers, Series 1.1, Box 92, Folder 22.
11. Kathryn Young to Church, April 7, 1961, Church papers, Series 1.1, Box 93, Folder 5.
12. Church to Glenn Brewer, Feb. 9, 1961. Church to A.D. Greene, Feb. 8, 1962. Ward Hower to Church, undated memo, Church papers, Series 1.1, Box 93, Folder 5.
13. Church to Orville Freeman, Feb. 21, 1963. Church to Len Jordan, May 9, 1963, Church papers, Series 1.1, Box 93, Folder 6.
14. Church to Seth Burstedt, July 19, 1963, Church papers, Series 1.1, Box 93, Folder 6. Ralph Harding to Church, July 12, 1963. Church to Harding July 23, 1963, Church papers, Series 1.1, Box 93, Folder 7.
15. *Three Congressmen Offer opposition to Sawtooth Wilderness Designation*, Idaho Statesman, Sept. 5, 1963, Page 16. *Harding to Offer Bill on Sawtooths*, Idaho State Journal, Aug. 24, 1963, Page 31.
16. Kenneth Reynolds to Ralph Harding, Sept. 3, 1963.
17. Congressional Record, Sept. 30, 1963, Volume 109, No. 155, Church papers, Series 1.1, Box 93, Folder 7.
18. Max Edwards to Frank Church, Aug. 28, 1963. Nelson and Barnes memos, Church papers, Series 1.1, Box 93, Folder 7.
19. Len Jordan to Church, Sept. 23, 1963. Robert E. Smylie to Church, Sept. 16, 1963, Church papers, Series 1.1, Box 93, Folder 7.

20. Church to Jack Mullowney, Oct. 10, 1963. Mullowney to Church, Oct. 13, 1963. O.J. Smith to Church, Sept. 13, 1963, Church papers, Series 1.1, Box 93, Folder 8.
21. Robert Wing to Frank Church, Sept. 19, 1963, Church papers, Series 1.1, Box 93, Folder 8.
22. Orville Freeman to Sen. Henry Jackson, March 18, 1964. Stewart Udall to Henry Jackson, March 23, 1964, Church papers, Series 1.1, Box 93, Folder 9.
23. Church to John Scott, Oct. 7, 1964. Church to John Scott and Eugene Dorsey, Feb. 9, 1965. *At Last a National Park*, Idaho Statesman, Feb. 3, 1964, Page 4, Church papers, Series 1.1, Box 93, Folder 9.
24. Douglas W. Dodd, *Preserving Multiple Use Management*, PhD Thesis, University of California 2000, Pages 227-234.
25. Porter Ward to Church, Dec. 28, 1965, Church papers, Series 1.1, Box 93, Folder 9. Church to Gus Kelker, Jan. 6, 1966, Church papers, Series 1.1, Box 93, Folder 10.
26. *Hearings Before the Subcommittee on Parks and Recreation of the Senate Interior Committee on S3294, a bill to establish the Sawtooth National Park, and S3295, a bill to establish the Sawtooth National Recreation Area*, June 13-14, 1966, U.S. Government Printing Office, 1966. Ernest Day to Idaho Wilderness Committee and friends, June 1, 1966, Church papers, Series 1.1, Box 56, Folder 11.
27. Hearing Record, Page 26.
28. Robert Smylie statement, hearing record, Pages 7-9.
29. Ted Trueblood, hearing record, Pages 38-40.
30. Bruce Bowler testimony, Pages 156-157. Stanley Burns testimony, Pages 53-58.
31. Art Manley, hearing record, Pages 16-21.
32. Clifford Hansen, hearing record, Pages 107-109.
33. Franklin Jones, hearing record, Pages 66-70.
34. Roger Pegeus, hearing record, Pages 25-37.
35. Clifford Merritt, hearing record, Pages 58-66.
36. John Corlett, *'National Park' Seems Extinct*, Idaho Statesman, June 17, 1966, Page 18.

Chapter 11

A dagger in the White Clouds

1. Keith Whiting, The Idaho Forester 1970, Page 8. *Geologist Predicts White Clouds Mine Will Have $1 Million Payroll*, Idaho State Journal, May 8, 1969, Page 7. The original find was made by Jess Baker and Lester Fallen.
2. *Crews Commute by Helicopter to Hunt Molybdenum at Remote Castle Peak*, Idaho Statesman, Sept. 27, 1968, Page 1, section 2.
3. Bob Johnson letter to author, Oct. 22, 2008.
4. J. Robb Brady e-mail, Oct. 17, 2008.
5. J. Robb Brady, *Miners and Idaho's Castle Peak*, Idaho Falls Post Register, Sept. 25, 1968, Page 4.
6. *Threat of Mine in White Clouds Deplored by Idahoan*, Idaho Statesman, Sept. 28, 1968, Page 15.
7. H. Tom Davis e-mail, Sept. 27, 2008.
8. *Mining Firm Asks Road to White Clouds*, Idaho Statesman, March 9, 1979, Page 1.
9. *A Dagger in the White Clouds*, Intermountain-Observer, March 15, 1969, Page 1.
10. *Mining Firm's Address Listed*, Idaho Statesman, March 23, 1969, Page 4.

11. *Boise Engineering Firm Hired as Firm Speeds Plans for Road to Ore Deposits*, Idaho Statesman, March 16, 1969, Page 3B.
12. *The Beauty of the White Clouds Should Be Preserved*, Idaho Statesman, March 20, 1969, Page 4. Rollie Bruning, *Another View of Castle Peak*, Idaho Statesman, April 7, 1969, Page 4.
13. Greater Sawtooth Preservation Council newsletter, April 1969, Gerald Jayne papers, University of Idaho library.
14. Kathryn Merriam e-mail, Oct. 28, 2008.
15. Russell Brown interview, Sept. 23, 2008.
16. Gerald Jayne to Frank Church, Feb. 27, 1969, Gerald Jayne papers.
17. Frank Church to Gerald Jayne, March 20, 1969. Orval Hansen to Jayne, March 8, 1969, Jayne papers.
18. *Meets Set to Discuss Mine Road*, Idaho Statesman, March 27, 1969, Page 10D.
19. Brock Evans to Bruce Bowler, April 5, 1969, Bowler papers, Box 39, Folder 25.
20. *Study Probes Status of White Clouds*, Idaho Statesman, April 4, 1969, Page 1B.
21. *Help Save the White Clouds*, display ad, Idaho Statesman, May 4, 1969, Page 4C.
22. *Mining Firm Outlines White Clouds Plans*, Idaho Statesman, May 8, 1969, Page 1.
23. Don Samuelson to Frank Church, Feb. 1, 1960, Church papers, Series 1.1, Box 92, Folder 20.
24. *Governor Backs Plan for Mine*, Idaho Statesman, May 10, 1969, Page 1.
25. *Parks Board Chief Resigns at Hearing*, Idaho Statesman, May 10, 1969, Page 1.
26. Bowler statement, Brock Evans statement, Bowler papers, Box 39, Folder 24.
27. In 1983 the state of Idaho sued mining companies for damage at Panther Creek. In 1993 the U.S. Justice Department joined in the case on behalf of the National Oceanic and Atmospheric Administration (NOAA). In a settlement announced in 1995 mining companies agreed to pay $60 million for cleanup and restoration, NOAA news release 1995.
28. *White Clouds Called Spur to Gem Wealth*, Idaho Falls Post-Register, May 11, 1969, Page 1. Ernie Stites, *Ernestly Yours*, Idaho State Journal, May 19, 1969, Page 4.
29. *Sacrifice Idaho Needn't Make*, Idaho Statesman, May 11, 1969, Page 4.
30. *The White Clouds*, Idaho Falls Post-Register, reprinted in Idaho Statesman, May 24, 1969, Page 4. *Ah Wilderness*, Twin Falls Times-News, May 11, 1969, Page 1. *The Sportsmen Vs. the Spoilers*, Lewiston Tribune, May 11, 1969, Page 4.
31. Perry Swisher, *Rape on Castle Peak*, Intermountain Observer, May 17, 1969, Page 4. Bowler papers, Box 39, Folder 24.
32. Ot Power, *Ex Mining Official Says 'Engage Brain'*, Idaho Statesman, June 2, 1969, Page 4.
33. *Cascade Chamber Votes to Back Mine in White Clouds Region*, Idaho Statesman, June 2, 1969, Page 5.
34. Joe Jemmett, *The Case for the ASARCO Road*, Intermountain Observer, April 26, 1969.
35. John Merriam, Intermountain Observer, April 26, 1969, Bowler papers, Box 39, Folder 23.
36. Russell Brown, Intermountain Observer, May 3, 1969, Page 6.
37. H. Tom Davis, Intermountain Observer, May 3, 1969, Page 6, Bowler papers, Box 39, Folder 23.
38. Ted Trueblood, *Tourism Termed Better for State*, Idaho Statesman, June 2, 1969, Page 5.
39. *Forest Service Reports Little Control of Mines*, Idaho Statesman, June 13, 1969, Page 1.
40. Tom Ochiltree, *Law Aids Mine Firm in White Clouds Fuss*, Idaho Statesman, June 1, 1969, Page 1. *Buying Claim Could Block Mining Plans*, Idaho Statesman, June 2, 1969, Page 1
41. Greater Sawtooth Preservation Council newsletter, May 28, 1969, Bowler papers, Box 39, Folder 23.
42. *Sawtooth Preservation Council Urges White Clouds Legislation*, Idaho Statesman, June 29, 1969, Page 5A.

43. *Idaho Wildlife Group Requests Laws to Protect White Clouds*, Idaho Statesman, June 24, 1969, Page 20.
44. Ernest Day to Roger Hansen, June 30, 1969, Bowler papers, Box 39, Folder 25. John Merriam to Roger Hansen, July 5, 1969, Jayne papers.
45. Congressional Record, July 2, 1969.
46. Church news release, July 1969, Bowler papers, Box 39, Folder 25.
47. Statement by Rep. James McClure to the Subcommittee on Parks and Recreation of the House Interior Committee on S853, July 10, 1969, Bowler papers, Box 39, Folder 26.
48. *McClure Opposes White Clouds Plan*, Idaho Statesman, July 11, 1969, Page 1. *White Cloud Area Project Opposed*, Idaho Falls Post-Register, July 11, 1969, Page 1.
49. *McClure Seems to Stand With Miners,* Idaho Falls Post-Register, July 25, 1969, Page 4. *McClure Didn't Back White Clouds*, Lewiston Tribune, July 12, 1969, Page 4. *No Time for Delay on White Clouds*, Idaho Statesman, Aug. 31, 1969, Page 4.
50. James McClure to Richard Hronek, Aug. 12, 1969, Bowler papers, Box 39, Folder 27.
51. *Hike Into White Clouds Confirms Worst Suspicions of Damage*, Idaho Statesman, July 8, 1969, Page 11.
52. David Frazier, *Serenity, Survey Stakes in White Clouds Create Mixed Emotions for Observers*, Idaho Statesman, July 8, 1969, Page 10. *ASARCO May Begin White Clouds Road This Summer*, Idaho Statesman, July 9, 1969, Page 6.
53. Walter Johnson, *$6.75 a Day Buys Luxury Trek Through Spectacular White Clouds,* Idaho Statesman, Aug. 31, 1969, Page 1B.
54. Ken Robison, *Patrolman for U.S. Forest Service Keeps Tabs on Visitors, Wildlife, Mine Operations*, Idaho Statesman, Aug. 31, 1969, Page 6B.
55. Bill Platts interview by author, March 15, 2008.
56. John Corlett, *Legal Remedy Sought to Halt Denver Firm's Alleged Pollution of White Clouds Lake*, Idaho Statesman, Aug. 16, 1969, Page 13.
57. *Little Boulder Lake in White Clouds Clears After Bentonite Flow Curbed*, Idaho Statesman, Aug. 21, 1969, Page 9C.
58. *Hysterical Preservationists, Ore in White Clouds Termed Significant,* Idaho Statesman, Aug. 2, 1969, Page 9C.
59. John Corlett, *Samuelson Scores Forest Service for Publicizing Road Application by Mining Firm*, Idaho Statesman, July 31, 1969, Page 9B.
60. *Sagebrush and Scraggly Trees*, Idaho Statesman, Aug. 3, 1969, Page 4A. *Local Groups Say Governor Denies Voice for Mines,* Idaho Falls Post-Register, Aug. 3, 1969, Page 2.
61. *Forest Service Charged With Deceptive Tactics, Samuelson Says Idahoans Hoaxed,* Idaho Statesman, Aug. 6, 1969, Page 1.
62. Greater Sawtooth Preservation Council newsletter, August 1969, Bowler papers, Box 39, Folder 25.
63. Russell Brown to Len Jordan, Aug. 6, 1969, Gerald Jayne papers.
64. *A Champion for Idaho's Environment,* Idaho Falls Post-Register, Jan. 9, 2001.
65. Paul Fritz to Bruce Bowler, Aug. 8, 1969, Questions on Sawtooth NRA bill, Bowler papers, Box 39, Folder 27.
66. John Merriam to Bruce Bowler, Sept. 8, 1969, Bowler papers, Box 59, Folder 28.
67. *Mine Geologist Tells Offer To Assure Restoration in White Clouds Area,* Idaho Statesman, Aug. 14, 1969, Page 1D.
68. *ASARCO Geologist's White Clouds Comments Draw Fire from Wildlife Federation Director*, Idaho Statesman, Aug. 15, 1969, Page 1D.
69. Jim McClure Reports, Summer 1969, Bowler papers, Box 39, Folder 28.
70. John Corlett, *Miners to Thank Gov. Samuelson,* Idaho Statesman, Aug. 28, 1969, Page 2B.

71, *Budget Bureau Says No to Parks, Recreation Areas,* Outdoor News Bulletin, Wildlife Management Institute, Sept. 26, 1969, Bowler papers, Box 39, Folder 28.
72. *Sawtooth Freeze Makes No Sense,* Idaho Statesman, Sept. 21, 1969, Page 4A.
73. *Samuelson Rips Policy of USFS,* Idaho Statesman, Sept. 12, 1969, Page 12.
74. *Boisean Hits Mine Potential of White Clouds,* Idaho Statesman, Sept. 12, 1969, Page 12.
75. *Governor Says U.S. to Grant Mine Road,* Idaho Statesman, Sept. 26, 1969, Page 1D. Samuelson's meeting with Hardin alarmed Thomas Kimball, director of the National Wildlife Federation. He asked that Hardin meet with him, Ernie Day and NWF director Stewart Udall before any road decision was made. Kimball to Hardin, Sept. 24, 1969, Gerald Jayne papers.
76. *Ogden Forester Denies Mining Road Approved,* Idaho Statesman, Sept. 27, 1969, Page 17.
77. *Proposed Access Route for Mining Reportedly Located in White Clouds,* Idaho Statesman, Oct. 1, 1969, Page 27.
78. *Forester Says Claims Valid By White Clouds Mine Firm,* Idaho Statesman, Oct. 6, 1969, Page 15.
79. *Governor Says Law Orders Road Permit,* Idaho Statesman, Oct. 1, 1969, Page 27.
80. *ASARCO Delays Road Plans Pending Further Ecological Study,* Idaho Statesman, Dec. 4, 1969, Page 5C.
81. *Mining Plan for Clouds Defended*, Idaho Statesman, Dec. 4, 1969, Page 5C.
82. *Group Asks Road Permit In Area of White Clouds,* Idaho Statesman, Nov. 13, 1969, Page 1D. *Another Threat to White Clouds,* Idaho Statesman, Nov. 15, 1969, Page 4A.
83. Greater Sawtooth Preservation Council newsletter, October 1969.
84. Alice Dieter, *Silent Mountain Peaks Presided Over Idaho's Biggest Battle of 1969,* Intermountain Observer, Dec. 27, 1969, Page 1, Bowler papers, Box 39, Folder 28.
85. *The White Clouds – Rich or Happy,* Lewiston Tribune, July 4, 1969, Page 4.
86. Forest Service news release, Jan. 5, 1970, Bowler papers, Box 39, Folder 28.
87. *Whose Wilderness?* Life Magazine, Jan. 9, 1970, Page 109.
88. *Letters,* Life Magazine, Feb. 6, 1970, page 16A.

Chapter 12

Stopping the ASARCO mine

1. Greater Sawtooth Preservation Council, Boise, newsletter, July 1970, H. Tom Davis papers, University of Idaho library.
2. Tom Kovalicky, Stanley Forum, August 2008.
3. Forest Service Sawtooth brochure, Bruce Bowler papers, Box 39, Folder 29.
4. H. Tom Davis, notice of first meeting, Greater Sawtooth Preservation Council, Boise. First newsletter, GSPC Boise, February 1970, Bowler papers, Box 39, Folder 29.
5. Tom Kimball to Clifford Hardin, Jan. 16, 1970. Edward Weinberg to Edward Shulman, Feb. 6, 1970, Bowler papers, Box 39, Folder 29.
6. Edward Weinberg to Tom Kimball, Jan. 30, 1970, Bowler papers, Box 39, Folder 29.
7. Tom Kimball to Walter Hickel, Feb. 13, 1970, Bowler papers, Box 39, Folder 2.
8. *Bills Propose to Control Idaho Pit Strip Mining, Require Restoring Site,* Idaho Statesman, Feb. 4, 1970, Page 1D. *Industry Spokesmen, Conservationist Rap Bill to Regulate Surface Mining, Water Pollution,* Idaho Statesman, Feb. 20, 1970, Page 19.
9. *Mines, Power, Construction Industries Oppose Bill to Regulate Surface Digging in Idaho,* Idaho Statesman, Feb. 24, 1970, Page 17.

10. John Corlett, *GOP Neglects Mine Study Need,* Idaho Statesman, March 6, 1970, Page 11A. Art Manley to Bruce Bowler, March 6, 1970, Bowler papers, Box 39, Folder 30.
11. Travis Roberts to Ed Weinberg, March 4, 1970, Bowler papers, Box 39, Folder 30. *U.S. Wildlife Bureau Says White Clouds Mining Could Stop Fish Runs on Salmon's East Fork*, Idaho Statesman, March 10, 1970, Page 1C.
12. *Governor Denies Pollution Probe Role*, Idaho Statesman, March 11, 1970, Page 9.
13. Bruce Bowler to John Findley, March 12, 1970. Walt Blackadar to Findley, March 17, 1970, Bowler papers, Box 39, Folder 30.
14. *Push Mapped for Bill for Better Protection of Sawtooth Range,* Idaho Statesman, March 8, 1970, Page 1D.
15. *White Clouds Inclusion in New U.S. Park Called Better Than Mining 'Quick Buck'*, Idaho Statesman, March 16, 1970, Page 1C. GSPC Boise newsletter, July 1970, Bowler papers, Box 40, Folder 1.
16. *A Non-Emotional Case Against Mine*, Idaho Statesman, March 29, 1970, Page 4A.
17. *ASARCO to Delay White Clouds Project,* Idaho Statesman, March 25, 1970, Page 1.
18. *Wildlife Group Endorses Park, Recreation Area,* Idaho Statesman, April 7, 1970, Page 16. Franklin Jones to Len Jordan, April 8, 1970. Idaho Wildlife Federation Sawtooth-White Clouds Park and Recreation Proposal, Sen. Len B. Jordan papers, Boise State University Library, Series 6, Box 37, Folder 16.
19. *Growing Concern for the White Clouds,* Idaho Statesman, April 12, 1970, Page 4A.
20. E.M. Bacon to Franklin Jones, May 6, 1970, Bowler papers, Box 39, Folder 31.
21. GSPC Boise newsletter, May 1970, Bowler papers, Box 39, Folder 31. *Court Suit Threatened on Mining,* Idaho Statesman, May 14, 1970, Bowler papers, Box 39, Folder 21.
22. *Simplot Tells Press Club Growers Lost Potatoes, Money in Withholding Action*, Idaho Statesman, May 13, 1970.
23. *Forest Service Reports Significant Use and Activities in Sawtooth Area*, Idaho Statesman, June 11, 1970, Page 11B.
24. *Foresters Ban Gear in Mining, Earth Movers Ruled Out in White Clouds*, Idaho Statesman, July 9, 1970, Page 1D.
25. *White Clouds Becomes Focus of Court Tests to Protect Area*, Idaho Statesman, July 16, 1970, Page 1D. Ernest Day to Tom Kimball, July 14, 1970, Bowler papers, Box 40, Folder 1.
26. *ASARCO Official Says Ways Viewed for Post Mining Restoration in White Clouds*, Idaho Statesman, July 23, 1970, Page 1D.
27. *State Solon Backs White Clouds Road as Sportsman Aid*, Idaho Statesman, July 21, 1970, Page 7. John Peavey would later switch from the Republican to the Democratic Party. He would also become a friend of conservation.
28. *Mine Firm Activity in White Clouds Appalls Pocatellans Visiting Area*, Idaho Statesman, July 22, 1970, Page 2D.
29. *Senate Told Park in Sawtooths Would Benefit Nation*, Idaho Statesman, August 20, 1970, Page1B.
30. *Best Answer for White Clouds*, Idaho Statesman, August 13, 1970, Page 4.
31. *Governor Balks at Sawtooth Park Plan*, Idaho Statesman, August 20, 1970, Page 1B.
32. John Corlett, *Samuelson's Views Put Dent in Sawtooth Plan*, Idaho Statesman.
33. Robert E. Smylie, *Governor Dynamites the Sawtooth Park*, Intermountain Observer, August 22, 1970.
34. *Miners Oppose Unused Land,* Idaho Statesman, Aug. 21, 1970, Page 27. *Mine Sites to Remain, Panel Told*, Idaho Statesman, Aug. 27, 1970, Page 2A.
35. *Chairman's Gavel Halts Minton's Lengthy Talk,* Idaho Statesman, Aug. 27, 1970, Page 1. *Andrus, Samuelson Differ in Testimony on Sawtooth Plan,* Idaho Statesman, Aug. 27, 1970, Page

2A. *Crowd of 500 Packs Opera House at Sun Valley to Hear Pro-Con Testimony on National Park Status for Sawtooths,* Idaho Statesman, Aug. 27, 1970, Page 2A.
36. Hearing Before the Subcommittee on Parks and Recreation of the Committee on Interior and Insular Affairs, House of Representatives on HR 5999, HR 1890 and S 853, Aug. 26, 1970, U.S. Government Printing Office.
37. *A Formula for Sawtooth Country,* Idaho Falls Post-Register Aug. 30, 1970, Page 4.
38. Frank Church newsletter, October 1970, Church papers.
39. *Public Land Users Organize to Push Multiple Use Idea,* Idaho State Journal, Oct. 11, 1970.
40. *Andrus Backer Responds to Critics, Emphasizes White Clouds Concern*, Idaho Statesman, Oct. 30, 1970, Page 4.
41. *Chamber Elects*, Idaho Falls Post-Register, Oct. 18, 1970. Newsletter, Bowler papers, Box 40, Folder 6.
42. *Samuelson Accused of False Statements*, Idaho Falls Post-Register, Oct. 2, 1970.
43. *Andrus Reaffirms White Clouds Opinion, Other Issues in Visit*, Gooding County Leader, Oct. 8, 1970, Page 1.
44. *Democrat Hopeful Knocks Park Proposal at Gooding Luncheon,* Gooding County Leader, Oct. 8, 1970.
45. *Andrus disputes hunting end if Sawtooth Park established*, Lewiston Tribune, Oct. 13, 1970, Bowler papers, Box 40, Folder 6.
46. Bob Leeright, *Environmental Control Major Campaign Issue*, Idaho Falls Post-Register, Oct. 22, 1970.
47. *Environmental Council Denounces Statement*, Idaho Falls Post-Register, Oct. 22, 1970.
48. H. Tom Davis memo, 1971, Davis papers.
49. *Cecil Andrus, Politics Western Style*, Sasquatch Books 1999, Page 19.
50. *Andrus, Politics Western Style*, Page 22.
51. *New Park-Recreation Area Proposal for Idaho's Sawtooth Mountains Outlined*, Idaho Statesman, March 2, 1971, Page 24.
52. H. Tom Davis to Frank Church, March 4, 1971, Davis papers.
53. Don Zuck to Len Jordan, April 8, 1972, Jordan papers, Series 6, Box 42, Folder 17.
54. James McClure, Orval Hansen joint press release, March 30, 1971, Jordan papers, Series 6, Box 46, Folder 48. Frank Church, Len Jordan joint news release, March 30, 1971, Church papers, Series 7.4, Box 4, Folder 8.
55. John Merriam to Frank Church, Len Jordan, Orval Hansen, April 22, 1971, Jordan papers, Series 6, Box 42, Folder 9. John Merriam to Cecil Andrus, April 8, 1971, Andrus papers, Series 141-1, Box 15, Folder 12. *The Sawtooth Bill, a Step Backward for Conservation*, Greater Sawtooth Preservation Council Bulletin, April 1971.
56. Frank Church to Darrell Hirte, June 28, 1971, Church papers, Series 1.1, Box 93, Folder 11.
57. House Subcommittee on Parks and Recreation Hearing Record HR 6957, June 7-8, 1971, U.S. Government Printing Office.
58. *Sawtooth Recreation Area Bill Approved by House Panel*, Idaho Statesman, Nov. 11, 1971, Page 1. James McClure to Bruce Bowler, Jan. 3, 1972, Bowler papers, Box 40, Bolder 10.
59. *Sawtooth Recreation Area Bill Now Goes to Senate*, Idaho State Journal, Feb. 7, 1972. Greater Sawtooth Preservation Council Hearing Alert, April 1972, Bowler papers, Box 40, Folder 10.
60. *Study Urges No Mines in White Clouds Until Molybdenum Needed*, Idaho Statesman, April 5, 1972, Page 1.
61. Cecil Andrus news release, April 5, 1970, Bowler papers, Box 40, Folder 10.
62. *White Clouds Issue Returns*, Idaho Statesman, April 20, 1972, Page 4A.
63. *Andrus Hits White Clouds Photos Cut*, Idaho Statesman, April 28, 1972.
64. *Rug-Pulling in the White Clouds*, Idaho Falls Post-Register, May 8, 1972, Page 4.

65. *Church, McClure Split Over Mine Protection in White Clouds Area*, Idaho Statesman, April 13, 1972, Page 1D. *Church rejects Firm's Offer to Return Mined "Clouds" Land*, Idaho Statesman, April 13, 1972.
66. Church, Jordan news release, May 17, 1972, Church papers, Series 7.4, Box 56, Folder 43.
67. Church news release, July 24, 1972, Bowler papers, Box 40, Folder 10.
68. Richard Hronek. *Scenic Sawtooth Recreation Area Dedicated by Top Idaho Officials*, Idaho Statesman, Sept. 2, 1972, Page 1.
69. U.S. Forest Service, *Sawtooth National Recreation Area Progress Report 1975*, Church papers, Series 1.1, Box 93, Folder 12. *Sawtooth Recreation Area Still Faced by Problems*, Idaho Falls Post-Register, Nov. 20, 1975, Page 1.
70. Study Report and Plan, *Proposed Sawtooth National Park-National Recreation Area Idaho*, National Park Service, March 1,1975, Idaho Historical Society Library.
71. Cleve Corlett to William McKnight, Sept. 23, 1974, Jordan papers, Box 69, Folder 4.
72. Letter from Kathryn Merriam, Oct. 28, 2008.
73. *White Clouds Open Pit Mulled*, Idaho Statesman, July 28, 1981, Page 1, Bowler papers, Box 40, Folder 13. *Evans Rips mining Idea*, Idaho Statesman, July 29, 1981, Page 8A. John Corlett, *Protect White Clouds from Mine*, Idaho Statesman, Aug. 17, 1981, Page 6A.

Chapter 13

Saving Hells Canyon

1. Russ Mager, telephone interview by author, Jan. 24, 2009.
2. Russ Mager, Talmon's Miscellany (unpublished manuscript 2002).
3. Bill Platts, *High Dams Against the Sturgeon*, Idaho Wildlife Review, September 1965, Pages 3-5.
4. Richard Solomon to Russ Mager, Dec. 20, 1965, Mager papers.
5. Russ Mager to Justice William O. Douglas, Nov. 30, 1966. Louise Covington to Mager, March 3, 1967, Mager papers.
6. Jerry Jayne Memoirs, unpublished manuscript, 2008, Pages 25-36. Jayne interview by author, Sept. 23, 2008.
7. Russ Mager to Stanford Tepfer, April 23, 1967, Mager papers.
8. Floyd Harvey, telephone interview by author, Nov. 3, 2008. Floyd Harvey interview with Clark Hansen, Center for Columbia River History, October 1999, Pages 11-12.
9. Floyd Harvey, telephone interview by author, April 15, 2009.
10. Brock Evans, *A Hells Canyon Story*, Hells Canyon Preservation Council 1999. (The original HCPC disbanded in 1976. The current HCPC based in LaGrande, Oregon, established in 1982, continues to monitor management of the Hells Canyon National Recreation Area.)
11. Udall, Secretary of Interior vs. Federal Power Commission, U. S. Supreme Court, June 5, 1967.
12. Russ Mager to Justice William O. Douglas, June 27, 1967, Mager papers.
13. James M. Hockaday, *History of the Payette National Forest,* 1968, Page 122.
14. Brock Evans to Russ Mager, June 17, 1967, Mager papers.
15. Brock Evans, *A Hells Canyon Story*.
16. Russ Mager telephone interview by author, Jan. 24, 2009.
17. Jerry Jayne memoirs, unpublished manuscript, 2009. Russ Mager interview by author, Jan. 24, 2009.

18. Hells Canyon Preservation Council newsletter, December 1967, Mager papers.
19. James Campbell to Bill Platts, Dec. 19, 1967, Jerry Jayne papers, University of Idaho Library. (The Tom Davis of the early HCPC should not be confused with H. Tom Davis, the Boise engineer and a leader in the campaign to stop an open pit mine in the White Clouds.)
20. Hells Canyon Preservation Council newsletter, December 1967. William Ashworth, *Hells Canyon, The Deepest Gorge on Earth,* Hawthorn Books, 1977, Pages 148-149.
21. Brock Evans to Russ Mager, Oct. 26, 1967, Mager papers. Hugh Smith, Answer to Petitions for Intervention, Pacific Northwest Power Co., Bruce Bowler papers, Box 7, Folder 4.
22. Brock Evans to James Campbell, Nov. 1, 1967, Jerry Jayne papers. Art Manley to John G. Wilson, Jan. 17, 1967, Bowler papers, Box 7, Folder 6.
23. Hells Canyon Preservation Council newsletter, February 1968, Mager papers.
24. Hells Canyon Preservation Council newsletter, May 1968, Mager papers.
25. *Attorney says Dam Won't Harm Salmon, Steelhead Fishing*, Lewiston Tribune, April 1, 1968, Page 14. Morton Brigham to Russ Mager, April 3, 1968, Mager papers.
26. Cyril L. Slansky, *The Case Against High Mountain Sheep Dam*, presented at the annual meeting of the Northwest Conservation Council, May 5, 1968, Mager papers.
27. William Blair, *Riding the Rapids of the Snake River in Hells Canyon*, New York Times, June 2, 1968. *The Last Dam,* New York Times, June 2, 1968. Hells Canyon Preservation Council newsletter, May 1968.
28. Department of Interior news release, May 15, 1968, Bowler papers, Box 7, Folder 8.
29. Hells Canyon Preservation Council newsletter, August 1968, James Campbell to Don Samuelson, Feb. 2, 1968. Mager papers.
30. Jordan, Church joint news release, Sept. 12, 1968, Church papers, Series 1.1, Box 156, Folder 13. *Idaho Senators Pursue Dam Moratorium After Colorado Bill Protects Water,* Idaho Statesman, Sept. 13, 1968, Bowler papers, Box 40, Folder 23.
31. *Grace E. Jordan, The Unintentional Senator*, Syms-York Company, Boise, 1972, Page 46. (Mrs. Jordan's book chronicles Len Jordan's political career. An earlier book, *Home Below Hells Canyon*, describes the family's life at the Kirkwood Bar sheep ranch in Hells Canyon during the depression.)
32. *Dam Opponents Have Their Say*, Lewiston Tribune, Sept. 18, 1968, Page 18.
33. Hells Canyon Preservation Council newsletter, January 1969, Mager papers.
34. A Bill to Establish the Hells Canyon-Snake National River in the States of Idaho, Oregon and Washington and for Other Purposes, Jerry Jayne papers. *Outdoor Leaders Propose Hells Canyon Protection,* Idaho Falls Post-Register, Nov. 11, 1968, Page 12.
35. HCPC letter to members of Congress, Nov. 11, 1968, Mager papers.
36. Brock Evans to Russ Mager, Jan. 10, 1969, Mager papers.
37. Russ Mager to Oregon and Washington HCPC members, Jan. 12 1969, Mager papers. Brock Evans, *A Hells Canyon Story.*
38. Hells Canyon Preservation Council newsletter, January 1969, Mager papers. Frank Church to Russ Mager, April 29, 1969, Mager papers.
39. Hells Canyon Preservation Council newsletter, Aug. 4, 1969, Mager papers.
40. Brock Evans to Lew Bell, May 27, 1969, Jayne papers. Ted Trueblood to Al McGlinsky, June 9, 1968, Jayne papers.
41. Russ Mager to Ernie Day, Al Klotz, Jim Calvert, Feb. 23, 1969, Mager papers. Idaho Wildlife Federation brief, Oct. 14, 1970, Bowler papers, Box 8, Folder 8.
42. Brief of Sierra Club, Federation of Western Outdoor Clubs and Idaho Alpine Club to Federal Power Commission, October 1970.
43. Invitation to join the IEC, summer 1969, Bowler papers.

44. Boyd Norton, HCPC and Hells Canyon Reflections, Hells Canyon Preservation Council. Arthur Godfrey to Walter Hickel, July 9, 1969, Mager papers. Floyd Harvey interview with Clark Hansen, Oct. 22, 1999. Russ Mager, phone interview by author, April 29, 2009.
45. Arthur Godfrey to Walter Hickel, July 1969. Ashworth, Page 163.
46. Russ Mager to HCPC directors, November 1969, Mager papers.
47. HCPC newsletter, Feb. 2, 1970, Jayne papers.
48. Floyd Harvey, Clark Hansen interview, Page 19.
49. Hearing Before the Subcommittee on Water and Power Resources of the Committee on Interior and Insular Affairs United States Senate, Feb. 16, 1970, U.S. Government Printing Office.
50. James Campbell, PNP Recreation Proposal A Joke, Says Hells Canyon Council, HCPC news release, March 20, 1970, Mager papers.
51. Ashworth, Pages 163-164.
52. Stacy Gebhards, *Wild Things*, Washington State University Press, Pullman, 1999, Pages 42-43.
53. *Hickel Gives No Indication of Feelings About Dam*, Lewiston Tribune, May 26, 1970, Page 16.
54. *Linkletter Favors New Land Use*, Lewiston Tribune, 1970. Ashworth, Pages 164-165.
55. William Levy, Examiner's Recommendation to Federal Power Commission, Feb. 23, 1971.
56. Cecil Andrus, Tom McCall, Dan Evans to Federal Power Commission, June 15, 1971.
57. Sam Day, *Is Church Soft on Conservation?,* Intermountain Observer, June 5, 1971, Page 4.
58. Robert Packwood to Frank Church, June 18, 1971, Church papers, Series 1.1, Box 68, File 17.
59. HCPC newsletter, August 1971, Jayne papers.
60. Frank Church to Russ Mager, July 16, 1971, Mager papers. Frank Church to Clifford Hardin, June 10, 1971, Sen. Len Jordan papers, Box 36, Folder 19.
61. *Diverse Groups Form Coalition to Save Snake*, Lewiston Tribune, June 27, 1971, Page 14.
62. *Len Jordan's Little Bombshell*, Intermountain Observer, Aug. 28, 1971, Page 3.
63. Hearings Before the Subcommittee on Parks and Recreation of the Committee on Interior and Insular Affairs, United States Senate, Sept. 16, 17 and 30, 1971, U.S. Government Printing Office.
64. Pete Henault, *A Setback on the Middle Snake*, Intermountain Observer, Sept. 25, 1971, Page 1. Jerry Jayne, *Environmentalist Calls Irrigation Issue Red Herring*, Idaho Statesman, Oct. 1, 1971, Page 4.
65. Virginia Wildlife Federation to Len Jordan, Aug. 14, 1971. Mrs. Thomas Waller to Jordan, Aug. 26, 1971. Florida Wildlife Federation to Jordan, Aug. 19, 1971, Jordan papers, Box 36, Folder 19.
66. HCPC newsletter, April 1972, Jayne papers. *Jury Ups Valuation of Pittsburg Land*, Idaho Statesman, March 16, 1975, Page 1. *Jury Ups Canyon Land Value,* Idaho Statesman April 25, 1975, Page 7C.
67. HCPC newsletter, November 1972, Jayne papers. Ashworth, Pages 179-180.
68. *Most Answering McClure Poll Want No New Dams on Snake*, Idaho Statesman, Sept. 8, 1971. HCPC newsletter, November 1972, Jayne papers.
69. HCPC newsletter, April 1972, Jayne papers. Ashworth, Pages 182-183.
70. Pete Henault to Frank Church and Robert Packwood, Dec. 5, 1972, Church papers, Box 92, File 2.
71. Mike Wetherell to William Ashworth, Oct. 5, 1976, Church papers, Series 1.1, Box 153, Folder 2.
72. Church, McClure, Packwood, Hatfield news release, July 23, 1973, Church papers, Series 7.4, Box 5, Folder 7.
73. *Water Users Battle Canyon Plan at Senate Hearings*, Lewiston Tribune, Dec. 16, 1973, Page 14. *Recreation Users Dominate Hearing*, Lewiston Tribune, Dec. 16, 1973, Page 14. Cecil Andrus statement, Dec. 14, 1973.

74. *Ed Williams, Jack Bowman Missing in Snake River*, Lewiston Tribune, April 24, 1973, Page 12.
75. Church-McClure news release, June 2, 1974. *The Hells Canyon Hearing*, Idaho Statesman, July 18, 1974, Page 6A. *Jordan Says Position on Dams Unchanged*, Idaho Statesman, Aug. 16, 1974, Page 5.
76. *The Hells Canyon Hearing*, Idaho Statesman, July 18, 1974, Page 6A. *Scaled Down Scenic Role Asked for Canyon*, Lewiston Tribune, July 11, 1974, Page 14. *Andrus Outline Heard by Panel*, Lewiston Tribune, July 11, 1974, Page 14. *McClure Is Confident of 'Sensible Bill'*, Lewiston Tribune, July 11, 1974, Page 14.
77. *Officials Disagree on Hells Canyon*, Idaho Falls Post-Register, July 16, 1974, Page 1. Hells Canyon Preservation Council newsletter, May 1974, Jayne papers.
78. Ashworth, Pages 192-194. HCPC newsletter, January 1975, Jayne papers.
79. *Lewiston man files lawsuit in burning of Hells Canyon camp buildings,* Idaho Citizen, August 1977, Page 13. Ashworth, Pages 189-190. Floyd Harvey interview by author, Nov. 4, 2008.
80. Leroy Ashby and Rod Gramer, *Fighting the Odds, the Life of Senator Frank Church*, Washington State University Press 1994, Pages 448-449.
81. *Utility Offers Hells Canyon Compromise*, Idaho Statesman, April 11, 1975.
82. Len Jordan, *An Open Letter to the Citizens of Idaho*, Idaho Statesman, May 1, 1975, Page 7A, Bowler papers.
83. *Utility Firms Denied Two New Snake Dams*, Idaho Statesman, March 26, 1975, Page 1. *Power Combine Wages Battle to Dam Snake,* Idaho Statesman, May 17, 1975, Page 21, Bowler papers, Box 8, Folder 9.
84. Congressional Record, *Proceedings and Debates of the 94th Congress,* First Session, Volume 121, Part 29, U.S. Government Printing Office 1975, Pages 3057-3061.
85. HCPC newsletter, January 1976, Jayne papers.
86. *Power Commission Drops Snake River Dam Proposals,* Idaho Statesman, June 9, 1976, Page 3B.
87. *Recreation Area Dedicated*, Lewiston Tribune, June 21, 1976, Page 1. *A Toot on the Trumpet,* Lewiston Tribune, June 22, 1976, Page 4. *Its Complete! Hells Canyon NRA Dedicated*, Lewiston Tribune, Aug. 1, 1976, Page 1.

Chapter 14

Saving the River of No Return Wilderness

1. Address of Brock Evans to the organizational meeting of the Idaho Environmental Council, Oct. 19, 1968, Church papers, Box 152, File 17.
2. Minutes of the IEC meeting in Caldwell, Dec. 13, 1969.
3. James Calvert, Record of the meeting held at Hamilton, Nov. 1 and 2, 1969 on the Salmon River Breaks and Idaho primitive areas, Gerald Jayne papers, University of Idaho Library.
4. James Calvert, recommendations on the classification of the Salmon River Breaks area under the Wilderness Act, Dec. 15, 1969, Jayne papers.
5. Notice of public meetings on the Idaho Primitive Area, Idaho Environmental Council, March 30, 1971, Jayne papers.
6. Carl Hocevar, Idaho Primitive Area information meeting, Idaho Falls, April 1, 1971, Jayne papers.
7. Proposed Idaho Wilderness and Salmon River Wilderness, U.S. Department of Agriculture, March 1974.

8. Walt Blackadar to Conservation Friends, Feb. 7, 1973, Jayne papers.
9. Pete Henault, *Conservationists Take A Stand,* Intermountain-Observer, March 10, 1973, Page 12.
10. Gerald Jayne memo, Jan. 4, 2008.
11. A Proposal, Idaho Wilderness and Salmon River Wilderness, U.S. Department of Agriculture, July 18, 1974.
12. *Boise Cascade Favors Middle Road*, Idaho Falls Post-Register, Nov. 15, 1979.
13. Idaho Environmental Council newsletter, November 1973.
14. Mindy Cameron, *Hundreds Jam Forum to Debate Future of Wilderness in Idaho*, Idaho Statesman, Nov. 27, 1973, Page 15, second section.
15 River of No Return Wilderness Council newsletter, March 1974, Jayne papers.
16. Cecil Andrus to Vern Hamre, June 1, 1974. Vern Hamre to Cecil Andrus, June 4, 1974, Andrus papers 141-2, Box 78, Folder 15.
17. Robert Long to Cecil Andrus, Andrus papers 141-2, Box 78, Folder 14.
18. *Andrus Protests 1,143,000-acre Wilderness Plan,* Idaho Statesman, Dec. 5, 1974, Page 1.
19. *Idaho Primitive Area Plan Draws More Fire*, Idaho Statesman, Dec. 6, 1974, Page 10.
20. *Idaho Wilderness, A Tragic Decision*, Idaho Falls Post-Register, Dec. 6, 1974, Page 4.
21. Gerald Jayne to Gerald Ford, Dec. 14, 1974, Jayne papers.
22. Duke Parkening to Earl Butz, Feb. 13, 1975, Church papers, Box 157, Folder 8.
23. Sen. David Little to Gerald Ford, March 21, 1975, Church papers, Box 157, Folder 25.
24. H. Tom Davis to Jerry Jayne and others, February, 1975, Jayne papers.
25. Ted Trueblood to Frank Church, Jan. 23, 1975, Church papers, Box 157, Folder 8.
26. Ted Trueblood to Frank Church, April 28, 1975, Church papers, Box 157, Folder 8.
27. Douglas Scott to Frank Church, March 31, 1975, Church papers, Box 157, Folder 8.
28. Ben Yamagata to Frank Church, June 5, 1975, Church papers, Box 15, Folder 8.
29. Douglas Scott to wilderness supporters, July 2, 1975, Ralph Maughan papers, University of Idaho Library.
30. Cecil Andrus to James M. Cannon, Sept. 1, 1976, Andrus papers, Box 389, Folder 31.
31. *Chamberlain Inclusion Seen*, Idaho Statesman, Sept. 29, 1976, Page 1
32. *Poison Pen Letter Smirches Andrus*, Idaho Statesman, Dec. 6, 1976, Page 1.
33. *Idahoans Push for Andrus*, Idaho Statesman, Dec. 8, 1967, Page 15.
34. *Idaho Conservation Group Shocked At Andrus Letter*, Idaho Press-Tribune, Dec. 4, 1976.
35. Cecil Andrus to Ted Trueblood, Trueblood papers, Box 84, Folder 13.
36. H. Tom Davis e-mail to author, Oct. 8, 2012.
37. Ted Trueblood, *Inside the Interior's Superior*, Field and Stream magazine, May 19, 1977.
38. Ted Trueblood to River of No Return directors, Jan. 8, 1977, Trueblood papers, Box 1, Folder 11.
39. Ethel Kimball to Frank Church, April 30, 1979, Church papers, Box 154, Folder 6.
40. Charles Creason, *The Gospel Hump Controversy*, unpublished paper for environmental law seminar, University of Idaho 1977, Church papers, Box 157, Folder 2.
41. Church news release, April 6, 1977, Church papers, Box 6, Folder 9.
42. Dennis Baird to Frank Church, July 23, 1977, Church papers, Box 153, Folder 10.
43. *Hundreds Listen to Gospel Hump Testimony*, Idaho County Free Press, Aug. 31, 1977, Page 1.
44. Testimony of C. H. and Virginia Ketcham, Church papers, Box 157, Folder 3.
45. *Forest Factions to Seek Compromise*, Idaho Statesman, June 5, 1977, Page 1B.
46. Opening statement by Sen. Frank Church, hearing before the Parks And Recreation Subcommittee, Grangeville, Aug. 24, 1977, Church papers, Box 157, Folder 1.
47. *Senate Panel Ok's Wilderness Region for Gospel Hump*, Idaho Statesman, Oct. 7, 1977, Page 4B.

48. Ted Trueblood memo to RNR directors, Oct. 17, 1977, Trueblood papers, Box 1, Folder 11.
49. Ted Trueblood to Frank Church, Oct. 12, 1977, Trueblood papers, Box 1, Folder 11.
50. Ernest Day to Frank Church, Oct. 14, 1977, Trueblood papers, Box 1, Folder 11. Nelle Tobias to Frank Church, Oct. 18, 1977. Phillip Fairbanks to Frank Church, Nov. 9, 1977, Church papers, Box 157, Folder 3.
51. Ted Trueblood to Frank Church, Dec. 3, 1977, Trueblood papers, Box 1, Folder 11.
52. Church letter included in Trueblood memo for RNR directors, Dec. 20, 1977, Jayne papers.
53. Ted Trueblood to Frank Church, Dec. 20 1977, Trueblood papers, Box 1, Folder 11.
54. Ted Trueblood to RNR members, Feb. 13, 1978, Jayne papers.
55. River of No Return Wilderness, present status, IEC newsletter, June 1978, Jayne papers.
56. Morton Brigham to Ted Trueblood, June 18, 1978, Jayne papers.
57. Idaho Environmental Council news release, Jan. 22, 1979, Jayne papers.
58. *Environmentalists Dominate Hearing,* Lewiston Tribune, April 3, 1979.
59. *Carter Proposes Wild Areas,* Idaho Statesman, April 17, 1979, Page 1.
60. *Preservation or logging for Salmon River country?*, Idaho Statesman, May 20, 1979.
61. *2.3 Million Wilderness Plan Favored 2-to-1*, Idaho Statesman, May 22, 1979, Page 1.
62. *Loggers, Hikers Battle Over Wilderness*, Idaho Falls Post-Register, May 22, 1979, Page 1. *Wilderness Hearings Extended*, Page A13.
63. *Wilderness Group Says Timber Industry Lets Logs Leave Idaho,* Idaho Statesman, May 23, 1979, Page 6B.
64. *Church, McClure Anticipate Compromise on Wilderness*, Idaho Statesman, May 25, 1979, Page 1.
65. Memo to River of No Return campaigners from Steve Payne and Pat Ford, Sept. 7, 1979, Jayne papers.
66. *Panel Ok's Wilds Bill for Idaho*, Idaho Statesman, Nov. 6, 1979, Page 1.
67. IEC Thanks Church, Criticizes McClure for RNR bill, news release, Nov. 7, 1978, Jayne papers.
68. Scott Reed, *Some Salmon River riddles: Why was door to dams left open?,* Idaho Citizen, August 1980.
69. Norm Brewer, *Senate Ok's wilds area for Idaho*, Idaho Statesman, Nov. 21, 1979.
70, Church news release, Nov. 20, 1979, Church papers, Box 7, Folder 15.
71. *Environmentalists Applaud Senate Wilderness Action*, Idaho Statesman, Nov. 21, 1979, Page 3A.
72. Norm Brewer, *Wilderness Bill Provides Campaign Forum*, Idaho Statesman, Nov. 22, 1979, Page 1B.
73. *Church Raps Symms Over Wilderness*, Idaho Statesman, Dec. 7, 1979, Page 1.
74. *Wilderness Hearings Begin in D.C.,* Lewiston Tribune, Dec. 7, 1979, Page 1.
75. Ralph Maughan statement before House Subcommittee on Public Lands, Dec. 6, 1979, Ralph Maughan papers, University of Idaho Library.
76. Congressional Record, April 16, 1980.
77. LeRoy Ashby and Rod Gramer, *Fighting the Odds, The Life of Senator Frank Church*, Washington State University Press, 1994, page 604.